Sharing Network Leadership

Volume 4 in
LMX Leadership: The Series

Series Editor:
George B. Graen, *University of Louisiana*

LMX Leadership: The Series

George B. Graen, Series Editor

Volume 1: Dealing with Diversity (2003)
edited by George B. Graen

Volume 2: New Frontiers of Leadership (2004)
edited by George B. Graen

Volume 3: Global Organizing Designs (2005)
edited by George B. Graen and Joni A. Graen

Sharing Network Leadership

edited by

George B. Graen
University of Louisiana

and

Joni A. Graen
Graen and Associates

Greenwich, Connecticut • www.infoagepub.com

Library of Congress Cataloging-in-Publication Data

Sharing network leadership / edited by George B. Graen and Joan A. Graen.
   p. cm. — (LMX leadership)
  Includes bibliographical references.
  ISBN-13: 978-1-59311-529-6 (pbk.)
  ISBN-13: 978-1-59311-530-2 (hardcover)
  1. Leadership. 2. Business networks. 3. Organizational behavior. 4. Interorganizational relations. I. Graen, George B. II. Graen, Joni A. III. Series.
  HD57.7.S4755 2006
  658.4'092—dc22

                                                2006015683

ISBN 13: 978-1-59311-529-6 (pbk.)
         978-1-59311-530-2 (hardcover)
ISBN 10: 1-59311-529-6 (pbk.)
         1-59311-530-X (hardcover)

Copyright © 2006 IAP–Information Age Publishing, Inc.

All rights reserved. No part of this publication may be reproduced, stored in a retrieval system, or transmitted, in any form or by any means, electronic, mechanical, photocopying, microfilming, recording or otherwise, without written permission from the publisher.

Printed in the United States of America

                         **Library
                    University of Texas
                       at San Antonio**

CONTENTS

Foreword
   George B. Graen and Joni A. Graen   vii

Preface
   George B. Graen and Joni A. Graen   ix

1. Communication Strategies for Sharing Leadership Within a Creative Team: LMX in Theater Groups
   Michael W. Kramer   1

2. To Share or Not to Share Leadership: New LMX-MMX Network Leadership or Charismatic Leadership on Creative Projects
   George B. Graen   25

3. Expanding The Scope: Social Network and Multilevel Perspectives on Leader-Member Exchange
   David M. Mayer and Ronald F. Piccolo   37

4. Network Factors in Leader-Member Exchange Relationships
   Deborah E. Gibbons and Steven L. Grover   63

5. Pushing the Frontier of LMX Research: The Contribution of Triads
   Evan Offstein, Ravindranath (Ravi) Madhavan, and Devi R. Gnyawali   95

6. An Exploration of the Relationship Between Communication Network Structures Team-Member Exchange Quality and Teamwork
   Alex M. Susskind, Kristin Behfar, and Carl P. Borchgrevink   119

7. Macrostrategic, Mesostrategic, and Microstrategic Leadership
   Processes in Loosely Coupled Networks
   James Douglas Orton and Gurpreet Dhillon — *137*

8. Emotional Intelligence, Leader-Member Exchange and
   Individual Contributions to Organizational Social Capital
   Melvin L. Smith — *169*

9. Organizational Cynicism: A Field Examination Using Global and
   Local Social Exchange Relationships and Workplace Outcomes
   Pamela Brandes, Diya Das, and Michael Hadani — *191*

10. Leader-Member Exchange and Solidarity Behavior:
    A Study of Reciprocity and Performance
    Birgit Schyns, Brigitte Kroon, and Karin Sanders — *225*

11. The Role Of LMX and Communication in
    the Goal Setting Process
    David J. Henderson, Tanguy Dulac, and Robert C. Liden — *245*

12. Post Simon, March, Weick, and Graen:
    New Leadership Sharing as a Key to Understanding Organizing
    George B. Graen — *269*

About the Authors — *279*

FOREWORD

The future is now for research on relational leadership as described by the first three volumes of this series (Graen; 2002, 2003; Graen & Graen, 2004). The twenty-first century's turbulent knowledge economy with its rapidly changing demands on organizational life has seen the emergence of new ways of organizing and new forms of organizations. The innovative construction of informal and network-like organizations, the morphing changes of networks among participants, the fading of formal boundaries defining organizations, and evolving employment contracts, demand the conceptualization of organizations as sets of dynamic relationships. As such, the product of organizing that we call organization is shorthand for human sense-making taking place in a social context that is constantly changing as a result of human interaction in organizational environments.

This meso approach of understanding organizations as sets of dynamic relationships has been employed by leader-member exchange theory (LMX) since its discovery by Graen and his students in the early 1970s. It avoids the common problems of reification of organization and the need to postulate that humans and organizations are independent. Perhaps, because of the advances of this meso approach, many scholars are seeing it with a new appreciation. This volume continues our development of this dynamic relationship approach by highlighting the team and the network applications of leadership sharing dynamics via LMX and takes the next step to the macro marriage of formal and informal organizations.

In this book, we elaborate on the dynamic process of leadership sharing in creative project networks by pointing out that the boundaries and relationships of the networks change over time. As the project requirements evolve, new leaders emerge, make their contribution, and move into support positions. This leadership sharing dynamic is a necessary condition for mature LMX and member-member exchange (MMX). This insight about the sharing of leadership within networks directs us to the process of microbehavior being transformed to meso-options and being converted to macrostrategies. This sequence of micro to macro directs us to a marriage of the formal with the informal organization. At this stage we are post Simon, March, and Weick.

Organizational practices are already ahead of us in focusing on the integration of formal and informal maps of organizations (*Business Week*, February 27, 2006, pp. 48-49). The legality of collecting informal network information by promising confidentiality and then drawing network maps of organizations with names for managers use has not been adjudicated yet, but consultants are busy collecting this informal network information from employees and comparing it to formal network plans to target and punish people for unwanted deviations. This invites abuse until regulated by law based on solid research.

What is needed is an open and honest program in organizations that allows undesired deviation to be corrected informally by the network members involved. Such an in-house program was reported by Graen (1989) in which the executive pyramid of about 100 officers of a commercial bank negotiated new and improved work roles and formal networks to bring what they should do in line with what they actually did on their jobs. The future is now in this area and we need to perform needed research without delay or this healthy development may become another of our fads, fashions and folderol.

PREFACE

This book is about putting authentic people back into the social creations we call productive organizations—warts and all. The design of these organizations is as old as human civilization. It helped construct ancient Greece, Egypt, and China. It was improved in the West by the Romans and in the East by the Chinese. During more recent times it was improved by the British Empire whose command and control models gradually gave way to the knowledge models of today. This book is about how we can discover the alternative processes by which fallible humans use sense making to continuously improve organizations at the macrostrategy level.

We would like to thank the contributors to volume 4 for their great work, patience, and dedication to the completion of the volume. A special thanks to one of our authors, Deborah Gibbons, who shared leadership with us. Also, we thank George Johnson, publisher of Information Age Publishing for his guidance, patience, and production assistance.

On behalf of the contributors to this project, we dedicate this volume to our grandchildren, Stephanie, Andrew, Lauren, Jessica, and Joseph Graen. They are our pride and joy.

Graen Bear Circle
Beaver Lake, Arkansas

CHAPTER 1

COMMUNICATION STRATEGIES FOR SHARING LEADERSHIP WITHIN A CREATIVE TEAM

LMX in Theater Groups

Michael W. Kramer

This study examines supervisor-subordinate communication in a creative team, the directors and performers involved in a theatrical production. Using ethnographic methods, it explores how the director and the performers interacted to create and maintain high leader-member-exchange (LMX) relationships of shared leadership throughout the group's history. Comparisons to other theater groups furthers the understanding of the process of creating and maintaining leader member relationships. Implications of this deep-level investigation for other settings where shared leadership can occur in team settings with fixed deadlines are discussed.

INTRODUCTION

Research on leader-member exchanges (LMX) has greatly enhanced the understanding of superior-subordinate relationships. Originally conceptualized by George Graen and his various coauthors, extensive research explores the LMX topic both in the management and the organizational communication literature. Indicative of the breadth of research along these lines, this study appears in the fourth of a series of volumes exploring LMX. Most LMX research has used quantitative research methods to measure LMX and then tested the relationship between LMX and a variety of other variables (Gerstner & Day, 1997). Such an approach provides invaluable information, but fails to capture the lived experience of the LMX relationship (Fairhurst & Hamlett, 2003). The purpose of this study was to explore the experience of high LMX relationships from the perspective of the participants, both the leader and the members. In particular, using ethnographic methods of participant observation and interviews, this study explored how the director and cast members of a theater group communicated to create and maintain the shared leadership indicative of high LMX relationships.

REVIEW OF LITERATURE

Since comprehensive reviews of leadership in organizations (e.g., Fairhurst, 2001; Yukl, 1989) and groups (e.g., Pavitt, 1999; Shaw, 1981) exist elsewhere, what follows is only a brief overview of that scholarship. Typically, leadership scholarship is presented as a progression from trait to style to contingency approaches to leadership, followed by more contemporary models. Trait approaches assume leaders have certain characteristics that make them effective, although it has been difficult to determine any traits that are consistent across situations (Stodgill, 1948). Style approaches assume that leaders have a particular approach to leadership that they use consistently across settings (e.g., Blake & Mouton, 1964). Contingency approaches assume that as situations change, effective leaders adapt their leadership styles accordingly (e.g., Hersey & Blanchard, 1988). Some of the contemporary models of leadership are actually reminiscent of trait approaches to leadership since they attempt to identify the characteristics of charismatic leaders (e.g., Trice & Beyer, 1986), visionary leaders (e.g., Larwood, Falbe, Kriger, & Miesing, 1995), and transformational leaders (e.g., Keller, 1992), among others.

Consistent across most of this research is an assumption that leaders and supervisors have an average leadership style (ALS) and that they treat all of their subordinates roughly equally. As a result, research on supervisor-subordinate communication has focused on the impact of communication behaviors of supervisors on subordinates as a collective group. Typical of research along these lines, subordinates generally rated supervisors as more effective and were more satisfied with them when they were more communication minded, more willing to listen, asked or persuaded rather than ordered, passed on information from their supervisors, and provided feedback (Jablin, 1979).

In contrast to research assuming an ALS, Graen and his associates proposed LMX (and its precursor vertical dyad linkage model) which recognizes that supervisors do not treat all their subordinates the same. Since extensive reviews of the LMX literature exist in other scholarly venues (e.g., Gerstner & Day, 1997; Graen, 2003a,b; Graen & Uhl-Bien, 1995; Schriesheim, Castro, & Cogliser, 1999), what follows is only a brief summary and critique of the LMX literature. For example, Graen and Schiemann (1978) found that supervisors displayed three distinct patterns of communication with their subordinates; these three levels of relationships, a low, medium, and high level of LMX, explained supervisor-subordinate relationships better than ALS. In contrast to low LMX relationship which are task-oriented with limited personal relationship, high LMX relationships are characterized by mutual trust, respect, commitment, and bonding that creates and enables new opportunities for development for members (Graen, 2003b). Research has demonstrated that not only do supervisors treat their subordinates differentially, consistent with conceptualizations of LMX, but that subordinates are keenly aware of the differential treatment, discuss the differential treatment, and respond differently depending on whether the treatment is viewed as deserved or not (Sias & Jablin, 1995).

Building on this conceptualization of differential supervisor-subordinate relationships, a large number of studies have been conducted, using either two or three levels of LMX. For example, Graen, Liden, and Hoel (1982) found that those receiving the more supportive communication of a high LMX relationship were less likely to turnover than those in the more contractual communication relationship of a low LMX relationship. In summarizing research up to that time, Graen and Uhl-Bien (1995) concluded that the more open and inclusive communication of a high LMX partnership relationship was associate with a wide range of positive outcomes such as increased satisfaction, increased commitment, and decreased turnover, as well as various affective and productivity outcomes for the leaders, work units, and the organizations.

In recent years, there has been a gradual shift away from viewing supervisor-subordinate relationships as a primarily a vertical process of hierarchical influence to viewing leadership as more of an interdependent process in which leaders share leadership and decision making with subordinates (Pearce & Conger, 2003). Particularly in teamwork settings, leaders work in relation with group members rather than through strict hierarchical influence; shared leadership involves dialogue in which power differences are minimized (Fletcher & Käufer, 2003). Such descriptions of shared leadership are consistent with high LMX relationships.

Scholars have begun to focus on LMX within teamwork settings as a way of examining shared leadership indicative of high LMX relationships. Viewed through the LMX lens, role making in team settings is viewed as a bottom-up process in which the team values and structure emerge through the interaction of leaders and members as the leaders empower team members rather than control them (Graen, 2003a,b). Successful project team leaders develop work relationships with and among their team members early in the process so that when deadlines approach, team members already have the motivation and commitment to the team to successfully meet "drop dead" completion dates without leaders relying on hierarchical power (Graen, Hui, & Taylor, 2004). These successful work relationships develop when one member of the dyad, usually the leader, offers to move the relationship to a higher level of trust and sharing of leadership indicative of a high LMX relationship (Hiller & Day, 2003). Graen and Lau (2005) conclude that team leaders may be classified as one of three types: (1) Team Makers who work to create high LMX relationship with all team members; (2) Cherry Pickers who choose to develop high LMX relationships only with select team members deemed most likely to develop highly collaborative relationships; and (3) Job Enforcers who choose not to develop high LMX relationships with any team members. Teams in which leadership is shared through high LMX and coworker relationships are expected to be more successful over time (Hiller & Day, 2003).

Despite this focus on shared leadership, very little is actually known about the communication processes or the experience of team development (Graen et al., 2004). The vast majority of LMX research has relied on quantitative measures collected through self-report interviews and questionnaires. Although a wide variety of measures have been used by scholars to measure LMX, ranging from single item measures to multiple items scales, the LMX7 is the most commonly used measure (Gerstner & Day, 1997). Regardless of the measure, the focus on measuring the relationship tends to obscure the actual experience and communication behaviors of the LMX relationship (Fairhurst & Hamlett, 2003).

In contrast to such quantitative approaches, a few communication studies have been conducted using discourse analytic techniques. Fairhurst and Chandler (1989) examined micro-analytic conversational patterns and found that supervisors in low LMX relationships were more likely to interrupt their subordinates than those in high LMX relationships, thus limiting the low LMX subordinates' ability to develop high LMX relationships. In a similar approach, Fairhurst (1993) found that supervisors used aligning behaviors such as insider joking, supporting, and coaching to minimize distance with subordinates in high LMX relationships, but used polarizing behaviors such as competitive conflict and power games to maintain or increase distance with subordinates in low LMX relationships. The use of narrative discourse also varied according to the nature of the LMX relationship and was particularly complex because in using organizational narratives, the supervisor represents the organization, as well as the individual (Fairhurst & Hamlett, 2003).

Together, the quantitative and discourse analytic approaches provide a rich understanding of LMX relationship, and yet do not provide a complete picture of the communication processes of developing and maintaining shared leadership in supervisor-subordinate relationships from the beginning to the end of a team's history. This study was designed to help create an increased understanding of the ongoing process of developing and maintaining high LMX relationships within a team by examining a group's entire history.

RESEARCH QUESTIONS

An educational theater production provided an opportunity to explore shared leadership and team development from beginning to end of a group's history. Theater productions are temporary systems that combine the various talents and resources of the team members in short time periods often less than six weeks (Goodman & Goodman, 1976). This makes them similar to project teams that have "drop dead" deadlines (Graen et al., 2004), since performance dates are set in advance. Since the interactions between the director and eventual group members begin around the time of tryouts and end shortly after the final performance, it is possible to view the group process from start to finish.

The creative nature of a theatrical production seems like an ideal setting for shared leadership. Traditional managing or controlling leadership techniques work well in business as usual setting, but more team-oriented, high LMX leadership is needed when dealing with less favorable situations (Graen et al., 2004). This would suggest that most theater directors should use the more team-oriented leadership of high LMX relationship to create a quality performance.

Instead, due to a short time frame, directors typically rely on standard ways of working together as a group rather than promoting creativity so that the production process actually constrains professional and human development (Goodman, 1981). As a result, there is a fairly consistent process for producing theatrical presentations across productions; the leadership structure is designed so that a variety of secondary leaders, such as assistant directors, costumers, technicians, choreographers and the like, work together to produce the primary director's image or idea of the show (Goodman & Goodman, 1972). This constraining approach to leadership seems particularly ironic given the creative nature of a theater production.

As an alternative to a controlling style indicative of low LMX relationships, directors may choose to create a shared or collaborative leadership style that provides opportunity for cast members to actively share in the creative process of producing the final performance. Collaborative directing involves the director relinquishing some of the control to the actors so that power is redefined and there is less of a traditional director to actor hierarchy (Herrington, 2000). Since little is known of the actual processes by which the shared leadership of a high LMX teamwork setting is developed in a theater setting, this study explored this first research question:

- **RQ1**: What are the general communication processes and strategies used by leaders and members to create a high LMX shared leadership style of team management in a theater group?

A common concern with shared leadership in team work is the tendency for groups to begin with shared leadership, but to gradually create hierarchal leadership over time. This somewhat troubling pattern frequently occurs in both naturally groups such as self-managed work teams (Barker, 1993) and zero-history, leaderless groups (Seers, Keller, & Wilkerson, 2003). So creating a shared leadership setting at the beginning of a group's history does not ensure that the group will maintain a teamwork atmosphere over time or as deadlines approach. Communication processes must also maintain the shared leadership approach. As a result, the study addresses the second question as well:

- **RQ2**: What are the general communication processes and strategies used by leaders and members to maintain a high LMX shared leadership style of team management in a theater group rather than reverting to more hierarchal leadership styles?

METHOD

Ethnography was a particularly appropriate method to use to address the two research questions since as a qualitative method, ethnography allows the researcher to develop thick, rich descriptions of a group's culture

(Fetterman, 1989). Through active participation in a culture, ethnographers gain an understanding of a group's culture by walking about in it rather than by examining reports or maps about it (Rubin, Rubin, & Piele, 2000). As such ethnography provided a valuable method for gaining understanding of communication that develops, supports, and maintains a culture of shared leadership.

Primary Data

Fetterman (1989) suggests four processes involved in conducting an ethnography: (1) gaining entrance to the group or culture of interest; (2) creating a research trail; (3) analyzing the data; and (4) verifying the data. Each of these is described below.

Gaining Entrance. While attending a community event, Carl,[1] a director in a local university theater department, asked whether I would consider taking a role in a production he was directing the next semester. This particular theater group allowed members of its community to tryout along with students. A mutual colleague had told him of my previous acting experience (see Kramer, 2002, 2004). He explained that he was particularly interested in having someone my age portray the role of an older, middle-aged character instead of a college student to provide more realism to the production. After reading the script, I agreed to tryout for the production. When I requested the opportunity to conduct research as part of my participation, Carl readily agreed. I subsequently tried out for the production along with other interested actors and actresses. No one else tried out for the part of the older man and I was cast in the role giving me access to the group as a participant.

Creating a Research Trail. After receiving permission to conduct this research from the Institutional Review Board and all members of the production, I collected two forms of data for this study. First, I generated field notes for all activities related to the production including tryouts, rehearsals, performances, and strike (removing the set after the last performance). During the early rehearsals I made "scratch notes," brief reminders of observations, in the script I was carrying, and during later rehearsals and other activities I consciously made "headnotes," mental notes of details, conversations, and impressions of what occurred; I then expanded both of these into extensive field notes as soon as possible after each activity (Lindlof, 1995). This process resulted in 180 pages of field notes detailing the activities of the production.

After the final performance, I conducted semi-structured interviews with all the principal participants involved in the production, including the director, assistant directors, and all of the performers. I also interviewed all the designers and technicians involved in the production as part of a broader study of communication processes in theatrical productions. These interviews were transcribed verbatim resulting in 157 pages of interview data.

Analyzing the Data. The first step of the data analysis was data reduction (Lindlof, 1995). The data included a significant amount of information peripheral to the process of creating and maintaining the shared leadership style of a high LMX relationship, such as participants' past experience and future plans. These data, part of the broader research project, but tangential to the focus of this study, were separated from those which focused on the interactions among the director, two assistant directors, and five performers.

A thematic analysis was conducted on the remaining data. Although a researcher cannot approach data without some preconceived ideas (Lindlof, 1995), the categories were allowed to emerge by reading and rereading the field notes and interview data repeatedly, rather than by trying to force the data into predetermined categories. Through a constant comparison method themes were developed and category labels applied (Glaser & Strauss, 1967). Exemplars of each of the major themes are presented below.

Verifying the Data. In keeping with Creswell's (1997) recommendations, I used two forms of verification for this study. First, direct quotes from interviews and field notes are provided. This allows the reader to make their own assessment of the face validity of the findings. Second, I conducted member checks by having two other members of the group read and comment on a draft of the manuscript. Since they both agreed with the analysis and conclusions, no changes were made based on their reactions.

Secondary Data

To provide additional insight into the experience of shared leadership, I made use of data collected in two previous ethnographic studies of theater groups (Kramer, 2002, 2004). The data for these two studies were collected in essentially the same manner as those in this study. Comparing and contrasting the experiences of these various theater groups provides addition understanding of shared leadership in theater groups.

PRIMARY DATA FINDINGS

The analysis of the primary data identified communication processes in answer to the two research questions. In answer to RQ1, three themes emerged to explain how shared leadership was created for the production. In answer to RQ2, several others themes emerged to explain the process of maintaining shared leadership once it was established. Unexpectedly, a final theme emerged that indicated that although shared leadership was normative in this production, there were some tensions related to enacting shared leadership.

RQ1: Creating Shared Leadership

Three themes indicated how Carl and the members of the production created the high LMX relationships of shared leadership for this group. Because it takes an invitation by one of the members to develop high LMX relationship (Hiller & Day, 2003), it is not surprising that the director was the most active in creating this team management, but that other group members also played an important role in creating these relationships.

A Shared Leadership Philosophy. High LMX relationships develop only if the leader is committed to creating them. In his interview, Carl clearly expressed a philosophy of sharing leadership with his performers. He said:

> I'm just not talented enough or egotistical enough to work in an autocratic way.... So in production, I need to learn from the actors what the show will look like—and I base most of my direction of the play on what we find in rehearsal. I believe that my casting is driven by an instinct for interrelationships between performers. And the concept [of the play] grows out of that group of actors.... I need input—lots of it, from my actors, my assistant directors, my designers, my fight choreographers, my stage manager, and sometimes even a member of the running crew, about what's working and what's not. To me it's much more fun that way—and I reserve the right to reject or accept whatever I receive and use it in the way I'd like in the production.

Here Carl clearly explicated an approach to directing that involved the shared leadership of high LMX relationships. He understands leading as interrelationships with his performers, not control. He desired input from the performers and expected to extend his understanding of the production through interaction with them. He retained a leadership role by reserving the right to reject or accept suggestions, but by and large, his philosophy was to share leadership with the members of his cast and production crew.

Selecting Team Membership. Carl recognized that in order for his philosophy of shared leadership to work, he needed to select assistants and cast members comfortable with such an approach. In his interview he commented on some previous experiences in which he had limited success in developing shared leadership with student actors:

> The students were very uncomfortable with a director who liked to experiment at rehearsals, who wanted to collaborate with them on the blocking and acting, and who expected them to bring something to the process.

As he indicates, the students in that production were uncomfortable sharing in the leadership process; he found that they preferred to be told what to do. Based on that experience, he approached this production differently. He told me:

> One way of avoiding the experience of [the other show] was working with a more expertly crafted script, but that was also paired with selecting actors who I felt would be much more able and interested in having the freedom to experiment. To have that freedom, I needed to work with more experienced performers—and ... I knew that this was the case.

Carl selected cast members whom he felt would be comfortable and confident enough to participate in sharing the leadership. He recruited assistant directors and most of the performers, including me, prior to tryouts based on his belief that they would be comfortable actively sharing in the process of creating the show.

The selection of team members is a mutual process. The assistant directors and performers joined this production because they were confident it would be a collaborative process rather than a hierarchical control process with Carl as the director. Steve, one of the actors, commented, "I like working with Carl. I find him to be a brilliant guy.... He tends to want us to explore our characters more than him telling us." Like others, Steve indicated here that he liked being able to participate in creating his portrayal of the character rather than being told what to do by the director. A number other group members mentioned wanting to be involved in this production due to Carl's style of sharing leadership and mentioned avoiding certain other directors due to their more controlling styles. So not only did Carl select individuals for the production because he thought they would work well with his team-oriented philosophy, but those individuals choose to participate because they preferred that style of shared leadership.

Communicating Shared Leadership. Certainly having a commitment to creating high LMX relationships and mutual selection of group members comfortable and committed to such an approach are important components in creating shared leadership. However, those commitments must be communicated to create a group atmosphere of shared leadership. Carl explicitly communicated his philosophy to the group as we began rehearsals. I recorded these observations in my field notes during the first rehearsal:

> Carl said it was up to us to decide what a person's history and so forth was and that we should spend a lot of time thinking about this. He said, "You have a say in what the person was." He said he wanted to know what we thought. Sometimes we would have to agree on things since it affected other characters as well. He also mentioned that as we add things during rehearsals and discussions we are free to take something away if we don't like it…. He said he did not have any preconceived notions about how the characters might develop.

At this very first rehearsal Carl invited the performers to participate as team members in creating the production during this initial performance. He specifically invited them to play a role in deciding how the characters would be portrayed and encouraged them to develop them. In this way he communicated his shared leadership style.

Group members accepted Carl's invitation to share in the leadership at the same rehearsal. Carl asked each of the performers about their character's motivation and then listened to their explanations. For example, I recorded the following in my field notes:

> Next Carl asked me what my character wanted. I said I wanted to see how they [the other characters who had grown up] turned out … and that I wanted to make sure someone else took the blame for what happened. He asked what I wanted from the character Barry. I said that I wanted Barry to speak for me, tell my side of the story. Then he asked what I wanted from Florence. I said I wanted some sympathy from her, so that she doesn't blame me. He seemed satisfied with my answers.

Here I was invited to develop my own interpretation of my character. By providing my interpretation, I communicated my willingness to share in the leadership. By conveying that he was satisfied with my response and the responses of others, Carl created and reinforced high LMX relationships within the group.

RQ2: Communication Strategies for Maintaining Shared Leadership

Establishing shared leadership during the initial rehearsal was an important first step, but only through continual communication would a cooperative, shared leadership continue throughout the groups' history. The director, assistant directors, and performers used a variety of strategies to maintain this shared leadership throughout.

Direct Strategies. A common strategy for maintaining shared leadership was for the director, assistants, or performers to directly challenge something that they were not satisfied with during a rehearsal and then collaborate with others on a solution to the problem. My field notes recorded this sequence of interactions:

> Alice (assistant director) announced, "I'm just not happy with that." Carl said, "Okay, A.D. What don't you like?" Alice explained that she didn't like Ellen at a middle distance from Randy.... She wanted her either far away or right in his face.... Carl said, "Okay, let's try it. You're supposed to be an extra set of eyes." But Ellen said, "I don't understand what you want." Carl said, "Alice, get up and show her...." So Alice ... got up and really got in Randy's face. Ellen said, "I see what you mean, but I'm not sure." Both Carl and Alice said, "It has to be what works for you. Try it." So Ellen did it.

This example illustrates how people initiated shared leadership during rehearsals by directly challenging some choice that had been made. Here, Alice participates in the leadership by voicing her disagreement with the blocking (positioning of the actors). Later Ellen challenges Alice's suggestion by saying she's not sure she likes it, but agrees to try it. Carl supports the initiative of both of them by having Ellen try the new blocking but by leaving the final decision up to her. The three of them are sharing leadership. Repeatedly during rehearsal a member of the production directly expressed dissatisfaction with something; this was followed by a discussion and resolution that satisfied the people involved. In this way the participants shared responsibility for deciding how the particular moment in the play would be performed.

Indirect Strategies. Rather than directly voicing dissatisfaction, participants often initiated shared leadership through indirect communication, often a question rather than a direct challenge. Questions were less threatening than a direct challenge. I record this typical indirect request for collaboration:

> Ellen asked, "Why do I get up?" Carl said, "Motivation is a good thing." Ellen said, "I just sat down; why would I get up right away?" Carl suggested that she was getting up and down because she didn't know what to do with herself because Barry is there. After she tried it ... she said it still feels weird. He said it's what he'd prefer, and that she shouldn't rush it and then it would work.

In this case Ellen's question initiates a discussion of the blocking. She shares in the leadership by voicing her dissatisfaction through a series of questions. Even though she is eventually convinced to do it the way Carl suggested, she participated in the decision making in a more tentative manner than if she had directly announced that she did not like the blocking. She is more likely committed to the blocking because she has had the opportunity to voice her idea in this indirect manner.

Suggestions or Demonstrations. At first glance, making suggestions or demonstrating how something should be done would appear to be more of a controlling style of leading rather than shared leading. In an early rehearsal I observed this:

> During the second part of the monologue Carl decided that blocking was too repetitious and so he demonstrated an idea of Ellen sitting on the bed differently. After he did that he said, "Do it better than me. Do a better job of acting than me." Ellen tried it, but actually did something a little differently, and David said, "That was great." She ended up standing on the bed when she said her mother was standing in the middle of the kitchen. It worked quite well.

By demonstrating what he wanted, Carl seemed to be controlling rather than sharing the decision making. However, because Carl encouraged Ellen to do it better, he allowed her to actually do something different which she did. He reinforces her ability to collaborate by complimenting her choice. Thus, even when Carl made suggestions or demonstrated those suggestions, he still maintained shared leadership by allowing performers to adapt and change his ideas. In this way both the director and the performers participated in the leadership.

Experimenting. Due to the creative nature of theater, performers frequently experimented with blocking or interpretation of lines as a way of participating in developing the final performance. For example, during one rehearsal, Randy chased Steve around the bed for the first time during one scene. In my interview, I asked Randy if he had consciously decided to make this change, but he admitted that it happened somewhat randomly simply because Steve was in a slightly different position. Carl gave them positive feedback on the blocking innovation and it became a permanent part of the production. Although some experiments were the result of conscious decisions rather than chance, the experiments served that same purpose of sharing in the leadership of the group. By experimenting with interpretations and blocking, performers shared in creating the production of the play.

Permission to Lead. In contrast to experimenting, performers sometimes requested permission to try something. A particularly significant example of this was my request that my character play the guitar during portions of the performance. Carl immediately liked the idea and through the first weeks of rehearsals we discussed when I should play and when I should not. On opening night Carl gave each member of the production a hand written thank-you card. My card included the following:

David thanked me "for a fantastic job on the old man." I gave him "color and nuances I never imagined." The guitar "completely reshaped my understanding of the play." He thanked me for being in a play that "defies traditional dramaturgy" and for making it possible "for the production to take flight and sing!"

By granting my request to experiment with guitar playing in the background of scenes, Carl affirmed by role in the shared leadership. As we negotiated when to play, we experienced mutual influence. In his thank you note, he reaffirmed that my contribution had helped shape the production of the play. Other performers asked permission for a variety of changes from blocking to interpretation to costuming. In each case, they participated in the decision making that led to the quality of the final performance.

Tensions Over Shared Leadership

The previous analyses might suggest that shared leadership occurred without any tensions and that the director, assistant directors, and performers worked in harmony. A final theme concerning shared leadership was that, although shared leadership was the norm for this group, there were occasional problems with it. This was especially true when Carl demonstrated an idea rather than explaining or suggesting it. Ellen expressed her concerns about demonstrations (line reads) in her interview:

> Carl had a tendency to do line readings where if you weren't saying it the way he wanted, he would be like "Give me the script. Here. This is how it needs to be done." And I don't deal well with that because it's, then what's the, why am I there?

Ellen saw these demonstrations or line reads as contrary to shared leadership. Line reads suggested that her input was not important and that she was simply to follow Carl's suggestions. In his interview Carl commented on why he occasionally did line readings:

> I will give a line reading if the actor is just not getting it. And I rarely do it. I don't like to do it. But I will do it if it's, if they're not getting it. And most of the time, what I say to an actor is don't do it the way that I'm doing it. Do it with the intension or play the action that I'm playing.

Carl tried to downplay the tension over line reads by suggesting he rarely used them and by telling the actors not to do it exactly like he had. This allowed the actors to still share in creating the interpretation of the particular lines. Steve was cognizant of the tension about line readings:

> I came to realize that, especially once she (Ellen) almost broke down and said, "No, you can't come up on stage and do line readings." And he (Carl) knows there's no bigger insult to an actor than doing that. So after that I think was his big turning point of giving us free rein.

Steve seemed to suggest that line reads were ineffective, but recognized that eventually the actors were given more input, even after a number of line reads. So the demonstrations or line reads created some tension because they seemed contrary to shared leadership, and yet eventually, shared leadership occurred as Carl still allowed performers to work off of and change what he had suggested.

In addition to some tension over the use of demonstrations as part of shared leadership, there were times when participants felt there were limits to their participation in the decision making. One of the assistant directors, Chris, never liked one particular aspect of the staging when two characters exchanged props as part of the play. He felt that it dragged down the show at that particular moment. He never volunteered his idea although he said he would have if he had been specifically asked. He was waiting for a specific invitation to discuss that moment in the play before he would share in the leadership. When the invitation did not come, he did not initiate the collaboration.

This final theme suggests that although a high LMX relationship of shared leadership was created and maintained in the group in general, there were limits to its enactment. At times, the director seemed to be more controlling than sharing in style and at other times the performers and assistant directors failed to participate in the shared leadership.

Summary of Primary Analysis

The analysis suggested that the development of a high LMX relationship of shared leadership was the direct result of the director having a shared leadership philosophy and selecting production members who would embrace the opportunity to share in the leadership process. The director communicated this philosophy to the members of his production, who accepted the invitation to participate in shared leadership. The shared leadership approach was maintained throughout the production as the director and other participants used a variety of communication strategies to sustain shared leadership, such as direct and indirect strategies and experiments. Finally, although shared leadership worked relatively smoothly and consistently throughout the production, there were tensions at times as demonstrations sometimes seemed to represent hierarchical leadership and members were sometimes reluctant to voluntarily participate in sharing leadership.

ANALYSIS OF SECONDARY DATA

The analysis of primary data revealed that the director, Carl, created and maintained shared leadership in his production with all of the performers and assistant directors. In this way, Carl represented the team maker in which the leader develops high LMX relationships with the entire group (Graen & Lau, 2005). However, theater directors often do not create such relationships with their production group. Carl recognized that a team maker approach is often not the case in educational theater when he said this:

> And it is true that a director working primarily with younger actors should expect to have to be very explicit about how a moment should be played; how it should look ... even offer line readings, if the students don't get it. And after watching my colleagues work both here and in the various festivals and conferences where plays are produced, it's clear that this is often the modus operandi of directing in educational theater.

Carl suggests here that directors often cannot use a shared leadership approach especially with inexperienced performers who lack the skills and understanding to contribute at the level needed for a more collaborative environment. He went so far as to suggest that most educational directors use a more controlling style instead of a high LMX relationship.

My previous experience with theater productions (Kramer, 2002, 2004) indicates that directors frequently develop other types of relationship with their performers. A variety of individual and situational constraints lead to directors using other types of LMX relationships. Secondary data analysis of these previous theater productions provided examples of enforcer and cherry picker styles of team leadership, as well as possible explanations as to why directors of other production may be unable to create shared leadership situations.

Communicating an Enforcer Philosophy

Whereas Carl clearly held and communicated a shared leadership philosophy, the director in one group I participated in did not have such a philosophy and clearly communicated it to the cast. At one point in a rehearsal, the director, Darryl, announced, "Remember you're the actors. I'm the director." He went on to tell us to quit making suggestions to him because he knew what he was doing and what he wanted done. He repeated that same line again later. He did not develop high LMX relationships with any of the performers, indicative of an enforcer (Graen & Lau, 2005). Not only did he not invite performers to develop a higher level of relationship (Hiller & Day, 2003), he actively discouraged them from trying to develop such a relationship. As a result, the performers stopped offering suggestions and resigned themselves to the problems in the production. In private conversations, they discussed ways of improving the staging or creating faster scene changes, but they no longer offered their suggestions to Darryl. Recognizing their limited role, many offered only minimal assistance even when they could have done significantly more. Overall, the result of communicating an enforcer philosophy of not sharing leadership was that the group withdrew from participating in leadership, their creative talents were underutilized, and the quality of the final production was negatively impacted.

Maintaining the Cherry Picker Philosophy of Differential Treatment

As suggested by Fairhurst (1993) and Fairhurst and Chandler (1989), differential treatment of subordinates is maintained through communication strategies. In the same way that Carl created a team in which all members had high LMX relationships with him through various communication strategies, the directors of other productions maintained differential treatment through communication strategies. The director of another production, Gwen, (Kramer, 2002) established her role as leader by structuring the rehearsals and determining the blocking. Although she allowed cast members to make some suggestions, she only created high LMX relationships with some and more enforcer relationships with others by allowing for influence outside of rehearsals. She particularly listened to the more experienced performers. I recorded this interaction after a rehearsal:

> I told Gwen that I am quite uncomfortable with John getting so close to me at one point. I told her that my character would hit him or shove him if he actually got that close. He also should be intimidated by my character, not willing to approach me. I also told her that I think it slows the tempo of the play down. She says that she will hold him back.

Through this conversation outside of rehearsal, I was allowed to share in the leadership as the director listened to my ideas, and then she told John at a subsequent rehearsal to do that particular blocking the way I preferred. It was evident throughout the production that certain people were insiders who could influence Gwen and others were outsiders who simply did what she suggested. Thus, the differential treatment created a dialectical tension of inclusion and exclusion (Kramer, 2004). Some members of the cast were insiders with high LMX relationship and others were outsiders with low LMX relationships.

Uncontrolled Selection Process

Although the differences in LMX across these productions could be explained as a leadership style difference (Blake & Mouton, 1964), careful comparison of the primary and secondary data sets provides an alternative explanation for the differences. Whereas Carl actively recruited performers that he felt would conscientiously participate in shared leadership, the directors of the community theater productions had limited control over who auditioned for their productions since tryouts were open to the community. Although community theater directors may encourage certain individuals to audition, they largely must use the talent that attends the auditions. The resulting cast members may experience dialectical tensions between those who prefer ordered rather than emergent activities (Kramer, 2004). For example, a soloist in a musical voiced this complaint:

> You know, I wanted somebody to say stand here, shake your hips. Walk over here, look at the crowd, wiggle your head. Walk over here and do this. And when you say that line, move your hands like this. You know, that's what I wanted. I didn't get any of that. I just had to go figure it out myself.

This soloist clearly wanted a more controlling style of leadership, an enforcer who told him what to do and when to do it down to minute details. He found it frustrating to have to share in the collaboration and participate in developing his own interpretation and movements for his character. He wanted more direction from the leader.

Another cast member said almost the opposite thing:

> I think that if you're going to have people be a role ... you should allow them to feel like how they would play it ... You know there wasn't a whole lot, you know, experimenting I thought, that I, I didn't think there was a lot of latitude.

In contrast to the previous soloist, this performer wanted more freedom to participate in the interpretation of his role. He wanted to be invited to develop a more participatory role with the director so that he could experiment and contribute to the production.

This suggests that the uncontrolled selection process resulted in a group that did not equally value participation in the team process of sharing in the leadership. The directors then seemed to revert to either an enforcer or cherry picker approach to leadership (Graen & Lau, 2005). Darryl communicated and maintained an enforcer role. Gwen created high LMX relationships with selected members of the group deemed capable of participating in the leadership and then maintained low LMX relationships with others. The result was the type of differential treatment of group members noted in much of the LMX research (e.g., Graen & Schiemann, 1978; Sias & Jablin, 1995).

Summary

Overall, the secondary analysis of data from previous studies provides a picture of the strikingly different leadership relationships that can develop in theatrical productions. The directors of these other productions used communication to develop either enforcer or cherry picker relationships with their team members (Graen & Lau, 2005). The analyses suggested that Carl's ability to recruit production members who embraced shared leadership played an important role in his ability to work collaboratively with them; the inability of Darryl and Gwen to control the recruitment process may have contributed to their use of the enforcer and cherry picker styles of leadership.

DISCUSSION

This participant observation research provided an opportunity to examine the process by which a director created and maintained shared leadership with his assistants and performers as they worked together as a team to create a theatrical production. By communicating a shared leadership philosophy at the beginning of the group's history and reinforcing shared leadership throughout the process, he was able to be a team maker in which all members of the group participated and collaborated in leading the group. The examination of the previous participant observation data on other theater groups provided additional insight into how other types of LMX relationships are developed through communication. The results provide a number of insights.

It is clear that developing high LMX relationships takes more than complimenting subordinates or group members regularly. Certainly Carl gave the performers plenty of positive feedback throughout the production, but so did the directors of the others productions. What created the high LMX relationships was that he communicated his shared leadership philosophy by requesting and welcoming input, and then he maintained that approach throughout the production. By allowing group members to directly and indirectly challenge decisions, he invited them to participate in the leadership. By stating that even his own suggestions or demonstrations had to work for the cast members, he empowered them to make decisions with him. The high LMX relationships with the whole group were the result of sustained efforts to create and maintain shared leadership through interaction, not simply positive feedback generously spattered on the group.

The analyses of the various productions provide compelling evidence that LMX relationships are created mutually, not by one member of the dyads. One member of the dyad may invite another member to move the supervisor-subordinate relationship toward the more shared leadership approach of a high LMX relationship (Hiller & Day, 2003), but the members must reciprocate. Carl invited the performers to join him in high LMX relationships of shared leadership, but the members established and maintained the relationship by actively initiating ongoing discussions of appropriate interpretation and blocking throughout the group process. Darryl discouraged high LMX relationships and the cast members reciprocated by withdrawing their suggestions and enthusiastic support. Thus, the level of team work is mutually created and maintained. It is not imposed on the group by the leader.

The analyses also suggest that there are negative impacts when there is a mismatch of relationship expectations, such as when the leader seeks high LMX relationships but members desire low LMX relationships, or a leader seeks low LMX relationships but the members desire high LMX relationships. Carl's experience on a previous production, in which student actors preferred a more controlling style of directing than he did, suggests that such mismatches are dissatisfying for the leader and most likely the members as well. Darryl's desire for a low LMX relationship may have satisfied him, but clearly created dissatisfaction among the group members. However, neither example provides insight into effective communication strategies to use when mismatches of expectations occur. Further research could examine this and perhaps identify strategies that can be used to bring expectations of leaders and members closer together.

The problem of mismatched expectations between leaders and members can be particularly difficult when directors have limited control over the selection process for their cast. Many individuals prefer the more controlling type of leadership of an enforcer who limits their creative involvement. For example, organizational newcomers tend to experience less stress, less role ambiguity, and more satisfaction when they receive institutionalized socialization that promotes custodial rather than innovative roles (e.g., Jones, 1986; Ashforth & Saks, 1996). While Carl was able to recruit and cast individuals who preferred his shared leadership approach, other directors, such as Gwen, could not. This suggests that the ability to recruit individuals who share directors' preferences in leadership style may be a key to creating a match between leaders' and members' expectations.

The results of these analyses suggest that in theatrical groups leaders may develop into team makers with high LMX relationship with all team members, cherry pickers with high LMX relationships only with select team members, or job enforcers who maintain low LMX relationships with all team members (Graen & Lau, 2005). These analyses do not give a definitive answer concerning leaders' ability to choose the type of relationship they develop with the group members. Carl was able to select members amenable to high LMX relationships, but the other directors had limited control over the selection process and so may have been unable to be team makers. In addition, Carl worked with only five performers, whereas the other directors worked with more than 20 performers each. It is likely that the size of the group has a significant impact on whether a team maker, cherry picker, or enforcer leadership style develops. Limitations of resources, time and energy, may lead to different types of leader to team member relationships.

Due to the ethnographic method used in this study, it is difficult to determine other settings where the results might apply. The results appear to transfer to other creative settings which have been explored through other lenses, such as a collaborative orchestra (Seifter, 2001), or a jazz ensembles (Bougon, Weick, & Binkhorst, 1977; Eisenberg, 1990). Beyond similar creative endeavors, the results may transfer to other temporary groups such as ad hoc committees, short term projects, and other groups with clear start and finish dates. Future research can determine if similar processes occur elsewhere and if similar communication strategies occur in those other settings.

It seems that the communication strategies used by the director and performers in this study would be useful ones for inviting and sharing in leadership in many contexts. Direct strategies, such as stating discomfort with a decision or policy, would seem to open lines of communication for sharing in decision making. Indirect strategies, such as asking why are we doing this or can you explain this to me, would also create situations in which discussions can lead to shared leadership. Similar hypothetical examples can be generated for the other strategies defined here. And of course, announcing that input is not desired would seem to have the same chilling effect on leader member relationships in many contexts like it did with Darryl. Further research can explore this in other contexts.

The extensive research on LMX has made significant contributions to our understanding of supervisor-subordinate communication. The research has identified LMX relationships and their impact on a variety of individual and organizational outcomes. This study advances the understanding of LMX relationships by providing insight into the experience of sharing leadership in the process of creating and maintaining LMX relationships in a particular group setting, theatrical productions.

NOTE

1. The names of the personnel and characters involved in the production have been changed to protect their anonymity.

REFERENCES

Ashforth, B. E., & Saks, A. M. (1996). Socialization tactics: Longitudinal effects on newcomer adjustment. *Academy of Management Journal, 39,* 149-178.

Barker, J. R. (1993). Tightening the iron cage: Concertive control in self-managing teams. *Administrative Science Quarterly, 38,* 408-437.

Blake, R. R., & Mouton, J. S. (1964). *The managerial grid.* Houston: Gulf.

Bougon, M., Weick, K., & Binkhorst, D. (1977). Cognition in organizations: An analysis of the Utrecht Jazz Orchestra. *Administrative Science Quarterly, 22,* 606-639.

Creswell, J. W. (1997). *Qualitative inquiry and research design: Choosing among five traditions.* Thousand Oaks, CA: Sage.

Eisenberg, E. M. (1990). Jamming: Transcendence through organizing. *Communication Research, 17,* 139-164.

Fairhurst, G. T. (2001). Dualisms in leadership research. In F. M. Jablin & L. L. Putnam (Eds.), *The new handbook of organizational communication: Advances in theory, research, and methods* (pp. 379-439). Thousand Oaks, CA: Sage.

Fairhurst, G. T. (1993). The leader-member exchange patterns of women leaders in industry: A discourse analysis. *Communication Monographs, 60,* 312-351.

Fairhurst, G. T., & Chandler, T. A. (1989). Social structures in leader-member interaction. *Communication Monographs, 56,* 215-239.

Fairhurst, G. T., & Rhea Hamlett, S., (2003). The narrative basis of leader-member exchange. In G.B. Graen (Ed.), *Dealing with diversity: LMX leadership: The series* (Vol. 1, pp. 117-144). Greenwich, CT: Information Age.

Fetterman, D. M. (1989). *Ethnography: Step by step.* Newbury Park, CA: Sage.

Fletcher, J. K., & Käufer, K. (2003). Shared leadership: Paradox and possibility. In C. L. Pearce & J. A. Conger (Eds.), *Shared leadership: Reframing the hows and whys of leadership* (pp. 21-47). Thousand Oaks, CA: Sage.

Gerstner, C. R., & Day, D. V. (1997). Meta-analytic review of leader-member exchange theory: Correlates and construct ideas. *Journal of Applied Psychology, 82,* 827-844.

Glaser, B., & Strauss, A. (1967). *The discovery of grounded theory.* Chicago: Aldine Press.

Goodman, R. A. (1981). *Temporary systems: Professional development, manpower utilization, task effectiveness, and innovation.* New York: Praeger.

Goodman, L. P., & Goodman, R. A. (1972). Theater as temporary system. *California Management Review, 15,* 103-108.

Goodman, R. A., & Goodman, L. P. (1976). Some management issues in temporary systems: A study of professional development and manpower—the theater case. *Administrative Science Quarterly, 21,* 494-501.

Graen, G. B. (2003a). Interpersonal workplace theory at the crossroads. In G. B. Graen (Ed.) *Dealing with diversity: LMX leadership: The series* (Vol. 1, pp. 145-182). Greenwich, CT: Information Age.

Graen, G. B. (2003b). Role making onto the starting work team using LMX leadership: Diversity as an asset. In G. B. Graen (Ed.), *Dealing with diversity: LMX leadership: The series* (Vol. 1, pp. 1-28). Greenwich, CT: Information Age.

Graen, G. B., Hui, C., & Taylor, E. T. (2004). A new approach to team leadership: Upward, downward, and horizontal differentiation. In G. B. Graen (Ed.), *New frontiers of leadership: LMX leadership: The series* (Vol. 2, pp. 33-66). Greenwich, CT: Information Age.

Graen, G. B., & Lau, D. (2005). Proper levels of analysis, hierarchical linear models, and leadership theories. In G. B. Graen (Ed.), *Global organizing designs: LMX leadership: The series* (Vol. 3, pp. 237-271). Greenwich, CT: Information Age.

Graen, G. B., Liden, R. C., & Hoel, M. (1982). Role of leadership in the employee withdrawal process. *Journal of Applied Psychology, 67,* 868-872.

Graen, G., & Schiemann, W. (1978). Leader-member agreement: A vertical dyad linkage approach. *Journal of Applied Psychology, 63,* 206-212.

Graen, G. B., & Uhl-Bien, M. (1995). Relationship-based approach to leadership—development of leader-member exchange (LMX) theory of leadership over 25 years—applying a multilevel multidomain perspective. *Leadership Quarterly, 6,* 219-247.

Herrington, J. (2000). Directing with viewpoints. *Theatre Topics, 10,* 155-168.

Hersey, P., & Blanchard, K. H. (1988). *Management of organizational behavior: Utilizing human resources* (5th ed.). Englewood Cliffs, NJ: Prentice-Hall.

Hiller, N. J., & Day, D. V. (2003). LMX and teamwork: The challenges and opportunities of diversity. In G. B. Graen (Ed.), *Dealing with diversity: LMX leadership: the series* (Vol. 1, pp. 29-57). Greenwich, CT: Information Age.

Jablin, F. M. (1979). Superior-subordinate communication: The state of the art. *Psychological Bulletin, 86,* 1201-1222.

Jones, G. R. (1986). Socialization tactics, self-efficacy, and newcomers' adjustments to organizations. *Academy of Management Journal, 29,* 262-279.

Keller, R. T. (1992). Transformational leadership and the performance of research and development project groups. *Journal of Management, 18,* 489-501.

Kramer, M. W. (2002). Communication in a community theater group: Managing multiple group roles. *Communication Studies, 53,* 151-170.

Kramer, M. W. (2004). Toward a theory of dialectics in group communication: An ethnographic study of a community theater group. *Communication Monographs, 71,* 311-332.

Larwood, L., Falbe, C. M., Kriger, M. P., & Miesing, P. (1995). Structure and meaning of organizational vision. *Academy of Management Journal, 38,* 740-769.

Lindlof, T. R. (1995). *Qualitative communication research methods.* Thousand Oaks, CA: Sage.

Pavitt, C. (1999). Theorizing about the group communication-leadership relationship: Input-process-output and functional models. In L. R. Frey, D. S. Gouran, & M. S. Poole (Eds.), *The handbook of group communication theory and research* (pp 313-334). Thousand Oaks, CA: Sage.

Pearce, C. L., & Conger, J. A. (2003). All those years ago: The historical underpinnings of shared leadership. In C. L. Pearce & J. A. Conger (Eds.), *Shared leadership: Reframing the hows and whys of leadership* (pp. 1-18). Thousand Oaks, CA: Sage.

Rubin, R. B., Rubin, A. M., & Piele, L. J. (2000). *Communication research: Strategies and sources* (5th ed.). Stamford, CT: Wadsworth.

Schriesheim, C. A., Castro, S. L., & Cogliser, C. C. (1999). Leader-member exchange (LMX) research: A comprehensive review of theory, measurement, and data-analytic practices. *Leadership Quarterly, 10,* 63-113.

Shaw, M. E. (1981). *Group dynamics: The psychology of small group behavior* (3rd ed.). New York: McGraw-Hill.

Seers, A., Keller, T., & Wilkerson, J. M. (2003). Can team members share leadership? Foundations in research and theory. In C. L. Pearce & J. A. Conger (Eds.), *Shared leadership: Reframing the hows and whys of leadership* (pp. 77-102). Thousand Oaks, CA: Sage.

Seifter, H. (2001). *Leadership ensemble: Lessons in collaborative management from the world's only conductorless orchestra.* New York: Times Books.

Sias, P. M., & Jablin, F. M. (1995). Differential superior-subordinate relations, perceptions of fairness, and coworker communication. *Human Communication Research, 22,* 5-38.

Stodgill, R. M. (1948). Personal factors associated with leadership: A survey of the literature. *Journal of Psychology, 25,* 35-71.

Trice, H. M., & Beyer, J. M. (1986). Charisma and its routinization in two social movement organizations. *Research in Organizational Behavior, 8,* 113-164.

Yukl, G. (1989). Managerial leadership: A review of theory and research. *Journal of Management, 15,* 251-289.

CHAPTER 2

TO SHARE OR NOT TO SHARE LEADERSHIP

New LMX-MMX Network Leadership or Charismatic Leadership on Creative Projects

George B. Graen

The new LMX-MMX leadership theory is described using Michael Kramer's participant observer documentation over the life cycle of the productions. As illustrated by Kramer the necessary exchange for a mutually trusting, respecting and committed working relationship is the authentic sharing of and acceptance of leadership. These are of two types: between leader and member (LMX) and between members (MMX). For each type both exchange parties must understand and accept the risks and rewards of this emergent working relationship. Moreover, both parties must agree that equity is defined by not what the giving party of the relationship thinks is fair but what the receiving member thinks is fair. In both LMX and MMX relations, the parties provide what the other wants and not what they should want (Buckingham & Coffman, 1999). This maximizes individual growth need fulfillment. A team leadership sharing decision tree is presented and discussed.

INTRODUCTION

According to the research literature, those who seek the basic strategies of team leadership have a choice of two: They can share or not share leadership with their team (Northhouse, 2001). If they choose to share leadership, they need to proceed in the manner described by Graen and his colleagues in their new Leader-Member Exchange-Member-Member Exchange (LMX-MMX) network theory of leadership, (Graen, 2003a,b; Graen, Hui, & Taylor, 2004; Graen & Lau, 2005; Uhl-Bien, Graen, & Scandura, 2000). Some benefits of this new network LMX-MMX leadership style are trust in and respect for the leader and commitment to and efficacy toward the network outcomes of effective team functioning and the achievement of network objectives (Graen, Hui, & Taylor, 2004; Seers, 2004). Additional benefits are improved network morale and more positive network attitudes toward work and the organization (Graen, 2003a,b).

Mechanisms for Leadership Sharing

Leadership sharing among employees in a group or team is not new (Katz & Kahn, 1978), but the mechanisms by which influential acts are shared had not been specified in detail until Graen's recent revision of LMX-MMX network theory of leadership sharing (Graen, 2003a,b). These mechanisms are further elaborated in the present book.

Leadership sharing process via role making is conceptually and empirically different from leader empowerment (Conger & Kanungo, 1988), Vroom and Yetton's (1973) participative decision making, self leadership (Manz & Sims, 1980), and transformational leadership (Bass & Avolio, 1990). In contrast to these above theories, Graen defines leadership sharing as the exchange of volunteered responsibility accepted by a follower and in reaction to revocable influence given informally by a leader for a particular purpose and with constraints. For example, a follower or coworker who volunteers to drive the bus containing the group is granted this mission until an accident happens or the destination is reached.

This leadership sharing process is different from dumping unwanted tasks, formal or informal delegation, and getting someone to do your work (pseudo leadership sharing). It requires that both parties share risks and rewards equitably. Hence, it requires progressively increasing levels of trust, respect, and commitment to maintain its growth. This translates into progressively stronger interpersonal work relationships. Although people differ in their risk taking propensity, very few would share leadership with relative strangers. Clearly, without strong trust, respect and commitment, little leadership sharing can be expected. According to

Graen's theory, leadership sharing is a necessary condition for mature LMX-MMX network leadership.

Leadership sharing must be authentic to produce the full and lasting power of enriched exchange. Artificial leadership sharing, while sometimes temporarily successful, in a short time destroys the reputations of would be leaders. "Fool me once" becomes the tag for one who falsely shares leadership. The signals of authentic and artificial leadership sharing were described by Graen (2003a,b). Both leaders and would be leaders should study these signals and use them as tests of authentic leadership sharing.

Getting Started

As Kramer (2006) described the communication strategies for authentic sharing of leadership influence, leaders admitted to being human, to not having all of the great answers and they asked for help from the team in terms of identifying potential problems, making suggestions for improvement, and sharing ideas. Leaders make clear that team members will share praise but not criticism with them. As the process proceeds, leaders progressively seek more significant responsibility from team members and progressively reward them for their augmented contributions. A critical part of leadership sharing is called "Role Making" by Graen (2003b) and involves the informal negotiated but functional redefinition of the respective roles of both leader and particular team member through a leader-member exchange of leadership. Clearly, role making is the driver of all mature LMX dyadic relationships and all LMX team leaderships. For those potential team leaders who seek the follower-granted influence we call leadership but who refuse to share leadership out of fear or arrogance cannot employ LMX-MMX leadership but must rely on their charismatic leadership. As Kramer (2006) describes this charismatic leadership communication strategy, leaders tell their teams that they do not need any help from them to lead the team and that they want no suggestions about this. When the team responds positively to this style of leadership over the life cycle of the team, we assume that the leader has charisma.

Strategies for Developing Team Leadership

As Kramer (2006) pointed out, these two styles of leadership work better with the appropriate team members and leaders try to select their appropriate followers. LMX team leaders prefer followers with clearly defined self-concepts and some experience who want to make helpful suggestions for improvements. In contrast, charismatic team leaders seek followers with more ambiguous self-concepts and little experience, who want to be told what to do (Graen & Lau, 2005).

Potential leaders should assess the characteristics of their team members in terms of these two leadership styles. If they prefer to make suggestions and seek to enrich their contributions, they are predisposed to LMX leadership sharing through role making. In contrast, if they prefer to be told what to do and to avoid the responsibility of enriched roles through role making, they are predisposed to charismatic leadership. Unfortunately for potential leaders, team's characteristics often fall between the two extremes with some team members preferring much or some leadership sharing and others preferring none. In these cases, leaders must work harder over time to enact a workable compromise. It is not hard to understand how most teams settle on a combination of both "asking for suggestions" and "telling what to do." Team members' role-making preferences about this are difficult to change and leaders can only share leadership with those who accept and enact the opportunity. As discussed by Graen and Lau (2005), leaders may prefer a strategy to share leadership with all (Team Makers), some (Cherry Pickers), or none (Job Enforcers), and followers may readily accept shared leadership (Career Makers), resist it (Conflicted), or reject it (Job Takers). Leaders must determine early in the team-making process, both the motivations of their team members (career makers, conflicted, and job takers) and their strategy (team makers, cherry pickers, or job enforcers). Consequently, for teams on creative projects, those with higher proportions of shared LMX-MMX team leadership perform more effectively internally and achieve greater success (Graen et al., 2004). According to this leadership theory, the monotonically increasing advantage of higher proportions of mature LMX-MMX relationships is derived from the enhanced investments in social capital by team members exchange for a share of leadership. This sharing of influence over the way the team functions can be highly motivating to those who prefer it.

Leadership in teams, according to this theory, is the increment in influence over team functions greater than the sum of prescribed parts. It is influence over that prescribed by formal team descriptions that give team members strictly limited influence in the team. Team leaders can enhance the total amount of influence in their teams by sharing it with followers and the more they share the better. Total social capital growth for a team is a function of total team leadership sharing with its larger interdependent networks.

Potential leaders who choose to tell all their teammates what to do forgo the above benefits of influence sharing and must rely on the team's formal design and their own charisma to direct and motivate the team to successful outcomes. This may be a comfort for these leaders, but it may be a source of team dissatisfaction and under achievement for team members.

In sum, the choice of leadership strategies is clear: Leaders can choose to share leadership with their team members or to lead without sharing leadership with their team. Under the leadership sharing strategy, the leader benefits from extra-role contributions of followers who enact leadership opportunities. Followers may work harder, think deeper, assume greater career risks, and do unexpected helpful things to ensure team success. In this sense, leadership sharing can get the most out of a creative team. In contrast, under a charismatic leadership strategy, team performance on all dimensions rests on the leader's talents. The leader makes all of the decisions and asks only that the team members do what they are told without protest. This may work for the truly gifted, but it also may yield serious underutilization of team members' collective talents and job experience.

In a series of team life cycle studies of engineering design project teams, Graen et al. (2004) found that LMX leadership sharing was strongly related to team performance as judged by a panel of experts and users. Performance of the teams was predicted by the leader's view of LMX leadership sharing and independently by the team member's views of LMX and MMX. In addition, leadership sharing was strongly related to team cooperation and fairness. On all of those measures from both leader's and teammate's points of view, 100% LMX or 100% MMX leadership sharing was clearly superior to 50% leadership sharing that was superior to 0% sharing. Hence, whether viewed from the leader (down) the followers (up) or the followers (across), 100% was superior to 50% that was superior to 0% sharing.

Overcoming Fears

With all of these benefits of leadership sharing, why do so many leaders of creative teams fail to fully engage the process? As was described by Kramer (2006), one communication strategy to initiate team leadership sharing is for the leader to admit that he or she doesn't have all of the answers and ask for suggestions from team members. Those who readily offer suggestions are encouraged and recognized for good ideas but are protected from criticism for poor ideas. Those team members who resist offering suggestions can be asked again and again. This process is self correcting as the team will help sort out the more useful from the less useful ideas when given the opportunity. One question that arises from this is: What factors inhibit the easy acceptance of this promising method of building a creative team of leadership sharing teammates?

We find that managers we have trained to become leaders usually have several doubts about entering a process of leadership sharing. First, they fear a loss of control by giving team members too much latitude in decision making, and coordination of the team may become too difficult and make them look bad. Second, they fear that team members will ask for personal favors and create embarrassing obligations for leaders. Third, they fear that team members will find out that they do not have all of the answers and lose respect for them. Finally, although many more fears have been expressed, the last resort is that their teammates do not want to share leadership with them. These fears must be addressed and worked through before leaders will test the unknowns of leadership sharing.

Fortunately, these fears can be overcome with proper training in the strategies of leadership sharing. Trainees come to understand that the process of sharing leadership is a successive approximation process in which successively more significant opportunities are reinforced when successful with progressively more meaningful recognition and resources. Also, they learn that followers must be made to succeed especially early in the development.

As the process unfolds, followers who share leadership grow into leaders within the team and share equitably in the success of the team. They grow out of their old roles and into new roles within the team. They come to understand that team leadership can be multiplied by following appropriate strategies. Team leaders come to recognize that sharing too much leadership too soon is a strategic mistake. They learn that until a follower is prepared to respect and enact a leadership sharing opportunity, it should not be given. After they are given, opportunities need to be supported as necessary to ensure success, because success invigorates the growth of shared leadership. Clearly, the benefits out weigh the risks in building a creative leadership sharing team. Even when a leader develops only one member into a leadership sharing partner, the benefits are worth the effort.

Sharing Leadership is More Than Delegation

Sharing leadership is the process of enriching an LMX relationship by including a follower in a meaningful higher-level project for the first time and giving the follower opportunities to develop new and valuable leadership competences. This process permits followers to share in leadership of higher-level projects and learn from them. In contrast, delegation is the process of assigning a new project to a follower without any necessary leadership component. The "more than" component is the actual sharing of leadership influence between leader and member on high-level projects. For example, it is the leader's reaching out to the follower for suggestions, analysis and cooperation on making the solution effective.

Leadership sharing involves professional risks for both parties as well as consequent personal and professional rewards. The risks for both are misjudging the capacity and motivation of the other to make the project successful. One failed attempt at leadership sharing because of misjudgment of the other may make another attempt less likely to occur. A successful attempt should make another attempt more likely. The benefits for members are career enhancing opportunities beyond the formal fast-track development path and acceptance into exclusive competence networks throughout the enterprise via new LMX and MMX relationship networks. Similarly, the benefits for leaders are career enhancing opportunities upstairs and acceptance into upstairs competence networks via new LMX and MMX relationships. Both leaders and members benefit appropriately by growing new dyadic leadership capacity. Over their entire careers, leaders and members who share leadership at every higher position tend to be more pleased with their careers, promoted faster, and rise higher in the organization (Graen & Wakabayashi, 2005).

Given that leadership sharing between leaders and members has been shown to result in such valuable outcomes for those practicing it consistently, the question is: Why isn't it universally practiced? One answer appears to be fear of charges of unfairness and favoritism. Leaders and their followers must have assurances from the top of the organization about the legitimacy of leadership sharing before it can be more widely practiced. Without such assurances, fears dominate the average leader, and only the self-confident leaders and members enact leadership sharing by accepting the risks and reaping the invaluable benefits. In these organizations, power sharing becomes the selection test for the fast track and the executive suite. The business decision rule is clear: Share leadership when the benefits outweigh the risks.

Our experience in organizations in which CEOs support of managerial leadership sharing is communicated through an active management development program shows that at all levels most followers readily seek greater leadership sharing but many leaders had to be reassured by their CEO before they shared leadership with their followers. Once these reluctant leaders were reassured and trained, many were amazed at the enthusiasm of their followers for progressively more significant leadership sharing. Not surprisingly, not all followers who were offered greater leadership opportunities enacted them. However, those that did made their teams better.

COMPLEXITY OF LMX LEADERSHIP IN PRACTICE

An LMX team maker will seek to develop 100% high quality relationships with his or her direct and indirect colleagues who are interdependent in terms of team effectiveness. However, this is not always possible for a variety of reasons including refusal to augment one's contribution to the team for any reasonable inducement.

In such cases the team maker is forced to become a cherry picker and develop a series of contingency plans. These plans involve identifying the critical players in each of the defining scenes, whether they be actors or crew members, and rating them first, second, third, etc. choice. The director tries to share leadership with the first choices and depending on his or her success may need to go to second or third or no choices. Later, depending on the success of the development of the first round of selected relationships, leaders may need to develop a second, third or fourth round of leadership sharing.

Further complexity is added when the leader finds that each leadership sharing relationship is different depending upon the personality of the partner. Partners may value different opportunities in terms of valence and instrumentality. Moreover, partners may react to the nature of others relationship with the leader. These potential sources of felt inequity must be dealt with by leaders as they arise. For example, when one sought complete and final say over a defining scene, the director had to demonstrate that this was not leadership sharing. The director must be given an alternative that is better for the project and not just better for the actor. Thus, compromise and creative problem solving must be substituted for my way only.

Other complexities involve changing the original project into a superior project through a process of team creative problem solving (Graen, 1989). A team with leadership sharing contributor's defining scenes allows a leader to guide his or her team in a creative process of shaping the project to best fit the team's strength and create the better production. Clearly, leader's sharing contributors must be supported and guided in ways that differ from non-sharing contributors. Leaders must carefully mold his or her contributors in manners that are seen as professionally growth enhancing (Graen, 2003a,b).

A final complexity involves the proper network of leadership sharing. Although most leadership research arbitrarily defines this proper network as the direct reporting relationships in a two-level unit, the proper network is seldom this confined. It usually involves at least three levels and interdependent roles outside of the direct reporting relationships. In fact, team leadership is defined as providing resources from outside of the team as needed for team effectiveness (Hackman & Walton, 1986).

According to Hackman and Walton, as long as the team has adequate resources, the leader should stay out of the way and anticipate the teams future needs. Team leaders who have influence with the outside resource providers are often the most effective in terms of team performance. Thus, a leadership sharing team leader must understand the team's resource needs and where and how the resources may be obtained to keep the team project on time and on budget. We have a good understanding of intrateam leadership using LMX-MMX leadership theory as tested by research, but we have more to learn about appropriate network leadership for team success. This book is a start in the direction of developing LMX leadership beyond team leadership to effective network leadership based on the prime directive of sharing leadership.

To go beyond team leadership to network leadership requires the integration of network and leadership theory. This mission is initiated in this book. According to LMX-MMX theory, network theory separates formal and informal organizing networks by distinguishing between the standard operating procedures of the formal (written and mechanistic) legal organization and the informal (unwritten and organic) human organization. Network theory further maps informal networks of trust, respect, commitment, liking, competence, and influence. The new LMX-MMX leadership theory (Graen 2003a,b; Graen & Lau, 2005; Uhl-Bien et al., 2000) incorporates relevant parts of both formal and informal organizations including mapping the networks and their influence on behavior, performance, and social capital of individuals, teams, and networks.

Decision Tree

The team leadership sharing decision tree as shown in Figure 2.1, prescribes that all potential followers, who are functionally involved in the teams mission, be given the opportunity to participate beyond their job descriptions to enhance the team mission. Next, the followers respond with acceptance, rejection or indecision regarding the opportunity. Their responses are evaluated in terms of each follower's talent and social capital relevant to the team mission. The LMX leadership theory's suggested actions are as shown. Considering both the follower's motivation to share leadership and the talent and social capital to be gained for the project, the leader's time and energy will be well served by following the recommendations.

Those that volunteer and possess high talent and social capital deserve the most leadership sharing attention and support as do those who have the resources but are reluctant to try. Next, the most deserving should receive a soft sell with more indirect persuasion. Finally, the least likely

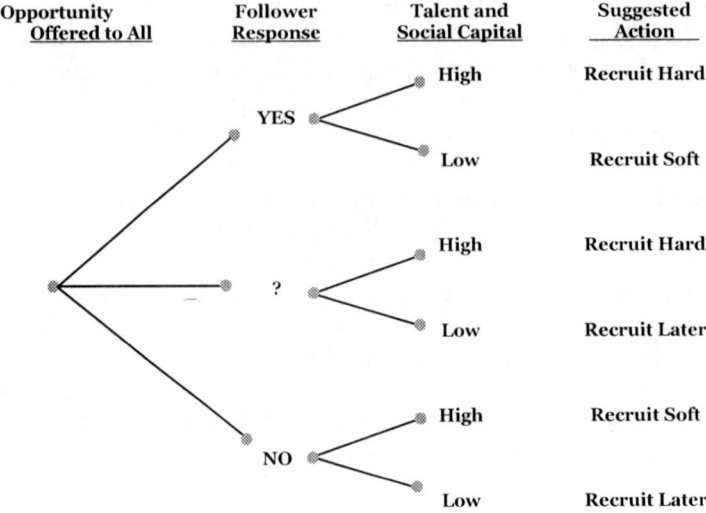

Figure 2.1. Leadership sharing decision tree.

and valuable followers are left to do their prescribed jobs with the leadership sharing invitations open.

Recent research by Sparrowe and Liden (2005) shows that a person's influence in the organization (social capital) as judged by coworkers at all levels was a function of two different components of the leader and member work relationship. The first component was the extent that both leader and member (direct report) were participants in the "same competence networks" in the organization. A competence network (Graen, 2003a,b) is a network of people who are functionally interdependent and accomplish the most difficult operations in often extra-organizational manners. The second component is the sharing of power as indexed by an LMX measure. Those employees who experienced both a strong overlap in participation in competence networks and mature leader-member exchange relationships were those judged with the most clout and influence in getting things done within the company. LMX-MMX leadership theory postulates that the process of shared leadership can spread far outside the home unit to parts of the entire human environment was supported.

Caveat

This paper does not suggest that leadership sharing cannot be done by highly charismatic leaders who can control their egos. In fact, we are suggesting that team leaders employ leadership sharing, regardless of their leadership charisma, when they must lead a project team on a creative project. The wise-team leader should multiply the team leadership base by programmed sharing with as many members as feasible. This should be especially good advice for the top management team that must choose wisely.

REFERENCES

Bass, B. M., & Avolio, B. J. (1990). *Transformational leadership development: Manual for the MLQ*. Palo Alto, CA: Consulting Psychologist Press.

Buckingham, M., & Coffman, C. A. (1999). *First break all the rules: What the world's greatest managers do differently*. New York: Simon and Schuster.

Conger, J. A., & Kanungo R. N. (1988). Conclusion: Patterns and trends in studying charismatic leadership. In J. A. Conger & R. N. Kanungo (Eds.), *Charismatic leadership: The elusive factor in organizational effectiveness*. San Francisco: Jossey-Bass.

Graen, G. B. (1989). *Unwritten rules for your career: 15 secrets for fast-track success*. New York: Wiley.

Graen, G. B. (2003a). Role making onto the starting work team using LMX leadership diversity as an asset. In G. B. Graen (Ed.), *Dealing with diversity, LMX leadership: The series* (Vol. 1, pp. 1-28). Greenwich, CT: Information Age.

Graen, G.B. (2003b). Interpersonal workplace theory at the crossroads. In G.B. Graen (Ed.), *Dealing with diversity, LMX leadership: The series* (Vol. 1, pp. 145-182). Greenwich, CT: Information Age Publishing, Inc.

Graen, G. B., Hui, C., & Taylor, E. T. (2004). A new approach to team leadership: Upward, downward and horizontal differentiation. In G. B. Graen (Ed.), *New frontiers of leadership, LMX leadership: The series* (Vol. 2, pp. 33-66). Greenwich, CT. Information Age.

Graen, G. B., & Lau, D. (2005). Hierarchical linear models and leadership theory. In G. B. Graen (Ed.), *Global organizing designs, LMX leadership: The series* (Vol. 3, pp. 235-269). Greenwich, CT. Information Age.

Graen, G. B., & Wakabayashi, M., (2005). Japanese models of managerial progress: Sponsored, tournament and two-stage mobility. In G. B. Graen (Ed.), *Global organizing designs, LMX leadership: The series* (Vol. 3, pp. 153-172). Greenwich, CT. Information Age.

Hackman, J. R., & Walton, R. E. (1986). Leading groups in organizations. In P. S. Goodman (Ed.), *Designing effective work groups*. San Francisco: Jossey-Bass.

Katz, D., & Kahn, R. (1978). *The social psychology of organizations* (2nd ed.). New York: Wiley.

Kramer, M. W., (2006). Communication strategies for sharing leadership within a creative team: LMX in theater groups. In G. B. Graen (Ed.), *Sharing network leadership, LMX leadership: The series* (Vol. 4). Greenwich, CT: Information Age.

Manz, C. C., & Sims, H. P. (1980). Self-management as a substitute for leadership: A social learning theory perspective. *Academy of Management Review, 5*, 361-367.

Northhouse, R .G. (2001). *Leadership: Theory and practice* (2nd ed.). Thousand Oaks, CA: Sage.

Seers, A. (2004). Leadership and flexible organizational structures: The future is now. In G. B. Graen (Ed.), *New frontiers of leadership, LMX leadership: The series* (Vol. 2, pp. 1-31). Greenwich, CT: Information Age.

Sparrowe, R. T., & Liden, R. C. (2005). Two routes to influence integrating leader-member exchange and network perspectives. *Administrative Science Quarterly, (50)*4.

Uhl-Bien, M., Graen, G. B., & Scandura, T. A., (2000). Implications of leader-member exchange (LMX) for strategic human resource management systems: Relationships as social capital for competitive advantage. In G. R. Ferris (Ed.), *Research in personnel and human resource management* (Vol. 18, pp. 137-185). Stamford, CT: JAI Press.

Vroom, V. H., & Yetton, P. W. (1973). *Leadership and decision-making*. Pittsburgh, PA: University of Pittsburgh Press.

CHAPTER 3

EXPANDING THE SCOPE

Social Network and Multilevel Perspectives on Leader-Member Exchange

David M. Mayer and Ronald F. Piccolo

Leader-member exchange (LMX) theory focuses on the *dyadic* relationship between a leader and follower, and research has identified numerous advantages for followers who develop high quality relationships with their leaders. However, despite calls from prominent LMX scholars, the majority of this research does not take the broader social context into account when studying LMX. Taking a contextual approach is important because it most closely mirrors the theoretical foundations of LMX and provides the most accurate depiction of how relationships exist in real world work organizations. In this chapter we further solidify the argument that it is critical to examine the broader social context when studying LMX, review the literature on two contextual approaches (social networks and multilevel thinking) that seek to move beyond studying individual relationships devoid of context, and conclude by presenting a model that integrates these two approaches in an effort to summarize the extant literature and inspire future LMX research to consider the social context.

INTRODUCTION

Few leadership theories have received more theoretical and empirical attention over the past three decades than leader-member exchange (LMX) theory (for reviews see Dienesch & Liden, 1986; Erdogan & Liden, 2002; Gerstner & Day, 1997; Graen & Scandura, 1987; Graen & Uhl-Bien, 1995; Liden, Sparrowe, & Wayne, 1997; Schriesheim, Castro, & Cogliser, 1999). Originally termed vertical dyadic linkage (VDL) theory, LMX distinguishes itself from many other leadership theories by focusing primarily on the *dyadic* relationship between a leader and his or her followers (Dansereau, Graen, & Haga, 1975). LMX theory originally posited that leaders *differentiate* among their followers due to the actions of leaders, followers, or both by developing high quality relationships with subsequently high achieving followers and spending less time and resources with subordinates that are subsequently less able; although more recent perspectives suggest that leaders should seek enriched relationships among their followers by attempting to develop high quality relationships with all or as many as feasible (Graen, 2003a,b). Research has demonstrated that when a follower develops a high quality relationship with his or her superior, a number of valuable outcomes emerge such as increased job performance, satisfaction, commitment, role clarity, decreased turnover intentions (Gerstner & Day, 1997).

While there is a considerable amount of interest in LMX and most leadership scholars acknowledge the value in examining the relationships between a leader and his or her followers within a group, unit, or team, unfortunately, the majority of research on LMX has focused solely on individual dyadic relationships without taking the social context fully into account. As an example, even though the theoretical stance of LMX is that enriching relationships among followers in a team improves *workgroup* productivity, only recently has research actually examined how the composition (i.e., proportion of high quality relationships in a group) of a group impacts group performance (Graen, Hui, & Taylor, 2004). Similarly, with the exception of an early study by Graen and his associates (Cashman, Dansereau, Graen, & Haga, 1976), only recently has research explored the effect of the network of relationships that leaders and followers have and how such networks may directly impact individual and group outcomes or how network variables may strengthen or weaken the effects of high quality relationships (see Sparrowe & Liden, 2006). Many scholars have called for the expansion of LMX research to consider examining such relationships within a broader social environment reflecting more appropriately what exists in real world work settings (Balkundi & Kilduff, 2005; Erdogan & Liden, 2002; Gertsner & Day, 1997; Graen & Uhl-Bien,

1995; Uhl-Bien, Graen, & Scandura, 2000; Zaccaro, Rittman, & Marks, 2001).

In this chapter we seek to build on the going momentum for studying LMX within a broader social context by integrating LMX with two perspectives: (1) *social networks* and (2) *multilevel thinking*. Many scholars have noted that it is important to integrate *social network* perspectives in LMX theory and research (Liden et al., 1997; Sparrowe & Liden, 1997, 2006). Prompting some of the interest in this integration is early work on LMX that found the relationship a leader had with his or her superior impacted how useful a high quality relationship would be for a subordinate (Cashman et al., 1976; Graen, Cashman, Ginsburgh, & Schiemann, 1977). In addition to the importance of leaders' and followers' social networks, recent advances in *multilevel thinking* have also begun to influence the LMX literature (Graen & Uhl-Bien, 1995; Schriesheim et al., 1999). Given that LMX is a theory about dyads in work groups and networks, it is essential for research to be true to the theory and to study LMX relationships within the context of such groups. By doing so, a host of interesting questions emerge regarding when having a high quality relationship is most beneficial to a leader and/or follower, as well as how the composition of relationships within a group impacts group performance. As theoretical, empirical, and methodological strides regarding social networks and multilevel influences have been made in recent years, leadership scholars are increasingly calling for leadership research, and LMX research in particular, to take this broader context into account.

There are three primary goals of this chapter. First, we seek to build interest in taking context into account when studying LMX. While a lot is known about the effects of having a high quality relationship for followers, we presently do not have a good understanding of how LMX relates to social network variables, how such variables placate or exacerbate LMX effects, or how group level variables directly or indirectly impact individual and group outcomes of LMX. Second, in our attempt to build interest, we provide a comprehensive review of the theoretical and empirical work integrating LMX with social networks and multilevel thinking. Such a review is important as considerable work has been done in these areas in the past decade and it's important to take stock in what we presently know. Third, we present a model that integrates social network and multilevel perspectives on LMX by summarizing past empirical research and highlighting a number of important areas of future research with the goal of studying LMX within a broader social context. As the theoretical work largely outweighs the empirical work, it is essential to make some recommendations about potentially fruitful future empirical investigations.

In the pages that follow, we begin our discussion by drawing on recent work to build the case that it is important for LMX research to take the broader social context into account—specifically focusing on social network and multilevel perspectives. We then review the theoretical and empirical literatures integrating LMX and networks and multilevel thinking. Finally, we conclude the chapter by suggesting a number of potential avenues for future research.

INTEGRATING CONTEXT: THE IMPORTANCE OF SOCIAL NETWORK AND MULTILEVEL PERSPECTIVES

LMX theory has steadily developed over the past three decades. Reichers and Schneider's (1983) work on the evolution of constructs posits that constructs and theories go through a series of developmental stages. In the first stage the theory is initially articulated and initial empirical articles emerge (called *introduction and elaboration*). In the second stage there are critical reviews of the research and the research grows more complex such as the examination of moderating and mediating variables (called *evaluation and augmentation*). The third and final stage involves general acceptance of the theory and a thorough knowledge of nearly all relevant boundary conditions for the effects (called *consolidation and accommodation*). It would be hard to argue that LMX theory is still in its infancy but it would also be imprudent to suggest that LMX theory has reached its zenith and there is little else to understand. Certainly, LMX theory and research are in the *evaluation and augmentation* stage in which scholars seek to understand more fully the causal mechanisms and boundary conditions of LMX effects.

A useful approach to examining mediating and moderating variables affecting LMX effects is to examine contextual variables—variables that take into account the social context in which leaders and their followers find themselves in work organizations (Balkundi & Kilduff, 2005). Until recently, very little leadership research had taken a contextual approach. In their influential review, House and Aditya (1997, p. 445) sum up this lack of attention to contextual factors: "It is almost as though leadership scholars, including the first author of this article, have believed that leader-follower relationships exist in a vacuum. While it is unlikely that scholars believe this, the fact is that the organizational and environmental context in which leadership is enacted has been almost completely ignored." More recently, empirical research has begun taking such a perspective (see Bono & Anderson, 2005; Sparrowe & Liden, 2006).

This movement to explore context, particularly with regard to social networks, is prevalent within the LMX literature. Even some of the early reviews of the LMX literature called for the examination of context. For example, Dienesch and Liden (1986, p. 630) called for more research on contextual influences on LMX and noted, based on Cashman and his associates work (1976), that "... leaders who do not have a good relationship with their immediate supervisor tend to have less to offer their subordinates than leaders who have cultivated good relationships with their immediate supervisors." Thus, even as far back as 20 years ago, scholars reviewing the literature on LMX argued for the importance of considering the broader social and organizational context.

Subsequent reviews have also pleaded for more research integrating the social context into LMX research. Gerstner and Day (1997, p. 839) stated that, "Researchers should continue to examine the role of organizational context," and "... much empirical research is needed to understand how the LMX model operates at different levels of analysis." Erdogan and Liden (2002, p. 98) noted that "LMX is imbedded within a larger system of relationships," and cite research integrating LMX and social networks. Sparrowe and Liden (1997, p. 523) make an important insight that, "...both of the perspectives used in the development of LMX theory, role theory and social exchange theory, recognize how dyadic relations develop within a social context," but that research has generally not been in line with these theoretical foundations. Graen and Uhl-Bien (1995, p. 233) agree with Graen and Scandura (1987) that, "... LMX should be viewed as systems of dyadic relationships, or network assemblies." Finally, Liden et al. (1997, pp. 90-91) provide perhaps the clearest explanation for why the broader social context is essential to keep in mind: "The quality of a member's exchange with his or her leader is, however, embedded in a larger relational context that includes peers, the member's own subordinates, the leader's peers and superiors, as well as others beyond the boundaries of formally constituted work groups."

It is no coincidence that nearly every major review of the LMX literature within the past two decades makes the point that to be consistent with the theoretical foundations of LMX and to develop a theory that most accurately maps onto real world work organizations, it is important to consider the broader social context in examining dyadic relationships between a leader and a follower. Some scholars focus their concerns on a lack of research integrating LMX with social networks and others focus on the dearth of research examining LMX from a multilevel perspective. Given that there is little doubt that prominent LMX researchers subscribe to the importance of taking a contextual perspective, in the succeeding sections we first detail the theoretical and empirical work integrating LMX and social networks and then detail the LMX work employing a multilevel framework.

LMX AND SOCIAL NETWORKS

In this section, we consider the literatures on leader-member exchange theory and social network analysis, with the intention of encouraging new research that utilizes a network perspective in leadership research. The purpose of the current section is to describe, from a theoretical perspective, how LMX has been associated with network centrality and how a network perspective on leadership is critical to the advancement of leadership research in general, and LMX research in particular. Whereas much of the existing research on LMX theory has centered on the single dyadic relationship that exists between a leader and follower (Sparrowe & Liden, 1997), significant strides have been made in articulating theoretical justification for assessing leader effectiveness in terms of high quality leader-member exchanges from a social networks perspective. In addition, we will introduce and summarize the conclusions from several studies that have successfully examined LMX and social networks. We first begin by highlighting important related trends in the broader leadership literature.

Trends in the Broader Leadership Literature: Relationships and Social Networks

In the last two decades, the leadership concept and much of the scholarly research on leader effectiveness has evolved beyond the simple examination of leadership traits or behaviors. Modern approaches to understanding excellent leadership recognize that leadership is an influence process that is not limited to positions of formal authority within an organizational structure (Uhl-Bien, 2003). Instead of defining leadership as a set of outstanding individual qualities or a specific set of motivating behaviors, those in academia and in the popular press regard leadership as a process by which one individual develops and exercises influence on others (Maxwell, 1993; Yukl, 1989).

Whereas traditional approaches have described leadership as a set of specific behaviors (e.g., Ohio State studies; Fleishman, 1973) or as a follower's cognitive evaluation of the leader's vision (e.g., transformational leadership; Bass, 1985), modern thought about leadership emphasizes an individual's ability to develop strong ties with members of the organization and to facilitate the development of "distributed intelligence" (Marion & Uhl-Bien, 2001). Indeed, effective leadership is not assigned exclusively to those who occupy formal positions of authority within an organization, nor is leadership limited to the interactions between two specific parties (leader and follower). Rather, successful leaders in an organization may be those who build social capital with co-workers and develop effective relationships among organizational members (Marion & Uhl-Bien, 2001).

Beyond the progression in our definition of leadership, there is a growing need to conduct leadership research with consideration of the social context within which a leader is placed. Certainly, leadership in most modern organizations is tied to the development of influential relationships with others (Geletkanycz, & Hambrick, 1997). As such, research on the leadership process needs to (a) estimate correspondence between a leader's behavior and the development of social capital (i.e., social networks), and (b) determine the extent to which network characteristics shape observed effects of leadership on individual (e.g., performance, satisfaction, and commitment) and group outcomes (e.g., group performance). Indeed, much of the work in today's business is done in teams or work groups (Devine, Clayton, Philips, Dunford, & Melner, 1999; Ilgen, Hollenbeck, Johnson, & Jundt, in press; Kozlowski & Bell, 2003), so it is natural for researchers to pursue a reconciliation of leadership thought with consideration of the social network that develops among members of the work group.

The broad literature on leadership has certainly provided extensive evidence of an effective leader's influence on individual attitudes and work behavior, but while most modern theories of leadership are specified at the group-level (e.g., transformational leadership; Bass, 1985), many studies of the leadership process examine interactions and causal effects at the individual level (Gerstner & Day, 1995; Judge & Piccolo, 2004). That is, studies of leadership tend to isolate one particular leadership style with a focus on single, dyadic relationships. Contextual boundaries of a leader's influence have been examined (e.g., Shamir & Howell, 1999), but additional study is needed to identify how characteristics of an individual's social network shape subsequent job related behaviors and attitudes. Thus, the next steps in the development of leadership thought is to consider leadership as a method of relationship development, to determine how individual leadership behaviors shape a follower's position and influence in the organization's social network, and how a follower's position within that network shapes important organizational outcomes.

Theoretical Work

There is considerable theoretical work linking LMX and social networks. LMX is based, in part, on the quality of leader-member interactions and the quality of relationships that a leader develops with each member of his or her work group. Social network analysis offers a meaningful framework for assessing the structure and composition of an individual's pattern of informal relationships in an organization (Baker, 1992), and is thought to have an effect on the individual's success in the organization (see Kilduff & Tsai, 2003 for a review). As relationships and interactions are at the center of each concept, a natural linkage exists between LMX and social network analysis (Wellman, 1988).

Several authors (e.g., Burt, 1992; Graen & Uhl-Bien, 1995) have proposed an integration of LMX and social networks by explaining how high quality leader-member interactions are embedded in a work context (Liden et al., 1997), and by emphasizing the importance of the structure of informal relationships on important organizational outcomes (Sparrowe & Liden, 1997). In their influential summary of the LMX literature, for example, Graen and Uhl-Bien (1995, p. 233) called for the expansion of the dyadic partnership between leader and follower to group and network levels, suggesting that leader-member exchanges be "… viewed as a system of interdependent dyadic relationships of network assemblies." Further, Sparrowe and Liden (1997, p. 527) argued, "social network analysis, through its emphasis on the effects of the structure of relationships on important outcomes, offers a means for extending the domain of LMX research beyond the vertical dyad linkage."

As such, the integration of LMX theory and social network analysis is critical (e.g., Graen & Uhl-Bien, 1995; Sparrowe & Liden, 1997) with recognition of the value that exists for the extension of LMX research beyond the analysis of a single dyadic relationship and the prediction of individual-level outcomes (e.g., member satisfaction and commitment). By examining LMX theory with a social network perspective, it is expected that researchers are more likely to identify the impact of group or work context on individual and group outcomes, more capable of explaining why the observed effects of high quality exchange exist, more willing to examine how relationships outside the immediate work group matter, and more able to say how leaders create positive relations among their followers.

A natural question that follows then is "how can we integrate LMX and social network analysis?" Several existing reviews offer compelling guidance (Liden et al., 1997; Graen et al., 2004; Graen & Uhl-Bien, 1995; Sparrowe & Liden, 2006), and in each case, the connection between leader-member exchanges and the structure of informal relationships has been grounded in social exchange theory. Our potential to draw a link between LMX and social network analysis rests primarily on the idea that relationships are at the heart of LMX theory and social networks. Indeed, *relational* theories of leadership (Murrell, 1997) define human interactions at the center of effective leadership, with an emphasis on the development of non-hierarchical, non-formal relationships among agents both internal and external to the organization. LMX theory, with its emphasis on the quality of relations between organizational members and its recommendations for the development of differentiated relationships with members of a work team, is consistent with a relational approach.

A social network perspective on leadership would require that leaders be skilled at building strong networks among subordinates, peers, and superiors, and skilled at accurately identifying those relationships and network subassemblies that are particularly useful (or harmful) to one's effectiveness. As Balkundi and Kilduff (2005, p. 946) theorized, effective leaders must accurately perceive aspects of the social network, including "relations between actors in [the work] unit and the extent to which [these] relationships involve embedded ties (kinship, friendship)." According to these authors, the accurate perception of and constructive management of informal social networks within an organization is "intrinsic to the leadership role" (p. 942). In this way, a leader's effectiveness is contingent on his or her ability to identify, foster, and maintain a powerful network of formal and informal relationships. Given the theoretical grounding for an integration of LMX theory and social network analysis, several studies have directly (or indirectly) derived a link between LMX and network centrality. In the following section, we review the handful of studies that have recognized social network development as part of the LMX leadership process.

Empirical Research

The theoretical work linking social networks and LMX far outweighs the amount of empirical work that has tested such notions. However, there is some research that was conducted soon after LMX theory was developed and some recent research that speaks to the importance of examining relationships outside the work group and social networks in particular. Specifically, there are four major sets of findings: (1) research linking a leader's relationship with his superior to member outcomes, (2) research exploring how leader and member centrality influence perceptions of LMX quality, (3) research examining the effects of having a high quality relationship with member centrality, and (4) research examining a leader's social network and whether a member has been incorporated into that network as boundary conditions for the effects of LMX. We review this empirical research below.

Despite a call by leading scholars to integrate LMX and social network analysis, only a handful of studies have specifically considered a relationship between the two concepts. First, some research has demonstrated that a leader's relationships with his or superior matters. For example, Cashman et al. (1976) and Graen et al. (1977) found that the quality of a leader's relationship with his or her own boss has a direct positive influence on the leader's resources to develop enriched exchange relationships with his or her own subordinates. Indeed, if a leader had a poor relationship with his or her boss, employees were less likely to benefit from high quality relationships with their leader.

Second, in a study of 91 professionals in a nonprofit organization, Goodwin, Whittington, and Bowler (2004) found significant interactions between aspects of a leader's network centrality and a follower's perceptions of LMX quality. For example, when the leader maintained high *influence* centrality in the organization's social network, the leader's advice centrality had little impact on followers' ratings of LMX quality. However, when the leader did not have influence centrality, the leader's advice centrality had a direct and significant effect on ratings of LMX quality. Further, when a leader was not regarded as central in the organization's social network, followers were less likely to report similarity with the leader or high levels of relationship quality. Similar results were reported for leader perceptions of LMX quality. That is, a follower's position in the organization's influence and advice networks shaped leader ratings of similarity with the follower and ratings of LMX quality. If a member was regarded as non-central, leaders were less likely to report favorable leader-member relations. Thus, according to Goodwin and his associates, network centrality has an important influence on how dyadic interactions are judged from both the leader and follower's perspective. The Goodwin et al. study provides further support for an integration of LMX theory and social network analysis.

Third, some recent research has linked LMX quality with network centrality. Sparrowe and Liden (2006) suggested that a relationship between LMX and a member's influence in his or her network could not be understood apart from consideration of the organization's larger social network. In a sample of 212 employees across three separate organizations, the authors reported a positive and significant relationship between LMX and member advice centrality and sponsorship, providing support for the notion that high quality leader-member relations shape the member's status in the organization's larger social network.

Fourth, Sparrowe and Liden also found support for a social network moderator of the effects of having a high quality relationship on member influence. Further, sponsorship and leader advice centrality each acted as moderators of the relationship between LMX and member influence. According to the authors, the value of a high quality relationship (i.e., high LMX) depended on the leader's own centrality in the broad organizational network and the extent to which a member shared networks with his or her leader.

Similar research is present within other leadership domains such as transformational leadership theory. For example, Bono and Anderson (2005) surveyed 39 managers and 130 employees in 6 separate organizations to determine how transformational leadership behaviors affect the leader's centrality in advice and friendship networks. Consistent with expectations, the authors found positive associations between behaviors that characterize the transformational approach (e.g., intellectual stimulation and charisma) and the leader's centrality in advice and influence networks.

Although sparse, these studies illustrate how leadership can be integrated with social network analysis to understand how leadership effects are revealed. In this section, we attempted to build a case for the integration of LMX and social network analysis. In the next section, we continue our discussion on the extension of LMX theory by introducing the literature on LMX and multilevel thinking.

LMX AND A MULTILEVEL PERSPECTIVE

In addition to examining LMX with a social network paradigm, another strategy for understanding contextual effects on leader-follower relationships is by taking a multilevel approach. Indeed, one trend in the organizational sciences is that scholars are increasingly taking a multilevel approach to understand a variety of phenomena (Klein, Dansereau, & Hall, 1994; Klein & Kozlowski, 2000). Taking a multilevel approach acknowledges that relationships traditionally examined at the individual level of analysis can be impacted by higher-level variables (e.g., group, team, unit, store, branch, organization, industry, etc.) and encourages scholars to consider not only individual-level dependent variables but also outcomes at the aggregate level of analysis. Within the leadership literature, a growing amount of literature is taking a multilevel perspective (For a review, see Yammarino, Dionne, Jae, & Dansereau, 2005).

Within the LMX literature specifically, a burgeoning literature is emerging. LMX theory was initially premised on the assumption that the best way for a leader to head a productive group is by differentiating among his or her followers and creating high quality relationships with some members and spending less time and resources with those less willing to grow (Graen, Novak, & Sommerkamp, 1982; Graen, Scandura, & Graen, 1986) and less capable members (Dansereau et al., 1975). Thus, LMX as a theory is inherently multilevel. Leader-member relationships take place within a broader social context—that of the work group. In addition, such relationships are likely to be impacted by forces outside of the work group itself (e.g., the leader's relationship with his or her supervisor). Further, the dependent variable of interest in LMX theory—group performance—is not at the individual level of analysis (although it is almost exclusively tested at this level). In what follows we highlight theoretical and empirical LMX work that takes a multilevel perspective.

Theoretical Work

Two reviews of the LMX literature within the past decade raise the important issue of using a multilevel perspective to understand LMX. In perhaps the most comprehensive review, Graen and Uhl-Bien (1995) suggest that the next wave of LMX research should take a multilevel perspective. They point out that leader-follower relationships do not exist within a vacuum but rather within a work group and an organization. They also acknowledge that informal relationships between peers, teammates, and other organizational members are also relevant. Specifically, they propose that a multilevel approach includes, "investigating patterns of relationship quality within the leadership structure, taking into consideration the criticality of relationships for task performance, as well as the effects of differentiated relationships on each other and the entire structure" (Graen & Uhl-Bien, 1995, p. 234).

Graen and Uhl-Bien (1995) go on to pose a variety of questions that emerge when taking a multilevel perspective at various levels of analysis. At the *workgroup* level, questions regarding why differentiating occurs, how differentiating impacts member relationships, and individual and group performance, and what is the best combination of relationships within a group are posed. At the *organizational* level, the impact of having a high quality relationship with a leader and his or her ability to make friendships throughout the organization are pertinent issues. At a *cross-organizational* level, questions emerge regarding how the pattern of relationships in a group or organization impacts employee interactions with individuals outside the organization. The work by Graen and Uhl-Bien provides a great introduction into the possible questions that can be asked when studying LMX from a multilevel perspective.

Another recent review by Schriesheim et al. (1999) highlights some of the level of analysis issues that have plagued the LMX literature. Indeed, these authors noted, "the level of analysis issue is not a minor or trivial one for LMX research" (p. 78). They highlight how early work on LMX (then referred to as VDL), departed from the prevailing assumptions of average leadership style (ALS) which posited that leaders treat all followers the same way. LMX on the other hand posited that leaders differentiate among their subordinates. They go on to say that while most assume that LMX is predicated on the differentiation process, the work by Graen and Uhl-Bien (1995) provides a departure from the traditional dyadic level of analysis to consider LMX from multiple levels of analysis. In response, Dansereau and colleagues have distanced themselves from LMX per se and have examined a new approach referred to as "Individualized Leadership," which focuses on dyadic relationships without a group or organizational context (Dansereau et al., 1995; Graen & Lau, 2005 for a review). While this approach has been critiqued (see Graen, 2005), it still presents one of the current perspectives on LMX.

Both of these theoretical reviews point to the importance of specifying the level of analysis before conducting LMX research. While there is not complete consensus about the appropriate level of analysis LMX should be tested at, there appears to be momentum to study LMX from multiple levels. Below we review LMX research that has taken a multilevel approach. One set of research examines the differentiation process (i.e., Do all group members have high or low quality relationships or is there variance?), and the other set of research examines the effects of LMX at the group level with a specific focus on group-level outcomes.

Empirical Research

Testing the differentiation hypothesis. The majority of research exploring LMX from a multilevel perspective has sought to examine whether groups are differentiated or whether leaders treat all of their followers the same. Schriesheim and colleagues (Schriesheim, Neider, & Scandura, 1998; Cogliser & Schriesheim, 2000; Schriesheim et al., 2000; Schriesheim, Castro, Zhou, & Yammarino, 2001) have put together an impressive body of research using a multilevel analytical approach to test predictions of LMX. The premise of this multilevel research is to test whether within-group effects proposed by LMX are indeed stronger than between-group effects. For example, if followers have different perceptions of their relationship quality with their leader then it supports the within-group approach as originally espoused by LMX. However, if members of a group rate their relationship quality similarly to other group members then this supports a between-group effect and substantiates the presumptions of average leadership style (ALS)—a theory that posits that leaders treat all of their members similarly.

To test whether the LMX or ALS approach is most appropriate, Schriesheim and colleagues have used a statistical approach called WABA (within and between analysis; Dansereau, Alutto, & Yammarino, 1984). There are three primary steps to WABA. First, in WABA I, each variable is assessed to determine whether its variation is primarily attributable to within or between group entities. Second, in WABA II, relationships are assessed to determine whether their variation is primarily attributable to within-group entities, between-group entities, or none at all. Third, raw score correlations are separated into within and between-group entities and the results from the first two steps are combined with the third step to determine the most appropriate level of analysis of the relationship.

The results of these multilevel examinations have generally found support for both within- and between-group effects (Graen, 2003a; Schriesheim et al., 1998; Cogliser & Schriesheim, 2000; Schriesheim, Castro, & Yammarino, 2000; Schriesheim et al., 2001). Thus, while there is some variation in how followers rate their relationships with a particular leader, the variation within groups appears to be smaller than the variance between groups. These results suggest that aspects of both the ALS and LMX approaches have credence. While these results are potentially interesting, scholars have noted the potential weaknesses of WABA as a statistical approach because it is highly sample size dependent (Bliese, 2000) and LMX scholars have critiqued this analytical approach (Graen & Lau, 2005).

Despite the possible limitations of WABA as an analytical tool, recent work by scholars using other multilevel frameworks have also found both within and between-group effects using aggregation statistics and random coefficient modeling (RCM), commonly referred to as hierarchical linear modeling (HLM). The use of RCM as an analytical technique to study LMX relationships has been praised in the literature (Graen & Lau, 2005). Calculating aggregation statistics is an important first step before using RCM because it is important to determine if there is a between-group effect such that it makes sense to partition the variance attributable to within and between-group effects. In an empirical demonstration of this approach, Hoffman, Morgeson, and Gerras (2003) found an ICC(1) value for LMX ratings of .39, which suggests that there is a significant between-group effect for LMX indicating that 39% of the variance in an individual's LMX score is attributable to the specific group in which that member resides.

The results of this emerging body of multilevel research on LMX is very useful in partly substantiating the claim of LMX theory that not all members in work groups feel like they have the same level of quality in their relationships with a particular leader and that aspects of groups impact individual LMX perceptions. Thus, the aforementioned multilevel studies provide support for the need to understand the effects of differentiation in groups. These WABA and ICC(1) findings are important because they provide evidence that LMX does in part operate at the group level of analysis, and thus provides evidence for why it is important to take the group context into account.

Testing Group-Level Dependent Variable

As highlighted previously in this chapter, research on LMX was initially conceptualized as producing group-level outcomes, but the empirical research has focused mainly on the more unexpected individual-level outcomes. Below we highlight some of the research that has been conducted.

The first paper to examine group-level outcomes associated with LMX was conducted by Liden, Erdogan, and Wayne (2002). They found that variance in group members' perceptions of LMX was positively related to group performance (i.e., leader ratings of the group). In other words, the more variance in LMX relationship quality across group members the higher the group performance. This is consistent with initial LMX theorizing that because of limited time and resources, a leader was forced to differentiate between his/her employees and thus to create higher and lower quality relationships. In addition, this relationship was moderated by the LMX median. The authors dichotomized LMX using a median split and found that for groups with a low LMX median, differentiation improved performance, whereas, for groups with a high LMX median, differentiating did not impact performance. This finding suggested that when group members are above the median with regards to high quality relationships, differentiation has less of an impact, but when group members are below the median in terms of being in the in-group, it is important to have a few trusted people who leaders can count on to perform. Finally, while not predicted, they found that LMX median was positively related to group performance. Thus, while it is not entirely clear whether the effects are partly attributable to the high correlation between LMX median and LMX variance, the notion that having a group of individuals with high quality relationships is advantageous did receive some support.

More recent studies have also examined the effects of LMX on group outcomes. Graen et al. (2004) found that when a higher percentage of members of a team had high quality relationships with their leader both team performance and team development were more favorable. Dotan, Goldstein, Nishii, and Mayer (2004) found that the group median on LMX positively related to group sales performance but that, in contrast to the differentiation hypothesis, variance in group members' LMX perceptions was not related to group sales performance. Further, when there was low differentiation and the group was cohesive and synergistic, group sales performance was most favorable. Nishii, Mayer, Goldstein, and

Dotan (2004) examined LMX quality (mean levels of LMX within a group) as a moderator of the relationship between group diversity and group performance (e.g., profits, customer satisfaction, turnover). The results indicated that group profits and customer satisfaction were higher and turnover was lower when diverse groups had high LMX ratings. Stewart and Johnson (2005) also examined LMX as a moderator of group diversity effects on group performance. They found that LMX quality (group mean on LMX) and LMX differentiation (group variance on LMX) interacted with group diversity to predict group performance. High quality and differentiation attenuated the potential deleterious effects of diversity, whereas low quality and differentiation were associated with decreased performance. Finally, Mayer (2006) found that higher mean levels of LMX were positively related to procedural and interactional justice climates, whereas variance in LMX perceptions was negatively related to these justice climates—especially when the groups were high on task interdependence.

In this section we reviewed the theoretical and empirical work on LMX that took a multilevel perspective. In the next section we present a model that integrates social network and multilevel approaches to the study of LMX.

INTEGRATIVE MODEL AND FUTURE DIRECTIONS

Thus far we have tried to make the case that integrating social network and multilevel perspectives into LMX research is important because such approaches take the social context into account, and we have reviewed relevant theoretical and empirical work using this framework. We now present a model that pictorially summarizes existing research and seeks to promote new research taking a social network and/or multilevel approach to LMX (see Figure 3.1). The model is partitioned into individual- and group-level sections to elucidate how a multilevel perspective can enrich the LMX literature. Specifically, for each level (individual and group), we describe direct effects, then mediating effects, and finally moderating effects indicated in the model—with a particular focus on integrating social network variables. We first discuss the empirical research that has been conducted within each subsection and then present potential research questions to stimulate empirical work integrating LMX, networks, and multilevel perspectives. Although this model is not meant to be exhaustive, its purpose is to clarify what research has been done and bring to light a number of potential research questions.

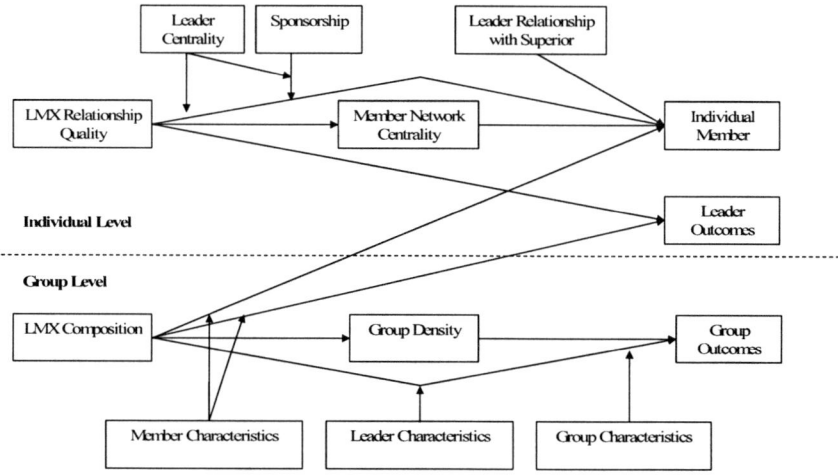

Figure 3.1. A multilevel social network model of leadership.

Individual Level

Direct effects. At the individual level of analysis there is considerable research to draw upon. For example, a plethora of past research has linked LMX relationship quality with a variety of individual outcomes (Gerstner & Day, 1997). In addition, although less research has focused on leader outcomes per se there is some research to support the idea that having a high quality relationship with a follower results in improved leader outcomes. However, given that LMX is a theory about leader effectiveness, we suggest more research on this link is needed. Integrating the social network perspective, work by Cashman et al. (1976) and Dansereau et al. (1975) provide support for the notion that a leader's relationship with his or her own boss is positively related to member outcomes. The integration of social network variables here prompts potential research questions. For example, does a leader's relationship with other team members impact an individual team member's or leader's outcomes? Does a leader's relationship with other leaders outside the immediate work group impact individual member or leader outcomes?

Mediating effects. Although much research has been conducted to link high quality relationships with member outcomes, there is a dearth of research examining why such relationships occur. We propose in this model that one explanation for the effects of high quality relationships on individual outcomes is because members that develop good relationships with their leaders are likely to be more central in their group's networks.

Indeed, if a member is "in good" with a leader she or he is likely to have better access to resources and information—and thus more likely to be a central player in the group's network. Preliminary support for this notion comes from the work of Sparrowe and Liden (2006) who found a positive relationship between having a high quality relationship and network centrality. And, many studies have linked network centrality to a variety of individual outcomes (Borgatti & Foster, 2003). Thus, it may be that network centrality serves as a mediator of the LMX quality to outcomes relationships. By testing this mediated path, scholars could uncover another explanation for why members' with high quality relationships reap a variety of benefits. Extending this logic, a variety of questions emerge. For instance, does member network centrality mediate the effects of LMX relationship quality on individual outcomes? Is this more likely to be the case for certain dependent variables? Does it matter what type of network a member is central in? Do high quality relationships result in being central in advice networks as opposed to friendship networks? Are individuals with low quality relationships more central in adversarial networks or do individuals with high quality relationships alienate fellow team members and subsequently become central in adversarial networks? Does having a high quality relationship impact what type of centrality index is higher (e.g., in-degree, out-degree, betweeness)? All of these questions would be interesting to address in future research.

Moderating effects. As LMX theory and research continue to evolve, it is important to identify boundary conditions of LMX effects. Sparrowe and Liden (2006) used a social networks paradigm to examine two moderators of LMX effects. They found that the relationship between having a high quality relationship with a leader and member influence is moderated by both sponsorship and leader centrality—the relationship is stronger when leaders are central in their network and when members are ushered in as apprentices by their leader. Further, there is a three-way interaction between relationship quality, sponsorship, and leader centrality such that members do not get positive outcomes if they have a high quality relationship and are sponsored by a leader who is not central. This research suggests that the effects of having a high quality relationship are in part dependent on aspects of the leader's centrality and whether a member is engulfed into that network. Unanswered questions include whether a member's perceived (or actual) similarity with his or her leader impacts whether he or she is sponsored.

In addition, future research should examine the extent to which follower centrality shapes leader-member exchange quality and observed outcomes of high quality exchange. The study by Goodwin et al. (2004) offered evidence that a follower's position within an organization's social network has an influence on perceived similarity with the leader and judgments of LMX quality. According to the authors, outcomes of LMX quality (e.g., organizational commitment, job satisfaction, in-role performance) are not independent of the follower's network. These observations are consistent with studies in the leadership literature that have emphasized the role of followers in the leadership process (e.g., Ehrhart & Klein, 2001; Howell & Shamir, 2005). Thus, characteristics of the follower and the follower's network are likely to influence the development of LMX quality and the existence of valuable organizational outcomes.

Group Level

Direct effects. While some research has used a social networks perspective to link the existence of a high quality relationship with member outcomes, there is a dearth of research integrating both social networks and a multilevel approach to LMX. Although there is a shortage of research on this issue, it is likely that team composition (meaning both the group mean and variance on LMX) could have direct effects on member and leader outcomes. For example, if the group mean is high, one would expect individual outcomes to also be more favorable. However, when differentiation (i.e., variance) is high, it is unclear if team composition has an effect on member and leader outcomes or if it is an artifact. Looking at these cross-level direct effects raises the question of how group composition of LMX impacts individual and leader outcomes. In addition to the direct effect of group composition of LMX on individual outcomes, one can examine its relationship with group outcomes. For example, research by Dotan et al. (2004) and Liden et al. (2002) suggests that LMX composition impacts group performance. However, Dotan et al.'s results suggest that having a higher group mean on LMX leads to the most favorable outcome, Liden et al.'s findings suggest that differentiation (under the right contexts) is most effective. A fundamental question that needs to be answered in the LMX literature is whether differentiation leads to positive individual and group outcomes or whether it is better for all team members to have high quality relationships.

Mediating effects. Just as we posited that network features could mediate the relationship between high quality relationships and member outcomes, we also believe this process could operate at the group level. Indeed, the integration of social network analysis may be essential to extending the scope of LMX beyond the examination of individual outcomes to those that reflect results at a higher-level (e.g., group performance, cohesion, cooperation). At its core, LMX theory provides a compelling explanation of how leader-member interactions shape follower attitudes, cognition, and behaviors. To understand how high quality

LMX relates to outcomes at the group level, network features may emerge as a valuable explanatory mechanism.

It is reasonable to suggest, for example, that when most members of a group have high quality relationships, it is likely that such individuals will have more access to information and resources and will share that information with one another. In other words, an inclusive environment where there are frequent positive interactions between members is likely to emerge. Such a situation exemplifies what network scholars call a *dense* network. Density refers to the number of actual links to the number of possible links in a network. Thus, the more members are connected, the denser the network. And, considerable research has demonstrated that groups with dense networks tend to be more effective—both in terms of viability and performance (Balkundi & Harrison, in press). Given the links between group composition of LMX and group density, and the relationships between density and group outcomes, it is likely that one way LMX impacts group performance is by creating dense networks where information and resources are shared. Thus, group density may help to explain the observed effects of high quality exchange. To our knowledge no research has examined this possibility.

Moderating effects. Just as we examined boundary conditions of individual effects, we also highlight a few boundary conditions at the group level. Because research has generally not addressed this issue, many ideas are speculative and we try to highlight areas of future research. Specifically, we discuss three classes of variables—member, leader, and group characteristics.

It is likely that member characteristics moderate the relationship between LMX composition and individual outcomes. One pertinent question is: Which type of person most objects to differentiation? Indeed, members that value an equality rule will likely have less favorable attitudes when group members are treated differently. There is also support for the notion that women and collectivists tend to value equal treatment and thus might object more to differentiation (Major & Deaux, 1982). However, if group members are solely interested in group outcomes and they believe differentiation is an acceptable and appropriate means to improve group performance they may accept such differentiation. Thus, it is important to understand how different types of people react to differentiation.

In addition to member characteristics, leader characteristics are also an important moderator of the relationship between LMX composition and group outcomes. For example, Liden et al. (1997) suggested that competent leaders will be more effective when differentiating because they will choose the right members with which to develop high quality relationships. In addition, social and communication skills also might be important for a leader who needs to justify why group members are getting differential access to high quality relationships. Thus, certain leaders may be able to thrive when differentiating while others may not.

Finally, characteristics of the group may also matter. For example, Dotan et al. (2004) found that low differentiation led to the best outcomes when groups were cohesive and synergistic. In addition, Mayer (2006) found that differentiation had a particularly negative effect on justice climates when the group was high in task interdependence. Thus, characteristics of the group appear to have an impact on how LMX composition relates to group outcomes. This appears to be a fruitful area for research.

Studies of this nature are consistent with the broad leadership literature, which has attempted to emphasize the importance of context on the emergence, development, and effectiveness of various leadership styles. Fiedler's (1967) contingency theory, for example, rested on the notion that leaders could not adjust their behaviors according to the demands of the organization's environment and the leader's relationship with members of the organization's informal network. According to Fielder, when a leader maintains high position power (i.e., network centrality) and high quality leader-member relations (i.e., high quality LMX), a task-oriented style of leadership is most effective. On the other hand, when a leader maintains modest power within the organization and only marginal relations with co-workers, a people-oriented style is most desirable. In this way, Fiedler recognized that effective leader behavior should not be examined independent of the leader's centrality in the organization's social network.

Further, it has become widely accepted that societal (e.g., political, economic), organizational (e.g., mission, structure) and group (e.g., cohesiveness, norms) contingencies exist to impose meaningful constraints on the effectiveness of specific leader behaviors. This idea was recently articulated by Pawar and Eastman (1997), who described how an organization's mission and governance structure shaped the emergence of charismatic and transformational leadership styles. As the authors noted, organizational issues are particularly meaningful when researchers examine leadership effects at the group level. As such, future examinations of LMX should recognize the impact of those contextual and group characteristics that are widely proposed to influence the effectiveness of leader behavior and the development of high quality leader-member relations.

CONCLUSIONS

The goal of this chapter was to further integrate the social network structure into LMX research by drawing on social network and multilevel perspectives. There is clearly a trend within the larger leadership literature, and the LMX literature in particular, to take the social context into account when examining leadership effectiveness. By integrating these perspectives, LMX scholars will help develop a more ecologically generalizable theory of leadership that has important implications for how to lead a team or network. In addition, by including aspects of social network analysis in leadership research, researchers and practitioners will recognize network relationship building as a critical part of the leadership function. Such an enhancement to our view of the leadership process may move existing models of leadership forward.

REFERENCES

Baker, W. (1992). The network organization in theory and practice. In N. Nohria & R. Eccles (Eds.), *Networks and organizations: Structure form and action* (pp. 397-429). Boston: Harvard Business School Press.

Balkundi, P., & Harrison, D. H. (in press). Ties, leaders, and time in teams: Strong inference about network structure's effects on team viability and performance. *Academy of Management Journal*.

Balkundi, P., & Kilduff, M. (2005). The ties that lead: A social network approach to leadership. *The Leadership Quarterly, 16*, 941-961.

Bass, B. M. (1985). *Leadership and performance beyond expectations*. New York: Free Press.

Bliese, P. D. (2000). Within group agreement, non-independence, and reliability: Implications for date aggregation. In K. J. Klein & S. W. J. Kozlowski (Eds.), *Multilevel theory, research, and methods in organizations: Foundations, extensions, and new directions* (pp. 349-381). San Francisco: Jossey-Bass.

Bono, J. E., & Anderson, M. H. (2005). The advice and influence networks of transformational leaders. *Journal of Applied Psychology, 90*, 1306-1314.

Borgatti, S. P., & Foster, P.C. (2003). The network paradigm in organizational research: A review and typology. *Journal of Management, 29*, 991-1013.

Burt, R. S. (1992). *Structural holes: The social structure of competition*. Cambridge, MA: Harvard University Press.

Cashman, J., Dansereau, F., Graen, G., & Haga, W. J. (1976). Organizational understructure and leadership: A longitudinal investigation of managerial role—making process. *Organizational Behavior and Human Performance, 15*, 278-296.

Cogliser, C. C., & Schriesheim, C. A. (2000). Exploring work unit context and leader-member exchange. A multi-level perspective. *Journal of Organizational Behavior, 21*, 487-511.

Dansereau, F., Alutto, J., & Yammarino, F. (1984). *Theory testing in organizational behavior*. Englewood Cliffs, NJ: Prentice Hall.

Dansereau, F., Graen, G. B., & Haga, W. (1975). A vertical dyad linkage approach to leadership in formal organizations. *Organizational Behavior and Human Performance, 13*, 46-78.

Dansereau, F., Yammarino, F.J., & Markham, S.E. (1995). Leadership: The multiple level approaches. *Leadership Quarterly, 6*, 97-109.

Devine, D. J., Clayton, L. D., Philips, J. L., Dunford, B. B., & Melner, S. B. (1999). Teams in organizations. *Small Group Research, 30*, 678-711.

Dienesch, R. M., & Liden, R. C. (1986). Leader-member exchange model of leadership: A critique and further development. *Academy of Management Review, 11*, 618-634.

Dotan, O., Goldstein, H. W., Nishii, L. H., & Mayer, D. M. (2004). *Leader-member exchange, group-level process, and group performance*. Poster presented at the annual conference of the Society for Industrial & Organizational Psychology. Chicago, IL.

Ehrhart, M. G., & Klein, K. J. (2001).Predicting followers' preferences for charismatic leadership: The influence of follower values and personality. *Leadership Quarterly, 12*, 153-179.

Erdogan B., & Liden, R. C. (2002). Social exchanges in the workplace: A review of recent developments and future directions in leader-member exchange theory. In L. L. Neider & C. A. Schriesheim (Eds.), *Leadership* (pp. 65-114). Greenwich, CT: Information Age.

Fiedler, F. E. (1967). *A theory of leadership effectiveness*. New York: McGraw-Hill.

Fleishman, E. A. (1973). Twenty years of consideration and structure. In E. A. Fleishman & J. G. Hunt (Eds.), *Current developments in the study of leadership* (pp. 1-40). Carbondale, IL: Southern Illinois University Press.

Geletkanycz, M. A., & Hambrick, D. C. (1997). The external ties of top executives: Implications for strategic choice and performance. *Administrative Science Quarterly, 42*, 654-681.

Gerstner, C. R., & Day, D. V. (1997). Meta-analytic review of leader-member exchange theory: Correlates and construct issues. *Journal of Applied Psychology, 82*, 827-844.

Goodwin, V. L., Whittington, J. L., & Bowler, W. M. (2004). *LMX and social network analysis*. Paper presented at the Annual Conference of the Academy of Management. New Orleans, LA.

Graen, G. B. (2003a). Interpersonal workplace theory at the crossroads. In G. B. Graen (Ed.), *Dealing with diversity: LMX leadership: The series* (Vol. 1, pp. 145-182). Greenwich, CT: Information Age.

Graen, G. B. (2003b). Role making onto the starting work team using LMX leadership: Diversity as an asset. In G. B. Graen (Ed.), *Dealing with diversity: LMX leadership: the series* (Vol. 1, pp. 1-28). Greenwich, CT: Information Age.

Graen, G. B. (2005). Three dyadic leadership theories: Comparative multiple hypotheses testing. In G. B. Graen (Ed.), *Dealing with diversity: LMX leadership: the series* (Vol. 1, pp. 1-28). Greenwich, CT: Information Age.

Graen, G. B., Orris, D., & Alvares, K. (1971) Studies Testing The Contingency Model. *Journal of Applied Psychology, 55*, 202-204.

Graen, G. B., Alvares, K., Orris, D., & Martella, J. (1970). The contingency model of leadership effectiveness: Antecedent and evidential results. *Psychological Bulletin, 74*, 285-296.

Graen, G. B., Cashman, J. F., Ginsburg, S., & Schiemann, W. (1977). Effects of linking-pin on the quality of working life of lower participants. *Administrative Science Quarterly, 22*, 491-504.

Graen, G. B., Hui, C., & Taylor, E. T. (2004). A new approach to team leadership: Upward, downward, and horizontal differentiation. In G. B. Graen (Ed.), *New frontiers of leadership: LMX leadership: The series* (Vol. 2, pp. 33-66). Greenwich, CT: Information Age.

Graen, G. B., & Lau, D. (2005). Proper levels of analysis, hierarchical linear models, and leadership theories. In G. B. Graen (Ed.), *Global organizing designs: LMX leadership: The series* (Vol. 3, pp. 237-271). Greenwich, CT: Information Age.

Graen, G. B., Novak, M. A., Sommerkamp, P. (1982). The effects of leader-member exchange and job design on productivity and satisfaction: Testing a dual attachment model. *Organizational Behavior and Human Performance, 30*, 109-131.

Graen, G. B., & Scandura, T. (1987). Toward a psychology of dyadic organizing. In B. Staw & L.L. Cummings (Eds.), *Research in organizational behavior* (Vol. 9, pp. 175-208). Greenwich, CT: JAI Press.

Graen, G. B., Scandura, T., & Graen, M. R. (1986). A field experimental test of the moderating effects of growth need strength on productivity. *Journal of Applied Psychology, 71*, 484-491.

Graen, G. B., & Uhl-Bien, M. (1995). Relationship-based approach to leadership: Development of leader-member exchange (LMX) theory over 25 years: Applying a multi-level multi-domain perspective. *Leadership Quarterly, 6*, 219-247.

Hackett, R. D., Farh, J-L, Song, L.J., & Lapierre, L. M., (2003). LMX and organizational citizenship behavior: Examining the links within and across Western and Chinese samples. In G. B. Graen (Ed.), *Dealing with diversity, LMX leadership: The series* (Vol. 1 pp. 219-263). Greenwich, CT: Information Age.

House, R. J., & Aditya, R.N. (1997). The social scientific study of leadership: Quo vadis? *Journal of Management, 23*, 409-473.

Hoffman, D. A., Morgeson, F. P., & Gerras, S. J. (2003). Climate as a moderator of the relationship between leader-member exchange and content specific: Safety climate as an exemplar. *Journal of Applied Psychology, 88*, 70-178.

Howell, J. M., & Shamir, B. (2005). The role of followers in the charismatic leadership process: Relationships and their consequences. *Academy of Management Review, 30*, 96-112.

Ilgen, D. R., Hollenbeck, J. R., Johnson, M., & Jundt, D. (in press). Teams in organizations: From I-P-O models to IMOI models. *Annual Review of Psychology.*

Judge, T. A., & Piccolo, R. F. (2004). Transformational and transactional leadership: A meta-analytic test of their relative validity. *Journal of Applied Psychology, 88*, 70-178.

Kilduff, M., & Tsai, W. (2003). *Social networks and organizations.* London: Sage.

Klein, K. J., Dansereau, F., & Hall, R. J. (1994). Levels issues in theory development, data collection, and analysis. *Academy of Management Review, 19*, 195-229.

Klein, K. J., & Kozlowski, S. W. (2000). *Multilevel theory, research, and methods in organizations*. San Francisco: Jossey-Bass.

Kozlowski, S. W. J., & Bell, B. S. (2003). Work groups and teams in organizations. In W. C. Borman, D. R. Ilgen, & R. J. Klimoski (Eds.), *Comprehensive handbook of psychology: Industrial and organizational psychology* (Vol. 12, pp. 333-375). New York: Wiley.

Liden, R. C., Erdogan, B., & Wayne, S. J. (2002). *Leader-member exchange differentiation: Implications for group effectiveness*. Unpublished manuscript.

Liden, R. C., Sparrowe, R. T., & Wayne, S. J. (1997). Leader-member exchange theory: The past and potential for the future. In G. R. Ferris (Ed.), *Research in personnel and human resources management* (Vol. 15, pp. 47-119). Greenwich, CT: JAI Press.

Lord, R. G., & Emrich, C. G. (2001). Thinking outside the box by looking inside the box: Extending the cognitive revolution in leadership research. *Leadership Quarterly, 11*, 551-579.

Marion, R., & Uhl-Bien, M. (2001). Leadership in complex organizations. *Leadership Quarterly, 12*, 389-418.

Maxwell, J. C. (1993). *Developing the leader within you*. Nashville, TN: Thomas Nelson.

Major, B., & Deaux, K. (1982). Individual differences in justice behavior. In J. Greenberg & R.L. Cohen, (Eds.), *Equity and justice in social behavior* (pp. 43-76). New York: Academic Press.

Mayer, D. M. (2006). *A group-level examination of the relationship between LMX and justice*. Paper presented at the annual conference of the Society for Industrial & Organizational Psychology, Dallas, TX.

Murrell, K. (1997). Emergent theories of leadership for the next century: Towards relational concepts. *Organizational Development Journal, 15*, 35-42.

Nishii, L. H., Mayer, D. M., Goldstein, H. W., & Dotan, O. (2004). *Diversity and bottom-line performance: The moderating role of leader-member exchanges*. Poster presented at the annual conference of the Society for Industrial & Organizational Psychology, Chicago, IL.

Pastor, J. C., Meindl, J. R., & Mayo, M.C. (2002). A networks effect model of charismatic leadership. *Academy of Management Journal, 45*, 410-420.

Pawar, B. S., & Eastman, K. K. (1997). The nature and implications of contextual influences on transformational leadership: A conceptual examination. *Academy of Management Review, 22*, 80-109.

Reichers, A. E., & Schneider, B. (1990). Climate and culture: An evolution of constructs. In B. Schneider (Ed.), *Organizational climate and culture* (pp. 5-39). San Francisco: Jossey-Bass.

Schneider, B., & Reichers, A. E. (1983). On the etiology of climates. *Personnel Psychology, 36*, 19-39.

Schriesheim, C. A., Castro, S. L., & Cogliser, C. C. (1999). Leader-member exchange (LMX) research: A comprehensive review of theory, measurement, and data-analytic practices. *Leadership Quarterly, 10*, 63-113.

Schriesheim, C. A., Castro, S. L., & Cogliser, C. C. (1999). Leader-member exchange (LMX) research: A compresnsive review of theory, measurement, and data-analytic practices. *Leadership Quarterly, 10*, 63-113.

Schriesheim, C. A., Castro, S. L., & Yammarino, F. J. (2000). Investigating contengencies: An examination of the impact of span of supervision and upward controllingness on leader-member exchange using traditional and multivariate within-and between-entities analysis. *Journal of Applied Psychology, 85*, 659-677.

Schriesheim, C. A., Castro, Zhou, X., & Yammarino, F. J. (2001). The folly of theorizing "A" but testing "B." A selective level-of-analysis review of the field and a detailed leader-member exchange illustration. *The Leadership Quarterly, 12*, 515-551.

Schriesheim, C. A., Neider, L. L., & Scandura, T. A. (1998). Delegation and leader-member exchange: Main effects, moderatorss, and measurement issues. *Academy of Management Journal, 41*, 298-318.

Shamir, B., & Howell, J. M. (1999). Organizational and contextual influences on the emergence and effectiveness of charismatic leadership. *Leadership Quarterly, 10*, 257-283.

Sparrowe, R. T., & Liden, R. C. (1997). Process and structure in leader-member exchange. *Academy of Management Review, 22*, 522-552.

Sparrowe, R. T., & Liden, R. C. (2006). Two routes to influence: Integrating leader-member exchange and network perspectives. *Administrative Science Quarterly*.

Sparrowe, R. T., Liden, R. C., Wayne, S. J., & Kraimer, M. L. (2001). Social networks and the performance of individuals and groups. *Academy of Management Journal, 444*, 316-325.

Stewart, M., & Johnson, O. E. (2005). *Workgroup diversity and group performance: The moderating effect of leader-member exchange.* Paper presented at the annual meeting of the Academy of Management, Honolulu, HI.

Uhl-Bien, M. (2003). Relationship Development as a Key Ingredient for Leadership Development. In S. Murphy & R. Riggio (Eds.), *The future of leadership development* (pp. 29-147). Erlbaum.

Uhl-Bien, M., Graen, G. B., & Scandura, T. A. (2000). Implications of leader-member exchange (LMX) for strategic human resource management systems: Relationships as social capital for competitive advantage. In G. Ferris (Ed.), *Research in personnel and human resources management* (Vol. 18, pp. 137-185). Stamford, CT: JAI Press.

Wellman, B. (1988). Structural analysis: From method and metaphor to theory and substance. In B. Wellman & S. D. Berkowitz (Eds.), *Social structures: A network approach* (pp. 19-61). Cambridge, MA: Cambridge University Press.

Yammarino, F. J., Dionne, S. D., Jae, U. C., & Dansereau, F. (2005). Leadership and levels of analysis: A state-of-the-science review. *Leadership Quarterly, 16*, 879-919.

Yukl, G. (1989). Managerial leadership: A review of theory and research. *Journal of Management, 15*, 251-289.

Zaccaro, S. J., Rittman, A. L., & Marks, M. A. (2001). Team leadership. *Leadership Quarterly, 12*, 451-483.

CHAPTER 4

NETWORK FACTORS IN LEADER-MEMBER RELATIONSHIPS

Deborah E. Gibbons and Steven L. Grover

This chapter applies basic precepts of network theory to leader-member relationships and leadership exchanges that are embedded in broader social networks. The network concepts include relational attributes such as friendship, advice, or trust that may compose a relationship; formation and effects of triads and other subgroupings; patterns of relationship-building within and beyond the group or team, and centrality in the network. Each network concept is integrated with LMX theory to produce propositions about network structures including leader-member relationships. Finally, complementary effects of interpersonal relations, network structures, and LMX relationships on team process effectiveness are discussed.

INTRODUCTION

Social networks form the background in which leadership occurs. They provide the channels through which it unfolds, and they create the forum in which it will be evaluated. Formal leaders who develop positive relationships can be more effective and evaluated more highly by their team members than leaders who fail to build positive relationships (Graen & Uhl-Bien, 1995). As each leader-member relationship develops from the stranger phase toward maturity, surrounding relationships are likely to affect and be affected by it. Through ongoing communications, observations, comparisons, and adjustments, each new leader-member relationship becomes enmeshed in the social system to which it is a component. Established leader-member relationships then contribute to further developments in the existing network.

All relationships, including those between leaders and members of their teams, can be influenced by the nature and structure of embedding social networks. The nature of a network creates norms that must be upheld, and it establishes expectations for behavior between members of the network. Our perceptions of each other, evaluations of performance, and feelings about the relationship reflect social information obtained through networks. The amount of time we invest in a leader-member relationship is limited by the other relationships that we maintain, and the quality of the relationship may be assessed in comparison with those other relationships. Finally, the value of a leader-member relationship to a participant may depend on the availability of alternative relationships in the network. Given socially constructed behavioral expectations, social information processing, and comparison of relations among members, it is possible that perceptions of leader-member relationship quality may depend as much on the social network as on attributes or actions of the leader. The nature of each leader-member relationship can be shaped by the network in which it occurs, and people may build network connections to compensate or strengthen their leader-member relationships.

In this chapter, we situate current knowledge about leader-member relationships within the broader context of self-organizing informal social networks. Our goal is to identify aspects of social networks that influence or result from relationships and attitudes between leaders and team members. In this process, we will review basic concepts about network content and structure, then theorize about how they might influence the leader-member relationship. We will address circumstances within a leader-member exchange relationship that may trigger particular networking behaviors. Finally, we will produce a set of propositions that encapsulate the premises developed in the chapter.

BACKGROUND

The negotiated relationship between leaders and followers, or members, lies at the center of leader member exchange (LMX) theory. Leaders and followers work out their relationship together. Some leaders and their followers have positive, high quality relationships, but others have comparatively low quality relationships. Members with high quality relationships may share leadership and receive greater resources than members with lower quality relationships (Graen & Uhl-Bien, 1995).

The human context surrounding the leader and the member influences formation of their relationship, as does demographic similarity (Duchon, Green, & Taber, 1986; Green, Anderson, & Shivers, 1996). Additionally, a host of LMX literature shows that leaders who have resources to distribute, or discretion, have a greater ability to manipulate or control the quality of the LMX relationship (Graen & Scandura, 1987). Network theories indicate that interlaced social structures also affect the quality and perceptions of the LMX relationship. They further imply that the nature of the LMX relationship may impact some network-building behaviors by leaders or members. We begin our examination of these network effects by discussing attributes of relations such as friendship and advising, then we will move into structural concepts such as clique membership, ego networks, and centrality.

In order to apply network theories to leader-member relationships, an explanation of some essential terms will be helpful. First, "ego" refers to the focal person under discussion. We may refer to the set of all ties between ego and his or her alters as an "ego network." A tie could be an advice relation, a friendship relation, a trust relation, or a combination of relations between two parties. This list of ties is not meant to be exhaustive. In general, a relation*ship* refers to the tie between two parties, while a *relation* refers to a particular type of relationship between them. Each relationship combines one or more relations of varying strengths that together characterize the feelings, communication patterns, and behavioral propensities that occur between the two parties.

The nature of the tie is empirically assessed in network studies by asking each person in a population whether, or the degree to which, they have a particular relation with every other person in the population. For example, a friendship network instrument might list the name of every employee of a retail store, and ask each person to indicate which people on the list they regard as friends. Strength of the tie might be assessed using a response scale ranging from casual to close friend. The goal is to measure the dyadic relations, and to aggregate the set of all relationships to understand the structure of the system. The network can then be mathematically analyzed and graphically depicted by showing members as nodes connected by lines that represent friendship. Directed graphs use arrows to show who is sending the relationship to whom, with the direction of the arrow always going from sender to receiver. If Alice named Bob as her friend, an arrow in the friendship graph will proceed from

Alice to Bob. Similarly, if Alice goes to Bob for advice, the arrow in an advice graph will go from Alice to Bob. You can find more detailed information about networks analysis in works by Degenne and Forse (1999), Nohria (1992), and Wellman (1988), as well as through the International Network for Social Network Analysis website (www.INSNA.org).

CHARACTERISTICS OF RELATIONSHIPS

A relationship in network theory may include a variety of attributes, such as advice, affect, trust, dependence, or leadership exchange. It may be largely positive, as friendship and advice relations tend to be, or it may be largely negative, as competitive and enmity relations are likely to be. It may involve frequent interaction, but a relationship can also exist in the absence of direct contact, as when thousands of people interact as a group with another entity. The characteristics of a relationship influence subsequent expectations and interactions between the participants. Exchange behavior, traditionally held central to the leader-member relationship, is only one aspect of the potentially complex bundle of meanings, communications, and transmission channels that compose a relationship.

Leader member exchange is characterized by different qualities of leadership exchanges that can range from a great deal to none at all (Dansereau, Graen, & Haga, 1975; Graen & Cashman, 1975). A leader tends to have high quality relationships with some members and lower quality relationships with other members, as shown in Figure 4.1. Alice and Bob have weak relationships with the leader, while Charlie and Danielle have strong relationships. Weak relationships between leader and members tend to remain exchange-based, with little trust, positive affect, or long-term reciprocity. Higher quality relationships, sometimes termed "mature partnerships" include mutual respect, trust, and commitment that support open communication and helping behaviors (Lee, 2005). These relationships are subsets of the surrounding social networks, and the quality of the leader-member relationship is likely to be strongly influenced by the nature and structure of those networks.

Attributes of Direct Relationships

Figure 4.1a shows strength of relationships determined by LMX quality as defined by that literature. Figures 4.1b and 4.1c show friendship and advice ties that might be expected to contribute to LMX quality.

People with whom the leader has high quality LMX relationships are those whom he or she respects, likes, trusts, and includes in a leadership

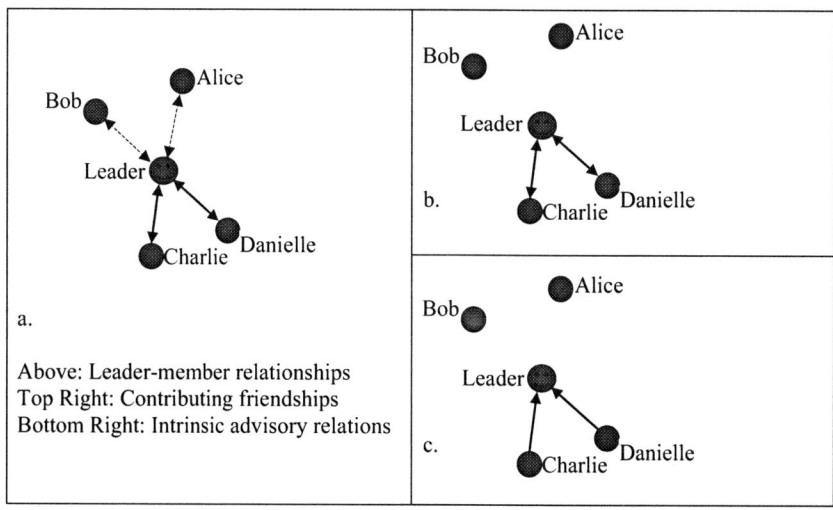

Figure 4.1. LMX relationships, friendship, and advice relations.

cadre. They are likely to have access to advice from the leader, while those who are not part of this cadre may be excluded from information sharing. At least two aspects of a leader-member relationship—friendship and an advisory role—may contribute to LMX quality, but they provide distinct avenues for influence and cooperation.

Friendship and advice relations each comprise multiple defining characteristics. For example, friendship includes positive affect, intimacy, altruism, and trust (Gibbons, 2004; Krackhardt, 1992). Positive affect increases helpfulness and involvement at work (George & Brief, 1992; Staw, Sutton, & Pelled, 1994), and interpersonal trust fosters cooperation (McAllister, 1995). A leader-member relationship that includes friendship is likely, therefore, to produce cooperation and mutual support. Friendship tends to be egalitarian and reciprocal (Bell, 1981), and therefore does not support power differential between leader and member.

An advice tie, in contrast, may include some of these attributes, but none of them are necessary components of the relation. The advice tie simply requires that someone with expertise consistently shares his or her knowledge with an advisee. Advice networks tend to create power for the advisors (Brass, 1992), particularly if they advise many people. Leaders who build strong advisory roles into their relationships with members are likely to be more influential with those individuals and in the overall system than leaders who are not seen as sources of advice. This relates to principles of dependence (Pfeffer, 1992): A leader on whom members depend for information builds a power base through the relationships. To the extent that the advice-giving is directed from leader to member and not reciprocated, power differential increases.

Power differential that develops within an advice relation does not happen naturally in a friendship, so co-occurrence of these two relations creates a unique, multiplex relationship. A multiplex relationship is one in which two or more relations are present. Given an advice relation and friendship in a leader-member relationship, there is potential for trust and altruism, but also for knowledge-based control. By combining relational attributes, multiplex relationships may expand opportunities for communication and exchange, even as they create limits on the kinds of interaction that are likely to occur.

The question has been raised, and only partially answered, whether multiplex relationships create more constraint or provide more interaction opportunities for participants. This question pertains to leader-member relationships within teams and informal social networks because friendship, informal advice relations, and formal structures tend to overlap in organizations (Brass, 1981). Certainly, the presence of positive interpersonal relations can facilitate successful working relationships (Jehn & Shah, 1997), but the added challenge of meeting friendship demands alongside advisory roles and leadership requirements may stress the leader-member relationship (see Graen, Hui & Taylor, 2004 for an example). The relative intensity of each component relation is likely to affect their overall impact on a working relationship between leader and member. The balance of benefits versus costs of maintaining such multiplex relationships may depend on a variety of relational and non-relational factors.

> **Proposition 1.** Leader-member relationships that include friendship relations are more likely to feature cooperation, altruism, and reciprocal influence than relationships that lack a friendship component.
>
> **Proposition 2.** Leader-member relationships that include an advice and consent role for the leader are more likely to feature power differential and nonreciprocal directed influence than relationships that lack such components.
>
> **Proposition 3.** Leader-member relationships that include both friendship and advice relations are likely to be stronger than those containing only one or the other, but they are also likely to constrain interpersonal behaviors to meet both friendship and advisory expectations.

LOCAL STRUCTURES IN A NETWORK

Local structures include arrangements of ties around a particular individual or within a subset of the network. Triads, indirect (2-step) relationships, cliques, and ego networks are all local structures that can affect dyadic leader-member relationships. People tend to form ties (or clump together) based on proximity (Monge & Eisenberg, 1987), preference for others who share salient characteristics (e.g., homophily, McPherson & Smith-Lovin, 1987), and shared attitudes or behaviors that draw people to meet and interact in particular settings (Feld, 1981). Some local structures are open, reaching into various parts of the network. Other local structures are closed, including densely connected members that form social clumps within the broader system. These clumps may range in size from triads to larger cliques or factions. Some clusters are insular, keeping most of their ties within the subgroup, and other clusters are more integrated into the broader social network. The pattern of ties within and among subgroups influences transfer of information (Gibbons & Sotnikov, 2004), acceptance of controversial ideas (Krackhardt, 1997), and formation of new dyadic relationships (Carley, 1991). Co-membership in a social subgroup may shape, strengthen, and support a positive leader-member relationship (Sparrowe & Liden, 2006).

Triads

Although dyads are the simplest social units for communications, coordination, leadership and so forth, triads are the simplest network structures. In any set of three people a variety of dyadic combinations among the three people may occur, including zero, one, two, or three dyadic ties. When all three individuals are tied, they form a triad, or three-person clique. Within this three-person clique, there are three dyadic relationships. This situation, in which dyads are embedded in a connected triad, may create stronger social influence than the dyad alone. The tendency to form shared attitudes through social information processing (Salancik & Pfeffer, 1978) may be strengthened because the triad provides a forum for discussion and convergence of ideas from all three members. The parties may tend to mutually reinforce shared beliefs and to exert normative pressure on each other to stick together. This pressure may be accepted or rejected.

Krackhardt has conducted several studies of dyads embedded in three-person cliques, with particular emphasis on friendship networks. Because the idea arises from the work of Georg Simmel (1950), he refers to these triad-embedded dyads as Simmelian ties. Simmelian ties are more stable than ties that are not embedded in a triad (Krackhardt, 1998), and they put more pressure on participants to adhere to normative behaviors (Krackhardt, 1999). Similar effects may arise in leader-member relationships, where it is proposed that two or more strong leadership sharing dyads create pressure for strong LMX triads (Graen et al., 2004).

Simmelian triads tend to strengthen and confirm members' shared attitudes regarding trust and distrust through positive and negative gossip. This amplification effect becomes particularly strong for negative gossip (Burt & Knez, 1996). Simmelian ties even influence perceptions about the network itself, such that people in them tend to agree more strongly about surrounding social structures than do people whose dyad is not part of a three-person clique (Krackhardt & Kilduff, 2002). In sum, these studies indicate that Simmelian ties are particularly strong dyadic links that shape participants' ideas, attributions, and behaviors.

A consequence of Simmelian ties for leader-member relationships is the potential for increased cognitive similarity, social identification, and altruistic behavior. Participation in the triad makes positive behavior more likely within each embedded leader-member dyad. At the same time as they are enacting positive behaviors, the leader and member are subject to social information processing with a third party who can reinforce agreement. Their ideas, attitudes, and knowledge base become more alike, and the developing history of positive interpersonal behaviors further increases trust. The result is a set of reinforced, higher-quality leader-member relationships. If Danielle's friend Ezekiel also becomes a friend to the leader (Figure 4.2), the leader-member relationship with Danielle is likely to become stronger as well. Ezekiel does not have to be a member of the leader's team for this effect to occur. Because of their participation in the triad, we also expect the relationship between the leader and Danielle to be more stable than the other leader-member relationships that are not embedded in a triad.

Proposition 4: Simmelian ties between leader and members improve the quality and stability of the leader-member relationships.

Social influence that is intrinsic to a triad may also lead to strategic development of Simmelian ties. Because joint connections to a third party can influence and reinforce dyadic behavior, developing a new LMX triad can be useful for a leader who is unsure about his or her ability to manage a subordinate relationship. Gargiulo (1993) found that managers built strong relationships with people who could constrain behavior by others on whom they depended. This demonstrates that people in organizations are able to identify helpful third-party relationships and to develop them

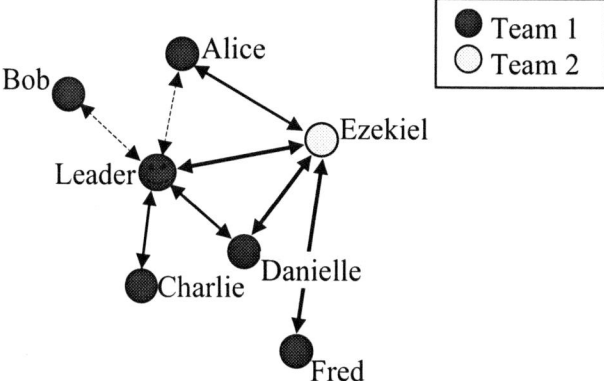

Above: The Leader of Team 1 shares a Simmelian tie with Danielle and a 2-step relationship (via Ezekiel) with Fred.

Figure 4.2. Triads, Simmelian Ties, and Indirect 2-step relationships.

strategically in order to affect their LMX dyadic relationships. Because Ezekiel and Alice are friends (Figure 4.2), the new friendship between the leader and Ezekiel may help the leader manage his/her relationship with Alice. Other strategic uses of triads may also arise. For example, competitive individuals may enter triads for their own purposes, without supporting a collaborative attitude among the parties. In such instances, a team leader is faced with the challenge of managing self-interested social behavior within the team (Offstein, Madhavan, & Gnyawali, 2006).

Cliques and Other Subgroups

Any subset of a network in which all members are connected to all other members is a clique. Cliques that include more than three members arise less frequently than triads, but their effects on member pairs may be similar. Because all members are connected to all other members, every clique that includes more than three people necessarily includes multiple triads. As a result, each person participates in multiple Simmelian ties, with potential for influence from each. This situation lends itself to iterative sensemaking, with the eventual result of shared beliefs, attitudes, and norms among members of the clique. In addition to the accumulated dyadic influences, the weight of agreement in the group presses members to uphold the group's norms and values. This effect is likely to occur more quickly and to continue longer if the clique remains largely separated from the rest of the social network. If subgroup members are somewhat less interconnected than in a clique, and if they interact more frequently with people outside the group, the forces toward unity and conformity are lessened.

The formation of cliques and other dense subgroups has a number of implications for leadership research generally and for LMX research more specifically. For purposes of exposition, we will examine cliques first as they relate to members, then to leaders, and finally to the leader-member relationship.

As noted above, in a closely aligned triad or larger clique, members of the group tend to form similar beliefs and attitudes. Information is shared, trust develops, and the embedding relationships strengthen and sustain dyadic relationships among clique members. Cohesiveness, or desire to stick together as a result of interpersonal attraction, can support individuals' desires to collaborate. Members of cohesive groups participate more in group activities, exhibit better attendance on the job (Cartwright, 1968), and are less likely to quit their jobs than people who are not members of cohesive groups (George & Bettenhausen, 1990). In these ways, clique membership could make people easier to lead. On the other hand, the power of agreement gives cliques an advantage in organizational decision making, especially if other people involved in the process are not united. Clique members can tackle political issues knowing that they have colleagues who will support them, which may be good or bad for a leader, depending on the quality of leader-member relationships. Whether aligned with the leader's agenda or not, the close overlapping ties within a clique increase the likelihood of cooperation and mutual support among members.

Members of cliques are tightly interwoven, and they tend to stick together. If the leader is outside of a clique and one member develops a strong relationship with the leader, she or he becomes a bridge between the clique and the leader. If the leader is outside of a clique and one member becomes offended at the leader, those feelings are likely to be shared within the clique. According to balance theory (Heider, 1946), a balanced state exists among three people only if all three share positive relations or if two who are positively related to each other both have a negative relationship with the third. The theory of transitivity in social networks follows from this line of thinking. It argues that given a tie from Person A to Person B and a tie from Person B to Person C, there is likely to be a tie from Person A to Person C (Wasserman & Faust, 1994). We can extend this reasoning to larger numbers of people who share close ties. Leaders who belong to cliques are subject to the values and influences of other clique members. Leaders whose followers form cliques must be continuously aware of the social influences and obligations arising from the social clustering. Balance will exist for clique members if all of them have positive relations with the leader or if all of them have negative relations with the leader. This enables consistency of thought and feelings in the entire clique.

When all clique members develop a positive relationship with the leader, the leader becomes a member of the clique. Clique dynamics should then strengthen the leader's relationships with all members as they interact repeatedly with each other. When the leader is a clique member, it should be feasible to include some members of the clique in leadership sharing while allowing others to opt out. Because of the feeling that everyone in the clique should be included in new opportunities, it would not be advisable for the leader to select some members for leadership sharing while excluding others. Over time, social pressure from participating clique members may lead less willing members to seek more responsibility. On the other hand, if some clique members have less than positive relations with the leader, this feeling is likely to spread to other clique members. Whether the relationship is positive, negative, or neutral, social information processing (Salancik & Pfeffer, 1978) should lead clique members to have similar attitudes toward a shared leader.

> **Proposition 5**: Clique members will tend to have a similar, high quality of relationship with a leader who is included in the clique.
>
> **Proposition 6**: A leader's relationships with members of a clique will tend to be more uniform compared to the leader's relationships with members that are not part of the same clique.

Because member cliques can influence leader-member exchanges positively or negatively, the extent to which a work group contains cliques impacts leaders' exchange options. Workgroups that have close ties among members may form stronger consensus, thereby placing leaders in potentially weaker exchange positions. The weaker exchange position arises as information asymmetry vanishes when members share information and form joint opinions. They gain power over the leader because what happens in organizations is not based on facts alone, but on social interpretations of facts. When the workgroup agrees on the social interpretation of facts, leaders have less influence within the exchange relationship. For example, if promotions are at stake, then with information asymmetry, the leader may use information in a secretive fashion with each individual employee in order to provide positive exchanges and to warrant actions in accordance with LMX theory. However, when the members themselves freely share the information, then the leader has lost that informational power.

> **Proposition 7**: A leader's ability to maintain information asymmetry diminishes as more cliques develop within the organization. Reduced information control, in turn, may diminish the leader's social influence and negotiating power.

Indirect Relations

Sometimes a leader needs to manage more followers than he or she can reasonably interact with. In other cases, team members may be physically distant and thus unable to interact frequently, or personal issues may have decreased the potential for positive LMX relationships. Under these circumstances, a third party relationship may partially compensate for the weak or absent leader-member relationship. Connecting with someone who has positive relationships with socially distant followers creates indirect (2-step) relationships between the leader and those followers. If the intervening relations are strong, the resulting 2-step relationship may serve many of the functions of a direct tie between leader and follower.

In Figure 4.2, Ezekiel may partially mediate the leader's relationship with Alice during the relation-building process. Ezekiel also connects the leader with Fred, who is not otherwise integrated into the social network. Through mutual links to Ezekiel, the leader and Fred now have a 2-step relationship. In this scenario, the need to manage leader-member exchanges is shaping the surrounding network, potentially triggering ripples of change. Intermediaries who connect the leader to several low LMX members may act as gatekeepers in the organization and obtain considerable influence in the system at large.

> **Proposition 8**: Leaders may choose to compensate for weak or absent relationships with members by creating strong ties to others who have relationships with those members. This strategy is expected to arise when the leader is unable to manage member relationships directly, whether because of interpersonal, organizational, or geographic circumstances.

Subgroup Partitions

In an organization where strong subgroup boundaries exist, membership in one subgroup may preclude active membership in another. Even when this does not occur, it is common for status differences to arise among subgroups of an informal network. The effect of subgroup structures on dyadic relations may be very subtle. Sometimes a dense network core receives most of the interaction from peripheral actors, while the peripheral actors maintain few ties to each other. In this situation, members of the social core have better information access and capacity to influence other network members, and people on the periphery may or may not realize it.

In LMX terms, both leaders and members are affected by strong subgroup boundaries. The nature of subgroup boundaries gives more power or influence to people who can span them. Therefore, we can conceptualize the network in ways that grant more power to either members or leaders who span boundaries. If we look at a larger organization with clear demarcations of cliques or subgroups, either members or leaders could connect them. For example, a clerk who simply knows people in another department becomes a link between the departments. This boundary spanning role may grant the clerk a certain amount of influence based on the ability to distribute information and coordinate interdepartmental action. A fundamental issue for LMX is that whoever spans subgroup boundaries has something to exchange in the LMX relationship.

Sometimes an informal network includes two or more factions. This naturally occurring tie structure creates clusters of people whose dense positive interconnections lead them to share ideas, values, and behaviors with cluster members while rejecting people and ideas from competing factions. Because these factions arise from the aggregation of informal ties, many members of the network may not even be aware of them. Nevertheless, relative position of a leader and team members in these substructures of the network may support or stress the relationship while facilitating or obstructing communications. It is particularly difficult to lead in a situation where competing factions actively oppose each other. The leader who aligns with one faction becomes immediately suspect by the other faction.

It is consistent with traditional LMX theory to consider that a leader could have high quality LMX relationships with multiple members of one faction and low quality LMX relationships with members of the other factions. The interesting practical question asks to what degree having differentiation is a viable leadership strategy. Because of the strong leadership sharing bias that is present when factions are involved, the leader may not have the option to develop strong positive relationships with all members of both groups. How can a leader strategically choose her ties in such a political context? The practical decision relies on more than the relative numbers of members in the different groups. It also relies on the connectedness of each group to other parts of the organization and its environment. In general, being involved with a faction that contacts many other groups will increase the leader's information access and avenues for influence. These, in turn, may facilitate relation building with members of the less integrated faction(s).

> **Proposition 9:** More effective leadership will emerge when members of a leaders' social group, compared to those not participating in the leaders' social group, have good quality network connections outside the unit.

Pattern of Ties in an Ego Network

A related way to explore networks is to examine how open or closed the ego network is. An ego network includes all of the focal individuals' contacts and the ties among those contacts. The ego network creates the immediate social context in which an individual works. Illustrated in Figure 4.3, an open ego network is one in which ego's contacts tend not to have ties with one another. For example, a sales representative may have an open professional network if the customer contacts have few ties with one another because they are competitors. A network with closure is one in which most of the individuals in ego's network have ties with one another.

Closure in one's ego network provides a comfortable social setting amid similar people who interact on a regular basis. Norms tend to be shared among members, and social support may be strong. Danielle's ego network, in Figure 4.3, includes many people who know each other. In contrast, an ego network that includes more people who don't have relationships with each other creates opportunities for brokering exchanges and information flows (Burt, 1992). People who occupy "structural holes"—places in the social network where ties among members are missing—may become gatekeepers of information and resources. Charlie's ego network includes many people who do not know each other; he occupies a structural hole in the organization's overall network. An ego network like Charlie's, which contacts a variety of social circles, accesses more information than does a more closed ego network like Danielle's. Because his ego network reaches into multiple sub-components of the surrounding social network, Charlie is likely to encounter a greater variety of norms and expectations among his contacts, and he may have access to a

Network Factors in Leader-Member Relationships 77

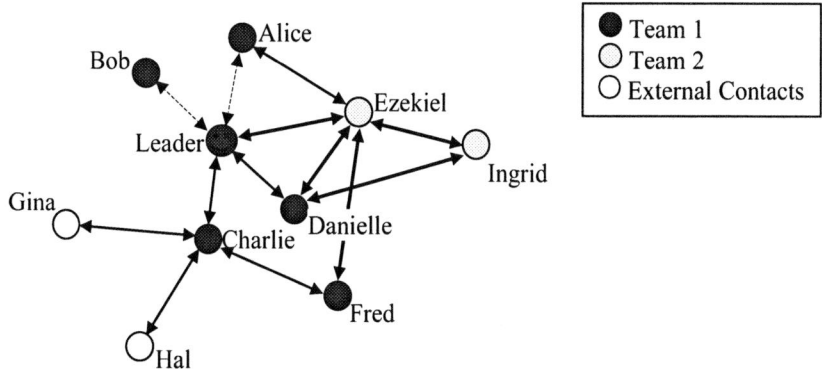

Above: Charlie's ego network is open;
Danielle's ego network has more closure.

Figure 4.3.   Closure versus Openness in Ego networks.

broader spectrum of resources. On the other hand, the increased social and exchange opportunities may come at the cost of social support, natural teamwork, and teammate trust that occur in social cliques.

Ego networks are often addressed with regard to instrumental ties, such as advice or exchange relations, but the pattern of overlap among instrumental and affective relations is also likely to impact the dyadic relationships. For example, a closed ego network that includes multiplex kinship and business ties creates a venue for strong affective and cognitive trust, cooperation, and high levels of peer monitoring. When personal and instrumental ties co-occur in a closed ego network, there is very little space for deviation from the group's norms regarding business or personal behavior. Everything—people, relations, finances—is interconnected and interdependent, with no alternative social channels for meeting personal or professional needs. All of Ego's relations are interwoven into the surrounding social fabric. On the other hand, a closed ego network that includes only instrumental ties may create trust and cooperation based on mutual benefits and potential punishment for defection. Because this network doesn't include affective relations, personal caring and accountability for personal behaviors are less likely to occur. The exchange nature of the network will create behavioral demands only within the realm of business. Personal relations that develop between members may be unsupported and unconstrained by group norms. In general, the potential effects of open versus closed ego networks on embedded relationships are likely to vary depending on the nature of the network.

In comparison with someone whose ego network is closed, an organization member who fills structural holes may have less need for a high quality relationship with the leader. A person in Charlie's position is less likely to depend on the leader for information and resources than is a person in Danielle's position. We therefore propose that members who occupy structural holes tend to invest less effort in developing high quality relationships with their leaders. Further, we propose that members who have lower quality relationships with their leaders, for whatever reason, will tend to develop broader ego networks as they search for alternative sources of information, resources, and opportunities.

Either or both mechanisms may affect network building behaviors by team members. Some people may realize they have low quality relationships with the leader, stimulating them to search for more contacts outside the workgroup. This suggests a cognitive and intentional networking agenda that would be interesting to examine empirically. Other people might naturally fill structural holes and, therefore, view the leader as one of many potential exchange contacts. Returning to the example of sales representatives, those who have broad ego networks may not need to develop high quality relationships with a boss who lacks access to unique customer bases.

> **Proposition 10**: In comparison with members whose ego networks are closed, those who fill structural holes will invest less effort in developing high quality relationships with their leaders.
>
> **Proposition 11**: Members who have lower quality relationships with their leaders, for whatever reason, will tend to develop broader ego networks as they search for alternative sources of information and resources.

Leaders' ego network patterns have implications for the nature of their leadership. Leaders who build open networks outside of the work group obtain novel information and opportunities to exchange with subordinate members. By developing broad contacts, they may increase their gatekeeping reputation and expert power in the group. Further, ties to people outside one's work group can be instrumental in obtaining resources under conditions of change or stress (Krackhardt & Stern, 1988). Leaders who develop open ego networks are better able to mobilize external resources than those who focus their relation building within the work group.

Supervisors who interact heavily among interconnected members of the immediate organization do not have as much information or resource access to offer in exchange relationships. They are less able to orchestrate innovation or expansion. They may, however, possess greater social influence through their close ties within the organization. If social knowledge and credits are needed to deal with internal politics, the supervisor who has developed close relationships that are deeply embedded in the organization's network may succeed where the external gatekeeper fails.

The tradeoff between open and closed ego networks may produce one leader who specializes in brokering opportunities and exchanges versus another leader who possesses social credits for obtaining resources and favor within the organizational hierarchy. The usefulness of each approach to leader networking depends on the environment in which the team is working. Under circumstances that demand new information, innovative ideas, and rapid adjustment to change, the leader who maintains a broad ego network will have more to contribute to the work group. In contrast, when work processes are stable and predictable, in mature organizations, and in highly political internal environments, closure in the leader's ego network may yield greater contributions to the work group.

> **Proposition 12**: In unstable or changing external environments, leaders with broad, open outside ego networks will be able to attract more high quality relationships with members due to the information and resources they offer.
>
> **Proposition 13**: In stable external environments, particularly given political internal environments, leaders with closed, deeply embedded ego networks will attract more high quality relationships with members due to their social knowledge and influence.

Relationships Resulting From Structural Similarity

People who interact with the same others in the same way are related by structural similarity. Because they occupy similar positions within the social network, they have comparable access to information, are subject to parallel social influences, and may see themselves and be seen by others as interchangeable. They tend to share attitudes and beliefs regarding the organizational context. For example, structural similarity can create similar attitudes toward tasks (Burkhardt, 1994), similar cognitive maps of linkages in organizational processes (Walker, 1985), and similar evaluations of other organizations (Galaskiewicz & Burt, 1991). Because they interact with many of the same others, people who are structurally similar in a friendship network have an increased chance of becoming friends (Gibbons & Olk, 2003). To the extent that structural similarity overlaps with direct relations, normative aspects of the relations may be reinforced. This follows from the presence of ties to third parties who may serve as monitors of behavior that passes between individuals.

An important consequence of structural similarity for leader-member relationships is that high quality relationships are likely to emerge from propinquity. Applying this idea to indirect leadership (Yukl, 2005), which does not always contain the intimate dyadic relationship, people who are structurally similar to the leader in a friendship network will have a much greater likelihood of developing a high quality leader-member relationship. For example, many business schools operate with a dean as an indirect leader. The dean will have high quality personal relationships with some faculty members and very limited relationships with others. Alongside formal structures and individual attributes that contribute to the nature of these relationships, structural similarity may build leader-member relationships. Some of the members of the business school are structurally similar to the dean and others are structurally dissimilar. Those who are structurally similar to the dean know many people who know the dean, and their mutual contacts are likely to bring them together. Because of their mutual relationships, the dean is more likely to have high quality relationships with the structurally similar members than with structurally dissimilar members. Over time, this process alone could lead to differentiation regarding the dean's leadership sharing in an organization. Density of ties would increase within each subcomponent of the network, but not between subcomponents (see Figure 4.4).

> **Proposition 14**: Structural similarity between leader and member will improve the quality of the leader-member relationship.
>
> **Proposition 15**: Over time, the naturally occurring tendency to develop relationships with people who are structurally similar will create LMX differentiation with the leader.

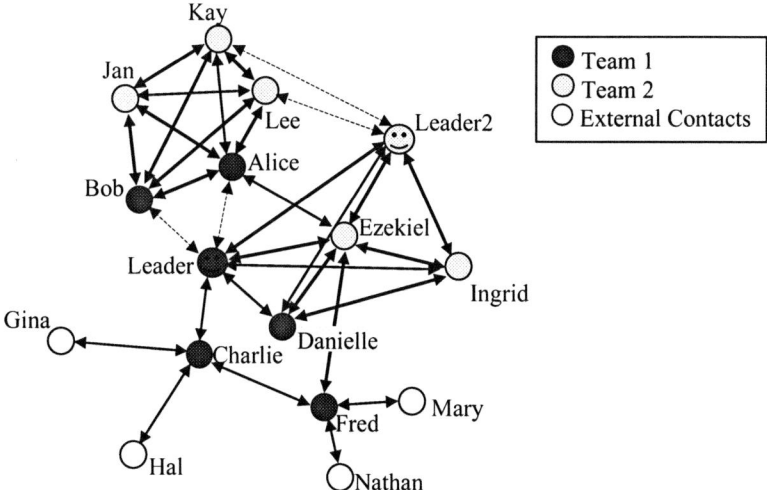

Above: Both team leaders, Danielle, Ezekiel, and Ingrid form a clique.
Alice, Bob, Jan, Kay, and Lee form a distinct clique that does not include the leaders.
Charlie and Fred are boundary spanners.

Figure 4.4.   Cliques and boundary spanners.

LEADERS' AND MEMBERS' CENTRALITIES WITHIN A SOCIAL NETWORK

An individual's position within a social network may be defined in terms of centrality and pattern of ties with and among others in the network. These distinctions in social position may affect the person's decisions (Kilduff, 1990), actions (Burt, 1987; Krackhardt & Porter, 1986), and impressions they make on others (Ibarra & Andrews, 1993).

Centrality in a network may be defined in several ways. The simplest concept is degree centrality, which indicates how many ties someone has. When ties are directed from one person to another, it can be useful to recognize the number of ties to and from each member of the social system. "In-degree" indicates the number of relations directed toward Ego, and "out-degree" indicates the number of relations directed by Ego toward someone else. In a friendship network, in-degree represents the number of people who see Ego as a friend, which could be considered an operationalization of popularity. Out-degree may reflect gregariousness in a friendship network. In general, friendship tends to be more symmetric than many other kinds of relations. Advice and dependence networks are more likely to contain significant asymmetries. In an advice network, in-degree represents the number of people who depend on Ego for information, and in-degree centrality is related to expert power. Out-degree indicates the number of persons on whom Ego depends for advice. The difference between in- and out-degree in an advice network may indicate power differential between Ego and his or her contacts.

This way of explaining network structure has parallels with LMX theory. Figure 4.1 illustrated the basic elements of LMX as strong or weak two-way ties. In the strong LMX ties, leaders and the members are exchanging leadership, and therefore should have common beliefs about the nature of their relationship. Nevertheless, the two-way exchange that occurs in a leader-member relationship does not, in itself, denote equivalent influence. If one party depends heavily on the other for information, that dependence may affect a leader's relationships with team members. Greater degree centrality tends to increase one's influence in a network, but if comparisons are being made, factions are forming, or votes are being taken, one's degree centrality *relative to others* may be the more important factor in shaping leadership outcomes. When an individual is recognized as a good source of advice, the behavior of advice-giving and the reputation from being sought can both contribute to organizational success. People with higher in-degree centrality in an advice network tend to receive higher performance ratings from supervisors (Sparrowe, Liden, Wayne, & Kraimer, 2001). This may follow from perceptions of power (Krackhardt, 1990) or from actual capacity to accomplish more because of increased influence and access to information in the system.

Being in a "between" or brokering position is another type of centrality that arises from placement of one's ties in a system. "Betweenness" measures the extent to which each person stands along the shortest paths connecting all other pairs in the network. In Figure 4.4, Alice and Ezekiel form a bridge that connects two subgroups of the network, so they have high betweenness. Information traveling through the grapevine from one subgroup of the network to the other must pass through them. Jan, Ingrid, and Danielle, in contrast, have low betweenness because nobody must go through them to obtain information from another person in the network. People who maintain very open ego networks tend to have high betweenness; people with closed ego networks tend to have low betweenness. Betweenness centrality affords influence because the individual serves as a conduit, a filter, or a stopper of transmissions among others in the social system. People with high betweenness centrality can act as gatekeepers for ideas, information, and resources, and they tend to receive higher performance ratings from their supervisors (Mehra, Kilduff, & Brass, 2001).

Many leaders occupy brokering positions to some extent as a result of their organizational roles. Formal leaders of workgroups act as links between their groups and the rest of the organization, and useful information that filters through a formal leader supports exchanges with members. Leaders may enhance team performance if they supplement their formal connections with informal ties that gather important and scarce information and facilitate positive exchanges across the team boundary.

Related to flow of information is the concept of "closeness" centrality in a network. Closeness centrality represents the overall ability of an individual to reach the rest of the social network through the existing network structure. Higher closeness indicates shorter paths to members of the network, which may increase capacity for obtaining and dispensing information or resources. To the extent that one is fewer steps away from other members of the system, he or she is better able to obtain information from or exert influence toward them. Closeness centrality captures the idea of overall access to the social resources in a complex organization. For example, in a large bureaucracy people have more power and influence to the extent that they know how to gather information. Closeness enhances one's ability to obtain information or resources from an organizational system.

This notion of closeness is essential to LMX. Some leaders have very little power or influence, or "discretion" in Graen's terms, and therefore followers have few reasons to engage in high quality exchange relationships. However, leaders with high closeness centrality can access resources and information from the greater organization. This gives them discretion, so they are in a better position to build high quality interactions with followers.

Closeness and betweeness power, then, combine to place leaders in a strong position to extract high quality relationships. Some organizations are relatively secretive, and others make information difficult to obtain due to the size and complexity of the organization. Leaders who understand and have good connections with the system can use this source of power to create good exchange relationships with subordinates.

> **Proposition 16:** A leader who has greater degree, betweenness, and closeness centralities in the organizational network possesses greater resources for enriching leader-member exchanges. As a result, leaders with greater centrality will tend to have a larger proportion of high quality leader-member relationships and more complete triads.

A very different kind of centrality arises from the positions of people to whom one is tied in a network. If a leader maintains positive relationships with people who maintain many positive relationships, these indirect relations may support the leader's image and influence among people with whom he or she has little or no direct interaction. Whether trying to promote new ideas, rally support for change, or simply maintain a positive organizational climate, positive relationships with central people increase a leader's potential to influence the social system. It is likely that attributes of the relationships will moderate this effect. Being a friend of someone who advises many people may not have the same effect as being an advisor of someone who is very popular. Minimal research has been invested to examine effects of compound friend-of-advisor or advisor-of-friend relations in organizations.

NETWORKS, LMX DIFFERENTIATION, AND TEAM PROCESS EFFECTIVENESS

We have thus far explained some primary concepts of network theory and tried to demonstrate how they inform leader-member exchange theory. Key relationships are summarized in Figure 4.5. We will now examine how LMX relationships and networks together affect team processes. Interpersonal relation qualities, network structures, and leadership sharing can all affect internal team processes such as cooperation, information sharing, and commitment. Relation qualities and configurations of boundary spanning ties may also influence team performance by limiting or facilitating resource and information acquisition. These effects of members' boundary spanning networks on team outcomes may combine with aspects of leadership sharing. Finally, social relations and network structures that impact leader-member relationships and leadership sharing may influence overall performance.

Strong interpersonal relations such as friendship can improve performance processes in teams whose tasks are interdependent. Friendship increases trust (Bell, 1981), information sharing (Zaccaro & Lowe, 1988), and willingness to discuss novel or controversial ideas related to one's job (Gibbons, 2004). Friendship leads people to help and support each other, even when there is no expectation of a tangible reward (Bell, 1981), and people invest much more effort in actions that affect their friends compared to mere acquaintances. In the context of team work, people are more likely to reveal new ideas or potential problems to friends among their team mates than to those with whom they lack a close personal relationship. This willingness to tackle difficult issues with friends could save time and prevent mistakes. Dense positive ties, such as those that occur in friendship cliques and closed ego networks, increase team communication and cohesiveness. Cohesiveness, in turn, increases participation in

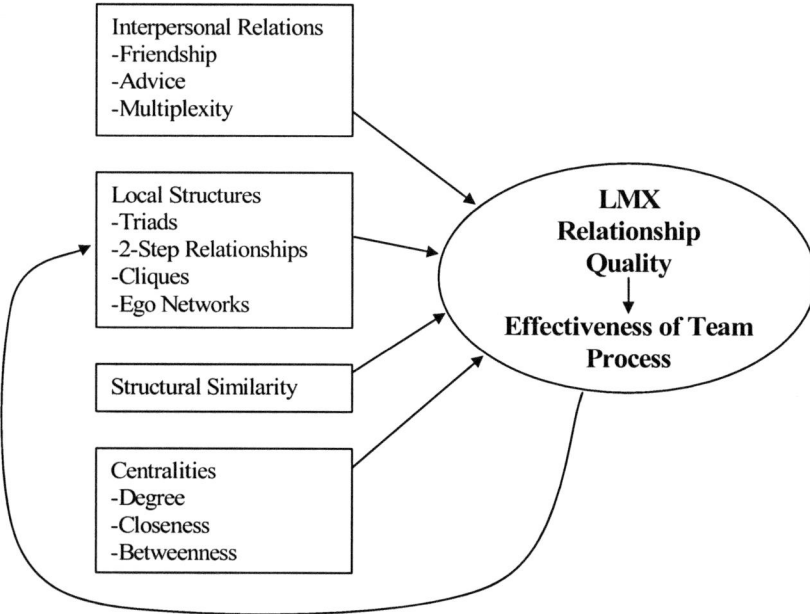

Figure 4.5. Overview of network interactions with leader-member relationships and team process effectiveness.

group activities and overall attendance on the job (Cartwright, 1968). Many effects of member relations and cohesiveness parallel outcomes of strong leader-member relationships, which can increase commitment, satisfaction, citizenship behaviors, and performance (Uhl-Bien, Graen, & Scandura, 2000).

Does this mean that strong member ties are interchangeable with strong LMX ties in teams? Not at all. Rather, vertical and horizontal dyads are likely to bolster each other as positive forces toward open discussion, good citizenship, and cooperation within a team. Dense positive interconnections among team members then reinforce and sustain cohesiveness that encourages people to take more responsibility for the team's performance. Furthermore, dense informal connections help groups to function by creating a team spirit, or mutual endorsement of goals. Triads, the more they occur in a team, strengthen those team effects. Additionally, strong lateral ties within a team are helpful when leadership is shared in the team or the leaders are chosen from the team. The trust, advice, and friendship ties one has as a team member will endure when one becomes a formal or informal leader. As people step into leadership positions, their centralities in the informal networks positively influence their ability to lead effectively (Krackhardt & Hanson, 1993). It is therefore useful for a leader to consider the informal network among team members when selecting people for leadership. Inclusion of central people in leadership may substantially improve the team's internal processes.

Boundary spanning relationships can also be crucial for team success, especially when innovation, problem solving, or stakeholder management are needed. To the extent that leaders share privileges and responsibilities with members, the potential network for team boundary spanning greatly increases. Rather than depending on one leader's ability to obtain resources, information, or partnerships through personal contacts, teams with leadership sharing use their members' networks for those purposes. For example, leaderless groups perform better under crisis conditions if one or more of their members have friends in other groups that control complementary resources (Krackhardt & Stern, 1988). Formally structured groups and teams may lose this advantage if members are not included in leadership. As leadership sharing increases, the team's potential for mustering resources, brokering deals, and establishing positive external relationships through members' ego networks increases dramatically. Even in day to day operations, professional ties between members and outside experts or agents may provide crucial sources for problem solving and bridge building. If those members are empowered to take action, if they feel some ownership of the team's projects, they may be more disposed to invest their social capital on the team's behalf. Because of this, members' network resources and leadership sharing amplify each other's contributions to the team.

NETWORKS ANALYSIS AS A TOOL FOR TEAM BUILDING

Careful use of networks analysis may assist managers in developing stronger teams. By mapping relationships among members, a team leader can identify communication gaps, weaknesses in the collaboration structures, or opportunities to share leadership with people who already hold influence in the informal social structures. With careful interventions, a thoughtful leader may use network analysis to increase the team's social capital. For example, Figure 4.6 depicts moderate and strong working relationships among students in a first-quarter MBA class, along with their boundary spanning ties to others in the university. The nodes are arranged using multidimensional scaling, which places people closer to similarly connected others and farther from dissimilarly connected others. To protect individuals, all names have been replaced by numbers. This is a good practice for two reasons. First, if people know that they will be identified in reports, they may not feel comfortable replying truthfully

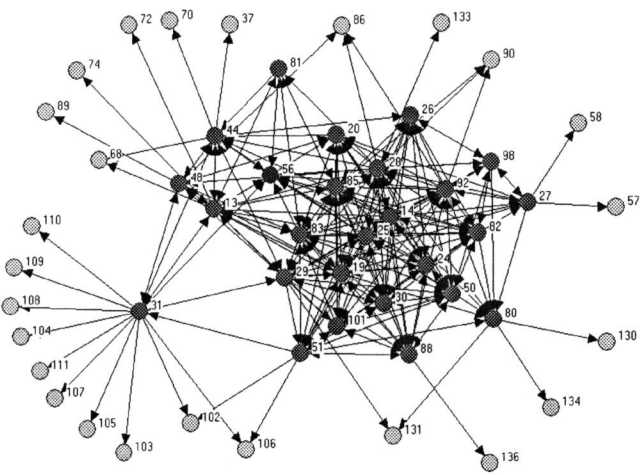

Note: * This graph was drawn using Netdraw (Borgatti, 2002).

Figure 4.6. Network among MBA class members, professor, and others in a university.*

about their relationships. Second, relationships invoke emotions and obligations, so releasing information about individuals' attitudes and interactions with others may endanger their future relationships. It is very important to protect the team members when using network analysis to aid team development.

One way to support team development using network analysis is by encouraging members to analyze their own interactions and collaborations. The students depicted in Figure 4.6 created personal graphs showing their own ego networks, including names, based on their perceptions of ties among their contacts. They were then able to analyze their own networking patterns, including closure versus openness, breadth and number of ties, and gatekeeping potential among their contacts. Each person also knew his or her own identification number in the complete graph, so members could look at the graph and see how their pattern of connection compared with others. This recognition can motivate further networking activities by members to strengthen their capacity for communication and collaboration within the team.

From the perspective of a team leader, understanding and discussing the network structure with members can support leadership sharing. People who already maintain good relationships with team members have more ability to coordinate team efforts than do people who lack these ties. Natural network-builders are good choices for leadership roles that require collaboration, while people on the periphery of the network probably need coaching before they should be expected to lead problem-solving or other heavily interactive tasks. In Figure 4.6, Persons 31 and 81may need help from a more central participant if they want to coordinate an interdependent whole-group effort. Even then, the lack of social influence with some subgroups may create obstacles to collaboration that will need to be overcome. On the other hand, person 31 has established many ties to people outside the class boundary, so this person has more potential for accessing external resources than any of the other members. Given a task that requires external collaboration, this person could work very successfully in joint leadership with internally integrated Persons 29 or 51, to whom she or he is connected. By understanding and addressing strengths and weaknesses in the network, a team leader gains an advantage in building and solidifying positive working relationships within and beyond the team.

The team leader may also obtain benefits from analyzing his or her own dyadic ties within the context of the network. In Figure 4.6, the professor is node number 56. Although the professor did not complete the self-analysis survey, we can use the network to identify strengths and weaknesses of this person's leader-member relationships. First, we see that 12 of the 25 students saw themselves as having moderate to strong working relations with the professor. Second, we see that the professor has many connections to people that appear toward the left half of the graph, but has limited access to people in the right half of the graph. By creating a strong tie to someone in that part of the network, the professor might access and influence the informal communications among this currently distant group of people. By building a few ties to that segment of the network, the professor might, thus, gain more understanding of the students' mentoring needs and performance challenges.

In this network, the professor has some ties to boundary spanning individuals (13, 31, and 44), but two boundary spanners (27 and 80) lack strong direct ties to the professor. If this group was a team with ongoing demands for coordination of information, action, and resources from external sources, the leader would depend on information from an intermediary about these potential partnering opportunities. Construction of stronger ties to these more distant parts of the network could enhance the professor's influence with the overall team while enabling more accurate assessment of members' readiness for leadership sharing. Alongside the need for greater personal connections to the more distant parts of the network, the professor could help some of the less integrated people become better connected by matching them with people like Persons 24 or 28 who are embedded within the team network. Having a clear map of the team's interaction patterns, thus, facilitates targeted interventions to help the team and its members develop their social capital.

CONCLUSION

Network analysis provides a rich vocabulary of how people interrelate. Because the nature and structure of a network provide the context in which leaders and followers develop relationships, deeper understanding of network growth and change may provide more richly articulated ways of describing relationships and understanding how they fit into larger social systems. This chapter has united some central concepts of network theory with exchange theory, developing propositions along the way. We hope that these propositions will be tested in ways that contribute to our understanding of how organizational members form relationships and how these relationships influence team processes. LMX relationships are more than just a matter of members who have high quality relations with the leader and others who have lower quality relations with the leader. Followers have relationships with one another and with the world outside the team. Together, interpersonal relations, local structures, and individual member centralities are likely to interact with LMX relationship quality and leadership sharing to impact team processes and outcomes. Team effectiveness is ultimately influenced by the nature and structure of networks that connect leaders and members with each other and the world beyond their team. Network theory provides a number of alternative platforms for articulating the attributes and consequences of these relationships that should be useful to LMX researchers.

ACKNOWLEDGMENT

Thanks to Jonathan Gibbons for help with the graphs. Development of this chapter was supported by a research fellowship from the University of Otago School of Business.

REFERENCES

Bell, R. R. (1981). *Worlds of friendship*. Beverly Hills, CA: Sage.
Borgatti S. P. (2002). *NetDraw: Graph visualization software*. Cambridge, MA: Harvard, Analytic Technologies.
Brass, D. J. (1981). Structural relationships, job characteristics, and worker satisfaction and performance. *Administrative Science Quarterly, 26*, 331-348.

Brass, D. J. (1992). Power in organizations: A social network perspective. In G. Moore & J. A. Whitt (Eds.), *Research in politics and society* (pp. 295-323). Greenwich, CT: JAI Press.

Burkhardt, M. E. (1994). Social interaction effects following a technological change: A longitudinal investigation. *Academy of Management Journal, 37*, 869-898.

Burt, R. S. (1987). Social contagion and innovation: Cohesion versus structural equivalence. *American Journal of Sociology, 92*, 1287-1335.

Burt, R. S. (1992). *Structural holes: The social structure of competition.* Cambridge, MA: Harvard University Press.

Burt, R. S., & Knez, M. (1996). Trust and third-party gossip. In R.M. Kramer & T.R. Tyler (Eds.), *Trust in organizations: Frontiers of theory and research.* Thousand Oaks, CA: Sage.

Carley, K. M. (1991). A theory of group stability. *American Sociological Review, 56*(3), 331-354

Cartwright, D. (1968). The nature of group cohesiveness. In D. Cartwright & A. Zander (Eds.), *Group dynamics: Research and theory* (3rd ed., pp 91-109). New York: Harper & Row.

Dansereau, F., Graen, G. B., & Haga, W. J. (1975). A vertical dyad linkage approach to leadership within formal organizations: A longitudinal investigation of the role making process. *Organizational Behavior and Human Performance, 13*, 46-78.

Degenne, A. & Forse, M. (1999). *Introducing social networks.* London: Sage.

Duchon, D., Green, S. G., & Taber, T. D. (1986). Vertical dyad linkage: A longitudinal assessment of antecedents, measures, and consequences. *Journal of Applied Psychology, 71*, 56-60.

Feld, S. L. (1981). The focused organization of social ties. *American Journal of Sociology, 86*, 1015-1035.

Galaskiewicz, J., & Burt, R. S. (1991). Interorganizational contagion in corporate philanthropy. *Administrative Science Quarterly, 36*, 88-105.

Gargiulo, M. (1993). Two-step leverage: Managing constraint in organizational politics. *Administrative Science Quarterly, 38*, 1-19.

George, J. M., & Bettenhausen, K. (1990). Understanding prosocial behavior, sales performance, and turnover: A group-level analysis in a service context. *Journal of Applied Psychology, 75*, 698-709.

George, J. M., & Brief, A. P. (1992). Feeling good—doing good: A conceptual analysis of the mood at work-organizational spontaneity relationship. *Psychological Bulletin, 112*(2), 310-329.

Gibbons, D. E. (2004). Friendship and advice networks in the context of changing professional values. *Administrative Science Quarterly, 49*(2), 238-262.

Gibbons, D. E., & Olk, P. M. (2003). Individual and structural origins of friendship and social position among professionals. *Journal of Personality and Social Psychology, 84*, 340-351.

Gibbons, D. E., & Sotnikov, S. (2004, June). *Interorganizational public health networks: structural effects on information diffusion.* Presented at the Public Health Systems Research Meeting of the AcademyHealth Annual Research Meeting, San Diego, CA.

Graen, G. B., & Cashman, J. F. (1975). A role-making model of leadership in formal organizations: A developmental approach. In J.G. Hunt & L.L. Larson (Eds.), *Leadership frontiers* (pp. 143-165). Kent, OH: Kent State University.

Graen, G. B., Hui, C., & Taylor, E. T. (2004). A new approach to team leadership: Upward, downward and horizontal differentiation. In G. B. Graen (Ed.), *New frontiers of leadership, LMX leadership: The series* (Vol. 2, pp. 33-66). Greenwich, CT: Information Age Publishing, Inc.

Graen, G. B., & Scandura, T. A. (1987). Toward a psychology of dyadic organizing. In B. M. Staw & L. L. Cummings (Eds.), *Research in organizational behavior* (Vol. 9, pp. 175-208). Greenwich, CT: JAI Press.

Graen, G. B., & Uhl-Bien, M. (1995). Relationship-based approach to leadership: Development of leader-member exchange (LMX) theory of leadership over 25 years: Applying a multi-level multi-domain perspective. *Leadership Quarterly, 6*(2), 219-247.

Green, S. G., Anderson, S. E., & Shivers, S. L. (1996). Demographic and organizational influences on leader-member exchange and related work attitudes. *Organizational Behavior and Human Decision Processes, 66*, 203-214.

Heider, F. (1946). Attitudes and cognitive organization. *Journal of Psychology, 21*, 107-112.

Ibarra, H., & Andrews, S. B. (1993). Power, social influence, and sense making: Effects of network centrality and proximity on employee perceptions. *Administrative Science Quarterly, 38*, 277-303.

Jehn, K. A., & Shah, P. P. (1997). Interpersonal relationships and task performance: An examination of mediating processes in friendship and acquaintance groups. *Journal of Personality and Social Psychology, 72*(4), 775-790.

Kilduff, M. (1990). The interpersonal structure of decision making: A social comparison approach to organizational choice. *Organizational Behavior and Human Decision Processes, 47*, 270-288.

Krackhardt, D. (1990). Assessing the political landscape: Structure, cognition, and power in organizations. *Administrative Science Quarterly, 35*, 342-369.

Krackhardt, D. (1992). The strength of strong ties: The importance of philos in organizations. In N. Nohria & R. G. Eccles (Eds.), *Networks and organizations: Structure, form, and action*. Boston: Harvard Business School Press.

Krackhardt, D. (1997). Organizational viscosity and the diffusion of controversial innovations. *Journal of Mathematical Sociology, 22*, 177-199.

Krackhardt, D. (1998). Simmelian ties; super, strong and sticky. In R. Kramer & M. Neale (Eds.), *Power and influence in organizations* (pp. 21-38). Thousand Oaks, CA: Sage.

Krackhardt, D. (1999). The ties that torture: Simmelian tie analysis in organizations. In S. B. Bacharach, S. B. Andrews, & D. Knoke (Eds.), *Research in the sociology of organizations* (Vol. 16, pp. 183-210). Stamford, CT: JAI Press.

Krackhardt, D., & Hanson, J. R. (1993, July-August). Informal networks: The company behind the chart. *Harvard Business Review*, 104-111.

Krackhardt, D., & Kilduff, M. (2002). Structure, culture and Simmelian ties in entrepreneurial firms. *Social Networks 24*, 279–290.

Krackhardt, D., & Porter, L. W. (1986). The snowball effect: Turnover embedded in communication networks. *Journal of Applied Psychology, 71*, 50-55.

Krackhardt, D., & Stern, R. N. (1988). Informal networks and organizational crises: An experimental simulation. *Social Psychology Quarterly, 51,*123-140.

Lee, J. (2005). Communication as antecedents and consequences of LMX development globally: A new strong inference approach. In G. Graen (Ed.), *LMX leadership: The series, Global organizing designs* (Vol. 3, pp. 1-41). Greenwich, CT: Information Age.

McAllister, D. J. (1995). Affect- and cognition-based trust as foundations for interpersonal cooperation in organizations. *Academy of Management Journal, 38*(1), 24-59.

McPherson, J. M., & Smith-Lovin, L. (1987). Homophily in voluntary organizations: Status distance and the composition of face-to-face groups. *American Journal of Sociology, 52,* 370-379.

Mehra, A., Kilduff, M., & Brass, D. J. (2001). The social networks of high and low self-monitors: Implications for workplace performance. *Administrative Science Quarterly, 46,* 121-146.

Monge, P. R., & Eisenberg, E. M. (1987). Emergent communication networks. In F.M. Jablin, L.L. Putnam, K.H. Roberts, & L.W. Porter (Eds.), *Handbook of organizational communication: An interdisciplinary perspective* (pp. 304-342). Newbury Park, CA: Sage.

Nohria, N. (1992). Is a network perspective a useful way of studying organizations? In N. Nohria & R. G. Eccles (Eds.), *Networks and organizations: Structure, form, and action* (pp. 1-22). Boston: HBS Press.

Offstein, E. H., Madhavan, R., & Gnyawali, D. R. (2006). Pushing the frontier of LMX research: The contribution of Triads. In G. Graen (Ed.), *Sharing network leadership, LMX leadership: The series* (Vol. 4). Greenwich, CT: Information Age.

Pfeffer, J. (1992). *Managing with power: Politics and influence in organizations.* Boston: Harvard Business School Press.

Salancik, G. R., & Pfeffer, J. (1978). A social information processing approach to job attitudes and task design. *Administrative Science Quarterly, 23,* 224-253.

Shrader, C. B., Lincoln, J. R., & Hoffman, A.N. (1989). The network structures of organizations: Effects of task contingencies and distributional form. *Human Relations, 42,* 43-66.

Simmel, G., (1950). Individual and society. In K. H. Wolff (Ed.), *The sociology of Georg Simmel.* New York: Free Press.

Sparrowe, R. T., & Liden, R. C. (2006). Two routes to influence: Integrating leader-member exchange and network perspectives. *Administrative Science Quarterly.*

Sparrowe, R. T., Liden, R. C., Wayne, S. J., & Kraimer, M. L. (2001). Social networks and the performance of individuals and groups. *Academy of Management Journal, 44,* 316-325.

Staw, B. M., Sutton, R. I., & Pelled, L. H. (1994). Employee positive emotion and favorable outcomes at the workplace. *Organization Science, 5*(1), 51-71.

Uhl-Bien, M., Graen, G. B., & Scandura, T. A. (2000). Leader-member exchange (LMX) for strategic human resource management systems: Relationships as social capital for competitive advantage. In G. R. Ferris (Ed.), *Research in per-*

sonnel and human resources management (Vol. 18, pp. 137-185). Stamford, CT: JAI Press.

Walker, G. (1985). Network position and cognition in a computer firm. *Administrative Science Quarterly, 30,* 103-130.

Wasserman, S., & Faust, K. (1994). *Social network analysis: Methods and applications.* New York: Cambridge University Press.

Wellman, B. (1988). Structural analysis: From method and metaphor to theory and substance. In B. Wellman & S.D. Berkowitz (Eds.), *Social structures: A network approach* (pp. 19-61). Cambridge: Cambridge University Press.

Yukl, G. (2005). *Leadership in organizations* (6th ed.). Upper Saddle River, NJ: Prentice Hall.

Zaccaro, S. J., & Lowe, C. A. (1988). Cohesiveness and performance on an additive task: Evidence for multidimensionality. *Journal of Social Psychology, 128,* 547-558.

CHAPTER 5

PUSHING THE FRONTIER OF LMX RESEARCH

The Contribution of Triads

Evan H. Offstein, Ravindranath Madhavan, and Devi R. Gnyawali

We propose extending LMX research beyond the dyad by introducing the triadic level of analysis. Recently developed statistical models such as $p*$ point the way toward multi-level analyses of organizational phenomena such as LMX. However, while such models are useful as investigative tools to identify and analyze triads, they cannot explain why particular triads form or how they function. We develop and explore the constructs of competitive and collaborative interdependence in order to better understand how LMX triads form and function. In addition to these constructs of competitive and collaborative interdependence, we introduce the notion of multiplexity within LMX triads. The idea of multiplexity suggests that the structure of a triad may be predicated on the content and nature of the relations that exist. In an effort to demonstrate the theoretical and methodological linkage for the study of LMX triads, we illustrate the use of $p*$ analysis to test for dyadic and triadic patterns. Practical implications and future directions for the triadic analysis of LMX relationships are outlined and discussed.

INTRODUCTION

To advance LMX to the next level of complexity, it is likely that some theoretical richness borrowed from triadic discussions in other disciplines may, in fact, add value to current conceptualizations of LMX. For instance, the triadic microstructure has been assumed implicitly in the larger business strategy domain of network theory—e.g., Burt (1992) popularized the notion of "structural holes" in which three actors share a specific type of relationship, where A is connected to B and to C, but B and C are not linked directly to each other. When structural and relational properties are borrowed from the larger strategic network perspective and juxtaposed with meaningful constructs from the current LMX literature such as fairness (Masterson, Lewis, Goldman, & Taylor, 2000, organizational politics (Douglas, Ferris, Buckley, & Gundlach, 2003), and social exchange (Graen & Uhl-Bien, 1995; Masterson et al., 2000), considerable theoretical richness is added to LMX theory.

Accordingly, in response to Graen's request to describe a triadic perspective to augment current LMX theory, we explore the following questions: (1) Why might a triadic relationship exist within LMX? (2) What are the main drivers or antecedents that might explain a triadic relationship? (3) What might a leader-member triad look like? (4) What are some possible interpersonal consequences ranging from the personal to the professional, from both a leader and member perspective that could result from a triadic perspective?

Apart from the reasons already identified, there is also a significant methodological rationale for incorporating triads into LMX theory. In parallel with the increasing interest in the multi-level modeling of organizational phenomena (e.g., Dansereau & Yammarino, 2003), innovative statistical models such as p^* (Wasserman & Pattison, 1996) have emerged recently, facilitating a more sophisticated understanding of triad microstructure than was previously possible. A key objective of triadic analysis, in general, and the p^* approach, in particular, is to capture the likelihood of observing particular triad structures (such as transitive triads; in a transitive triad, each of the three actors is directly tied to both of the others) and to identify the causal factors that influence that formation (Madhavan, Gnyawali, & He, 2004). As it relates to a deeper understanding of LMX, the p^* modeling approach helps confirm or deny the presence or absence of a tie between a pair of actors within a triad. In "graph-theoretic" terms, this analytical technique discerns structural tendencies in observed networks. More specifically, Contractor, Wasserman, and Faust (2006) describe p^* as helping to investigate whether hypothesized structural tendencies, such as transitivity, are present in the observed graph realization; this is done by estimating how the hypothesized structural property affects the probabilities of ties being present or absent in the network. While using the p^* model should expand and complement the methodological possibilities currently associated with LMX research, including the qualitative research tradition (Fairhurst, 1993) and multi-level analysis (HLM) (Graen & Lau, 2005), the core benefit of a p^* approach is to zero in on structural, as opposed to relational qualities of a given triadic relationship. Given this methodological consideration, we theoretically explore and offer conceptual arguments to explain the formation, maintenance, and consequences of these structural ties between members and leaders. Hence, our goal here is to further the triadic perspective of LMX on primarily a conceptual but also, in a more limited vein, methodological front. Since the triadic perspective of LMX on both theoretical and methodological fronts is rather recent, we hope to spark more refined and sophisticated future research on this topic of triads and LMX.

BACKGROUND

Tracing the historical roots of triads takes a scholar to a diverse array of disciplines to include psychology, sociology, and political science. Perhaps the most effective manner to trace the theoretical development is to begin chronologically. Simmel (1922) is one of the first to popularize the notion of triads, being among the first to logically argue that dyadic relationships are dramatically altered when a third party is added to the relationship. Specifically, three triadic forces distinguish triads from dyads: reduced individuality, reduced bargaining power, and reduced conflict. Within the dyad, an individual has greater individual leverage than in the triad, since there is no possibility of being outvoted by a majority. Also within the dyad, an individual has greater bargaining power, as a threat to leave the relationship is more potent than it would be in a triad. Finally, dyads may be characterized by more intense conflict, as the presence of a third party in the triad often serves to moderate positions as well as provides a mechanism for resolution.

It is important to note that Simmel (1922) conceptualized triads in a somewhat Machiavellian and competitive fashion. Specifically, Simmel's notion of *tertius gaudens* or "the third who benefits" is based on the assumption that a third party can enjoy a competitive advantage by breaking into a dyadic relationship. According to this perspective, a third party can capitalize on opportunities when two parties in a dyad are in conflict. One way in which this occurs is when members of a dyad hold each other in check while the third actor reaps benefits that otherwise would be denied by one of the two actors. It is important to note then that embedded in Simmel's (1922) idea of *tertius gaudens* is opportunism and the role of conflict. Thus, an interesting theoretical extension occurs when the triadic perspective explained here and the dyadic perspective largely contained within the LMX literature are integrated. Notably, if LMX theorists and researchers were to consider the triad more explicitly, there is a theoretical rationale to now include competition and opportunism within a triadic relationship. This, in itself, is a significant departure from mainstream LMX research that largely assumes the existence of, or movement to, a collaborative relationship (Uhl-Bien, Graen, & Scandura, 2000). Indeed, competition and opportunism embedded in a leader-member relationship have only been touched upon in such recent discussions on topics such as negative reciprocity (Uhl-Bien & Maslyn, 2003). This overarching emphasis on collaboration is prone to change when triadic as opposed to solely dyadic relationships are examined.

Balance Theory

Another theory that could inform how triads my influence LMX is Heider's balance theory. Heider (1958) was a German psychologist and tended to examine triads through an individual attitudinal lens. Unlike Simmel's (1922) notion of triads, which assumed conflict for gain, Heider (1958) reasoned that relationships should strive to stay in balance—and should not be in conflict. A balanced relationship exists when the attitudes of two people (A and B) and their respective attitudes towards another object (say person C) are aligned. When attitudes are dissimilar (A likes C, but B does not like C) a cognitive imbalance occurs *within* the individual (not between individuals). To remove the cognitive imbalance, an individual has three tactics at his/her disposal. First, person A can adjust his/her attitudes toward person C to align with person B's attitudes. Second, person A can adjust his/her attitudes toward person B to align with his/her attitudes toward person C. Finally, person A can try to influence person B to change his/her attitudes.

Note that if a researcher were to expand Heider's (1958) balance theory from an individual attitudinal perspective to that of three actors through an interpersonal lens, the conclusions drawn differ markedly from Simmel's (1922) *tertius gaudens* angle. Whereas Simmel (1992) implicitly described a relational imbalance from which a third party could gain advantage, Heider (1958) argues instead for harmony and balance within relationships. Using a metaphor of a three-legged stool, Heider (1958), however, appears to acknowledge the difficulty of keeping all legs or ties in balance. This explains, in part, his lengthy discussion into the tactics that a person can use to bring balance (i.e., change their attitude toward another person or attempt to influence another to change their attitudes). If this notion is extrapolated to the relationships between three actors, it becomes clear that some effort and management of the relationships will be necessary to first bring a relationship into balance and then to maintain that balance among the three actors.

Simmelian Ties

Krackhardt's (1998, 1999) *Simmelian ties* construct is an important development that situates many of Heider's ideas in the specific context of interpersonal triads. A Simmelian tie exists when two people are reciprocally and strongly tied to each other, and each is reciprocally and strongly tied to at least one third party in common (Krackhardt, 1998). The Simmelian ties construct illustrates the idea that the quality of a dyadic tie changes dramatically as a function of the overall structure in which the tie is embedded. Strongly backed up by the normative power of groups, Simmelian ties are qualitatively different from simple dyadic ties (Krackhardt, 1998). As it relates to LMX then, Heider's (1958) balance theory suggests that when a third actor is introduced into what was previously a dyadic relationship, the management of the interconnected relationships becomes more of a crucial responsibility of both the leaders and members. Otherwise, when relationships are not properly managed, they will gravitate toward imbalance.

Network Theory

Introducing the triadic concept into LMX can also be advanced by turning to early and more recent conceptualizations of network theory (Burt, 1992; Gnyawali & Madhavan, 2001; Pfeffer & Salancik, 1978). While dyadic links form the foundation of all networks, the presence of triads also exists within ego and larger networks. For this reason, some scholars contend that triads occupy an important "meso" level between dyadic ties and more complex network linkages (Madhavan et al., 2004). A consideration of triads in LMX is also consistent with prior calls in the literature to consider dyadic assemblies (Graen & Scandura, 1987) and to integrate LMX and network theories (Sparrowe & Liden, 2005). Generally speaking, the commonalities between network theory and the LMX perspective should enable, not detract from, the introduction of triads to mainstream LMX. For instance, rooted in both LMX and network theory is the notion of interdependence (Burt, 1992; Gnyawali & Madhavan, 2001; Uhl-Bien & Maslyn, 2003). Thus, the actors within a triad, whether they be firms or individuals, are interconnected and it is difficult to isolate causes and effects between a single dyad since all three actors are involved. Also, both network and LMX theories integrate behavioral and economic perspectives. While clearly LMX tends to the former, firmly rooted in the leader-member relationship is the notion of exchange, which begins predominantly from an economic notion of exchange to a more social type of exchange (Graen, 2003; Graen & Uhl-Bien, 1995; Uhl-Bien & Maslyn, 2003). Finally, the most elemental unit in both LMX (Graen & Uhl-Bien, 1995; Schriesheim, Castro, & Cogliser, 1999) and network theory (Granovetter, 1973) is that of a tie between two actors. Thus, the launching point of both theoretical perspectives, especially from a unit of analysis standpoint, is that of the dyad. Where network theory may be particularly germane to the integration of triads into LMX is the importance placed on position within a network and the controlling and resource advantages that arise to those that occupy key positions within a given network (Burt, 1992; Granovetter, 1973; Gnyawali & Madhavan, 2001). When network positioning is combined with current political perspectives of positioning with LMX (Douglas et al., 2003) insight is shed onto the questions of *why* triads form and *what* benefits arise from entering into a triadic structure. Importantly, this theoretical integration may offer more explanatory power due to the power imbalances that are known to exist between a leader and member (Uhl-Bien & Maslyn, 2003).

In summary, incorporating central tenets of *tertius gaudens*, balance theory, and the network perspective, frames LMX and triads in a different circumstance. In particular, a tension surfaces when a triadic angle is added to mainstream LMX theory. This tension arises due to the competing forces of competition, collaboration, and positioning within a triad. Thus, what follows is an exploratory examination of triadic LMX constructs, possible leader-member scenarios that account for these conflicting constructs, and the consequences that they bring about.

COLLABORATIVE AND COMPETITIVE INTERDEPENDENCE IN LMX TRIADS

Collaborative Interdependence

In developing a taxonomy for LMX triads, we begin with the notion of collaborative interdependence. Central to collaborative interdependence is a shared feeling that the triad is a bundle of resources. In this type of collaborative relationship, leaders and members enter and maintain a relationship based on the premise that each brings valuable knowledge, informational resources, and expertise in a complimentary fashion. Here, human capital, a private good, is fused into social capital as the leader and members share, refine, and develop knowledge in an iterative and integrative manner (Leana & Van Buren, 1999; Nahapiet & Ghoshal, 1998). This collaboration expands the resource capability beyond that of a dyad and also increases the number of opportunities available to both leader and member. Not surprisingly, when unique and diverse sets of human capital are added to the dyad through the formation of a triad, the collective expertise is broadened, which enables the collective to embrace and accept opportunities that otherwise would have been untenable in a strict dyadic relationship. Thus, a major driver of a collaborative interdependent LMX triad is likely to center on the realization that opportunities and resources increase in a multiplicative fashion when a third actor is introduced into the dyadic relationship.

While a collaborative interdependent triad may, indeed, go through similar stages of development common in dyad formation (Gerstner & Day, 1997), characteristics of a mature type of LMX triadic relationship include trust, mutual respect, and a longer temporal orientation—the same set of factors that determine a high quality dyadic relationship (Gerstner & Day, 1997; Masterson et al., 2000).

From a leadership vantage, the role of the leader is relatively straightforward here. In collaborative interdependent triads, the leader fosters a nonthreatening and comfortable context where members can freely exchange information and knowledge. The leader then works at maximizing the triad as a resource by combining, pooling, and marshaling member resources of information, knowledge, and skills to realize diverse and ever-increasing challenging outcomes.

Competitive Interdependence

Competitive interdependence and collaborative interdependence differ dramatically and that difference can be best explained by revisiting the core assumption of resource availability. Whereas in collaborative interdependence leader-members view resources in an expansive fashion, that is not the case in competitive interdependence. Instead, a driving force behind the formation and existence of this type of relationship is the premise that resources are scarce (Pfeffer & Salancik, 1978). This type of triadic formation is closely aligned with Simmel's (1922) *tertius gaudens*. For instance, members may perceive their reality as one of resource constraints. Constraints could be viewed as a limited number of promotions, pay raises, or even leader time. A member may purposefully try to preempt another member from achieving a monopoly on HR outcomes such as promotions and pay raises, which, incidentally, is likely highly correlated to the amount of time a member can obtain with their leader. While the scenario just described suggests competition initiated by members, either leader or member can also insert competition into a triadic relationship. Distinguishing this type of triad from a collaborative one is the drive to maximize individual goals even at the expense of the other members of the triad. While LMX theory suggests that some dyadic relationships may begin in this very fashion (Graen, 2003; Masterson et al., 2000), the presumption is that relationships seek to advance beyond this initial stage. Here, we suggest that driven by a relative permanent world view of resource scarcity, the competitive interdependent triad may be purposefully formed and purposefully maintained with no intent to advance the relationship to a more collaborative stage.

The role of the leader in a competitive interdependent triad is not as straightforward as that found in collaborative triads. First, competition between members may be implicit or explicit. If the competition is implicit, it may take longer for a leader to realize the presence of a competitive interdependent triad. An important caveat here is that while it takes all three actors of a triad to agree to collaborate and to stay in balance, it only takes one actor to view the triad as competitive and, as a result, to transform the triad into a competitively interdependent one. Thus, while the leader may, themselves, be collaborative in nature, if just one of the members views and acts within the triad in a competitive fashion, the triad becomes competitively interdependent. This poses special challenges to the leader who must now manage the competition, or the relational imbalance. In extreme cases or when the human capital is unusually talented, the leader might need to intervene to ensure that competition does not escalate to the point of creative destruction such as sabotage.

Borrowing from network theory (e.g., Gnyawali & Madhavan, 2001), it appears that there exists great advantage to the leader in competitive interdependent triads through a construct we term simply as positional privilege. A leader, through their positional power, can occupy the central node in a triad. Here, the leader, if driven by purely competitive motives, can use their position to play members against each other to reap benefits. For instance, one structural way to accomplish this is to purposefully create a structural hole between two members. We will discuss this more below in our explication of several triadic scenarios.

One may question why an actor (leader or member) would not choose to exit a competitively interdependent triad. There are two reasons that

Pushing the Frontier of LMX Research 103

suggest this is unlikely on both practical and theoretical fronts. Practically, leader-member relationships are different from mentor-protégé relationships. The latter tend to be voluntary, whereas leader-member relationships, in general, are more involuntary and are mandated by the organization (Baugh, Scandura, & Cogliser, 2003). Theoretically, the notion of resource scarcity explains why an actor would be reluctant to exit a competitive interdependent triad. Simply, if one actor leaves then two actors now share resources—the third actor is unable to gain access to limited resources if not involved in the triad.

TRIADIC SCENARIOS

In Figure 5.1, we present a hypothetical triad with or without links among all three of the actors. In our depiction, actor A is the leader while B and C are members. One of the primary benefits of attending to these different scenarios is to illustrate that while the structure of a triad may, on the surface, be structurally alike, the content and the purpose of any given triad can be markedly different.

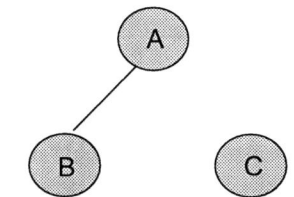

A, B, C triad with A-B dyadic ties (scenario 1)

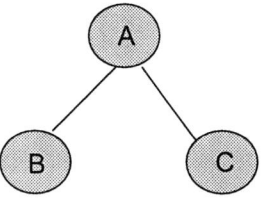

A, B, C triad with A-B and A-C dyadic ties and a structural hole between B and C (scenario 2)

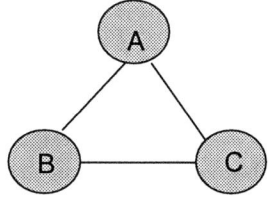

A-B-C transitive triad (scenario 3)

Figure 5.1. Illustration of triadic scenarios.

Leader Orientation

The leader orchestrates one possible scenario. Leader A may not be satisfied with member B's performance. While a leader could try behavioral techniques such as performance counseling or economic tools such as incentives, one possible mechanism to raise performance of member B is to insert direct competition into the dyadic relationship. Leader A achieves this by inviting member C. Leader A can control the amount of interdependence by either encouraging a transitive triad, where all actors have links to each other. Conversely, Leader A can create space or a structural hole between B and C. In this scenario, Leader A brokers information flow between B and C. Here, Leader A purposefully reduces interdependence in favor of dependence based on his or her position within the triad. Whether or not Leader A chooses to make this a transitive triad or not, embedded in this move by the Leader is a political positioning and signaling motive (Douglas et al., 2003; Ferris & Judge, 1991). Essentially, if member B has not followed the key counsel and warnings of Leader A, inviting C into a triad and then demonstrating that C values Leader A's expertise and suggestions may stimulate member B to improve efforts, outcomes, and, overall, performance. For sure, this scenario is driven by a competitive, not collaborative, force.

Alternatively, Leader A may know that C is talented and possess high levels of human capital. Leader A might then initiate a new tie with C to benefit from C's knowledge, skills, and abilities—not to signal a competitive tournament with member B. If the Leader keeps space between B and C and chooses to exercise a structural hole, the rationale for the triadic existence is neither fully competitive nor collaborative.

Finally, Leader A may opt to pool resources and try to create a synergistic experience by inviting C to form a triad. The rationale behind this move is primarily collaborative. Note that for a true collaborative experience to unfold, the triad must be transitive. A structural hole cannot exist since that would prevent information sharing and the development and creation of new knowledge. In this case, Leader A encourages interdependence and open dialogue to expand the capability of the triad, which, in turn, allows the collective to respond to more organizational and environmental opportunities (e.g., project work).

Interestingly, just because a leader is involved in a collaborative triad does not necessarily mean that there are no leader challenges. When no holes exist in a triad and it becomes transitive, information redundancy can result. Said differently, the leader may find that the same information is recycled among the legs of the triad. Indeed, this is one of the drawbacks mentioned by Burt (1992) and other network scholars. Also, the leader may need to renegotiate work patterns and tactics when a third actor is introduced. Indeed, whereas a dyad may have gone through the negotiation of expectations of roles and responsibilities (Sherman, 2002), this process may need to be repeated when a third actor is introduced. Moreover, this may require the leader to revisit tacit understandings and assumptions that may have been present during the dyad, but need to be made explicit when the triad forms. If C is newly introduced into what was previously a dyad between Leader A and member B, C may feel some initial discomfort due to a lack of understanding of work roles and existing norms. The leader, through formal and informal socialization techniques, can reduce this discomfort and can more speedily integrate the new member into the triad. This is particularly important since a collaborative triad cannot work at its optimum level if just one of the actors is not fully engaged.

To ensure that the "weakest link" does not prevent the advancement of the triad to accomplish its collaborative goals, the leader's primary and immediate duties revolve around selection and socialization. Selection is important since the formation of social capital is predicated on the input quality of the human capital (Offstein, Gnyawali, & Cobb, 2005). Socialization, especially that between C and B, is necessary so C feels comfortable sooner in his/her desire to freely contribute their human capital. Recall that if just one member of the triad chooses not to fully contribute, the triad, as a collective, is handicapped.

Member C Orientation

Members may possess differing motives, as well, to form a triad. For instance, C may form a tie with A to reduce B's advantage. In this scenario, C would strive for full interdependence, a transitive triad, based largely on informational reasons. If C cannot link with B, C is left to receive all information from the broker, Leader A. Realizing that to remain competitive C requires diverse, early, and full information, C will try to close all informational gaps. Also, realizing that leaders possess discretion (Offstein, Harrell-Cook, & Tootoonchi, 2005), resources (Pfeffer & Salancik, 1978), and power (Pfeffer, 1981), member C will attempt to engage in co-optation. Co-optation is neutralizing another's advantage through assimilation into an existing group or relationship. Thus, member C's agenda is to prevent member B from receiving the preponderance of benefits and resource advantages from Leader A.

In contrast to this competitive orientation, member C may seek a tie with A to create a triad and enhance common benefits. Under this scenario, C may seek to both contribute to and obtain benefits from the collaborative consequences associated with the deployment of social capital

(Nahapiet & Ghoshal, 1998). Unlike human capital, social capital is a public good that affords collective benefits, especially when the inputs are quality (Leana & Van Buren, 1998; Nahapiet & Ghoshal, 1998). Benefits include knowledge creation, innovation, and accelerated learning (Leana & Van Buren, 1999; Nahapiet & Ghoshal, 1998). This distinction is critical because collaboration simultaneously and positively affects *both* the individual and the larger collective, which in this case would be the triad.

Member B Orientation

We approach this scenario as if A and B were previously in and continue to remain in a traditional leader-member dyadic relationship. If collaboration is the dominant logic then the preceding argument as it relates to member C applies here. Specifically, B sees value creation from including a talented colleague into a triadic relationship. B then may consult with Leader A and offer an invitation of collaboration with member C. As long as Leader A agrees, the likelihood that a transitive triad will form is high.

If competition is the dominant logic, B will exert effort to purposefully block C from forming a tie, and in particular, a strong tie with Leader A. If the A to C tie does form, B may turn to politically motivated behaviors to create a favorable imbalance. For example, member B may employ impression management techniques to boost Leader A's assessment of B's value and performance, especially relative to member C. Other interpersonal tools at member B's disposal is that of ingratiation, which has received some attention in the LMX literature (Colella & Varma, 2001). To get noticed or to position, ingratiation can be a powerful tool evidenced by Wortman and Linsenmeier's (1977, p. 134) definition of ingratiation as "a class of behaviors employed by a person to make himself/herself more attractive to another." Of course, the underlying mechanisms described here are fueled by competition, and as a result, will form a competitively interdependent LMX triad.

Summary Comments on Scenarios

The above-mentioned scenarios serve only as a launching point to discuss the competitive and collaborative tensions that likely exist within LMX triads. This initial theoretical effort, while exploratory, does offer a framework to understand the reasons why LMX triadic relationships may occur and how the dynamics of such relationships would unfold. Earlier, we argued that a competitive interdependent triad could exist in perpetuity. While the driving force of competition, for example, could be the initiating and sustaining force behind triads, our discussion above also allows for the possibility of triadic states rather than triadic traits. Returning a moment to Heider's (1958) core principles underpinning balance theory, it is quite plausible that triads may shift in and out of balance over time. Conceivably, the competitive and collaborative tension found within these relationships could exist more as a state as opposed to a trait. This means that a triadic relationship is not constant and could fluctuate between the two tensions, with one force gaining at one particular point in time and ebbing at another.

Of particular note, procedural, distributive, and interactional fairness could be an important causal or moderating variable affecting the collaborative versus competitive nature of a triad. For instance, one can picture a scenario where three actors enter into a collaborative scenario and, as predicted by the theoretical discussions above, result in the achievement of several important outcomes. However, as success in meeting certain performance milestones occurs, the opportunities for one actor to feel slighted may actually increase. Here, the Leader must possess some strong social monitoring skills to ensure that rewards are doled out in a fair manner. Furthermore, the Leader must interact with the members fairly or risk the perception of interactional unfairness. Hence, a collaborative triad may evolve into a competitive one if, again, the leader does not take a proactive role in managing balance. In summary, while we have pursued competitive and collaborative interdependent triadic relationships as orthogonal for reasons relating to theoretical parsimony (Pedhazur & Schmelkin, 1991), further theory building and testing is necessary to support or refute the dimensionality of these constructs.

MULTIPLEX TRIADS

Multiplexity represents another interesting aspect of triads to consider in LMX relationships. In the scenarios described above, we have not explicitly accounted for the content of the relationship, i.e., whether the given tie between Leader and Members is a friendship tie, advice tie, etc. The idea that a given set of actors may be linked via multiple relations is well established in network studies (Ibarra, 1992; Wasserman & Faust, 1994). Specifically, any given trio of Leader (A) and Members (B, C) may be linked by more than one type of relationship—such as friendship and advice ties. For example, operational information may be shared equally between them, i.e., their *operational information sharing* triad may be transitive (See Figure 5.2).

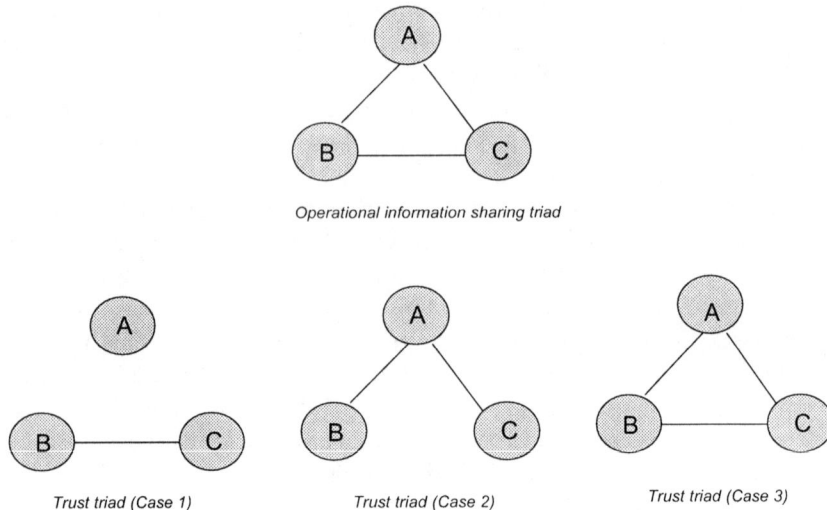

Figure 5.2. Multiplex triads.

However, it could well be that the trust network between the same individuals may have a different structure. For instance, A as a new Leader may find herself in the situation where she feels that she is not trusted by B and C, but that they have a strong trust tie between each other; in such a case, their *trust triad* belongs to the triadic isomorphism class[1] "102" (B-C linked, but A is an isolate), as depicted in Figure 5.2, Case 1. A triad characterized by a trusted Leader but intense competition between the two Members (and thus the absence of trust between them) may display a structure of *A-B, A-C* as depicted in Figure 5.2, Case 2. Of course, a reciprocally and strongly connected trust triad (Figure 5.2, Case 3) may exist in an LMX triad characterized by a fully collaborative and trust-laden set of relations. What is interesting about each of the cases sketched in Figure 5.2 is that they could each exist simultaneously with the transitive *operational information sharing triad*. Thus, three different LMX situations that look similar on the surface turn out to be quite different when multiplex triads are considered. For instance, one way to elaborate upon the scenarios described above would be to operationalize them in terms of more than one triad. If we were to contrast a competitively interdependent triad with a collaboratively interdependent triad in terms of multiplex relations, we propose that it will be possible to identify structural difference. The key here is the idea that when each content (e.g., operational information sharing) is taken one at a time, competitive and collaborative interdependence may lead to similarly structured triads. But a more sophisticated operationalization in terms of multiplex triads may show more. For example, Case 2 may be one possible manifestation of a competitively interdependent triad. The general takeaway is simply that multiplex triads may be a useful investigative tool to help understand LMX relations.

P ILLUSTRATION*

In this section, we illustrate how p^* analysis can be helpful in understanding the structural tendencies at work in a given network.[2] The ideas of collaborative and competitive LMX triads, developed above, become empirically testable if we assume that the dynamics of collaboration and competition will be manifested in the structural tendencies of the network. Specifically, we employ the simple intuition that collaborative triads are more likely to exhibit balance and closure, while competitive triads are more likely to be unbalanced and disconnected within triads comprising either friendship or trust relational content. In order to illustrate such an approach, we use a hypothetical trust[3] network in a small organization (13 actors at three different levels), as depicted in Figure 5.3. There are three hierarchical levels depicted: LL1 is at the highest level; L1 ... L4 are at the next level, and L1A ... L4B are at the third level. The line represents a trust relationship, with the arrow indicating direction—thus, e.g., L4 trusts LL1, but not vice versa.

Hypotheses

The theoretical arguments are fairly straightforward. A network that tends to collaborative LMX patterns (rather than competitive patterns) is likely to demonstrate two particular structural tendencies, one at the

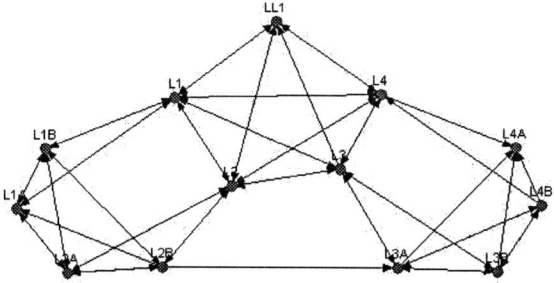

Figure 5.3. Illustrative trust network structure.

dyadic level and the other at the triadic level. At the dyadic level, we would expect to see *mutuality*, and at the triadic level, we would expect to see *transitivity*. Mutuality refers to the tendency of actors to engage in mutual, reciprocated ties, as opposed to unidirectional ties. Theories of exchange and resource-dependency suggest that actors are more likely to form ties with each other if they need resources from alters, and they, themselves, are in a position to offer something in return (Monge & Contractor, 2003). Arguably, such mutuality, as a reflection of reciprocal resource-dependence, is more likely to be found in a collaborative network. In contrast, actors in a competitive network would be less willing to engage in such mutual resource exchange. Thus, a structural tendency toward mutuality is an indication of a collaborative network.

At the triadic level, transitivity, referring to the tendency of actors to engage in "closed" triads, is a plausible marker of a collaborative network. If A-B and B-C, then the triad ABC is transitive if A-C also exists. Theories of consistency hold that individuals tend to be friends with the friends of their friends (Monge & Contractor, 2003). Thus, A and C are more likely to form a tie if the ties A-B and B-C already exist. However, this tendency is likely to be elevated in a collaborative network. There could be organizational incentives in such an organization to repeatedly form transitive ties; the spirit of collaboration acts as a positive force to enlarge each individual's circle of allies in this manner; and, by contrast, a competitively structured organization places barriers in the path of such transitivity. Thus, a structural tendency toward transitivity is an indication of a collaborative network.

An alternate structural tendency to consider at the triad level is *cyclicality*, which refers to the extent to which triads have a tendency to complete the cycle of ties—i.e., a triad is cyclical when A-B, B-C, and C-A. While both transitivity and cyclicality measure structural tendencies at the triadic level, the difference between them hinges on the directionality of the tie. In other words, transitivity and cyclicality are the same in a symmetric network. In our case, the trust network is directional, and thus, it would be interesting to see if the structural tendency to cyclicality is different from the structural tendency to transitivity, by means of an alternative hypothesis (as a "rule-out" tactic for cyclicality). It should also be noted that structural tendencies at the dyadic and triadic levels are meaningful only if the actors choose others in the network as partners—a structural tendency toward *choice* at the actor level, which thus becomes a baseline hypothesis.

Overall, if the network represented is collaborative, the following hypotheses should find support:

Hypothesis 1: The network demonstrates a structural tendency toward Choice. [Baseline]

Hypothesis 2: The network demonstrates a structural tendency toward Choice and Mutuality.

Hypothesis 3: The network demonstrates a structural tendency toward Choice, Mutuality, and Cyclicality. [Alternative]

Hypothesis 4: The network demonstrates a structural tendency toward Choice, Mutuality, and Transitivity.

Data and Method

The network represented in Figure 5.3 was analyzed using the program PSPAR, developed by Andrew Seary and Bill Richards to conduct p^* analysis. PSPAR is a standalone program that takes the network as input, does the pre-processing required for p^* analysis, and then conducts the necessary logistic regression.

Results

The results of the p^* analysis are presented in Table 5.1. The stepwise procedure shows that the additions of Mutuality and Transitivity result in a substantial reduction in the "Badness of Fit" measure, while the addition of Cyclicality does not. Among the 3-parameter models, the Transitivity model is clearly superior, thus ruling out the Cyclicality hypothesis (H3). Each of the other three hypotheses appears to be supported. The Wald statistics and associated p-values confirm that the illustration network demonstrates the structural tendencies of mutuality and transitivity. Thus, consistent with the theoretical arguments above, we conclude that this network tends to exhibit collaborative LMX patterns as opposed to competitive LMX patterns.

DISCUSSION AND IMPLICATIONS

Recently developed multi-level modeling tools such as p^* enable a researcher to identify the existence of structural triads within a given sample. This is a necessary, but not sufficient step in a more exhaustive under-

Table 5.1. Summary of *p** Analysis to Test for Illustrative Dyadic and Triadic Hypotheses

Hypothesis	Model	Number of Parameters	-2L ("Badness" of fit)	Wald Statistic (P-Value)		
				Mutuality	Cyclicality	Transitivity
1	Choice	1	201.250			
2	Choice + Mutuality	2	101.388	62.8585 (.001)		
3	Choice + Mutuality + Cyclicality	3	101.317	49.1504 (.001)	0.0719 (n.s.)	
4	Choice + Mutuality + Transitivity	3	93.098	49.5669 (.001)		8.0198 (.05)

standing of triads. After the triad is identified, it is important to discern the *nature* of that triad. In our theory building, we contend that triads are formed and exist to fulfill either competitive or collaborative motives. Depending on which of these tensions dominates, the management and outcomes of those triads are distinctly different.

In keeping with the spirit of exploring how LMX fits into the larger organizational context (Schriesheim et al., 1999), we briefly highlight some antecedents that likely influence the competitive versus collaborative nature of an LMX triad. Perhaps the appropriate starting point is to investigate the psychological composition of those members forming a triad. In fact, the personality profile of the members of a triad may be instrumental in shaping its charter. For instance, it would seem that members who are high on sociability and openness to learning personality dimensions might be more inclined to establish and promote a collaborative direction for the LMX triad. Also, the Thomas and Kilmann conflict resolution instrument suggests that individuals possess either a competitive or collaborative orientation or disposition (Thomas & Kilmann, 1974) Acknowledging these individual characteristics is particularly important because they are traits, and as such, are resistant to change and may help explain triadic behavior regardless of situation or context.

Good theory building should provide improvements in prediction and explanation of a given phenomenon (Pedhazur & Schmelkin, 1991) and from this improved understanding arises practical interventions of value to the practitioner. Armed with the knowledge of their members' dispositions, leaders, at the very least, are provided a more acute awareness of the make-up and composition of their triad. Since one of the major themes presented here is that management of a triad is more difficult than managing a dyad, this advanced and detailed compositional knowledge should be of particular value to organizational leaders.

For the reasons just described, Human Resources Management (HRM) seems particularly salient in influencing how triads within an organization come to exist and how they function. In particular, HRM wields control over the recruiting and selection process. Under these HRM functions, HRM can regulate the number of agents versus stewards that enter into and exit an organization. Davis and colleagues (1997) note that agents pursue self-interest first and foremost and, taken to an extreme, require considerable controls and safeguards to prevent agents from engaging in escalating opportunism to the detriment of others to include the organization as a whole. In contrast and, in general, stewards are concerned less with self-interest and seek, instead, to grow and expand an organization's resources through due care and prudence (Davis et al., 1997). Theoretically, then, it would appear that an organization comprised more of agents as opposed to stewards will produce more triads that are competitively interdependent. To this point, we have purposefully refrained from placing a pejorative label on a competitive or collaborative triad. Suffice to say, however, if organizational leadership desires more collaborative triads, policies and procedures should likely be designed to increase the selection and promotion of stewards while simultaneously reducing the selection rate and increasing the exit pace of agents.

HRM also frames the context in which people work, and because of that, shapes human behavior (Bowen & Ostroff, 2004; Lewin, Lippit, & White, 1939). Earlier we argued that resource availability helps shape the competitive versus collaborative orientation of a triad. To the extent that HR systems and processes enable the perception of resource scarcity through zero sum promotion and pay policies, the formation of competitive interdependent LMX triads are apt to increase. Conversely, if HRM shapes a more egalitarian culture through the design and enactment of their HRM policies, one would reason that collaborative interdependent triads would increase in kind. Extending this logic, HRM systems can be control or commitment oriented, with commitment oriented systems more highly correlated with superior firm performance (Arthur, 1994). It could be that a commitment HRM orientation may provide a context that sparks the development of collaborative, as opposed to competitive LMX triads. Another theme that resonates in our theory building, and which also applies to HRM, is the importance of fairness. Fairness in procedural, distributive, and interactional dimensions in the design and execution of various HR functions seems relevant in determining whether triads gravitate toward a competitive or collaborative purpose. For instance, perceived unfairness in compensatory and promotion practices may encourage individuals to join dyads for overly competitive, self-interested purposes. Hence, while individual dispositions likely shape the direction of LMX triads, research should attempt to control and account for organizational and environmental influences, especially variables related to HRM, to more fully specify their testable theoretical model.

One potentially intriguing area of research is to investigate this notion of collaborative and competitive LMX triads at the upper echelons of a firm. Indeed, empirical and theoretical investigation of this kind, even among traditional LMX research, is lacking—a vast majority of empirical LMX research is contained at the mid to lower levels of the firm. Investigating LMX in general, and triadic relations, in particular, at the upper-echelons is grounded in several important practical and conceptual reasons. First, the decision-making and strategic choice of the upper echelon has tremendous scope and any leadership development that affects the human capital of this select group is worthy of research attention (Offstein et al., 2005). Second, the triadic structure seems to naturally exist at these levels. For instance, triadic relationships often form between the CEO, the Board of Directors, and other members of the top management team (TMT). Thus, there is a natural and commonsensical setting to evaluate executive triads. But, most interesting, is that some evidence exists at this level to suggest that collaboration and competition work simultaneously, not sequentially (Henderson & Fredrickson, 2001). Specifically, Henderson and Fredrickson (2001) suggest that large pay gaps between the CEO and remaining members of the TMT spark a competitive tournament atmosphere (Lazear & Rosen, 1981) amongst a team that must coordinate and collaborate to achieve important firm outcomes that include driving firm performance. This is significant because it suggests that competition and collaboration can exist simultaneously, not just sequentially or in stages, amongst a team, to include a triad. Further examination into such a paradox is required to more fully develop the collaborative and competitive interdependent constructs we have outlined here and to achieve a better grasp of the dimensionality and construct validity of such constructs.

In conclusion, three decades and more than 200 empirical and theoretical articles have been devoted to advancing LMX theory. Indeed, the advances have been important on practical, empirical, and theoretical levels. In this chapter, we have suggested some ways to enrich our understanding of LMX relationships by paying attention to an important and relevant level of analysis—the LMX triad.

NOTES

1. In conventional triad analysis, there are 16 isomorphism classes of triads in general, such as 300 for a transitive triad. For an exhaustive description of

triad census and associated approaches, please refer to Wasserman and Faust (1994, ch. 14).
2. Our approach to illustrating p^* for this purpose is closely modeled after Monge and Contractor (2003, ch. 2), and Madhavan, Gnyawali, and He (2004).
3. The trust network has been chosen purely for illustration purposes—the argument here is about structural tendencies in any given relation, and thus should be applicable to any other relevant network as well.

REFERENCES

Arthur, J. B. (1994). Effects of human resource systems on manufacturing performance and turnover. *Academy of Management Journal, 37*, 670-688.

Baugh, G., Scandura, T. A., & Cogliser, C. C. (2003). LMX and mentoring diverse followers: Finding the competitive advantage for each. In G. B. Graen (Ed.,) *Dealing with diversity: LMX leadership—The series* (Vol. 1, pp. 59-90). Greenwich, CT: Information Age.

Bowen, D. E., & Ostroff, C. (2004). Understanding HRM-firm performance linkages: The role of the "strength" of the system. *Academy of Management Review, 2*, 203-221.

Burt, R. S. (1992). *Structural holes*. Cambridge, MA: Harvard University Press.

Colella, A., & Varma, A. (2001). The impact of subordinate disability on leader-member exchange relationships. *Academy of Management Journal, 44*, 304-315.

Contractor, N. S., Wasserman, S., & Faust, K. (2006). Testing multi-theoretical multilevel hypotheses about organizational networks: An analytic framework and empirical example. *Academy of Management Review* (forthcoming).

Dansereau, F., & Yammarino, F. J. (Eds.). (2003). *Multi-level Issues in Organizational Behavior and Strategy*. Amsterdam: Elsevier Science/JAI Press.

Davis, J. H., Schoorman, F. D., & Donaldson, L. (1997). Toward a stewardship theory of management. *Academy of Management Review, 22*, 20-48.

Douglas, C., Ferris, G. R., Buckley, M. R., Gundlach, M. J. (2003). Organizational and social influences on leader-member exchanges processes: Implications for the management of diversity. In G.B. Graen (Ed.,) *Dealing with diversity: LMX leadership—The series* (Vol. 1, pp. 59-90). Greenwich, CT: Information Age.

Fairhurst, G. T. (1993). The leader-member exchange patterns of women leaders in industry: A discourse analysis. *Communication Monographs, 60*, 321-350.

Ferris, G. R., & Judge, T. A. (1991). Personnel/human resources management: A political influence perspective. *Journal of Management, 17*, 447-488.

Gerstner, C. R., & Day, D. V. (1997). Meta-analytic review of leader-member exchange theory: Correlates and construct issues. *Journal of Applied Psychology, 82*, 827-844.

Gnyawali, D. R., & Madhavan, R. (2001). Cooperative networks and competitive dynamics: A structural embeddedness perspective. *Academy of Management Review, 26*, 431-445.

Graen, G. B. (2003). Role making onto the starting work team using LMX leadership: Diversity as an asset. In G.B. Graen (Ed.), *Dealing with diversity: LMX leadership—The series* (Vol. 1, pp. 59-90). Greenwich, CT: Information Age.

Graen, G. B., & Lau, R. (2005). Proper levels of analysis, hierarchical linear models, and leadership theories. In G.B. Graen & J.A. Graen (Eds.), *LMX leadership: The series, Global organizing designs* (Vol. 3, pp. 237-271). Greenwich, CT: Information Age.

Graen, G. B., & Scandura, T. A. (1987). Toward a psychology of dyadic organizing. In B.M. Staw & L.L. Cummings (Eds.), *Research in organizational behavior* (Vol. 9, pp. 175-208). Greenwich, CT: JAI Press.

Graen, G. B., & Uhl-Bien, M. (1995). Relationship-based approach to leadership. Development of leader-member (LMX) theory of leadership over 25 years: Applying a multi-level multi-domain perspective. *Leadership Quarterly, 6*, 219-247.

Granovetter, M. (1973). The strength of weak ties. *American Journal of Sociology, 78*, 1360-1380.

Heider, F. (1958). *The psychology of interpersonal relations*. New York: Wiley.

Henderson, A. D., & Fredrickson, J. W. (2001). Top management team coordination needs and the CEO pay gap: A competitive test of economic and behavioral views. *Academy of Management Journal, 44*, 96-117.

Ibarra, H. (1992, September). Homophily and differential returns: Sex differences in network structure and access in an advertising firm. *Administrative Science Quarterly, 37*, 422-447.

Krackhardt, D. (1998). Simmelian ties: Super strong and sticky. In R. Kramer & M. Neale (Eds.), *Power and influence in organizations* (pp. 21-38). Thousand Oaks, CA: Sage.

Krackhardt, D. (1999). The ties that torture: Simmelian tie analysis in organizations. In S. B. Andrews & D. Knoke (Eds.), *Research in the sociology of organizations* (Vol.16, pp. 183-210). Stamford, CT: JAI Press.

Lazear, E. D., & Rosen, S. (1981). Rank order tournaments as optimum labor contracts. *Journal of Political Economy, 89*, 841-864.

Leana, C. R., & Van Buren, H. J. (1999). Organizational social capital and employment practices. *Academy of Management Review, 24*, 538-556.

Lewin, K., Lippit, R., & White, R. (1939). Patterns of aggressive behavior in experimentally created social climates. *Journal of Social Psychology, 10*, 271-299.

Madhavan, R., Gnyawali, D. R., & He, J. (2004). Two's company, three's a crowd? Triads in cooperative-competitive networks. *Academy of Management Journal, 47*, 918-927.

Masterson, S. S., Lewis, K., Goldman, B. M., Taylor, M. S. (2000). Integrating justice and social exchange: The differing effects of fair procedures and treatment on work relationships. *Academy of Management Journal, 43*, 738-748.

Monge, P. R., & Contractor, N. S. (2003). *Theories of communication networks*. New York: Oxford University Press.

Nahapiet, J., & Ghoshal, S. (1998). Social capital, intellectual capital, and the organizational advantage. *Academy of Management Review, 23*, 242-267.

Offstein, E. H., Gnyawali, D. R., & Cobb, A. T. (2005). A strategic human resource perspective of firm competitive behavior. *Human Resource Management Review, 15*, 305-318.

Offstein, E. H., Harrell-Cook, G., & Tootoonchi, A. (2005). Top management team discretion and impact: Drivers of a firm's competitiveness. *Competitiveness Review, 15*, 82-92.

Pedhazur, E. J., & Schmelkin, L. P. (1991). *Measurement, design, and analysis: An integrated approach.* Hillsdale, NJ: Erlbaum.

Pfeffer, J. (1981). *Power in organizations.* Marshfield, MA: Pittman.

Pfeffer, J., & Salancik, G. R. (1978). *The external control of organizations: A resource dependence perspective.* New York: Harper & Row.

Schriesheim, C. A., Castro, S. L., & Cogliser, C. C. (1999). Leader-member exchange (LMX) research: A comprehensive review of theory, measurement, and data-analytic practices. *Leadership Quarterly, 10*(1), 63-113.

Seers, A. (1989). Team-member exchange quality: A new construct for role making research. *Organizational Behavior and Human Decision Processes, 43*, 118-135.

Sherman, J. D. (2002). Leader role inversion as a corollary to leader-member exchange. *Group and Organization Management, 27*, 245-271.

Simmel, G. (1922). *Conflict and the web of group affiliations.* (K. J. Wolff & R. Bendix, trans.). New York: Free Press.

Sparrowe, R. T., & Liden, R. C. (2005). Two routes to influence: Integrating leader-member exchange and network perspectives. *Administrative Science Quarterly* (forthcoming).

Thomas, K. W., & Kilmann, R. H. (1974). *Thomas Kilmann conflict mode instrument.* New York: XICOM.

Uhl-Bien, M., Graen, G. B., & Scandura, T. A. (2000). Implications of leader member exchange (LMX) for strategic human resource management systems: Relationships as social capital for competitive advantage. In G. Ferris (Ed.), *Research in personnel and human resources management* (Vol. 18, pp.137-185). Elsevier Science Press. Oxford: JAI Press/Elsevier Science.

Uhl-Bien, M., & Maslyn, J. M. (2003). Reciprocity in manager-subordinate relationships: Components, configurations, and outcomes. *Journal of Management, 29*(4), 511-532.

Wasserman, S., & Faust, K. 1994. *Social network analysis.* Cambridge, MA: Cambridge University Press.

Wasserman, S., & Pattison, P. E. (1996). Logit models and logistic regressions for social networks: An introduction to Markov random graphs and p^*. *Psychometrika, 60*, 401-425.

Wortman, C. B., & Linsenmeier, J. A. (1977). Interpersonal attraction and techniques of ingratiation in organizational settings. In B. Staw & G. Salancik (Eds.), *New directions in organizational behavior* (pp. 133-178). Chicago: St. Clair.

CHAPTER 6

AN EXPLORATION OF THE RELATIONSHIP BETWEEN COMMUNICATION NETWORK STRUCTURES TEAM-MEMBER EXCHANGE QUALITY AND TEAMWORK

Alex M. Susskind, Kristin Behfar, and Carl P. Borchgrevink

Scholars in the disciplines of management, psychology, and communication have spent a number of years examining team processes and team interaction in organizations. While these team-based examinations have greatly contributed to our knowledge of team-based communication, little attention has focused specifically on how communication network position relates to team members' perceptions and attitudes, such as team-member attitudinal cohesion (Stokes, 1983) and team-member exchange (Seers, 1989). In this investigation we integrate the theories of social contagion and social information processing to explore the relationships between formal and informal communication network structures and team members' perceptions and attitudes. We propose that, because frequent and fluid communication is believed to be vital to successful team interaction and process, a notable overlap between formal and informal communication network relationships will persist. Furthermore, we examine the team-based relationships between attitudinal cohesion, perceptions of information exchange, team effort sharing, and the network cohesion to assess how well these theories can ultimately predict team member performance through formal and informal network structure. These propositions are explored among participants from an 11-university, inter-organizational research alliance comprised of 11 intact research teams and the results are discussed.

INTRODUCTION

In recent years, teams have become a popular and effective way of managing and performing work tasks. The idea behind teams is that if they are structured to maximize communication density, connectivity, and minimize hierarchy, there will be greater flexibility in communicating, cooperating, and collaborating on work-related tasks, (Ibarra, 1992; Krackhardt & Hanson, 1993). However, a downside to teamwork is that it often takes longer than individual work, requires greater coordination of schedules, and sometimes more talented members feel burdened by low performers/contributors (Baldwin, Bedell, & Johnson, 1997). They found that among M.B.A. student teams, levels of communication were "directly and strongly associated with perceptions of team effectiveness and workload sharing." The same study found that workload sharing and team grades were negatively associated, and that students with higher cognitive ability reported lower satisfaction. This suggests that one or a few members of the team might be carrying the workload (Baldwin et al., 1997).

It has been suggested that social influence emerges as interdependent actors, who are senders and receivers of influence, share communication patterns (Rice, 1993). Recent research has found relationships between actor positions in their communication networks, such as constrained and non-redundant ties, and the degree to which they report satisfaction with their jobs and task-related peer interactions (Baldwin et al., 1997). Different elements of teamwork which are perceived, such as team members' flexibility, willingness to share work load, and equity and quality of member contributions, have also been shown to influence individual and team performance (Graen, Hui, & Taylor, 2004; Seers, 1989; Seers, Petty, & Cashman, 1995; Susskind, Odom, & Rutherford, 2004). Therefore, comparing structural attributes to attitude measurements is important to understanding why reciprocal behavior and team performance may vary between actors and their network characteristics.

This study will further investigate the relationships between team members' perceptions of teamwork, their attitudinal cohesiveness (perceived closeness to others) and their network cohesiveness (based on frequent and direct ties in their communication network). Social network analysis will be used for locating influential "source others," that is, the behaviors, attitudes, and influences to which an individual is exposed (Woelfel & Haller, 1971) and to get information about the intensity of exposure to social influence (Burt, 1983).

Seers' (1989) construct of team-member exchange (TMX) will be used to measure the dimensions of *information sharing* and *team effort sharing*, that is, the willingness to reciprocate a role in a working relationship, to contribute ideas, feedback and assistance, in return for the receipt of information, help, and recognition from other team members (Seers et al., 1995).

All analyses presented here were done at the dyadic level because of sample size and the fact that TMX measures *individual* perceptions of what is a "team player," not aggregated group perceptions as was used by Graen and his associates (2004).

BACKGROUND

Two theories, social contagion and social information processing, are useful in explaining how patterns in the communication network can influence a team member's attitudes, expectations, and behavior. Social contagion theory offers two explanations as to why members embedded in similar social contexts share similar attitudes: their cohesiveness (frequent, direct communication), or structural equivalence (like-others) (Burt, 1983). Membership in a subgroup narrows an individual's exposure to environmental stimuli and focuses attention on salient cues relevant to the group. It has been shown that frequent and repeated exchange between members increases group understanding of expectations for normative behavior (Burt, 1983; Hartman & Johnson, 1990). By identifying the structural boundaries of the social context in which an actor is embedded, it is possible to identify the actors and/or social influences that are most relevant in impacting attitudes.

Social information processing theory (Salancik & Pfeffer, 1978) explains how actors use expectations to interpret their environment and modify their behavior. It posits that many interactions have behavioral cues or "social information." Actors use this information to assess the rewards and consequences of "self" and "others'" behavior (Salancik & Pfeffer, 1978) and decide how to act or react.

However, individual perceptions of jobs and daily job related tasks are influenced by more than just the immediate exchange in which an actor is engaged (Emerson, 1992). Personal attributes, past experiences with individuals and with groups, and a variety of environmental factors have an influence on how actors act and react. Through communication exchange over time, team members come to understand norms and are able to predict how other members will act/react in different situations (Heimer, 1992). Through interacting with each other, members come to know the unique set of resources (ranging from skills, to contacts, to knowledge) and individual traits that each member brings to the team. Over time, the team members establish relationships and expectations of each other based on this knowledge.

If this relationship with other members offers enough benefits, members may be willing to tolerate or overlook costs of teamwork (Graen, 2003a,b; Saavedra & Van Dyne, 1999). For example, team members may be willing to endure longer task time, interpersonal conflict, or scheduling conflicts in return for leadership sharing, responsibility swapping or flexibility. If so, some members may perceive some other members as making greater contributions to the group's welfare as well as to the performance objectives (Graen & Uhl-Bien, 1995; Saavedra & Van Dyne, 1999). These extraordinary contributions likely lead to favorable perceptions, leader-member exchange and of team-member exchange quality and, therefore, should lead to defining fairness according to LMX, both attitudinal and network cohesion (Graen et al., 2004; Saavedra & Van Dyne, 1999). If team fairness is maintained and reciprocated appropriately, team members should share similar attitudes and interests in committing themselves to the group effort. If they are committed to the group effort, they should also perform well (Saavedra & Van Dyne, 1999).

SOCIAL INFORMATION AND INFLUENCE IN COMMUNICATION STRUCTURE

Formal network ties are associated with job duties, responsibility, and authority and usually carry communication exchange patterns about work related issues (Krackhardt & Hanson, 1993). They often come with a set of acceptable norms, such appropriate topics of discussion, language to be used, tone, and other characteristics of communication interaction imbedded and transferred through organizational culture or a job description. However, in a team setting, "these roles are meaningful only in the context of the loyalty they feel to one another and the knowledge they have of one another's needs, quirks, and whims" (Heimer, 1992, p. 143). Tichy (1981) and Ibarra (1992) note that these normative control mechanisms "tend to lead to the development of informal structures that are integrated and that overlap with formal structure" (Ibarra, 1992, p. 175).

The informal network is a way employees can meet their emotional needs by relating to those with common problems as they balance task demands with their individual social and emotional needs (Katz & Kahn, 1978). The informal networks **involving** team **members** serve important purposes in relation to perceptions of team member exchange quality. It is easy to see how the distinction can become blurred as teams work together, develop friendships, and influence each other's attitudes and expectations. Impressions about whether team members live up to their formal role responsibly, whether they are pleasant to work with, and if they trust one another as contributing to the group's goals are all issues that commonly discussed in the informal network of relationships (Krackhardt & Hanson, 1993). Therefore, it is hypothesized that social influence in the formal and informal networks are closely tied together in the team setting.

Proposition 1a: Formal and informal communication networks will be positively correlated.

Proposition 1b: Formal and informal network cohesion will be positively correlated.

NETWORK COHESION, ATTITUDINAL COHESION, AND TEAM MEMBER EXCHANGE

To describe how communication interaction affects individuals in a network, it seems necessary to examine the relationship between the patterns and relationships in the network to the attitudes of those within the network.

Identifying Strong Influences on Member Attitudes Toward Their Distributed Teams

By design, team boundaries are created with direct formal communication ties, which by definition, make them cohesive organizational subgroups (Wasserman & Faust, 1994). Cohesive communication ties are commonly used to explain how actors are socialized to accept subgroup norms and adopt similar attitudes (Burt, 1983; Hartman & Johnson, 1989). Direct ties carry *relational* influence intended to create behavior and attitudinal similarity among members' by focusing their exposure to group relevant stimuli (Hackman, 1992). This increases the team's ability to establish normative expectations about communicating, cooperating, and collaborating on formally prescribed tasks (Burt, 1983; Burt & Minor, 1983; Guzzo & Shea, 1992). These normative understandings serve as guides for team members to modify their attitudes and behaviors in order to perform in the best interest of the team (Salancik & Pfeffer, 1978; Burt, 1983; Hartman & Johnson, 1990; Heimer, 1992). Strong normative understandings about the way the group should operate have been shown to increase team performance (Guzzo & Shea, 1992; Hackman, 1992).

A good place to extend this discussion regarding a team-based environment is with cohesion, because it is manifested in two ways: network cohesion and attitudinal cohesion. First cohesion in a group characterizes direct/intense communication and influence and second, cohesion is a sense of "belonging" between team members and denotes similar feelings about the purpose and benefits of the team or group.

The first type of cohesion can be described in pure network terms relative to communication structure; that is, the amount of direct interactions between team members (Bovasso, 1996). Communication network cohesion is measured by the distance between two actors in a network (Borgatti, Everett, & Freeman, 2002), the shorter the path between any two actors, the more cohesive they are. The idea being that a direct tie or shorter connection between two actors in a network carries more direct social influence than an indirect tie or a longer chain of connections (such as a friend of a friend of a friend). The second type of cohesion is related to affective feeling toward the group (Witt, Hochwarter, & Hillman, 1999). With attitudinal cohesion the similarity in attitudes and expectations for group behavior and outcome influences how the members feel about being a member of the team (Hackman, 1992; Shah, 1998). It has been found that the more attitudinally cohesion among a group, the greater amount of homogeneity that exists in the way individuals perceive the behavior and attitudes of the other members of the group (Kincaid, 1993). If a member feels a sense of belonging to the group, or that the group meets his or her needs, the team member will feel more cohesive with the group (Stokes, 1983). As explained by social contagion theory, this should be reflected in communication patterns in the form of cohesive subgroups because more direct contacts make it more likely that the individual is under the influence of normative control mechanisms.

Proposition 2: Formal and informal network cohesion will be related to attitudinal cohesion.

Research has shown that elements of teamwork, such as team members' willingness to share workload and the equity and quality of others' contributions influence individuals' perceptions about the quality of their TMX (Seers, 1989; Seers et al., 1995; Susskind et al., 2004). In considering how external sources of influence impact members' attitudes about their teams, it is important to have an understanding of how much team members agree upon and are satisfied with the roles they play in their own team. Seers (1989) has proposed the construct of team-member exchange (TMX) to measure perceptions of how well other team members reciprocate working relationship roles. The construct identifies two dimensions that are especially relevant in the context of distributed teams: *information sharing* and *effort sharing* (Seers et al., 1995). The information-sharing dimension has to do with the degree to which members feel they receive social recognition, that they are allowed the opportunity to express opinions and needs, they feel others are sharing their expertise, and how well team members understand what is expected of them. The effort-sharing dimension has to do with the degree to which team members perceive each other as flexible about sharing responsibility for work and their willingness to help each other finish work that may have been assigned to other members. TMX is based on the idea that team members aggregate their perceptions of their team experience over time, and that this is how roles, norms, and attitudes toward the group are formed (Seers et al., 1995). Ideally, perceptions of internal TMX quality would be reinforced by external comparisons.

The TMX construct complements measurement of team cohesion because it focuses on the individual's role and his/her perception of the team's ability to share information and make a team effort (Seers, 1989; Witt et al., 1999). It moves beyond the attitudinal sense of belonging, and measures the degree to which members perceive their effort for the team goal as more of a benefit than a cost. In making this judgment, team members usually consider the group's performance, members' relationships with each other, and the benefits of belonging to the group (Saavedra & Van Dyne, 1999). For example, one of the TMX items measures the willingness of members to help others with work not assigned to them if their colleague gets too busy. This draws on the assumption that there are exchange values that have been established in the group and members know what is expected, rewarded, and their willingness to reciprocate a role in a working relationship. A team with a high TMX score exemplifies a group with members who have similar perceptions that they can contribute ideas, feedback, and assistance to other members, in return for the receipt of information, help, and recognition from other team members (Seers et al., 1995). In other words, they perceive each other as "team players."

Proposition 3: Network cohesion and attitudinal cohesion will be related to TMX.

The next logical question is one of how TMX and cohesion relate to individual performance. Social information processing explains how social cues observed in team interaction guide team members in choosing behaviors and attitudes that best suit the situation at hand. If team members are cohesive (attitudinally) communicate and share information fluidly, perceive to be sharing work in a fair manner, and feel that each member's effort is contributing to the group good, they should engage in behaviors that enhance their individual effort/performance as well as the group's performance.

> **Proposition 4:** Attitudinal cohesion and TMX will predict individual performance.

METHODS

Sample

This study examined communication network and attitude survey data of 11 autonomous work groups that were part of an inter-organizational research alliance between 11 universities in the United States. There were a total of 51 individuals in the alliance. Participants were research faculty in hospitality management programs. The sample size was $n = 44$ actors, yielding a survey response rate of 86 percent. In studies of networks and teams this is a normal and expected response rate.

Team Structure and Assigned Tasks

The purpose of each team was to conduct a study in one of the three "theme" areas identified by the research alliance: employee turnover, government regulation, and technology. Each team had the task of completing a comprehensive literature review, devising a theoretical foundation and methodology, and completing a pilot project for each study they undertook.

The teams were self-selected from the 11 universities by the 51 member alliance. Teams were composed of members who were believed to be most relevant or expert to one of the three main topic themes. Each team by necessity contained faculty from different universities and some of participants had multiple team memberships making the team boundaries loose by definition. Each team had a chosen leader, but in terms of the research alliance as a whole, each team and individual team member had a high degree of autonomy in structure and how they went about their work. Therefore, this sample is particularly attractive to measure TMX in because it has limited potential to be confounded by managerial interference (Seers, 1989) and would be clearly defined as autonomous works groups. In fact, self-managing teams have been shown to have higher levels of TMX (Seers et al., 1995) than traditional teams.

Measures

Early findings of this longitudinal program (Susskind et al., 2004) examined the communication dynamics of the research alliance described above. The communication network (formal and informal network ties and cohesion) and attitudinal (TMX and cohesion) data were used for this analysis. All analysis was done using UCINET (Borgatti et al., 2002).

Network Measures. Each participant was given a complete alphabetized directory of all research alliance members, which was organized by team and sponsoring university. The formal network was defined as *project related* contact with research alliance members. The informal network was defined as *non-project related* contact with research alliance members. Each respondent was asked to identify every other actor that he or she communicated during the first three stages of the project for each network over seven months. The seven Research Alliance members who did not return the survey were not included in the analyses.

A direct communication linkage was counted if an actor identified another as a contact. A contact was coded as either a zero or one, with a one representing a connection between two actors. The matrices were symmetrized because the direction of information flow was not important, but the existence of a social influence connection was. If one actor reported a connection, it is reasonable to assume the exchange between the two actors involved a flow of social information. By design, the team setting establishes patterns of communication, so it is highly likely that each participant gave an accurate report of their overall social influences. The matrices were symmetrized in UCINET by reporting the maximum linkage reported: the function that replaces xij and xji by max (xij,xji) (Borgatti et al., 2002).

Because teams are designed to maximize direct contacts, the main network property under consideration here was cohesion. Cohesion was calculated in UCINET using the Distance/Adjacency calculation, which by default records the shortest path length among all pairs. This was chosen over alternative cohesion calculations (such as reachability) because this study was interested in describing who each actor was directly connected to, not in *how* connected they were to the rest of the alliance. Since the attitude measures, cohesion and TMX, had to do with team-based perceptions, not positional roles, it was decided the most appropriate comparison was between team-based perceptions and formal and informal direct team communication ties.

Attitude Measures. Two attitudinal measures were considered in this analysis. Each construct was rated on a 5-point Likert scale ranging from: strongly agree, to neutral, to strongly disagree. The TMX construct had two dimensions which we used independently: *information sharing* and *effort sharing*. The information sharing dimension measured members' perceptions of inter-member feedback, comfort in communicating, and shared understanding in the team. The effort sharing dimension measured perceptions of members' willingness to "help" with workload sharing and reciprocate sharing favors. The reliability of the information sharing dimension of TMX was $\alpha = .77$ and the reliability of the effort sharing dimension of TMX was $\alpha = .89$. Because of the small sample size, factor analysis of the sub-scales was not possible.

The attitudinal cohesion scale was a six-item measure adapted from Stokes (1983) to measure how "close" or "together" the team members perceived themselves to be. It measured the degree to which each member felt included, how much he or she liked working with other team members, and overall impression of how rewarding belonging to the team was. The reliability of the scale was $\alpha = .87$.

Performance Scores. Individual performance (not aggregate team) ratings were considered in this study in order to keep the unit of analysis consistent. Each actor received performance ratings from the other members of his/her team. Those ratings were averaged to give each individual a performance score.

ANALYSIS

An average score for each attitude item (cohesion, TMX information sharing, TMX effort sharing, and performance) was computed and trans-

Table 6.1. Descriptive Statistics

Variable	Mean	Sd	(1)	(2)	(3)
1. TMX – Information	3.70	.64	1		
2. TMX – Effort	3.50	.77	.30*	1	
3. Cohesion	3.40	.89	.49**	.43**	1
4. Performance	4.37	.67	.34*	.13	.13

$N = 44$. * $p < .05$ level (2-tailed). ** $p < .01$ level (2-tailed).

formed into a 44 x 44 matrix of squared differences between the actor pairs.

The QAP correlation analysis in UCINET was used to test the association between networks (Borgatti et al., 2002). This test was used to assess the correlation between formal and informal communication patterns and formal and informal network cohesion, as hypothesized in Proposition 1a and Proposition 1b. QAP does not rely on the independence of data points.

The autocorrelation function in UCINET for interval data can be used to relate an actor-by-actor matrix to and interval-scaled attribute measure for each actor (Borgatti et al., 2002). This was used to test Proposition 2; to evaluate whether formal or informal communication in the networks were patterned by or associated with attitudinal cohesion.[1]

The QAP regression option in UCINET allows the regression of a "dependent matrix on one or more independent matrices, and assess[es] significance of the r-square and regression coefficients" (Borgatti et al., 2002). QAP regression analyses in UCINET was used to test Proposition 3, linear regression was used to test Proposition 4.[2]

RESULTS

Proposition 1a (*Formal and informal communication networks will be correlated*) was supported. The observed correlation was .579 between the two networks. The average random correlation was .000 with a standard error of .051. The percentage of random correlations that were as large as .579 was 0 percent on 1000 iterations, indicating, the correlation was deemed significant at the < .001 level.

Proposition 1b (*Formal and informal network cohesion will be correlated*) was also supported ($r = .520, p < .001$). These results show that cohesive subgroups (based on direct ties) have similar patterns in both the informal and formal networks.

Proposition 2 (*Formal and informal network cohesion will be related to attitudinal cohesion*) was not found to be statistically significant. Using autocorrelation, no significant correlations were found between attitudinal cohesion and the patterns of network cohesion in the formal network ($r = .07, p = .14$) or the informal network ($r = .027, p = .29$). However, after further analysis we determined that no relationship between them should be expected. The attitudinal cohesion matrix was constructed by squaring the differences in scores between actor pairs. Therefore, the scores ranged from 1 (for no difference) to 16 (the maximum squared difference between 1 and 5, the minimum and maximum possible average scores from the Likert scale ratings). The maximum distance in the formal communication network cohesion matrix was 2 (meaning one intermediary) and the maximum distance for the informal network was 4 (meaning 3 intermediaries). So, the correlation represents the relationship of distance between actors and differences in their average attitude scores. A positive relationship is expected because the larger the distance between actors in the network, the larger the difference in their attitudes should be. Although small and insignificant, a positive relationship was found. This insignificant result may be due to a range restriction problem and the use of squared difference scores; however, this is a common constraint when combining network and attitudinal data in matrix-based analyses in network analysis. The autocorrelation procedure was correlating values of one through four with the attitude scores, this leaves very little variation and is the equivalent of plotting points on top of points.

In testing Proposition 3 (*Network cohesion and attitudinal cohesion will be related to TMX*), QAP regression analysis was used. First we ran QAP once with the formal net and attitudinal cohesion as predictor variables, then again with the informal net and attitudinal cohesion as predictor variables—both times predicting TMX effort sharing. We then repeated the two regressions using TMX info sharing as the dependent variable. Overall, network cohesion was not related to TMX perceptions on both dimensions (information sharing and effort sharing), but attitudinal cohesion was as shown in Table 6.2.

Interestingly, small but significant relationships were found from a QAP correlation analysis done on the matrices of squared differences for attitudinal cohesion and TMX information sharing ($r = .291, p = .000$) and attitude cohesion and TMX effort sharing ($r = .225, p = .001$) (See Table 6.1).

Finally, in testing Proposition 4 (*Attitudinal cohesion and TMX will predict individual performance*), linear regression was used to assess how attitudinal cohesion, TMX information sharing, and TMX effort sharing related to performance. Interestingly, attitudinal cohesion was not a significant predictor ($ß = -.05, p = .71$), TMX effort sharing was not a significant predic-

Table 6.2. Predictive Ability of Network Cohesion and Attitudinal Cohesion for Similarity in TMX Perceptions Using QAP

TMX Effort Sharing				*TMX Information Sharing*			
Informal		*Formal*		*Informal*		*Formal*	
Network	Attitude	Network	Attitude	Network	Attitude	Network	Attitude
β p	β p	β p	β p	β p	β p	β Sig	β p
.21 .123	.17 .014	.04 .485	.18 .011	.04 .31	.28 .001	.02 .38	.29 .000

tor (ß = .04, p =.77), but TMX information sharing was a significant predictor (ß = .37, p =.05) of performance with an R^2 of .12.

DISCUSSION

Very little research, both in the network and management literatures, has examined the interplay between the formal and informal network (Ibarra, 1992). The results found here support the notion that they are interdependent and that social contagion is running through and between them. However, these results do not indicate a strong relationship between direct communication ties and similar attitudes. While it is clear that similarity in attitudinal cohesion is associated with TMX perceptions, these results fail to predict a relationship between network cohesion and TMX. One obvious explanation for this is that type of team and the natures of its task demands dictate different types of communication structures and group processes. These teams were geographically dispersed, working on interdependent, and had leaders to play the role of organizer. While they had to work together at the level of conceptualizing their studies, most of their work was done independently of one another for long periods. Typically, teams with low task interdependence do not have high-quality interaction processes (Wageman, 1995). Therefore, the fact that information sharing was a better predictor of performance than effort sharing is not surprising.

In this case, structural equivalence may have been a better predictor of social contagion's impact on attitude similarity than cohesion was, but we did not explore those relationships here. Shah (1998) found that employees in a large brokerage firm tended to rely on structurally equivalent referents for job-related information, but relied more on cohesive communication relationships for general information. Since performance was not predicted by effort sharing, but was by information sharing, it is possible that the purpose of other team members was to support and encourage independent work. It was found here that the informal and formal communication networks had similar patterns of cohesion. In addition, there was evidence that patterns in network cohesion and attitude were interdependent. However, they were not found to be significant predictors of similarity in TMX *job-related* perceptions. This indicates that social comparisons may not have been made against direct ties within teams, but rather against those with similar communication patterns in the rest of the research alliance. Since the alliance members shared joint team memberships and university affiliations, their referents for general information and social support may have been outside of their teams. Their roles as team members were more related information sharing tasks such as brainstorming, survey development, manuscript development and review. Therefore, it is understandable why it was difficult to find a relationship between direct ties and job-related perceptions. This analysis should certainly be replicated using structural equivalence as one of the correlates of network cohesion. As noted by Rice (1993), there are three mechanisms through which networks can be used to explain social influence: (1) Relational: the density and cohesion of a group that reinforces norms and values, (2) Positional: structural equivalence causes exposure to similar roles, values, status, activities, and attitudes, (3) Spatial: co-location makes it more likely that there will be interaction, exposure to similar influences.

LIMITATIONS AND FUTURE DIRECTIONS

There are several limitations to this analysis that suggest areas for further investigation. First, the influence of team leaders was not included. Therefore, the TMX construct may have been influenced by the atmosphere the team leader set for the team, rather than one the team members would have established for themselves (see Graen, 2006; Kramer, 2006). A future study might investigate the relationship between the strength, centrality, and power of communication ties and attitude variables, and if there are differences between the formal and informal network (e.g., there are multiple roles of friend, colleague, etc. the social influence may be different).

In addition, there was no measurement of the type of norms in that were established in the teams. In other words each team created and defined their own norms around the required tasks. Social contagion and social information processing may help explain and predict the influence of norms on team and network behavior. The findings of this study suggest that team leaders or managers might focus on different team-building activities and allocate resources differently depending on the *type and function* of social comparisons made by team members to each other and other actors in the network.

In addition, because this sample consisted of team members from different universities around the country, it would be interesting in the future to examine spatial effects. For example, actors from the same university may have more of an influence on each other than those who are not. Another special factor that may be worth investigating is the channel of communication that actors use (e.g., e-mail, phone, written). It is possible that the "richness" of the communication channels can have an affect on how a team's efforts take shape during the course of the project. In other words, did teams who met face-to-face perform any differently than teams that communicated primarily via email or telephone? This is particularly important today as teams are frequently "virtual" and span geographic distances. Data were collected in 1997 and 1998 from these project teams, virtual teams and the use of the Internet were just beginning to make stride as commonplace in our work lives. Given the findings of this study, it seems as though cohesion is an important factor for virtual teams as team members' attitudinal cohesion in this study was strongly related to both the information and effort sharing dimensions of TMX. Regardless of geographic location, team members who feel close to their team members will report higher levels interaction with their team in terms of TMX.

TMX information sharing was the only significant predictor of individual performance. Given the nature of the projects and the diversity of team membership in both geography and expertise—team members' espoused skill sets varied—it appears that higher performance resulted from bringing unique information to the team, rather than the perception of putting forth the effort to assemble that information. Also, because teams were geographically dispersed and members were specialized, effort sharing may not have been as easily identified as the flow of information into/from the team. This dynamic was most likely facilitated by the team leaders who coordinated information flow between and within teams. This is consistent with findings from the LMX literature (Graen et al., 2004) showing that information sharing is a predictor of performance.

Lastly, we did not examine the specific elements of the leader-member exchange among the teams. With geographically dispersed project teams, it is likely that leadership played an important role in how the work got done. We identified notable influences of individual performance and how teams functioned together. A next step for this research is to examine how leader-member relationships influenced or affected these teams. We are convinced that LMX would add to our understanding of how geographically dispersed project teams work together to complete complex tasks.

ACKNOWLEDGMENT

An earlier draft of this paper was presented at the Sunbelt XX conference, Vancouver, British Columbia April 15, 2000. Correspondence concerning this paper should be directed to Alex M. Susskind.

NOTES

1. The autocorrelation function in UCINET relates a dyadic binary variable (an actor-by-actor adjacency matrix) to a monadic variable (a vector representing an attribute of each actor). For example, if the dyadic variable consists of who are friends with whom, and the categorical variable is gender, the procedure tests whether friendship is patterned by gender (e.g., do boys prefer boys and girls prefer girls?). The routine is similar to performing a standard chi squared test except instead of using the chi squared distribution the underlying distribution is constructed using a randomization procedure (Borgatti et al., 2002, p. 103).
2. QAP procedure is principally used to test the association between networks. Often, one network is an observed network while the other is a model or expected network. The algorithm proceeds in two steps. In the first step, it computes Pearson's correlation coefficient (as well as simple matching coefficient) between corresponding cells of the two data matrices. In the second step, it randomly permutes rows and columns (synchronously) of one matrix (the observed matrix, if the distinction is relevant) and re-computes the correlation. The second step is carried out hundreds of times in order to compute the proportion of times that a random correlation is larger than or equal to the observed correlation calculated in step 1. A low proportion (< 0.05) suggests a strong relationship between the matrices that is unlikely to have occurred by chance (Borgatti et al., 2002, p. 99).

REFERENCES

Baldwin, T., Bedell, M., & Johnson, J. (1997). The social fabric of a team-based M.B.A. program: Network effects on student satisfaction and performance. *Academy of Management Journal, 40*(6), 1369-1397.

Borgatti, S., Everett, M. G., & Freeman, L.C. (2002). *Ucinet for windows: Software for social network analysis*. Harvard, MA: Analytic Technologies.

Bovasso, G. (1996). A network analysis of social contagion processes in an organizational intervention. *Human Relations, 49*(11), 1419-1435.

Burt, R. (1983). Cohesion versus structural equivalence as a basis for network subgroups. In R. Burt & M. Minor (Eds.), *Applied network analysis: A methodological introduction* (pp. 262-280). Beverly Hills, CA: Sage.

Burt, R. S., & Minor, M. (1983). *Applied network analysis: A mathematical introduction*. Newbury Park, CA: Sage.

Emerson, R. (1992). Social exchange theory. In M. Rosenberg & R. Turner (Eds.), *Social psychology: Sociological perspectives* (pp. 30-65). New Brunswick, NJ: Transaction.

Graen, G. B. (2003a). Interpersonal workplace theory at the crossroads. In G.B. Graen (Ed.), *Dealing with diversity: LMX leadership: The series* (Vol. 1, pp. 145-182). Greenwich, CT: Information Age.

Graen, G. B. (2003b). Role making onto the starting work team using LMX leadership: Diversity as an asset. In G. B. Graen (Ed.), *Dealing with diversity: LMX leadership: The series* (Vol. 1, pp. 1-28). Greenwich, CT: Information Age.

Graen, G. B., (2006). To share or not to share leadership: New LMX-MMX network leadership or charismatic leadership on creative projects. In G. B. Graen (Ed.), *Sharing Network Leadership. LMX leadership: The series* (Vol. 4). Greenwich, CT: Information Age.

Graen, G. B., Hui, C., & Taylor, E. T. (2004). A new approach to team leadership: Upward, downward, and horizontal differentiation. In G. B. Graen (Ed.), *New frontiers of leadership: LMX leadership: The series* (Vol. 2, pp. 33-66). Greenwich, CT: Information Age.

Graen, G. B., & Uhl-Bien, M. (1995). Relationship-based approach to leadership: Development of leader-member exchange (LMX) theory of leadership over 25 years: Applying a multi-level multi-domain perspective. *Leadership Quarterly, 6*(2), 219-247.

Guzzo, R. A., & Shea, G. P. (1992). Group performance and intergroup relations in organizations. In M. D. Dunnette & L. M. Hough (Eds.), *Handbook of industrial and organizational psychology* (Vol. 3, 2nd ed., pp. 269-314). Palto Alto, CA: Consulting Psychologist Press.

Hackman, R. (1992). Group influences on individuals in organizations. In M. Dunnette & L. Hough (Eds.), *Handbook of industrial and organizational psychology* (2nd ed., Vol. 3, pp. 199-267). Palo Alto, CA: Consulting Psychologists Press.

Hartman, R., & Johnson, D. J. (1990). Formal and informal group communication structures: An examination of their relationship to role ambiguity. *Social Networks, 12*, 127-151.

Heimer, C. (1992). Doing your job and helping your friends: Universalistic norms about obligations to particular others in networks. In N. Nohria & R. Eccles (Eds.), *Networks and organizations* (pp. 143-164). Boston: Harvard Business School Press.

Ibarra, H. (1992). Structural alignments, individual strategies, and managerial action: Elements toward a network theory of getting things done. In N. Nohria & R. Eccles (Eds.), *Networks and organizations* (pp. 165-188). Boston: Harvard Business School Press.

Katz, D., & Kahn, R. (1978). *The social psychology of organizations* (2nd ed.). New York: Wiley.

Kincaid, L. (1993). Communication network dynamics: Cohesion, centrality, and cultural evolution. In W. Richards & G. Barnett (Eds.), *Progress in communication sciences* (Vol. 12, pp. 111-134). Norwood, NJ: Ablex.

Krackhardt, D. (1990). Assessing the political landscape: Structure, cognition, and power in organizations. *Administrative Science Quarterly, 35*, 342-369.

Krackhardt, D., & Hanson, J. (1993, July-August). Informal networks: The company behind the chart. *Harvard Business Review*, 104-111.

Kramer, M. W., (2006). Communication strategies for sharing leadership within a creative team: LMX in theater groups. In G.B. Graen (Ed.), *Sharing network leadership: LMX leadership: The series* (Vol. 4). Greenwich: CT Information Age.

Rice, R. (1993). Using network concepts to clarify sources of mechanisms of social influence. In W. Richards & G. Barnett (Eds.), *Progress in communication sciences* (Vol. 12, pp. 43-62). Norwood, NJ: Ablex.

Saavedra, R., & Van Dyne, L. (1999). Social exchange and emotional investment in work groups. *Motivation and Emotion, 23*(2), 105-123.

Salancik, G., & Pfeffer, J. (1978). A social information approach to job attitudes and design. *Administrative Science Quarterly, 23*, 224-252.

Seers, A. (1989). Team-member exchange quality: A new construct for role-making research. *Organizational Behavior and Human Decision Making Processes, 43*, 118-135.

Seers, A., Petty, M., & Cashman, J. (1995). Team-member exchange under team and traditional management. *Group and Organization Management, 20*(1), 18-38.

Shah, P. (1998). Who are employees' social referents? Using a network perspective to determine referent others. *Academy of Management Journal, 41*(3), 249-268.

Stokes, J. P. (1983). Components of group cohesion: Intermember attraction, instrumental value, and risk taking. *Small Group Behavior, 14*(2), 163-173.

Susskind, A. M., Odom, P. R., & Rutherford, D. G. (2004). *Do liaisons have a role in teams? Examining the influence of liaisons in inter-organizational networks.* Paper presented at the Annual Conference of the International Communication Association, May 2004, New Orleans, LA.

Tichy, N. M. (1981). Networks in organizations. In W. H. Starbuck & P. C. Nystrom (Eds.), *Handbook of organizational design: Remodeling organizations and their environments* (Vol. 2, pp. 225-249). New York: Oxford University Press.

Wageman, R. (1995). Interdependence and group effectiveness. *Administrative Science Quarterly, 40*, 145-180.

Wasserman S., & Faust, K. (1994). *Social network analysis.* Cambridge, England. Cambridge University Press.

Witt, L., Hochwarter, W., & Hillman, C. (1999). Team-member exchange and commitment to a matrix team. *Journal of Social Behavior and Personality, 14*(1), 63-74.

Woelfel, J., & Haller, A. (1971). Significant others, the self-reflexive act and the attitude formation process. *American Sociological Review, 36*, 74-87.

CHAPTER 7

MACROSTRATEGIC, MESOSTRATEGIC, AND MICROSTRATEGIC LEADERSHIP PROCESSES IN LOOSELY COUPLED NETWORKS

James Douglas Orton and Gurpreet Dhillon

Our studies of the U.S. intelligence community and other information-technology-enabled organizations suggest a rising need for leadership research to merge with strategy research, moving strategy researchers into the study of microstrategic leadership processes, and moving leadership researchers into the study of macrostrategic strategy processes. We build on three premises from LMX publications to make this case. First, we build on Seers' observation that there is movement away from rigid organizational forms to flexible organizational forms; we describe this as a movement from tightly coupled firms to moderately coupled bureaucracies to loosely coupled networks. Second, we build on Seers' observation that there is coevolution in organizational forms research/practice and leadership research/practice; we describe this condition as "schizoid incoherence" and suggest that this condition is fed by five streams: technology, speed, changefulness, globalization, and chaos. Third, we build on

Uhl-Bien, Graen, and Scandura's observation that LMX theory helps explain the creation of strategic capital, and a broader call from Boal and Hooijberg for more research on the behavioral, cognitive, and social complexity that helps create strategic advantage; we participate in this conversation by reanalyzing three studies—Quinn's early discussion of logical incrementalism, Pascale's and others' writings on the Honda motorcycle case, and our own research on the John Brown Engineering and Construction case.

INTRODUCTION

Our studies of the U.S. intelligence community (Orton, 2000) and other information-technology-enabled organizations (Dhillon & Orton, 2001) have convinced us of the need for better research and better theory on the intersection of strategy processes and leadership processes. Some conceptual tools that help us explain the environments that we study are loosely coupled networks, schizoid incoherence, and microstrategies.

In this chapter, we (1) review some of the history on strategy-making, decision-making, and sensemaking processes in loosely coupled networks (March & Olsen, 1976; Simon, 1976; Weick, 1976); (2) provide further explanation of our earlier research on the topic of "schizoid incoherence" (Dhillon & Orton, 2001; Greenwood & Hinings, 1988); (3) explain the importance of microstrategic leadership in schizoid incoherent contexts (Orton & Weick, 1990); and (4) conclude with some observations on how of the emerging field of strategic leadership research can be developed more quickly (Boal & Hooijberg, 2000).

TIGHTLY COUPLED FIRMS, MODERATELY COUPLED BUREAUCRACIES, AND LOOSELY COUPLED NETWORKS

One of the intriguing challenges that leadership theory faces, as Seers noted in the lead chapter of last year's LMX volume (Seers, 2004) is a coevolution problem. Much of leadership theory is locked into an organizational world that no longer exists—a pre-World-War II world of multidivisional bureaucratic organizations (Chandler, 1962; Taylor, 1911; Weber, 1946), in which leadership "in" the organization emphasized control through a variety of levers (French & Raven, 1959) within a mechanistic system (Burns & Stalker, 1961). Driven by the competitive advantages created by historical uniqueness, causal ambiguity, and social complexity (Barney, 1991), firms have been racing away from tightly coupled firms and moderately coupled bureaucracies toward loosely coupled networks.

To put a sharp point on this movement, we often tell our executive education clients that 1500-1865 was the era of tightly coupled firms, 1865-1944 was the era of moderately coupled bureaucracies, and 1944-2006 is the era of loosely coupled networks (March & Olsen, 1976; Nohria & Eccles, 1992; Simon, 1976; Weick, 1976).

We often simplify the last sixty years of management research as the era of Simon, March, and Weick. Together they shifted the focus of research from management, administration, and mechanistic organizational forms to strategy-making, decision-making, and sensemaking processes within loosely coupled networks. Herbert Simon argued that as ambiguity, uncertainty, and turbulence increase at the macrostrategic level, we should expect to see a reduction of strategic comprehensiveness through such mechanisms as logical incrementalism, small wins, action rationality, and sequences of actions (Simon, 1976). This relationship suggests that at some point, strategy researchers are likely to see their topic of study split into three fields: macrostrategizing, mesostrategizing, and microstrategizing. Simultaneously, leadership theorists might expect to see their topic of study split into three similar fields: macrostrategic leadership, mesostrategic leadership, and microstrategic leadership (Boal & Hooijberg, 2000).

One concise historical treatment is suggested by the writings of Coase, Chandler, Williamson, Ouchi, and Powell. Coase, by focusing on the differences between market transactions (between firms) and hierarchical transactions (within firms), helped create a dividing line between treatments of organizations as firms and treatment of organizations as bureaucracies (Coase, 1937, 1960, 1974). Williamson built on Coase's distinction between firms and bureaucracies to create a universe focused on the reduction of transaction costs: bounded rationality, opportunism, small numbers, moral hazard problems, and asset specificity were called into service to explain the historical shift from firms to bureaucracies (Williamson, 1975, 1978, 1981, 1985, 1991a,b, 1994, 1996a,b,c; Williamson & Ouchi, 1981). Chandler, in contrast, said very little about firms, but provided the historical documentation for the study of bureaucracies: railroads, General Motors, DuPont, Sears, and Standard Oil (Chandler, 1962, 1977, 1990, 1991; McCraw, 1988). In contrast to Chandler's archival studies of 1920s multi-divisional bureaucracies, Ouchi studied Hewlett-Packard in the 1970s (Ouchi, 1981) and expanded the markets-hierarchies discussion (Ouchi, 1980) by incorporating ambiguity into the discussion. Ouchi showed that when norms of rationality hold, the firms-bureaucracies continuum is an adequate representation of organizational forms, but under conditions of high ambiguity, the model needed to be expanded to include network organizations, such as Hewlett-Packard's loosely coupled structure being kept coherent by a tightly coupled culture (Ouchi, 1978,

1980, 1981; Ouchi & Wilkins, 1978, 1983; Wilkins & Ouchi, 1983). Powell expanded the model further by pointing out that new organizational forms were neither firms nor bureaucracies, but could be described as networks that transcend organizational boundaries (DiMaggio & Powell, 1983; Powell, 1989, 1986, 1990; Powell & Brantley, 1992; Powell & DiMaggio, 1991).

To put a sharp pedagogical edge on this economic-history discussion of the evolution of organizational forms, we place dates on the three organizational eras: tightly coupled firms (1500-1863), moderately coupled bureaucracies (1863-1944), and loosely coupled networks (1944-2001). The era of firms lasted until 1863, when the rise of telegraphs and trains allowed the conglomeration of small firms into large bureaucracies like General Mills, General Foods, and General Motors. (This is the transition that Coase and Williamson study as "market failure.") The era of bureaucracies lasted until June 6, 1944, when (if one believes Cornelius Ryan's account of *The Longest Day*) a strict command-and-control German bureaucracy was defeated by a loosely coupled, emergent, organic system in which John Wayne, Sean Connery, and Robert Mitchum were autonomous, empowered actors united under a common objective (Ryan, 1959). (This is the transition that Ouchi and Powell study as "bureaucratic failure.") Since 1944, we find ourselves in the era of loosely coupled networks, when CNN, the European Community, and the Internet have come into power, leading to disaggregation, disintermediation, virtual organizations, and the network economy. This leads to studies such as Browning, Beyer, and Shetler's study of the Sematech research and development consortium in the semiconductor industry (Browning, Beyer, & Shetler, 1995). Browning, Beyer, and Shetler found that participants made one-way transfers or gifts into the network to establish a "moral community" based on trust and cooperation.

Several other researchers have built on Simon and have tracked the evolution of organizational forms from simple to complex—or from macrostrategic, to mesostrategic, to microstrategic leadership. Allison presented his model as three independent pedagogical decision-making lenses—a simplistic Rational Actor model, a barely comprehensible Organizational Processes model, and a "just right" Bureaucratic Politics model (Allison, 1969, 1971; Allison & Zelikow, 1999). Weick presented an important process model of enactment-selection-retention, with a variety of complex feedback loops (Weick, 1979). Weick's expanded model can be summarized as a theory of organizational sensemaking processes (Weick, 1995) within loosely coupled systems (Weick, 1976). Smircich and Stubbart described an Objective World of strategy, a Subjective World of strategy, and an Enacted World of strategy (Smircich & Stubbart, 1985). Martin, in her analysis of the corporate culture literature, captured these important movements from the simple to the complex (Martin, 1992). In the early stages of culture research, researchers believed in Paradigm 1, an Integration Paradigm, in which organizational members were presumed to share a common set of values and beliefs. In the middle stages of culture research, researchers believed in Paradigm 2, a Differentiation Paradigm, in which organizational culture was presented as the interaction of several subcultures. In late stages of culture research, researchers believed in Paradigm 3, a Fragmentation Paradigm, in which individual organization members manage a portfolio of subcultures that slice through the organization (Martin, 1992).

Fortunately, LMX theory is grounded in theories of enactment, in which leaders/managers and members jointly construct the environment to which they must then respond (Weick, 1979)—a process referred to by Graen and his colleagues as "role-making" (Uhl-Bien, Graen, & Scandura, 2000). Because LMX is grounded in enactment theories, it is better able than most theories of leadership to explain how leadership influences strategy, and how strategy influences leadership. Enactment theories explain how microstrategic actions shape the creation of portfolios of mesostrategic options, and how portfolios of mesostrategic options shape the creation of macrostrategic organizational directions (Mintzberg & McHugh, 1985). Enactment theories also explain how integrated macrostrategic cultures can influence differentiated mesostrategic subcultures, and how differentiated mesostrategic subcultures can explain fragmented microstrategic individual networks (Martin, 1992; Meyerson, 2001; Meyerson & Martin, 1987). Recent developments in LMX theory show that "scaleability," or the ability to explain leadership phenomena at multiple levels of analysis, and the additional ability to explain interactions between those levels of analysis, are continuing advantages of LMX theory (Graen, 2004).

FIVE STREAMS THAT CONTRIBUTE TO SCHIZOID INCOHERENCE

We characterize the last 50 years as a time of increasing "schizoid incoherence," a term originally introduced in Hinings and Greenwood's thorough analysis of strategic change processes (Greenwood & Hinings, 1988; Hinings & Greenwood, 1988; Ranson, Hinings, & Greenwood, 1980). Hinings and Greenwood mapped a series of "organizational tracks" by which organizations changed from one design archetype to another design archetype. In an idealized linear transformation from Design Archetype A to Design Archetype B, there is a theoretical midpoint where the organization is presumed to be half-A and half-B. Hinings and Greenwood referred to this point on the organizational track as a brief period of "schizoid incoherence." In our research on the U.S. intelligence community and other information-technology-enabled networks, we have come to believe that schizoid incoherence is no longer a temporary condition in complex organizations. Instead, we notice firms in a constant state of schizoid incoherence. The organizations we study do not know if they are currently in Design Archetype A, B, C, D, E, F, or G, and they do not know whether they should try to move toward Design Archetype T, U, V, W, X, Y, or Z (Dhillon & Orton, 2001). Four presidential commissions, for example, have criticized the U.S. intelligence community for its inability to create an effective post-Cold-War managerial structure: the Aspin-Brown commission of 1996, the Hart-Rudman commission of 2001, the Kean-Hamilton commission of 2004, and the Silberman-Robb commission of 2005.

The U.S. intelligence community is not in a brief transition point between Design Archetype A and Design Archetype B. Like many other organizations, it is in a constant state of schizoid incoherence about where it comes from and where it is headed.

Weick and Quinn have done a good job describing this change in the organizational environment in a recent review of literature on organizational change (Weick & Quinn, 1999). Our theories of change dating back to Kurt Lewin have been built on the model of "unfreeze-move-refreeze" (Lewin, 1943). Hinings and Greenwood's 1988 description is entirely consistent with Lewin's model of change—there are long periods of stability punctuated by brief moments of chaos, and the track from one design archetype to another briefly passes through a point labeled "schizoid incoherence." An important point for our notes here about strategic leadership—consistent with Seers' observations (Seers, 2004)—is that the "unfreeze-move-refreeze" model might no longer apply. Instead, we seem to be increasingly likely to have long periods of schizoid incoherence that are punctuated by brief moments of order (Orton, 2000). Theories of strategic leadership processes need to take into account a change commented on by several observers—there seems to have been a movement from infrequent and short periods of schizoid incoherence to constant, long periods of schizoid incoherence (Orton, 2000; Seers, 2004; Weick & Quinn, 1999).

A wide variety of observers have contributed to an emerging vocabulary about this macrolevel environment that we are calling schizoid incoherence. One stream emphasizes technology, a second stream emphasizes speed, a third stream emphasizes changefulness, a fourth stream emphasizes globalization, and a fifth stream emphasizes chaos.

Technology

The first stream describes the increasingly complex nature of technology. There have been many important studies of near catastrophes (Allison, 1971), normal catastrophes (Perrow, 1984), and normalized catastrophes (Vaughan, 1996). Allison's study of the Cuban Missile Crisis was grounded in Simon's, March's, and Weick's world of loosely coupled networks and consequently provided an early prototype for catastrophe studies (Allison, 1969, 1971; Allison & Zelikow, 1999). Later, Perrow described a dangerous world of interactive complexity caused by unpredictable interactions between complex technical systems and complex human systems, with his prescient prediction that the Chernobyl, Challenger, and Bhopal catastrophes would become "normal" in our era (Perrow, 1981, 1983, 1984, 1986). More recently, Vaughan's extraordinary analysis of decision processes in the Challenger launch decision introduces the idea of repeated decision cycles creating an organizational culture in which deviations become normalized (Vaughan, 1982, 1990, 1992, 1996, 1997). Other important studies by Weick and Gephart help explain the complex interactions between loosely coupled human networks and increasingly complex technologies (Gephart, 1997; Weick, 1985, 1988, 1990, 1993).

Speed

A second stream of research emphasizes the acceleration of macroenvironmental conditions. Peters described how managers can "thrive on chaos" through "liberation management" and "necessary disorganization for the nanosecond nineties" (Peters, 1992). D'Aveni captured the shift from one macrostrategy to a series of microstrategic plays in his discussion of hyperturbulent environments (D'Aveni, 1995). Brown and Eisenhardt, building on Eisenhardt's studies of strategic decision-making in high-velocity environments, refer to "managing on the edge of chaos" (Bourgeois & Eisenhardt, 1988; Brown & Eisenhardt, 1997, 1998; Eisenhardt, 1989; Eisenhardt & Bourgeois, 1988; Eisenhardt & Zbaracki, 1992).

Changefulness

A third stream emphasizes "changefulness" or frequency of organizational restructuring. Several "reconnaissance people" with front-line consulting experience report that the frequency of reorganizing has accelerated. Peters' explanation is that the "conventional approaches" to organizational structure are not working (Peters, 1987): "Today's structures were designed for controlling turn-of-the-century mass production operations under stable conditions, with primitive technologies. They have become perverse, action-destroying devices, completely at odds with current competitive needs" (p. 355). Torbert added that reorganizing is moving from an infrequent event to a constant process (Torbert, 1987): "During the 1980s, companies have been restructuring ... faster than a snake sheds skins. These changes are beginning to be understood, not as a onetime phenomenon for a given company but as a continuing condition of business" (p. xv). Kanter used a complementary metaphor to make a similar point (Kanter, 1989): "Shuffling and reshuffling the organizational deck to deal a better hand for the company has always been a fact of life for American business. But today companies are changing their shape more frequently and more dramatically" (p. 57). Ulrich and Lake also noticed the increasing pace of reorganizing (Ulrich & Lake, 1990): "No one organizational structure will fit all situations or provide an ideal resolution to the conflict of competing demands ... Once management accepts that the process of organizational design is a fluid, ongoing one and implements the procedures that make it most effective, the ability to adapt to change—and thus to compete successfully—will be enormously enhanced" (p. 167).

Globalization

A fourth stream emphasizes the confusion caused by globalization. Clegg and Gray conclude from their analyses that globalization is making the world more complex rather than less complex: "Globalization, then, rather than foreclosing these questions of identity in convergence on one form, opens them all up in a thoroughly postmodern way. Failure to appreciate this, or the tendency to focus on one aspect of this relativism, the virtual exclusion of relativity, is a form of theoretical fundamentalism that fails to reflect the current global conjuncture as one that is postmodern. The postmodern global world is simultaneously one of compression of space and time and, consequent upon this, an exacerbation of relativities between narratives of self, society, the globalizing world, and the increasingly transparent ways of being human, one to the other, that this complex of compression and relativization presents" (Clegg & Gray, 1996). Gergen and Whitney describe globalization as a force that moves organizations from "monologic" to "polyphonic" forms: "In his literary work, Bakhtin identifies what he views as a major creative turn in the form of the novel, from the traditional novel, in which the singular view of the author prevailed, to that of the multivoiced, or polyphonic, novel. In the polyphonic novel, such as Dostoevsky's *The Brothers Karamazov*, there is no singular vantage point, dominated by the author. Rather, there are multiple voices of enchantment, a plurality of characters, each given the space to make his/her actions and beliefs intelligible; the ultimate reality of the novel is that which issues from the interchange" (Gergen & Whitney, 1996).

Chaos

A fifth stream emphasizes meltdowns in meaning. Hatch described organization theory in general as moving from a classical period, to a modernist period, to a symbolic-interpretive period, and now into a postmodern period characterized by collages of theories, none more "privileged" than the others (Hatch, 1997). Gephart, Boje, and Thatchankery (1996) distinguished three types of emerging crises: legitimation crises, cultural crises, and representation crises. "Legitimation crises occur where the state apparatus fails to secure mass loyalty, and this can lead to disintegration of the state, changes in the organizing principles of the state, or social control through authoritarian repression" (p. 4). "The challenges, crises, and limits of modernism have led to the emergence of postmodernism as a cultural or social movement that critiques modernism and offers alternative institutional and aesthetic forms. These social movements can themselves produce crises by challenging the status quo of cultural processes and institutional forms and by seeking radical, disjunctive, social and organizational changes" (p. 6). "The delegitimation of science as totalizing knowledge or grand narrative has been associated with the emergence of views in which scientific methods are problematized. That is, there has been a loss of grand theory in all disciplines" (p. 7) (Gephart, Boje, & Thatchenkery, 1996).

The point we are trying to make is that macrostrategic environments are characterized by increasing technology, speed, changefulness, globalization, and chaos.

Strategic management rarely taps into the work of European social science philosophers Anthony Giddens, Pierre Bourdieu, and Ulrich Beck. We find, though, that Beck's work is especially helpful in building a better understanding of the causes of macrostrategic schizoid incoherence. Beck's writings explore a shift from an economy based on capital to an economy based on risk, a shift from nation-states to transnational organizations, a shift from highly traditionalized local lifestyles to highly detraditionalized global lifestyles, and a shift from high supplies of required compensated labor to automated low supplies of compensated human labor (Beck, 1992, 2000). What determines whether these four emergent forces will yield positive or negative outcomes? Beck argues that the future will be determined by the reallocation of individuals' energies away from paid compensation toward two other forms of labor: local or family-level labor and regional or transnational-level labor. In other words, in a theme which will be developed in the next section, the response to the macrostrategic environment of schizoid incoherence will be found in logical incrementalism, small wins, and the maintenance of portfolios of microstrategic actions.

"ENHANCED LEADERSHIP": MICROSTRATEGIC LEADERSHIP PROCESSES

Several researchers described the transition from the bureaucratic era into the network era (Henderson & Clark, 1990; Nohria & Eccles, 1992; Orton & Weick, 1990; Powell, 1990). Orton and Weick suggested that "Enhanced Leadership" was an important topic of study for the era of loosely coupled networks, and argued for a focus on "subtle" leadership processes:

> Some theorists view the management of loosely coupled systems as a problem and call for "stronger" leadership. For example, Murphy and Hallinger (1984) argued that loose coupling research described "what is" and school effectiveness research described "what can be" (p. 10). They wrote that loose coupling research implies that organizational levels and components have limited influence on other organizational levels and components because of "the presence of multiple and often conflicting goals" and "the lack of a clear instructional technology" (p. 7). Murphy and Hallinger (1984) also stated that in contrast to loose coupling, "the teacher effectiveness literature portrays schools as possessing a clearly defined technology or means to reach goals" (p. 8) The solution, according to these authors, is strong leadership that unifies goals and clarifies technology (pp. 9-10).

We have seen this idea of "strong" leadership as a compensation for "loose" structure in several other studies (Ouchi, 1980; Perrow, 1979; Peters & Waterman, 1982).

What is less well developed is Orton and Weick's notion of "subtle" leadership. Although it is tempting to sort "strong leadership" into Graen's category of "leadership" and sort "subtle leadership" into Graen's category of "managership," a more accurate way to describe subtle leadership would be to connect it to the processes of role-making in which the manager builds social capital into the network one relationship at a time (Uhl-Bien et al., 2000). Orton and Weick described subtle leadership as the awareness of system fragmentation and a willingness to engage that fragmented system:

> Other researchers have suggested that loose coupling calls for subtle leadership. For example, Boynton and Zmud (Boynton & Zmud, 1987) counseled information systems professionals who, because of the dispersal of computer technology, will find themselves in more loosely coupled systems, to try "to simultaneously provide centralized direction and coordination while recognizing the value of increased discretion" (p. 62). Similarly, Weick (1982) counseled educational administrators to be more attentive to the "glue" that holds loosely coupled systems together: "since channels are unpredictable, administrators must get out of the office and spend lots of time one on one—both to remind people of central visions and to assist them in applying these visions to their own activities" (p. 676). Therefore, this one-on-one or subtle leadership implies sensitivity to diverse system components (Kaplan, 1982) and the ability to control systems through conversation (Gronn, 1983).

Another way to think about the difference between strong leadership and subtle leadership might be to borrow Polanyi's distinction between explicit knowledge and tacit knowledge (Polanyi, 1983), and add that strategic advantage is more likely to come from tacit, subtle leadership processes than explicit, strong leadership processes because they are more socially complex, causally ambiguous, and historically unique (Szulanski, 1996).

Herbert Simon's concept of "bounded rationality" can be disaggregated into two complementary concepts: an increase in schizoid incoherence coupled with a decline in strategic comprehensiveness. Simon was the first organizational scholar to create a link between increasing complexity and decreasing comprehensiveness, through the concepts of uncertainty and ambiguity, bounded rationality, and loosely coupled systems (Simon, 1976). March picked up many of these themes and developed them in notions such as prescriptions for a technology of foolishness (March, 1981) and a focus on the chaotic nature of garbage can decisionmaking (Cohen, March, & Olsen, 1972). Allison's landmark study of strategy formation in the Cuban Missile Crisis provided a strong case study in which to explore the significance of microstrategies in the creation of macrostrategies (Allison, 1969, 1971; Allison & Zelikow, 1999).

Following in this tradition is Tom Peters, whose 1978 dissertation was on "small wins" and whose subsequent writings reinforce the concept (Peters, 1978, 1980, 1981, 1987, 1992; Peters & Austin, 1985; Peters & Waterman, 1982). Karl Weick's research on enactment processes, loosely coupled systems, small wins, and organizing processes also has a great deal to say about microstrategies (Weick, 1976, 1979, 1984, 1995). One of the common assumptions people make about causality (Einhorn & Hogarth, 1986) is that small causes should lead to small effects and large causes should lead to large effects. This assumption is built around two variables—the size, effort, and cost of the cause ("small" or "large") and the size, importance, and impact ("small" or "large") of the effect. "Small wins" are cases in which small causes lead to disproportionately large positive effects. The mechanics of these "small wins" include the notion of deviation-amplifying loops, also referred to as vicious circles and virtuous circles (Weick, 1979, p. 72). The continuing development of the idea of small wins (Weick, 1984) is built on the premise of small enactments that can develop into larger benefits through organizational processes. The emerging studies referred to as "chaos theory" seem to reinforce the notion of small bracketed enactments cycling into larger bracketed enactments.

Henry Mintzberg has been an ardent critic of macrostrategies. Mintzberg also influenced Quinn's discussions of strategies as patterns of decisions. Mintzberg's award-winning book, *The Rise and Fall of Strategic Planning*, is a thorough argument for the dismantling of macrostrategic thinking (Mintzberg, 1978, 1994; Mintzberg & McHugh, 1985; Mintzberg & Waters, 1985). Sumantra Ghoshal and Christopher Bartlett's recent work on the management of transnational organizations has drawn them into a logic of microstrategies as well, as they try to redefine strategy to purpose, structure to people, and systems to processes in *The Individualized Corporation* (Bartlett & Ghoshal, 1989, 1994, 1995; Ghoshal & Bartlett, 1995).

Armed with this short introduction to microstrategies, we turn now to three longer discussions of microstrategic leadership by Quinn (1980), Pascale (1984), and Dhillon and Orton (2002).

Logical Incrementalism as a Microstrategic Leadership Process

Before introducing his model of logical incrementalism, Quinn summarized the prevailing hierarchical, military-influenced, rational actor model of strategy formation (Quinn, 1980). Quinn defined strategy ("a pattern or plan that integrates an organization's major goals, policies and action sequences into a cohesive whole"), and then defined goals, policies, and action sequences. Goals, or objectives, "state what is to be achieved and when results are to be accomplished, but they do not state how the results are to be achieved." Policies "are rules or guidelines that express the limits within which action should occur." Action sequences, or programs, "specify the step-by-step sequence of actions necessary to achieve major objectives." Finally, Quinn defines strategic decisions as "those that determine the overall direction of an enterprise and its ultimate viability in light of the predictable, the unpredictable and the unknowable changes that may occur in its most important surrounding environments." Even against this rational actor backdrop, however, microstrategic elements begin to appear: (1) the suggestion in the definition of strategy that a strategy could be a pattern or a plan; (2) the inclusion of action sequences as one of the three components of strategy; and (3) the shift from macro "strategy" to more micro "strategic decisions."

In differentiating between strategy and tactics, Quinn further tilts the emphasis away from deliberate macrostrategies toward emergent microstrategies. "Strategies may be looked at as either *a priori* statements to guide action or *a posteriori* results of actual decision behavior. In most complex organizations ... one would be hardpressed to find a complete a priori statement of a total strategy that actually is followed.... Whether it is consciously set forth in advance or is simply a widely held understanding resulting from a stream of decisions, this pattern becomes the real strategy of the enterprise. And it is changes in this pattern—regardless of what any formal strategic documents may say—that either analysts or strategic decision-makers must address if they wish to comprehend or alter the concern's strategic posture" (Quinn, 1980).

To introduce his research on strategy formation in ten major organizations, Quinn builds on Allison's trichotomous division of Rational Actor ("Formal Systems Planning Approach"), Bureaucratic Politics ("The Power-Behavioral Approach"), and Organizational Processes (Allison, 1969, 1971; Allison & Zelikow, 1999). Quinn dismisses the Formal Systems Planning Approach quickly (it "underemphasizes qualitative, organizational and power factors"). He shows a little more respect for the Power-Behavioral Approach, nesting his text with references to other researchers (Lindblom, 1959): "Another body of literature has enhanced our understanding of multiple goal structures, the politics of strategic decisions, bargaining and negotiation processes, satisficing in decision-making, the role of coalitions, and the practice of 'muddling' in public sector management" (Quinn, 1978). Quinn, though, will not be pulled into the chaos of "muddling" or Organizational Processes. Instead, he carves out a position of "logical incrementalism" somewhere between the Rational Actor model and the Bureaucratic Politics/Organizational Processes models: "Strategy deals with the unknowable, not the uncertain. It involves so many forces, most of which have great strengths and the power to combine, that one cannot, in a probabilistic sense, predict events. Therefore, logic dictates that one proceed flexibly and experimentally from broad ideas toward specific commitments. Making the latter concrete as late as possible narrows the bands of uncertainty, and allows the firm to benefit from the best available information. This is the process of 'logical incrementalism.' It is not 'muddling.' Logical incrementalism is conscious, purposeful, active, good management. It allows executives to blend analysis, organizational politics and individual needs into a cohesive new direction" (Quinn & Voye, 1994).

Macrostrategic Leadership, Microstrategic Leadership, and Mesostrategic Leadership in the Honda Case Study

The Honda case study, although created by several researchers over a twenty-year period, is primarily credited to Richard Pascale. In 1959-1960, Honda Motorcycle Company created a U.S. subsidiary that eventually—with Japanese competitors Yamaha, Suzuki, and Kawasaki—drove the European motorcycle manufacturers out of the U.S. market. The British government asked the Boston Consulting Group to explain the Japanese success in the U.S. market. Michael Goold, a coauthor of the 1975 BCG report, described the context in which the report was written: The report does not dwell on how the Honda strategy evolved and on the learning that took place. However, the report was commissioned for an industry in crisis, with the brief of identifying commercially viable alternatives. The perspective required was managerial ("what should we do now?"), not historical ("how did this situation arise?") (Goold, 1992, 1996a). Goold later provided more background data on the situation in 1975: "In 1973, the Tory government had promoted a merger of the main companies involved, which were all making losses, under the ownership of Norton Villiers Triumph (NVT). NVT subsequently announced a cost reduction program involving the closure of the Triumph Meriden factory. The unions at the factory then mounted a long protest sit-in, and were rewarded by funding from the new, incoming Labor government to establish a worker's cooperative at Meriden. In 1975, the cooperative was about to recommence production at Meriden in competition with NVT, which was continuing to lose money. It was in this strategically difficult and politically sensitive situation that BCG was called in to identify "commercially viable' alternatives for the future of the industry (Goold, 1996b, p. 100).

The BCG report concluded that the four Japanese motorcycle manufacturers had a shared three-stage strategy: (1) Aggressively search for market share (respond to market with product redesigns, set and cut prices to achieve market share goals, set up effective marketing systems, and look for long-term payoffs); (2) Maximize production; and (3) Benefit from cost-experience curves (BCG, 1975).

The BCG report entered the public domain and was quickly absorbed by Harvard Business School and other business schools as a case study illustrating learning curve cost leadership strategies (Purkayastha & Buzzell, 1978). Purkayastha and Buzzell asserted, based on data in the BCG report, that Honda had followed a five-point strategy designed in Japan before entering the U.S. market. First, Honda made a decision to enter the U.S. market. Second, Honda knew in advance that it would be pushing the lightweight motorcycles first, then use cost leadership advantages gained from experience curves to move through increasingly large sizes of bikes. Third, Honda chose to use Los Angeles as a starting point for their U.S. development, presumably because of the climate, the cultural leverage, the shipping costs, and the highway infrastructure. Fourth, Honda designed a consumer marketing strategy that would target average, middle-class Americans as consumers, using the advertising campaign, "You meet the nicest people on a Honda." Finally, Honda decided to commit to continuing R&D and advanced manufacturing to support the rise of the U.S. market. For many years, the Harvard Business School case study helped participants understand the implementation of learning curve strategies by non-U.S. firms in the U.S. market.

Harvard Business School professor Anthony G. Athos and Stanford Business School professor Richard T. Pascale collaborated on an important book published in 1981, *The Art of Japanese Management* (Pascale & Athos, 1981). The book is primarily a comparison of the Japanese Matsushita and the American ITT, but a reference at the beginning of Chapter 4 indicates that Pascale met with Taizo Ueda, senior economist for Honda Motor Company, in Tokyo on July 1, 1980, where he collected the following quotation from Honda cofounder Takeo Fujisawa: "Japanese and American management is 95 percent the same and differs in all important respects" (p. 131). Pascale and Athos argued that Japanese managers were doing a better job than American managers in focusing on the "soft" 7 S's: Superordinate Goals, Structure, Systems, Style, Staff, Skills, and Strategy (p. 326), but that Americans could catch up quickly if they wanted to. The book was quickly reinforced by similar publications by Ouchi (*Theory Z*) and Peters and Waterman (*In Search of Excellence*) (Ouchi, 1981; Peters & Waterman, 1982).

Pascale further developed his Honda interview data to update the Purkayastha and Buzzell case from 1978 in two cases: Honda (A), which continued the strand of argument from the BCG report and the "Note on the Motorcycle Industry" case, and Honda (B), which presented Honda executives' memories of "what really happened." The Honda (B) data undermine each of the five assertions in the Honda (A) case. The B case explains that the decision to enter the U.S. market was driven by a need to keep the CEO focused on a new challenge, by a faulty process of elimination of possible new markets, and by a lack of data on basic details such as the existence of an April-August market window for U.S. motorcycle purchases. The B case also explains that the strategy was skewed toward large bikes, rather than small bikes: the large bikes' eyebrows resembled the eyebrows of Buddha (which the CEO took to be a good sign), they were afraid of alienating the leather-jacket-wearing, Marlon Brando "Wild Ones," gangster market; their "no particular selection criteria" for $140,000 of inventory accidentally favored large bikes; the small Supercub seemed inappropriate for the U.S. market; and they only started to focus on small bike sales after their large bikes had oil leaks and clutch failures. The B case also challenges the assertion that Honda chose Los Angeles for rational reasons; in the initial tour of the U.S., through Texas, Ohio, New York, and Los Angeles, the executives found abuse in all the cities except Los Angeles, where they discovered a large Japanese-American community. The B case also rebuts the assertion of an early strategy to sell to average, middle-class consumers: an undergraduate at UCLA designed the "nicest people ad campaign," his professor showed it to a friend at an ad agency, the ad agency developed the campaign and pitched it to Honda, and the Honda junior executives had to persuade senior executives to change advertising firms. This improbable chain of events could have been disrupted at any of its links, which makes it improbable that the strategy was designed in Japan beforehand. Finally, the B case reframes the assumption that Honda "decided" to invest in R&D and advanced manufacturing: the 1946 founding of the one-person Honda Technical Research Institute, the 1949 engine redesign, the 1951 breakthrough design, the 1959 racing victories, and the 1960 opening of a 30,000 unit-per-month plant are all connected as a cultural history, or a substitute for strategy. To sum up the five-point rebuttal of the Honda A case, the Honda B case includes the chilling phrase (for professors and students wedded to the Honda A case): "We had no strategy other than the idea of seeing if we could sell something in the U.S."

Pascale explains the Honda cases in more detail in a 1984 publication, "Perspectives on strategy: The real story behind Honda's success," in the *California Management Review* (Pascale, 1984). Pascale first critiques the macrostrategic bias of the Honda A case: "Extensive reading of strategy cases at business schools, consultants' reports, strategic planning documents as well as the coverage of the popular press, reveals a widespread tendency to overlook the processes through which organizations experiment, adapt, and learn. We tend to impute coherence and purposive rationality to events when the opposite may be closer to the truth" (p. 57). Pascale next explains Honda B's microstrategic focus through the concept of cultural differences: "The Japanese don't use the term "strategy" to describe a crisp business definition or competitive master plan. They think more in terms of 'strategic accommodation,' or 'adaptive persistence,' underscoring their belief that corporate direction evolves from an incremental adjustment to unfolding events"

Macrostrategic, Mesostrategic, and Microstrategic Leadership 153

(p. 64). Finally, Pascale suggests that success may lie more along the Japanese microstrategic path than the American macrostrategic path: "Their success, as any Japanese automotive executive will readily agree, did not result from a bold insight from a few big brains at the top.... What saved Japan's near failures was the cumulative impact of 'little brains' in the form of salesmen and dealers and production workers, all contributing incrementally to the quality and market position these companies enjoy today" (pp. 63-64).

The Pascale research was discovered by Mintzberg, who wrote a commentary on the case in 1991. His 1991 comment emphasized the linkage between emergent learning and deliberate strategizing: "BCG's mistake was not in what it did describe so much as in what it left out; the critical period of emergent learning that had to inform the deliberate planning process. In other words, strategy had to be conceived informally before it could be programmed formally" (Mintzberg, 1996, p. 466). Gould, as cited above, responded in 1992 by giving more context from the BCG 1975 report, and asking, "Given such an interest, what would a Mintzbergian learning approach recommend? This is not clear from Mintzberg's article, but presumably it would be 'try something, see if it works and learn from your experience.'... For the manager, such advice would be unhelpful, even irritating" (Goold, 1996a, p. 169). Mintzberg replied defensively, and mostly through *ad hominem* ridiculing of BCG consultants, by documenting the continued decline of the British motorcycle industry after the BCG report in 1975 ("So much for the result of this practical managerial perspective," p. 97) and by citing from a 1981 book by a British motorcycle executive ("this huge slice of the total British motorcycle industry was busy embarking on a madness of management consultancy," p. 97). Mintzberg's response wasn't published until 1996, when Goold was given a second chance to provide more context, as cited above. Goold deflected the criticisms by Mintzberg and continued to argue for a synthesis of planning and learning, or Honda A and Honda B (Goold, 1996b).

Into the conflict, in 1996, floats the *deus ex machina*, the Prince of the Strategic Management Society, Richard P. Rumelt. Rumelt says "Peace Capulets, Peace Montagues." Rumelt finds a middle ground between Honda A and Honda B—Honda C—in the concepts of "strategic intent" (Hamel & Prahalad, 1989) and "core competence" (Prahalad & Hamel, 1990). "Thus, Prahalad and Hamel provide us with a third vision of Honda. In their view, the company's direction is deliberate and managed, but they reject BCG's approach of placing market share, volume, learning, and cost at the center of the story. In addition, they reject the efficacy of a detailed strategy for competition. Instead, they see Honda as pursuing a long-term vision of global leadership in internal combustion engines, constantly building competencies in design and manufacturing, and competing through innovating around competitors' product offerings" (Rumelt, 1996, p. 108).

The Honda case is significant for this study because it helps clarify the differences between a macrostrategic approach (Honda A), a microstrategic approach (Honda B), and a mesostrategic approach (Honda C). Rumelt's analysis also helps create a bridge between mesostrategic theory and the emergent fields of research on routines, capabilities, competencies, and resources.

John Brown Engineering and Construction Case

In an earlier publication, easily available on the Web through the online journal *Management* (November 2002 issue, http://dmsp.dauphine.fr/Management/papersMgmt/44Dhillon.html), we reported on the John Brown case (Dhillon & Orton, 2001). John Brown has a proud heritage dating back to the 1830s. John Brown was acquired in 1986 by Trafalgar House Group, which acquired Davy International in 1991 and combined the firms to create an engineering and construction firm ranked third in the world, after the U.S.-based firms Bechtel and Fluor Daniel. In 1991, John Brown had 25,000 employees in 182 offices in 30 countries. In the 1990s, John Brown adopted an explicit information technology strategy that allowed it to become one of a new-generation of information-technology-enabled success stories.

The key finding of the John Brown case is that the firm was effective because (1) the CEO sensed that the macrostrategic environment of globalization and technological advances suggested that the firm should respond with some sort of global information technology strategy, and (2) the firm was able to identify five microstrategic actions to create differentiation from other firms through internal linkages. We believe that the firm would have been less effective if they had not been able to link this macrostrategic environment with these microstrategic actions. Nevertheless, we believe the firm could have been more effective if they had been able to articulate the linkage through several layers of portfolios of strategic options. Specifically, we would like to have seen an elaborated decision tree of strategic options.

At the first level, we would expect John Brown to decide between a tightly coupled firm (business) strategy, a moderately coupled bureaucratic (corporate) strategy, or a loosely coupled network (cooperative) strategy. Although most strategy researchers recognize a difference between firm strategies (create and sustain competitive advantage) and corporate strategies (effectively allocate cash flow across diverse businesses), very few strategy researchers have made the step forward toward the idea of a third major category of strategies, network strategies (effectively allocate tasks across a network of bureaucracies). We expect that given this first decision point, John Brown would have chosen to explore a variety of mesostrategic options embedded within the category of "firms."

At the second level, we would expect John Brown to decide between a cost leadership strategy and a differentiation strategy (Porter, 1980). If John Brown had taken the "bureaucracies" mesostrategic option from level one, the choice would have been between mergers and acquisitions, vertical integration, diversification, and globalization strategies. If John Brown had taken the "networks" mesostrategic option from level one, the choice would have been between strategic groups and strategic alliances strategies. Since the primary task for John Brown was survival of the business firm in the face of strong competition from, among others, Bechtel and Fluor Daniel, we expect that John Brown would have chosen a differentiation strategy.

At the third level, we would expect John Brown to decide between a wide variety of differentiation strategies. According to Barney (1997), two reasonable lists of differentiation strategies, one by Porter (1980) and one by Caves and Williamson (1985), can be combined to create twelve sources of differentiation. The Porter list includes (1) product features, (2) linkages between functions, (3) timing, (4) location, (5) product mix, (6) links with other firms, and (7) reputation. The Caves and Williamson list adds (8) products customized for specific customers, (9) product complexity, (10) emphasis on consumer marketing, (11) different distribution channels, and (12) service and support. Similar lists of strategies can be created for cost leadership, mergers and acquisitions, vertical integration, diversification, globalization, strategic groups, and strategic alliance strategies. Given the description of what John Brown did and why they did it, they appear to have chosen to differentiate themselves from their competitors through internal linkages between functions and units in their organization (number 2).

It seems to us that four more specific findings can be drawn from the general finding that John Brown did well, but perhaps they could have done better. First, we attempt to move the case from strategy to strategizing by linking macrostrategies, mesostrategies, and microstrategies into several important models of strategy formation. Second, we argue that a tree of mesostrategies can be expanded vertically as "ladders." Third, we argue that a tree of mesostrategies can be expanded horizontally as "portfolios." Finally, we argue that through an expanded tree of mesostrategic options, strategy researchers and organization members can increase the effectiveness of strategy formation through three mechanisms: storage of options, frequency of interactions between macrolevels and microlevels, and self-efficacy effects.

1. Linking Strategy Content Models and Strategy Process Models

The case of John Brown demonstrates the importance of revisiting and reemphasizing Simon's (1976) discussions of bounded rationality. Assume a graph with two axes (Y-axis is degree of the three variables; X-axis is time) and three variables: macro (schizoid incoherence), meso (bounded rationality), and micro (strategic options). Simon posited that over time, human rationality is constant or "bounded," schizoid incoherence is increasing over time, and the ambition of strategies is decreasing over time (Simon, 1976). The combination of these three continuing trends will require strategy researchers to pay more attention to leadership theory (Dess, Lumpkin, & Eisner, 2007), and leadership theorists to pay more attention to strategy research (Boal & Hooijberg, 2000).

The analysis of the John Brown case teaches a three-stage model of strategy formation. In Allison's terms, we funnel in from a chaotic environment (Organizational Processes), to a repertoire of options (Bureaucratic Politics), to a specific strategy (Rational Actors) (Allison, 1971). In Weick's terms, we try to understand how a complicated environment is reduced through enactment and sensemaking processes to a retained organizational decision (Weick, 1979). In Smircich and Stubbart's terms, we move from an Enacted World of strategy formation to a Subjective world of strategy formation to an Objective World of strategy formation (Smircich & Stubbart, 1985). In Martin's terms, we move from a Fragmentation view of organizations, to a Differentiation view of organizations, to an Integration view of organizations (Martin, 1992).

2. Expanding the "Ladders of Options" Vertically

Our analysis of John Brown's "ladder of options" includes five levels, but there is no reason to expect all firms to have the same number of levels. Hierarchical effects suggest that people at the top of organizations will be involved at primarily institutional rungs of the strategy formation ladder, people at the middle of organizations will be involved at primarily managerial rungs of the ladder, and people at the bottom of organizations will be involved at primarily technical rungs of the ladder (Thompson, 1967). The ladder of strategic options can be shortened or expanded depending upon the height of the hierarchy, the range of the organization's accumulated experience, and the richness of the organization's vicariously acquired vocabularies. We predict that as more research energy moves into the task of connecting macrostrategies to microstrategies, the number of levels in the "ladders of options" will increase.

3. Expanding the "Portfolios of Options" Horizontally

Our analysis of John Brown's "portfolios" demonstrates the variance we can expect in the number of options available at different levels of the "tree of options." At level one, we identified three options; at level two, we identified two options; while at level three we identified twelve options. Through collapsing or expanding levels from a base of 64 options, we could have provided one level of sixty-four options, two levels of eight options, three levels of four options, three levels of two or three options, and five levels of two options. Specialization of labor effects suggest that different firms will have different degrees of width to their "portfolios of options." Another advantage of expanding the "portfolios of options" concept is that it provides an unexpected link between the emergence of "real options" metaphors in strategy research and the emergence of microstrategies in strategy research. We suspect that the valuation of options changes depending on the breadth of the portfolio of available options held by the firm, and we suspect that some of the same phenomena can appear in strategy process research.

4. Improving Firm Performance through Three Mechanisms: Storage, Iterations, and Efficacy

We see three ways in which the addition of trees of mesostrategic options can create increased effectiveness for firms of the future, and for the people who study them.

First, we see an enhanced storage mechanism. Our studies of the Cuban Missile Crisis have shown us that despite the rational model of decision-making, in which alternatives are "generated" after the crisis has emerged, organizations retain a wide variety of options in institutional memory. Thus options are not generated out of thin air, but they are remembered, retrieved, or activated, depending on the richness of the institutional memory. We suspect that many firms suffer from a poorly formatted institutional memory of mesostrategic options. If a firm learns to articulate its tree of options, it is more likely to be able to retain options that emerge for one problem, which are not chosen at that point, in a better-structured institutional memory, in order to activate that option for a later situation.

Second, we see more frequent iterations between macroenvironments and microstrategies. The key assertion of organization theory is that there are often loose couplings between environmental demands and organizational actions, which translates into our discussion here as a loose coupling between macrostrategic environments and macrostrategies and microstrategic actions and microstrategies. If the path between the levels is well articulated, well known, and well used, we should expect more rapid and more frequent iterations—in the form of thought experiments—by organizational members and organizational researchers. We believe that some of the literature on differences between novices and experts, with its focus on "chunking," may provide support for our expectation that clarity of the middle structures will make iterations between upper and lower structures more effective. We also expect that a focus on mesostrategic options will help strategy content researchers, who tend to focus on macrostrategies, communicate more easily with strategy process researchers, who tend to focus on microstrategies. Mesostrategies can serve as a "boundary object" to facilitate communication between these two groups (Carlile, 1998).

Third, we predict that self-efficacy effects will be triggered when organization members and organizational researchers feel that they have a starting point in a tree of options. We know from Weick's story about Hungarian soldiers lost in the Swiss Alps, who find their way out of a winter storm with a map of the Pyrennees, that "a little structure can go a long way" —by reducing stress, reminding people of basic principles, and reducing conflict. Related research on positive illusions suggests that if people believe that they have a well-articulated tree of mesostrategic options, they are more likely to act in ways that create a positive self-fulfilling prophecy.

In summary, judging from the John Brown case, firms of the future will need to build trees of mesostrategic options, by expanding vertical ladders and expanding horizontal portfolios in order to (1) more effectively store possible strategies in institutional memory, (2) increase the fluidity of interactions between macrolevels and microlevels, and (3) increase the self-efficacy of organizational members as they try to link complex macrostrategic environments to complex microstrategic actions.

THREE IMPLICATIONS FOR STRATEGIC LEADERSHIP RESEARCH

In conclusion, we find ourselves in agreement with the following premises from the LMX literature. First we agree with Seers' observation that organizational forms have moved from stable to flexible organizational forms (Seers, 2004), through a sequence that we describe as a movement from tightly coupled firms to moderately coupled bureaucracies to loosely coupled networks. Second, we agree with Seers' further observation that research on organizational forms and research on leadership processes must coevolve (Seers, 2004), and we describe five characteristics of this "schizoid incoherent" environment: technology, speed, changefulness, globalization, and chaos. Third, we agree with Uhl-Bien, Graen, and Scandura that LMX theory has a great deal to contribute to strategic human resource management because of its clear focus on social capital (Uhl-Bien et al., 2000), and we have reanalyzed the Quinn work on logical incrementalism, the Pascale work on the Honda motorcycle case, and our own research on the John Brown case to further develop the ideas of interactions between macrostrategies, mesostrategies, and microstrategies. Fourth, we agree with Boal and Hooijberg's larger argument that emerging strategic leadership theories of behavioral complexity, cognitive complexity, and social complexity can enrich the discussions of how competitive advantage is created and maintained (Boal & Hooijberg, 2000).

The workplace of the future is the natural outgrowth of events that have been in place since Simon created the field of strategy after World War II. As uncertainty, or schizoid incoherence, continues to increase, we should not be surprised to see strategic ambition and comprehensiveness decrease. This means that leadership researchers need to open up their protected enclaves as a long-established and well-funded island in the Organizational Behavior archipelago to the incoming foreigners from the more recently populated Strategic Management mainland. There are three interdisciplinary research projects that should help.

One implication for leadership researchers is that we need to recognize that the agenda has shifted from a pre-World-War-II focus on "leadership" to a post-World-War-II focus on "strategic leadership" (Boal & Hooijberg, 2000). LMX theory in particular is well-positioned to make this transition because of its roots in the enactment literature and its subsequent ability to explain leadership phenomena at multiple levels of analysis, and the interaction between those levels.

A second implication for leadership researchers is that we need to become more involved in the mapping of portfolios of mesostrategic options. The field of strategy has long championed the idea of "generic strategies" (Porter, 1980), or what we would relabel "macrostrategies." A typical strategy textbook reviews several generic business strategies, several generic corporate strategies, and the newer textbooks are struggling to review several generic network strategies (de Wit & Meyer, 2005). We know from research on specific firms, though, that they succeed or fail not by the application of generic macrostrategies, but by the discovery of thousands of microstrategic actions that collectively build a competitive advantage (Barney, 2002). In between generic theory and specific practice is a valuable research project—the identification of portfolios of mesostrategic options. Instead of strategy textbooks describing a cost leadership macrostrategy, they are now more likely to describe 15 mesostrategic options under the rubric of a cost leadership macrostrategy: learning by experience, learning vicariously, differential low-cost access to factors of production, manufacturing redesign, etc. The next logical step, given our analysis of the John Brown case, is for a wide variety of options trees to appear to bridge the gap between macrostrategies and microstrategies. Organizations will expect their members to play increasingly active roles in strategy formation and strategy implementation at all levels, which will increase the value of these diverse mesostrategic options trees. Different countries, different industries, and different managerial backgrounds will generate different options trees, and the interaction among options trees will create more complex hybrids than exist currently. LMX researchers, with their well-developed expertise in microsociological processes (e.g., Kramer, 2006), have a contribution to make in this ongoing project in mesostrategic management research.

A third implication for leadership researchers is that we need to try to understand the interactions of microstrategies, mesostrategies, and macrostrategies over time. Traditionally, the role of the strategy researcher has been to study large samples of organizations, and reduce the complexity of the firms so that they fit in relatively coarse macrostrategic categories (e.g., three types of strategic alliances). The agenda we propose is to study samples of one or fewer (March, Sproull, & Tamuz, 1991) to better understand sequences of options used over time (D'Aveni, 1995), options embedded in institutional memory (Walsh & Ungson, 1991), and virtual options not yet articulated by the firm (Weick, 1989). In the workplace of the future, we do not expect researchers to continue to have the luxury of choosing whether they will study strategy content or strategy processes. We believe the shift from stable strategies to dynamic strategizing will sweep researchers into the study of how macrostrategizing, mesostrategizing, and microstrategizing processes are connected in strategizing cycles.

In conclusion, we think that LMX theory, because of its roots in enactment research and "role-making," is well-positioned to attack the following three projects that we believe are necessary for the useful and emerging field of strategic leadership (Boal & Hooijberg, 2000): (1) help transform the leadership research from its outdated roots in command-and-control bureaucracies from before World-War-II to a post-Simon-March-Weick environment of loosely coupled networks and schizoid incoherence; (2) get more involved in the project of mapping a shared repertoire of mesostrategic options that are generated and maintained by organizations, consulting firms, and academia; and (3) start asking questions about the interaction of generic macrostrategies, mesostrategic options, and microstrategic actions over time. We hope that our notes here are a small win that can help LMX research and strategic leadership research move in a sensible direction (Weick, 1984).

REFERENCES

Allison, G. T. (1969). Conceptual models and the Cuban missile crisis. *The American Political Science Review, 63*(3), 689-718.
Allison, G. T. (1971). *Essence of decision: Explaining the Cuban missile crisis*. Boston: Little, Brown, and Company.
Allison, G. T., & Zelikow, P. (1999). *Essence of decision: Explaining the Cuban Missile Crisis* (2nd ed.). New York: Addison Wesley Longman.
Barney, J. B. (1991). Firm resources and sustained competitive advantage. *Journal of Management, 17*, 99-120.
Barney, J. B. (2002). *Gaining and sustaining competitive advantage* (2nd ed.). Engelwood Cliffs, NJ: Prentice-Hall.
Bartlett, C. A., & Ghoshal, S. (1989). *Managing across borders: The transnational solution*. Boston: Harvard Business School Press.
Bartlett, C. A., & Ghoshal, S. (1994, November-December). Changing the role of top management: Beyond strategy to purpose. *Harvard Business Review*, 79-88.
Bartlett, C. A., & Ghoshal, S. (1995, May-June). Changing the role of top management: Beyond systems to people. *Harvard Business Review*, 132-142.
BCG. (1975). Strategy alternatives for the British motorcycle industry.
Beck, U. (1992). *Risk society: Towards a new modernity* (M. Ritter, Trans.). London: Sage.
Beck, U. (2000). *The brave new world of work* (P. Camiller, Trans.). London: Polity Press.
Boal, K. B., & Hooijberg, R. (2000). Strategic leadership research: Moving on. *Leadership Quarterly, 11*(4), 515-549.
Bourgeois, L. J., III, & Eisenhardt, K. M. (1988). Strategy decision processes in high velocity environments: Four cases in the microcomputer industry. *Management Science, 34*, 816-835.
Boynton, A. C., & Zmud, R. W. (1987). Information technology planning in the 1990's: Directions for practice and research. *MIS Quarterly, 11*, 59-71.
Brown, S. L., & Eisenhardt, K. M. (1997). The art of continuous change: Linking complexity theory and time-paced evolution in relentlessly shifting organizations. *Administrative Science Quarterly, 42*, 1-34.
Brown, S. L., & Eisenhardt, K. M. (1998). *Competing on the edge: Strategy as structured chaos*. Boston: Harvard Business School Press.
Browning, L. D., Beyer, J. M., & Shetler, J. C. (1995). Building cooperation in a competitive industry: SEMATECH and the semiconductor industry. *Academy of Management Journal, 38*, 113-151.
Burns, T., & Stalker, G. M. (1961). *The management of innovation* (3rd ed.). Oxford: Oxford University Press.
Carlile, P. R. (1998). *Understanding knowledge transformation in product development: Making knowledge manifest through boundary objects*. Unpublished Dissertation, University of Michigan.
Chandler, A. D. (1991). The functions of the HQ unit in the multibusiness firm. *Strategic Management Journal, 12*, 31-50.

Chandler, A. D., Jr. (1962). *Strategy and structure: Chapters in the history of the industrial empire* (pp. xi-xiv, 1-17). Cambridge, MA: MIT Press.
Chandler, A. D., Jr. (1977). *The visible hand: The managerial revolution in American business.* Cambridge, MA: Harvard University Press.
Chandler, A. D., Jr. (1990). *Scale and scope: The dynamics of industrial capitalism.* Cambridge, MA: Harvard University Press.
Clegg, S. R., & Gray, J. T. (1996). Metaphors of globalization. In D. M. Boje, R. P. Gephart, Jr., & T. J. Thatchenkery (Eds.), *Postmodern management and organization theory* (pp. 293-307). Thousand Oaks, CA: Sage.
Coase, R. H. (1937). The nature of the firm. *Economica, 4,* 386-405.
Coase, R. H. (1960). The problem of social cost. *Journal of Law and Economics, 3,* 1-44.
Coase, R. H. (1974). The lighthouse in economics. *The Journal of Law and Economics, 17.*
Cohen, M. D., March, J. G., & Olsen, J. P. (1972). A garbage can model of organizational choice. *Administrative Science Quarterly, 17,* 1-25.
D'Aveni, R .A. (1995). Coping with hypercompetition: Utilizing the new 7S's framework. *Academy of Management Executive, 9*(3), 45-57.
de Wit, B., & Meyer, R. (2005). *Strategy: Process, content, context* (3rd ed.). London: Thomson Learning.
Dess, G. G., Lumpkin, G. T., & Eisner, A. B.(2007). *Strategic management: Creating competitive advantage* (3rd ed.). Boston: McGraw-Hill/Irwin.
Dhillon, G., & Orton, J. D. (2001). Schizoid incoherence, microstrategic options, and the strategic management of new organizational forms. *Management, 4*(4), 229-240.
DiMaggio, P. J., & Powell, W. W. (1983, April). The iron cage revisited: Institutional isomorphism and collective rationality in organizational fields. *American Sociological Review, 48,* 147-160.
Einhorn, H. J., & Hogarth, R. M. (1986). Judging probable cause. *Psychological Review, 99*(1), 3-19.
Eisenhardt, K. M. (1989). Making fast strategic decisions in high-velocity environments. *Academy of Management Journal, 32*(3), 543-576.
Eisenhardt, K. M., & Bourgeois, L. J. (1988). Politics of strategic decision making in high-velocity environments: Toward a midrange theory. *Academy of Management Journal, 31*(4), 737-770.
Eisenhardt, K. M., & Zbaracki, M. J. (1992, Winter). Strategic decision making. *Strategic Management Journal, 13*(Special Issue), 17-37.
French, J. R. P., Jr., & Raven, B. (1959). The bases of social power. In D. Cartwright (Ed.), *Studies in social power.* Ann Arbor: The University of Michigan, Institute for Social Research.
Gephart, R. P. (1997). Hazardous measures: An interpretive textual analysis of quantitative sensemaking during crises. *Journal of Organizational Behavior, 18*(Special Issue), 583-622.
Gephart, R. P., Jr., Boje, D. M., & Thatchenkery, T. J. (1996). Postmodern management and the coming crises of organizational analysis. In D. M. Boje, R. P. Gephart, Jr., & T. J. Thatchenkery (Eds.), *Postmodern management and organization theory* (pp. 1-18). Thousand Oaks, CA: Sage.

Gergen, K. J., & Whitney, D. (1996). Technologies of representation in the global corporation: Power and polyphony. In D. M. Boje, R. P. Gephart, Jr., & T. J. Thatchenkery (Eds.), *Postmodern management and organization theory* (pp. 331-357). Thousand Oaks, CA: Sage.

Ghoshal, S., & Bartlett, C. A. (1995, Jan.-Feb.). Changing the role of top management: Beyond structure to processes. *Harvard Business Review*, 86-96.

Goold, M. (1992). Research notes and communication. *Strategic Management Journal, 13*, 169-170.

Goold, M. (1996a). Design, learning and planning: A further observation on the design school debate. *California Management Journal, 38*(4), 94-95.

Goold, M. (1996b). Learning, planning, and strategy: Extra time. *California Management Review, 38*(4): 100-102.

Graen, G. B. (2004). *New frontiers of leadership, LMX leadership: The series* (Vol. 2). Greenwich, CT: Information Age Publishing.

Greenwood, R., & Hinings, C. R. (1988). Organization design types, tracks, and the dynamics of strategic change. *Organization Studies, 9*, 293-316.

Gronn, P. C. (1983). Talk as work: The accomplishment of school administration. *Administrative Science Quarterly, 28*, 1-21.

Hamel, G., & Prahalad, C. K. (1989, May-June). Strategic intent. *Harvard Business Review*, 63-76.

Hatch, M. J. (1997). *Organization theory: Modern, symbolic, and postmodern perspectives.* Oxford: Oxford University Press.

Henderson, R., & Clark, K. B. (1990). Architectural innovation: The reconfiguration of existing technologies and the failure of established firms. *Administrative Science Quarterly, 35*, 9-30.

Hinings, C. R., & Greenwood, R. (1988). *The dynamics of strategic change.* Oxford: Basil Blackwell.

Kanter, R. M. (1989). *When giants learn to dance: Mastering the challenges of strategy, management, and careers in the 1990s.* New York: Simon and Schuster.

Kaplan, R. E. (1982). Intervention in a loosely organized system: An encounter with non-being. *The Journal of Applied Behavioral Science, 18*(4), 415-432.

Kramer, M. W. (2006). Communication strategies for sharing leadership within a creative team: LMX in theater groups. In G. B. Graen (Ed.), *Sharing network leadership, LMX leadership: The series* (Vol. 4). Greenwich, CT: Information Age.

Lewin, K. (1943). Forces behind food habits and methods of change. *Bulletin of the National Research Council, 108*, 35-65.

Lindblom, C. E. (1959). The science of muddling through. *Public Administration Review, 19*(2), 78-88.

March, J. G. (1981). Footnotes to organizational change. *Administrative Science Quarterly, 26*, 563-577.

March, J. G., & Olsen, J. P. (1976). *Ambiguity and choice in organizations.* Bergen, Norway: Universitetsforlaget.

March, J. G., Sproull, L., & Tamuz, M. (1991). Learning from samples of one of fewer. *Organization Science, 2*, 1-13.

Martin, J. (1992). *Cultures in organizations: Three perspectives.* New York: Oxford University Press.

McCraw, T. K. (Ed.). (1988). *The essential Alfred Chandler: Essays toward a historical theory of big business*. Boston: Harvard Business School Press.

Meyerson, D. (2001). *Tempered radicals: How people use difference to inspire change at work*. Boston: Harvard Business School Press.

Meyerson, D., & Martin, J. (1987). Cultural change: An integration of three different views. *Journal of Management Studies, 24*, 623-647.

Mintzberg, H. (1978). Patterns in strategy formation. *Management Science, 24*(9), 934-948.

Mintzberg, H. (1994). *The rise and fall of strategic planning*. New York: Prentice-Hall.

Mintzberg, H. (1996). Learning 1, planning 0. *Strategic Management Journal, 12*, 464-466.

Mintzberg, H., & McHugh, A. (1985). Strategy formation in an adhocracy. *Administrative Science Quarterly, 30*, 160-197.

Mintzberg, H., & Waters, J. A. (1985). Of strategies: Deliberate and emergent. *Strategic Management Journal, 6*, 257-272.

Murphy, J. A., & Hallinger, P. (1984). Policy analysis at the local level: A framework for expanded investigation. *Educational Evaluation and Policy Analysis, 6*(1), 5-13.

Nohria, N., & Eccles, R. G. (Eds.). (1992). *Networks and organizations: Structure, form, and action*. Boston: Harvard Business School Press.

Orton, J. D. (2000). Enactment, sensemaking, and decision-making in the 1976 reorganization of U.S. intelligence. *Journal of Management Studies, 37*, 213-234.

Orton, J. D., & Weick, K. E. (1990). Loosely coupled systems: A reconceptualization. *Academy of Management Review, 15*, 203-223.

Ouchi, W. G. (1978). Coupled versus uncoupled control in organizational hierarchies. In M. W. Meyer & et al. (Eds.), *Environments and organizations* (pp. 264-289). San Francisco: Jossey-Bass.

Ouchi, W. G. (1980). Markets, bureaucracies, and clans. *Administrative Science Quarterly, 25*, 129-141.

Ouchi, W. G. (1981). *Theory Z: How American business can beat the Japanese challenge*. Reading, MA: Addison-Wesley.

Ouchi, W. G., & Wilkins, A. L. (1978). Organizational entitativity: The problem of boundaries, units, and loose couplings. In D. V. Gibson (Ed.), *Seminars on organizations at Stanford, academic year, 1977-1978, Vol. IV*, 17-21.

Pascale, R. T. (1984). Perspectives on strategy: The real story behind Honda's success. *California Management Review, 26*(3), 47-72.

Pascale, R. T., & Athos, A. G. (1981). *The art of Japanese management: Applications for American executives*. New York: Warner Books.

Perrow, C. (1981). Normal accidents at Three Mile Island. *Society, 18*(5), 17-26.

Perrow, C. (1983). The organizational context of human factors engineering. *Administrative Science Quarterly*, 521-541.

Perrow, C. (1984). *Normal accidents: Living with high-risk technologies*. New York: Basic Books.

Perrow, C. (1986). *Complex organizations: A critical essay* (3rd ed.). New York: Random House.

Peters, T. J. (1978). *Some applications of the loose coupling approach in managerial/organizational consulting practice.* Paper presented at the Seminars on organizations at Stanford University, Stanford, CA.

Peters, T. J. (1980, July 21). Putting excellence into management, *Business Week,* p. 19b

Peters, T. J. (1981, May/June). Stamp out risk taking and creativity. *Hospital Forum,* 1-5.

Peters, T. J. (1987). *Thriving on chaos: A handbook for a management revolution.* New York: Harper & Row.

Peters, T. J. (1992). *Liberation management: Necessary disorganization for the nanosecond nineties.* New York: Knopf.

Peters, T. J., & Austin, N. (1985). *A passion for excellence: The leadership difference.* New York: Random House.

Peters, T. J., & Waterman, R. H. (1982). *In search of excellence: Lessons from America's best-run companies.* New York: Harper & Row.

Polanyi, M. (1983). *The tacit dimension.* Gloucester, MA: Peter Smith.

Porter, M. E. (1980). *Competitive strategy: Techniques for analyzing industries and competitors.* New York: Free Press.

Powell, T. C. (1992). Strategic planning as competitive advantage. *Strategic Management Journal, 13*(7), 551-558.

Powell, W. (1989, May 18). Presentation at Michigan Instutional Theory conference.

Powell, W. W. (1986). *Interorganizational strategies, managerial perceptions, and firm performance.* Paper presented at the Academy of Management, Chicago.

Powell, W. W. (1990). Neither market nor hierarchy: Network forms of organization. In B.M. Staw & L.L. Cummings (Eds.), *Research in organizational behavior* (pp. 295-336). Greenwich, CT: JAI Press.

Powell, W. W., & Brantley, P. (1992). Competitive cooperation in biotechnology: Learning through networks? In N. Nohria & R.G. Eccles (Eds.), *Networks and organizations: Structure, form, and action* (pp. 366-394). Boston: Harvard Business School Press.

Powell, W. W., & DiMaggio, P.J. (1991). *The new institutionalism in organizational analysis.* Chicago: University of Chicago Press.

Prahalad, C. K., & Hamel, G. (1990, May-June). The core competencies of the corporation. *Harvard Business Review, 68,* 79-91.

Purkayastha, D., & Buzzell, R. D. (1978). *Note on the motorcycle industry—1975.* Boston: Harvard Business School.

Quinn, J. B. (1978). Strategic change: Logical incrementalism. *Sloan Management Review, 20*(1), 7-21.

Quinn, J. B. (1980). *Strategies for change: Logical incrementalism.* Homewood, IL: R. D. Irwin.

Quinn, J. B., & Voye, J. (1994). Logical incrementalism: Managing strategy formation. *The strategy process.* Engelwood Cliffs, NJ: Prentice-Hall.

Ranson, S., Hinings, C. R., & Greenwood, R. (1980). The structuring of organizational structures. *Administrative Science Quarterly, 25,* 1-17.

Rumelt, R. P. (1996). The many faces of Honda. *California Management Review, 38*(4), 103-111.

Ryan, C. (1959). *The longest day: June 6, 1944*. New York: Simon & Schuster.
Seers, A. (2004). Leadership and flexible organizational structures: The future is now. In G.B. Graen (Ed.), *New frontiers of leadership, LMX leadership: The series* (Vol. 2, pp. 1-32). Greenwich, CT: Information Age.
Simon, H. A. (1976). *Administrative behavior: A study of decision-making processes in administrative organization* (3rd ed.). New York: The Free Press.
Smircich, L., & Stubbart, C. (1985). Strategic management in an enacted world. *Academy of Management Review, 10*, 724-736.
Szulanski, G. (1996, Winter). Exploring internal stickiness: Impediments to the transfer of best practice within the firm. *Strategic Management Journal, 17*(Special Issue), 27-43.
Taylor, F. W. (1911). *The principles of scientific management*. (1967 paperback ed.). New York: W. W. Norton.
Thompson, J. D. (1967). *Organizations in action: Social science bases of administrative theory*. New York: McGraw-Hill.
Torbert, W. R. (1987). *Managing the corporate dream: Restructuring for long-term success*. Homewood, IL: Dow-Jones.
Uhl-Bien, M., Graen, G. B., & Scandura, T. A. (2000). Implications of leader-member exchange (lmx) for strategic human resource management systems: Relationships as social capital for competitive advantage. In G. R. Ferris (Ed.), *Research in personnel and human resources management* (Vol. 18, pp. 137-185). Stamford, CT: JAI Press.
Ulrich, D., & Lake, D. (1990). *Organizational capability: Competing from the inside out*. New York: John Wiley & Sons.
Vaughan, D. (1982). Toward understanding unlawful organizational behavior. *Michigan Law Review, 80*, 1377-1402.
Vaughan, D. (1990). Autonomy, independence, and social control: NASA and the space shuttle Challenger. *Administrative Science Quarterly, 35*, 225-257.
Vaughan, D. (1992). Theory elaboration: The heuristics of case analysis. In C. C. Ragin & H. S. Becker (Eds.), *What is a case? Issues in the logic of social inquiry*. New York: Cambridge University Press.
Vaughan, D. (1996). *The Challenger launch decision: Risky technology, culture, and deviance at NASA*. Chicago: The University of Chicago Press.
Vaughan, D. (1997). The trickle-down effect: Policy decision, risky work, and the Challenger tragedy. *California Management Review, 39*, 80-102.
Walsh, J.P., & Ungson, G.R. (1991). Organizational memory. *Academy of Management Review, 16*(1), 57-91.
Weber, M. (Ed.). (1946). *From Max Weber: Essays in sociology*. Oxford: Oxford University Press.
Weick, K. E. (1976). Educational organizations as loosely coupled systems. *Administrative Science Quarterly, 21*, 1-19.
Weick, K. E. (1979). *The social psychology of organizing* (2nd ed.). Reading, MA: Addison-Wesley.
Weick, K. E. (1982, June). Administering education in loosely coupled schools. *Phi Delta Kappan*, 673-676.
Weick, K. E. (1984). Small wins: Redefining the scale of social problems. *American Psychologist, 39*(1), 40-49.

Weick, K. E. (1985). Cosmos vs. chaos: Sense and nonsense in electronic contexts. *Organizational Dynamics*, 50-64.
Weick, K. E. (1988). Enacted sensemaking in crisis situations. *Journal of Management Studies, 25*, 305-317.
Weick, K. E. (1989). Theory construction as disciplined imagination. *Academy of Management Review, 14*, 532-550.
Weick, K. E. (1990). The vulnerable system: Analysis of the Tenerife air disaster. *Journal of Management, 16*, 571-593.
Weick, K. E. (1993). The collapse of sensemaking in organizations: The Mann Gulch disaster. *Administrative Science Quarterly, 38*, 628-652.
Weick, K. E. (1995). *Sensemaking in organizations*. Newbury Park, CA: Sage.
Weick, K. E., & Quinn, R. E. (1999). Organizational change and development. In J. T. Spence, J. M. Darley, & D. J. Foss (Eds.), *Annual Review of Psychology* (Vol. 50). Palo Alto, CA: Consulting Psychologist Press.
Wilkins, A. L., & Ouchi, W. G. (1983). Efficient cultures: Exploring the relationship between culture and organizational performance. *Administrative Science Quarterly, 28*, 468-481.
Williamson, O. E. (1975). *Markets and hierarchies: Analysis and anti-trust implications*. New York: Free Press.
Williamson, O. E. (1978). *Institutional economics and some conjectures about loose coupling*. Paper presented at the Seminars on organizations at Stanford University, Stanford, CA.
Williamson, O. E. (1981). The economics of organizations: The transaction cost approach. *American Journal of Sociology, 87*, 548-577.
Williamson, O. E. (1985). *The economic institutions of capitalism*. New York: Free Press.
Williamson, O. E. (1991a). Comparative economic organization: The analysis of discrete structural alternatives. *Administrative Science Quarterly, 36*, 269-296.
Williamson, O. E. (1991b, Winter). Strategizing, economizing, and economic organization. *Strategic Management Journal, 12*(Special Issue), 75-94.
Williamson, O. E. (1994). Transaction cost economics and organization theory. In N.J. Smelser & R. Swedburg (Eds.), *Handbook of economic sociology* (pp. 77-107). Princeton, NJ: Princeton University Press.
Williamson, O. E. (1996a). Economic organization: The case for candor. *Academy of Management Review, 21*(1), 48-57.
Williamson, O. E. (1996b). *The mechanisms of governance*. New York: Oxford University Press.
Williamson, O. E. (1996c). Transaction cost economics and the Carnegie connection. *Journal of Economic Behavior & Organization, 31*, 149-155.
Williamson, O. E., & Ouchi, W. G. (1981). The markets and hierarchies program of research: Origins, implications, prospects. In A. V. d. Ven & W. Joyce (Eds.), *Perspectives in organizational design and behavior* (pp. 347-370). New York: Wiley.

CHAPTER 8

EMOTIONAL INTELLIGENCE, LEADER-MEMBER EXCHANGE, AND INDIVIDUAL CONTRIBUTIONS TO ORGANIZATIONAL SOCIAL CAPITAL

Melvin L. Smith

In this chapter I discuss the suggested effects of leader-member exchange (LMX) on individual contributions to the social capital of their organization. In doing so, I introduce a new construct, organizational social capital investment behavior (OSCIB), representing specific individual behaviors suggested to lead to the creation and maintenance of organizational social capital. I also suggest that the nature of the leader-member exchange relationships that form in organizations may be significantly influenced by both leader and member emotional intelligence. The implications and future directions are discussed.

INTRODUCTION

Considerable organizational research in recent years has focused on the concept of social capital. Researchers have studied the social capital of individuals (e.g., Burt, 1992, 1997; Friedman & Krackhardt, 1997; McFadyen & Cannella, 2004; Seibert, Kramer, & Liden, 2001), groups/teams (e.g., Cummings & Cross, 2003; Oh, Chung, & Labianca, 2004; Reagans & Zuckerman, 2001; Reagans, Zuckerman, & McEvily, 2004), and organizations (e.g., Ahuja, 2000; Capelli, 2004; Koka & Prescott, 2002; McEvily & Zaheer, 1999; Tsai, 2000; Uzzi & Gillespie, 2002). Much of this research, however, has concentrated primarily on outcomes associated with possessing social capital in its various forms.

While the growing body of organizational research on social capital has informed our understanding of its effects on a variety of outcomes, less attention has been devoted to the examination of factors that lead to its creation. Additionally, while research has examined social capital at various levels of analysis, little previous research has considered possible antecedents of individual contributions to the social capital of their organization. Building the relationships that represent organizational social capital requires an investment of time and energy on the part of individuals. Such effort could alternatively be devoted to other activities from which individuals might personally benefit. Accordingly, an important question to be explored is *what motivates individuals to invest their time and energy in the creation and maintenance of relationships that build organizational social capital?*

In exploring this question I briefly discuss the distinction between individual and organizational social capital and then introduce a new construct, organizational social capital investment behavior (OSCIB), representing individual behaviors that facilitate the creation and maintenance of organizational social capital. Drawing on social exchange theory (Blau, 1964), and more specifically generalized exchange relationships (Molm, Takahashi, & Peterson, 2000), as well as the norm of reciprocity (Gouldner, 1960), I suggest ways in which leader-member exchange is likely to influence an individual's OSCIB. I further suggest that the quality of the social exchange relationship that develops between a leader and his or her employees is largely influenced by both leader and employee emotional intelligence. I conclude the chapter with a discussion of implications and suggestions for future research.

Social Capital In Organizations

Coleman (1988) suggested that social capital could be defined by its function. He asserted that it consists of social structures, facilitates actions of actors within the structure and, unlike other forms of capital, resides in the relations between actors and not in the actors themselves. While Coleman's initial work generated considerable interest in the concept, his definition of social capital has been criticized due to its vagueness, which has resulted in differing and in some ways contradictory conceptualizations of the construct (Portes, 1998; Portes & Sensenbrenner, 1993).

One conceptualization, which is most commonly associated with the work of Burt (1992, 1997) focuses on the "private goods" aspect of social capital (see Leana & Van Buren, 1999). Burt (1992) offers that social capital is a property of individuals as he defines it in terms of the information and control benefits that accrue to individuals who are able to fill what he calls *structural holes* or gaps between nonredundant contacts in a network. Researchers who have adopted this structural view of social capital based on network position have found that social capital is significantly associated with a variety of individual outcomes such as promotions and bonuses (Burt, 1992, 1997), CEO compensation (Belliveau, O'Reilly, & Wade, 1996), and managers' assessment of career potential (Friedman & Krackhardt, 1997). Changes in social capital as measured by structural holes, has also been linked to changes in employee attitudes and perceptions (Susskind, Miller, & Johnson, 1998).

Adopting a very different conceptualization and definition of social capital from that described above, Putnam (1995) referred to social capital as "features of social organization such as networks, norms and social trust that facilitate coordination and cooperation for mutual benefit" (p. 67). While this definition is consistent with Coleman's presentation of the concept, it differs from Burt's (1992) definition in that it singularly focuses on what has been referred to as the "public goods" aspect of social capital (Coleman, 1990; Leana & Van Buren, 1999). Social capital as described by Putnam is based on dense networks of social interaction that reduce incentives for opportunism and broaden the individual participants' sense of self from "I" to "we," thus enhancing the appeal of collective benefits. Whereas Burt's analysis and discussion are motivated by the individual benefits of social capital, Putnam's work is centered on the benefits to a collective. Researchers who have adopted this public goods view have found that social capital at the collective level may significantly impact collective outcomes (cf. Fukuyama, 1995; Putnam, 1993).

Looking at social capital from this public goods perspective, organizational social capital has been characterized as a dense network of multiplex ties based on shared norms and values of trust, reciprocity, and bounded solidarity (cf. Coleman, 1988; Leana & Van Buren, 1999; Oh, Kilduff, & Brass, 1999; Portes & Sensenbrenner, 1993; Putnam, 1993, 1995). This communal or "bonding" form of the social capital construct represents a potentially valuable resource to organizations in that it has been argued to foster the development of intellectual capital (Nahapiet & Ghoshal, 1998) and to facilitate successful collective action (Leana & Van Buren, 1999; Newell, Tansley, & Huang, 2004; Uzzi, 1997).[1]

In their articulation of the dimensions of organizational social capital, Nahapiet and Ghoshal (1998) draw on Granovetter's (1992) conception of both structural embeddedness, which refers to the impersonal linkages between individuals within a social system (see also Burt, 1992) and relational embeddedness, which considers the nature of personal relationships that individuals have developed with one another through a history of interactions. They further contend that social capital also has a cognitive component, representing systems of shared interpretations and meaning between individuals. They thus describe organizational social capital as a three-dimensional construct consisting of a cognitive, relational, and structural dimension. This three-dimensional view of organizational social capital presented by Nahapiet and Ghoshal serves as the basis for development of a new construct that I maintain represents individual contributions to (or investment in) organizational social capital.

Organizational Social Capital Investment Behavior

While organizational social capital has been described here and elsewhere as a macro-level construct, its creation and maintenance are in essence dependent upon the specific behaviors of individuals within the organization, as well as the nature of the interactions between those individuals. Drawing on the three-dimensional conceptualization of social capital presented by Nahapiet and Ghoshal (1998), I propose that organizational social capital is created in large part by observable, individual behaviors that contribute to the cognitive, relational, and/or structural elements of interactions within an organization.

Cognitive Dimension. The cognitive dimension of social capital consists of shared codes and language, as well as shared narratives (Nahapiet & Ghoshal, 1998). This dimension of social capital involves shared cognition, collective interpretation, collective mind, shared meaning, and shared mental models (Klimoski & Mohammed, 1994; Levine & Moreland, 1999). Shared mental models represent knowledge structures that, when held by members of a group, enable that group to accurately understand group tasks, coordinate their actions, and adapt their behaviors to the task demands, as well as to other group members (Cannon-Bowers, Salas, & Converse, 1993; Levesque, Wilson, & Wholey, 2001).

When members of work teams have different mental models about how tasks should be completed, they have a difficult time coordinating their activities (Levesque et al., 2001). When team members share knowledge (as well as attitudes and beliefs), however, it enables them to interpret cues in a similar manner, make compatible decisions, and take appropriate actions (Cannon-Bowers & Salas, 2001; Klimoski & Mohammed, 1994). Thus, it can be argued that knowledge or information sharing among group members contributes to group knowledge and facilitates collective action. Accordingly, an observable behavior on the part of individuals that contributes to the cognitive dimension of organizational social capital is the sharing of information with others in the organization. Greater information sharing among individuals is likely to facilitate the emergence of shared mental models as represented by common language (and codes), as well as shared understanding.

Relational Dimension. According to Nahapiet and Ghoshal (1998), the relational dimension of social capital includes trust (and trustworthiness), norms, obligations, and identification. One observable individual behavior that is likely to contribute to this dimension is behaving in ways that are interpreted as trustworthy by other members of the organization (e.g., keeping one's promises made to another), which facilitates the building of shared or collective trust (see Leana & Van Buren, 1999; Knez & Camerer, 1994). Another individual action that arguably contributes to the relational dimension of organizational social capital is engaging in organizational citizenship behavior (OCB), or more specifically, engaging in helping behavior that is not explicitly required or rewarded as part of one's employment contract. Several researchers have stressed the importance of norms and obligations as a relational element of social capital (e.g., Coleman, 1988; Nahapiet & Ghoshal, 1998). Additionally, Leana and Van Buren (1999) offer that associability, which they define as the willingness and ability to subordinate self-interests to those of the collective, is a key component of organizational social capital. The extent to which an individual engages in helping behavior should serve as an indicator of associability, as well as demonstrate an adherence to norms and obligations (specifically the norm of reciprocity).

Structural Dimension. The structural dimension of social capital consists of both individual network ties and the overall network configuration of the collective (cf. Burt, 1992; Nahapiet & Ghoshal, 1998; Putnam, 1993). The structural dimension also incorporates a feature of social capital that has been referred to as "appropriable social organization" (see Coleman, 1988). This aspect of network structure implies that ties of one type may be transferred to another use (e.g., receiving work advice from a friendship tie).

Although the structural dimension of social capital plays a central role in both the public and private goods conceptualizations of the construct, contrary to the private goods approach where social capital is said to be greater in sparse networks where one's direct contacts are not otherwise connected to one another (Burt, 1992, 1997), researchers adopting a public goods approach discuss the benefits of dense networks of redundant contacts, as well as the benefits of network closure (see, e.g., Coleman, 1988; Putnam, 1993). Coleman contends that, in addition to density, network closure leads to higher levels of social capital since it allows for collective sanctioning, promotes trustworthiness, and facilitates the proliferation of obligations and expectations. This structural view of social capital as dense networks of reciprocal relationships leading to norms of trust and mutual obligations/expectations represents the bonding form of organizational social capital discussed in this article. Further, it is the behavior of individuals toward one another within the organization that contributes to the overall configuration of the organization's social network. Therefore, by engaging in behaviors that lead to the creation and maintenance of specific relationships between themselves and others within the organization, I argue that individual employees are ultimately responsible for building organizational social capital.

Finally, given the suggested interrelatedness of each of the articulated dimensions of social capital (see Nahapiet & Ghoshal, 1998), I offer that OSCIB can best be represented by the extent to which an individual shares information, behaves in a trustworthy fashion, *and* engages in helping behavior within the organization. While the proposed OSCIB construct shares the helping behavior dimension with organizational citizenship behavior (OCB), it represents more than simply being willing to help others.[2] It also includes trustworthy behavior and the specific act of sharing information with others, consistent with Leana and Van Buren's (1999) conception of organizational social capital as trustworthiness and associability (the willingness *and* ability to subordinate self interests for those of the collective). A summary of these suggested components of OSCIB and how they contribute to the creation and maintenance of organizational social capital is presented in Figure 8.1.

PREDICTING ORGANIZATIONAL SOCIAL CAPITAL INVESTMENT BEHAVIOR

Although there is no prior research that has examined the construct of OSCIB as defined here, considerable research has been conducted on various antecedents and consequences of the individual components that I have suggested comprise the OSCIB construct (i.e., trustworthy behavior, helping behavior, and information-sharing). Drawing on this research, I develop a model of OSCIB offering propositions regarding its relationship to leader-member exchange. I also suggest that leader-member exchange relationships are likely to be significantly influenced by the

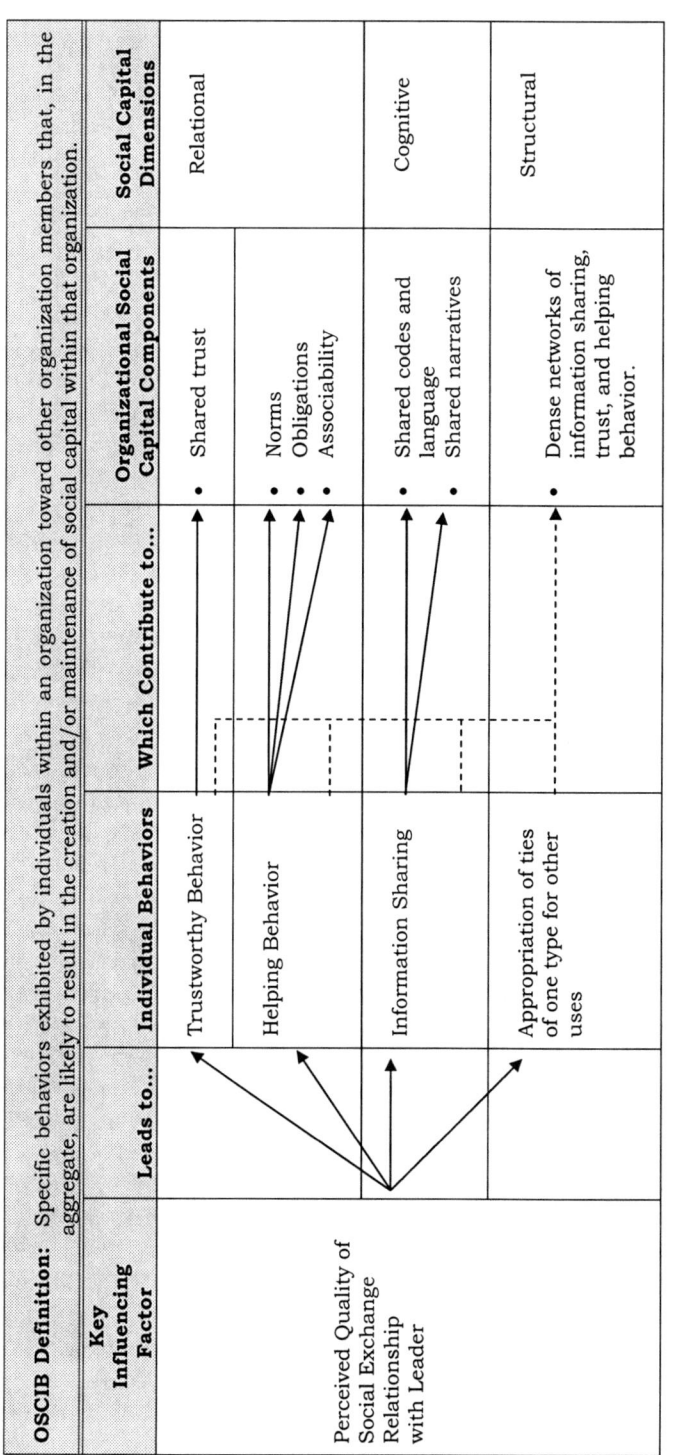

Figure 8.1. Organizational social capital investment behavior and the dimensions of social capital.

emotional intelligence of both parties of the relationship (i.e., both leader and member). This conceptual model is presented in Figure 8.2.

Leader-Member Exchange and Organizational Social Capital Investment Behavior

As suggested above, the creation and maintenance of organizational social capital are, in part, a function of the quality of the interactions between individuals in the organization. One potentially useful theoretical lens through which the quality of interactions may be examined is social exchange theory (Blau, 1964) and the associated norm of reciprocity (Gouldner, 1960), which suggest that supplying rewarding services to another obligates that individual to furnish benefits in turn, thus discharging the obligation. Organizational researchers have frequently drawn upon social exchange theory in their examinations of the employment relationship and other relationships between individuals in the work place. One of the most important and often studied forms of relationships in organizations is that between leaders and their subordinates. This relationship has generally been examined using the construct of leader-member exchange (Graen & Scandura, 1987).

LMX research draws on social exchange theory by suggesting that leaders, largely due to time pressures, are only able to develop close relationships with a few key subordinates (Graen, 1976). The LMX literature suggests that the quality of the relationship that develops between a leader and a subordinate significantly predicts a variety of work-related outcomes such as performance ratings (Duarte, Goodson, & Klich, 1993, 1994; Gerstner & Day, 1997; Graen, 2003; Howell & Hall-Merenda, 1999; Liden & Graen, 1980; Scandura & Schriesheim, 1994; Schriesheim, Neider, & Scandura, 1998; Wayne, Shore, & Liden, 1997), job satisfaction (Graen et al., 1982; Green, Anderson, & Shivers, 1996; Liden, Wayne, & Sparrowe, 2000; Major, Kozlowski, Chao, & Gardner, 1995; Schriesheim et al., 1998), organizational commitment (Duchon, Green, & Taber, 1986; Hackett, Farh, Song & Lapierre, 2003; Liden et al., 2000; Major et al., 1995), and team effectiveness (Graen, Hui, & Taylor, 2004). Uhl-Bien, Graen, and Scandura (2000) further suggest that LMX can help us understand the relational aspects of human resource functioning, ultimately leading to the systematic generation of social capital. I offer additional perspectives here regarding a potential process through which LMX may influence individual contributions to the important resource of organizational social capital.

I offer that the influence of LMX on individual contributions to organizational social capital occurs in part due to the principle of generalized

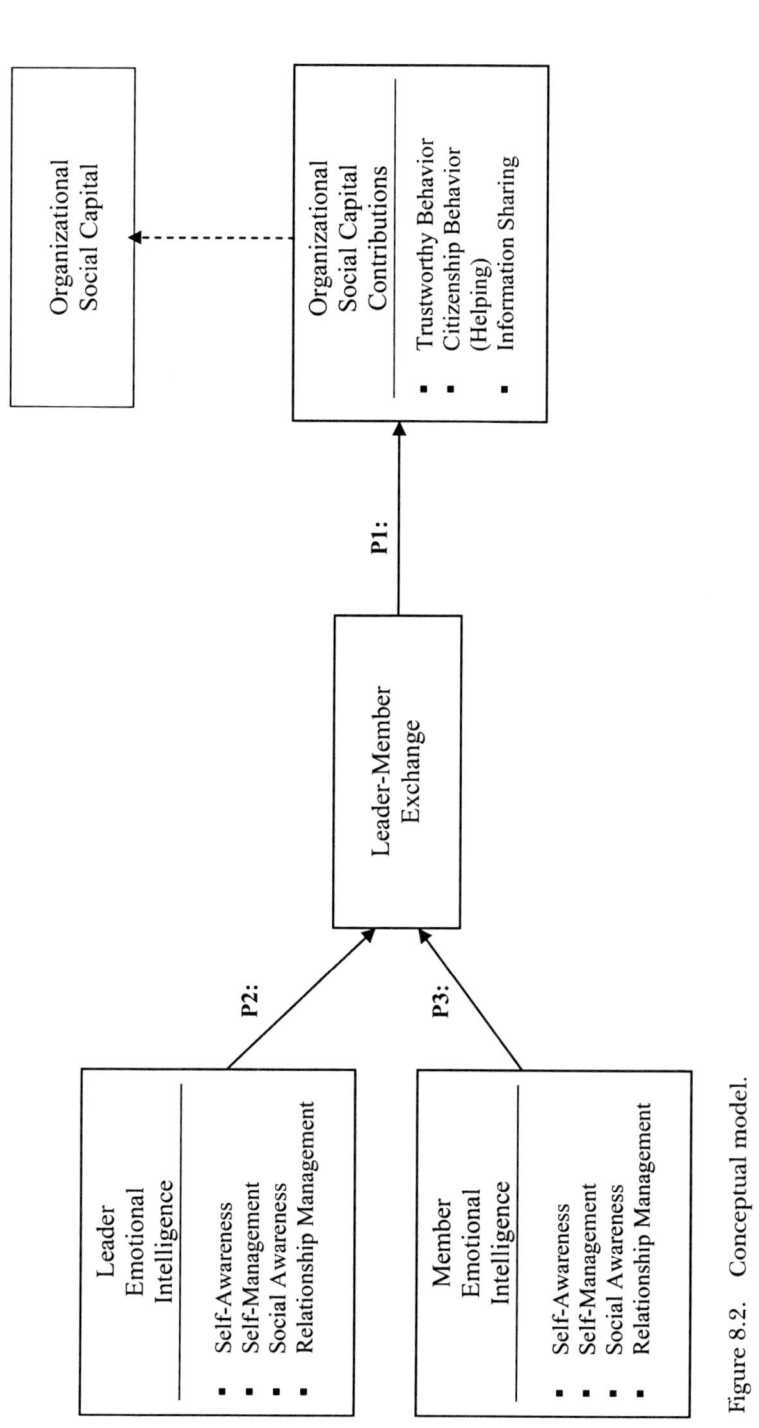

Figure 8.2. Conceptual model.

exchange, representing an indirect rather than a direct correspondence between what individuals give to and receive from one another. With this type of exchange, an individual's beneficial acts toward another may not necessarily be reciprocated by that person, but instead by a third party. For example, I may do you a favor and because of my generosity toward you, someone else may do me a favor. You may then at some point do someone else a favor to reciprocate the favor that I did for you. Following this process, within a defined social context everyone eventually both supplies resources and receives benefits, although not necessarily from the same person (see Takahashi, 2000 for a more detailed discussion of generalized exchange). Ekeh (1974) describes the process of generalized exchange as follows:

> The individual feels obligated to reciprocate another's action not by directly rewarding his benefactor, but by benefitting another actor implicated in a social exchange situation with his benefactor and himself. (p. 48)

Thus, the arguments relative to social exchange presented below do not apply exclusively to direct exchanges between a subordinate and his or her leader. I argue instead that perceived social exchange relationship quality with one's leader also influences one's exchanges with other individuals within the organization.

LMX and Trustworthy Behavior. Given that trust and trustworthiness are highly intertwined and reciprocally related constructs, perceptions of an exchange partner's trustworthiness are likely to influence one's willingness to trust that individual, as well as influencing one's own trustworthy behavior in the relationship. In his review of the trust literature, Kramer (1999) suggests that these perceptions of exchange partner trustworthiness are, among other things, based on the history of prior interactions with that particular individual. Kramer also states that, "a number of studies have demonstrated that reciprocity in exchange relationships enhances trust" (p. 575). Similarly, Graen and Scandura (1987) suggest that the development of the LMX relationship, which is shaped through role taking, role making, and finally role routinization, is essentially a trust building process. Therefore, high quality LMX relationships, which are characterized by mutual trust, loyalty, and behaviors that extend beyond the employment contract (Brower, Schoorman, & Tan, 2000), should be positively associated with trustworthy behavior on the part of individuals.

LMX and Helping Behavior. Liden and Graen (1980) contend that employees who perceive their LMX relationships to be of a high quality make contributions that go above and beyond their formal job duties. Those employees who report low-quality LMX relationships, on the other hand, according to Liden and Graen, are more likely to limit their performance to routine tasks specified in their employment contract. Brower et al. (2000) add that when a leader delegates authority and responsibility to a subordinate (as is the case with high quality LMX exchanges) the subordinate will likely value this behavior, and as a result be more satisfied, committed, and likely to engage in citizenship behaviors. A meta analysis by Hackett et al., 2003) and several previous studies have supported this suggested relationship between LMX and organizational citizenship behaviors (see Manogram & Conlon, 1993; Masterson et al., 2000; Settoon, Bennett, & Liden, 1996; Wayne & Green, 1993; Wayne et al., 1997). Prior research thus suggests a relationship between LMX and the helping behavior component of OSCIB.

LMX and Information Sharing. Graen and Scandura (1987) argue that the role-making phase of LMX development, in addition to being based on trust, is also built on the mutual contribution of valued resources between the leader and the subordinate. An important potential resource that may be exchanged during this phase is information, especially information that is not widely available to all members of the organization. Graen and Scandura contend that the leader has control of information as a resource and can decide what information is shared and not shared with various subordinates. Therefore, individuals with high-quality LMX relationships are likely to have greater access to valuable information due to the quality of their exchanges with their supervisor. In addition, due to the reciprocal nature of the LMX relationship, I argue that these individuals are also more likely to share valuable information with their supervisor and with others in the organization to the extent that such behavior is consistent with the role expectations established through the LMX relationship. Supporting this view, in a longitudinal study examining the vertical dyad linkage approach to leadership, which is the precursor to current LMX research, Dansereau, Graen, and Haga (1975) found that those members with high-quality LMX relationships reported receiving higher amounts of information from their superior as compared to those with low quality LMX relationships. These individuals with high-quality LMX relationships also spent more time and energy on activities classified as "communicating."

In sum, previous theoretical work together with the results of several empirical studies suggests that LMX perceptions on the part of an employee are likely to be positively related to each of the suggested components of OSCIB (i.e., engaging in trustworthy behavior, the performance of helping behaviors, and the sharing of information). Therefore, it follows that individuals who perceive their LMX relationship as high in quality should be more likely to engage in OSCIB.

> **Proposition 1.** Individuals' perceptions regarding the quality of their social exchange relationship with their immediate supervisor (LMX) will be positively related to their organizational social capital investment behavior.

The previous proposition suggests that LMX influences an individual's contributions to organizational social capital. Of additional interest, however, is the consideration of how the emotional intelligence of leaders, as well as their employees, might influence the leader-member exchange relationship.

EMOTIONAL INTELLIGENCE

Emotional Intelligence and Leader-Member Exchange

Kram and Cherniss (2001) argue that relationship quality is partially a function of the baseline level of emotional intelligence each person brings to the relationship. According to Kram and Cherniss, without certain emotional intelligence competencies, opportunities for relationship development may go unnoticed or be underutilized. They suggest that a number of competencies from the Social Awareness and Relationship Management domains of the emotional intelligence framework are essential for relationship development. These competencies, however, are built on other intrapersonal competencies in the domains of Self-Awareness

Table 8.1. Emotional Intelligence Competency Model

Personal Competence	*Social Competence*
Self-Awareness	*Social Awareness*
• Emotional self-awareness	• Empathy
• Accurate self-assessment	• Organizational awareness
• Self-confidence	• Service
Self-Management	*Relationship Management*
• Self-control	• Inspiration
• Transparency	• Influence
• Adaptability	• Developing others
• Achievement	• Change catalyst
• Initiative	• Conflict management
	• Teamwork and collaboration

Source: Goleman, Boyatzis, and McKee (2002).

and Self-Management as argued by Goleman (2001) and Goleman, Boyatzis, and McKee (2002). Thus, the full range of emotional intelligence competencies (demonstrated by both parties) is likely to have a significant influence on the quality of the leader-member exchange relationship that develops between a leader and his or her subordinates. Next, I draw on the work of Uhl-Bien et al. (2000) who discuss extensively the role-making process that occurs in high-quality LMX relationships, as well as the work or Goleman et al. (2002) who articulate the specific competencies that comprise their proposed model of emotional intelligence. In integrating these works, I offer arguments that suggest the importance of emotional intelligence on the part of the *leader* and the *member* in forming a high-quality leader-member exchange relationship.

Uhl-Bien et al. (2000) offer a model of relationship-building based on the parties of the relationship experiencing a series of interactions or exchanges. They suggest that the nature of these exchanges depends on (1) the characteristics each person brings to the relationship, (2) the individuals' expectations of the exchange, and (3) each person's assessment and reaction to the exchange (both during and after the exchange).[3] Each party's emotional intelligence can be viewed as one aspect of the personal attributes that they bring to the exchange relationship. Additionally, their emotional intelligence can serve to influence their expectations of, as well as their assessment of and reaction to, the exchange relationship as it develops.

From the perspective of the leader, there are a variety of emotional intelligence competencies that are likely to influence the role-making process and ultimately the quality of the LMX relationships formed with subordinates. Within the Self-Awareness and Self-Management domains (the intrapersonal competencies), competencies such as emotional self awareness (reading one's own emotions and recognizing their impact), self-confidence (a sound sense of one' self-worth and capabilities), emotional self-control (keeping disruptive emotions and impulses under control), transparency (displaying honesty, integrity, and trustworthiness), and optimism (seeing the upside in events, as well as seeing others positively and expecting the best of them) can all play an instrumental role in establishing high-quality relationships with subordinates. Demonstrating these competencies allows a leader to lead with authenticity and opens the door for the development of leader-member exchange relationships based on mutual respect, trust, and obligation. Gardner, Avolio, Luthans, May, and Walumbwa (2005) describe a similar effect as they discuss how self-awareness and self-regulation in a leader, which they label as authentic leadership, leads to authentic followership and ultimately authentic relationships between leaders and followers characterized by (a) transparency, openness, and trust, (b) guidance toward worthy objectives, and (c) an emphasis on follower development.

There are also a variety of emotional intelligence competencies within the Social Awareness and Relationship Management domains (the interpersonal competencies) that when demonstrated by a leader could significantly influence the development of high-quality LMX relationships. These include empathy (sensing others' emotions, understanding their perspective, and taking active interest in their concerns), developing others (bolstering others' abilities through feedback and guidance), and teamwork and collaboration (modeling cooperation and team building, as well as cementing close relationships beyond mere work obligations). Leaders who demonstrate these interpersonal competencies send the message to subordinates that they matter as individuals. Such leaders signal to subordinates that they understand and care about their concerns. They also signal that they recognize employees' personal development needs and are willing to assist them in their development efforts. Finally, leaders who demonstrate these competencies show that they are concerned about their subordinates as people not just employees. Individuals with leaders who consistently demonstrate the above emotional intelligence competencies in their ongoing interaction with them are likely to perceive the leader-member exchange relationship as one of high-quality. Thus, I propose the following:

> **Proposition 2.** Leader emotional intelligence will be positively related to leader-member exchange relationship quality as perceived by subordinates.

From the perspective of the subordinate, there are also a number of emotional intelligence competencies that are likely to influence the role-making process and the resulting quality of the LMX relationship formed with the leader (Gerstner & Day, 1997). Within the Self-Awareness and Self-Management domains, many of the same competencies important for leaders are also essential for subordinates when looking to develop high-quality LMX relationships. Emotional self-awareness, self-confidence, emotional self-control, and transparency are all competencies that should contribute to a subordinate's ability to act with authenticity and to build an authentic relationship with his or her supervisor. Additionally, the competencies of achievement (the drive to improve performance to meet inner standards of excellence) and initiative (readiness to act and seize opportunities) should contribute to the stage of the role-making process where individuals make an offer to engage in effort that goes beyond their formally defined role and continue as additional offers are made, accepted, and successfully acted upon as the relationship develops.

Along with demonstrating the above-mentioned intrapersonal competencies, when subordinates have the ability to sense the emotions of their supervisor and to understand their perspective on various matters (empathy), as well as have the ability to cultivate and maintain a relationship with them that goes beyond work obligations (building bonds, teamwork and collaboration), they should be able to develop a high-quality LMX relationship. This leads to the following proposition:

> **Proposition 3.** Member emotional intelligence will be positively related to leader-member exchange relationship quality as perceived by the leader.

IMPLICATIONS AND DIRECTIONS FOR FUTURE RESEARCH

In this chapter I have sought to explain how leaders can significantly impact the creation of social capital within their organizations. I have argued that through a process of reciprocity and generalized exchange, having a high-quality LMX relationship should make individuals more likely to engage in the types of behaviors that lead to the creation and maintenance of organizational social capital. Additionally, I have suggested that high-quality LMX relationships are more likely to develop when leaders and members exhibit higher levels of emotional intelligence demonstrated by displaying competencies in the areas of self-awareness, self-management, social awareness, and relationship management.

This chapter has potentially important implications for organizations. First, if LMX does indeed predict individual contributions to organizational social capital as suggested, then organizations could benefit by creating an environment that fosters the development of high-quality social exchange relationships between leaders and their subordinates. Second, I have argued that emotional intelligence may be a key factor in determining the quality of the LMX relationships that develop within an organization. To the extent that this holds true, incorporating certain emotional intelligence competencies into the selection criteria and/or the training and development activities of the organization could serve to enhance overall LMX relationship quality and ultimately lead to higher levels of organizational social capital.

Along those lines, there are a number of potentially fruitful avenues down which future research in this area might proceed. First, additional development of specific measures of the constructs discussed in this chapter, as well as testing of the propositions set forth, is needed to determine whether the suggested relationships are supported by empirical examination. Second, future researchers might also explore the implications of leader-member exchange relationship development over time. Conducting longitudinal studies of these relationships would allow for the examination of how changes in social exchange relationship quality between a leader and a subordinate as the relationship develops (or deteriorates) might potentially influence OSCIB. It could be the case that changes in relationship quality are as strong a predictor of individual contributions to organizational social capital as the actual quality of the relationship itself. Third, individual perceptions regarding other social exchange relationships in the workplace might also influence their contributions to organizational social capital. For instance, at the level of the work group or team, perceived team-member exchange (Seers, 1989) is likely to influence the level of information sharing, trustworthy behavior, and effort exhibited by an individual within the work group. Examining the extent to which perceived social exchange relationship quality at the team level might influence social capital contributions both within the team and within the broader organization represents another possible avenue for future research. Finally, while the focus of this chapter is on factors suggested to influence individual contributions to organizational social capital, the value of its contribution to the literature is partially predicated on the belief that higher levels of OSCIB, when aggregated, lead to higher levels of organizational social capital. Thus, future research that examines the relationship between the individual-level measure of OSCIB and an organizational-level measure of social capital across a number of organizations would provide a useful test of the link between these micro-and macro-level constructs.

CONCLUSION

The concept of social capital has received considerable attention in recent years in both the academic and practitioner communities. Organizational social capital has been described as a resource that creates organizational value by facilitating collective action (Leana & Van Buren, 1999). Given this increased attention and the perceived value of social capital as an organizational resource (Balkundi & Harrison, 2006), it is important that we develop a better understanding of potential processes though which social capital is developed in organizations.

This chapter represents an attempt to explore one such process by exploring why and how individuals contribute to the creation and maintenance of social capital in the organizations for which they work. In sum, I have suggested that in accordance with social exchange theory and the generalized norm of reciprocity, employees who have a perceived high quality exchange relationship with their immediate supervisor are more likely to engage in behaviors that lead to the creation and maintenance of organizational social capital. Further, I have proposed that high quality leader-member exchange relationships are more likely to develop when both parties of the relationship demonstrate high levels of emotional intelligence.

NOTES

1. See Adler and Kwon (2002) and Burt (2005) for a more extensive discussion of the bonding versus bridging perspectives of social capital and structural holes versus network closure.
2. See LePine, Erez, and Johnson (2002) and Podsakoff, MacKenzie, Paine, and Bachrach (2000) for extensive reviews of OCB and discussions of its suggested dimensions.
3. Uhl-Bien et al. (2000) also discuss the role of the context within which the relationship unfolds, as well as that of situational influences. Those aspects of their model are beyond the scope of the present discussion.

REFERENCES

Adler, P. S., & Kwon, S. (2002). Social capital: Prospects for a new concept. *Academy of Management Review, 27*, 17-40.

Ahuja, G. (2000). Collaboration networks, structural holes, and innovation: A longitudinal study. *Administrative Science Quarterly, 45*, 425-445.

Balkundi P., & Harrison, D. A. (2006, February). Ties, leaders, and time in teams: Strong inference about network structure's effects on team viability and performance. *Academy of Management Journal* (in press).

Belliveau, M., O'Reilly, C., & Wade, J. (1996). Social capital at the top: Effects of social similarity and status on CEO compensation. *Academy of Management Journal, 39*, 1568-1593.

Blau, P. (1964). *Exchange and power in social life*. New York: Wiley.

Brower, H. H., Schoorman, F. D., & Tan, H. H., (2000). A model of relational leadership: The integration of trust and leader-member exchange. *Leadership Quarterly, 11*, 227-250.

Burt, R. S. (1992). *Structural holes*. Cambridge, MA: Harvard University Press.

Burt, R. S. (1997). The contingent value of social capital. *Administrative Science Quarterly, 42*, 339-365.

Burt, R. S. (2005). *Brokerage and closure: An introduction to social capital*. New York: Oxford University Press.

Canon-Bowers, J. A., Sala, E., & Converse, S. (1993). Shared mental models in expert team decision making. In N. J. Castellan (Ed.), *Individual and group decision making: Current issues* (pp. 221-246). Hillsdale, NJ: Erlbaum.

Canon-Bowers, J. A., & Salas, E. (2001). Reflections on shared cognition. *Journal of Organizational Behavior, 22*, 195-202.

Capelli, P. (2004). Why do employers retrain at-risk workers? The role of social capital. *Industrial Relations, 43*, 421-447.

Cherniss, C., &.Goleman, D. (2001). *The emotionally intelligent workplace*. San Francisco: Jossey-Bass.

Coleman, J. S. (1988). Social capital in the creation of human capital. *American Journal of Sociology, 94*, S95-S120.

Coleman, J. S. (1990). *Foundations of social theory*. Cambridge, MA: Harvard University Press.

Conte, J. M., (2005). A review and critique of emotional intelligence measures. *Journal of Organizational Behavior, 26*, 433-440.

Cummings, J. N., & Cross, R. (2003). Structural properties of work groups and their consequences for performance. *Social Networks, 25*, 197-281.

Dansereau, F., Graen, G., & Haga, W. J. (1975). A vertical dyad linkage approach to leadership within formal organizations: A longitudinal investigation of the role-making process. *Organizational Behavior and Human Performance, 13*, 46-78.

Duarte, N. T., Goodson, J. R., & Klich, N. R., (1993). How do I like thee? Let me appraise the ways. *Journal of Organizational Behavior, 14*, 239-249.

Duarte, N. T., Goodson, J. R., & Klich, N. R. (1994). Effects of dyadic quality and duration on performance appraisal. *Academy of Management Journal, 37*, 499-521.

Duchon, D., Green, S. G., & Taber, T. D. (1986). Vertical dyad linkage: A longitudinal assessment of antecedents, measures, and consequences. *Journal of Applied Psychology, 71*, 56-60.

Ekeh, P.P . (1974). *Social exchange theory: Two traditions*. Cambridge, MA: Harvard University Press.

Friedman, R. A., & Krackhardt, D. (1997). Social capital and career mobility: A structural theory of lower returns to education for Asian employees. *Journal of Applied Behavioral Science, 33*, 316-334.

Fukuyama, F. (1995). *Trust: The social virtues and the creation of prosperity*. New York: Free Press.

Gardner, W. L., Avolio, B. J., Luthans, F., May, D. R., & Walumbwa, F. O. (2005). "Can you see the real me?" A self-based model of authentic leader and following development. *The Leadership Quarterly, 16*, 343-372.

Geher, G. (2004). *Measuring emotional intelligence: Common ground and controversy*. New York: Nova Science.

Gerstner, C. R., & Day, D. V. (1997). Meta-analytic review of leader-member exchange theory: Correlates and construct issues. *Journal of Applied Psychology, 82*, 827-844.

Goleman, D. (1995). *Emotional intelligence*. New York: Bantam.

Goleman, D. (1998). *Working with emotional intelligence*. New York: Bantam.

Goleman, D. (2001). Emotional intelligence: Issues in Paradigm building. In C. Cherniss & D. Goleman (Eds.), *The emotionally intelligent workplace* (pp. 13-26). San Francisco: Jossey-Bass.

Goleman, D., Boyatzis, R., & McKee, A. (2002). *Primal leadership: Realizing the power of emotional intelligence*. Boston: Harvard Business School Press.

Gouldner, A. W. (1960). The norm of reciprocity. *American Sociological Review, 25*,165-167.

Graen, G. (1976). Role making processes within complex organizations. In M. D. Dunnette (Ed.), *Handbook of industrial and organizational psychology* (pp. 1201-1245). Chicago: Rand McNally.

Graen, G., Novak, M., & Sommerkamp. (1982). The effects of leader-member exchange and job design on productivity and job satisfaction: Testing a dual attachment model. *Organizational Behavior and Humand Performance, 30,* 109-131.

Graen, G. B. (2003). Interpersonal Workplace Theory at the Crossroads. In G.B. Graen (Ed.), *Dealing with diversity, LMX leadership: The series* (Vol. 1, pp. 145-182). Greenwich, CT: Information Age.

Graen, G. B., Hui, C., & Taylor, E. T. (2004). A new approach to team leadership: Upward, downward, and horizontal differentiation. In G. B. Graen (Ed.), *New frontiers of leadership: LMX leadership: The series* (Vol. 2, pp. 33-66). Greenwich, CT: Information Age Publishing.

Graen, G. B., & Scandura, T. A. (1987). Toward a psychology of dyadic organizing. In B. M. Staw & L. L. Cummings (Eds.), *Research in organizational behavior* (Vol. 9, pp. 175-208). Greenwich, CT: JAI Press.

Granovetter, M. (1992). Problems of explanation in economic sociology. In N. Nohria & R. Eccles (Eds.), *Networks and organizations: Structure, form and action* (pp. 25-56). Boston: Harvard Business School Press.

Green, S. G., Anderson, S. E., & Shivers, S. L. (1996). Demographic and organizational influences on leader-member exchange and related work attitudes. *Organizational Behavior & Human Decision Processes, 66,* 203-214.

Hackett, R. D., Farh, J -L, Song, L. J., & Lapierre, L. M. (2003). LMX and organizational citizenship behavior: Examining the links within and across Western and Chinese samples. In G. B. Graen (Ed.), *Dealing with diversity, LMX leadership: The series* (Vol. 1 pp. 219-263). Greenwich, CT: Information Age.

Howell, J. M., & Hall-Merenda, K. E. (1999). The ties that bind: The impact of leader-member exchange, transformational leadership, and distance on predicting follower performance. *Journal of Applied Psychology, 84,* 680-694.

Klimoski, R., & Mohammed, S. (1994). Team mental model: Construct or metaphor? *Journal of Management, 20,* 403-438.

Knez, M., & Camerer, C. (1994). Creating exceptional assets in the laboratory: Coordination in "weakest-link" games. *Strategic Management Journal, 15,* 101-119.

Koka, B. R., & Prescott, J. E., (2002). Strategic alliances as social capital: A multidimensional view. *Strategic Management Journal, 23,* 795-816.

Kram, K. E., & Cherniss, C. (2001). Developing emotional competence through relationships at work. In C. Cherniss & D. Goleman (Eds.), *The emotionally intelligent workplace* (pp. 254-285). San Francisco: Jossey-Bass.

Kramer, R. (1999). Trust and distruct in organizations: Emerging perspectives, enduring questions. *Annual Review of Psychology, 50,* 569-598.

Leana, C. R., & Van Buren III, H. J. (1999). Organizational social capital and employment practices. *Academy of Management Review, 24,* 538-555.

LePine, J. A., Erez, A., & Johnson, D. E. (2002). The nature and dimensionality of organizational citizenship behavior: A critical review and mete-analysis. *Journal of Applied Psychology, 87*, 52-65.

Levesque, L. L., Wilson, J. M., & Wholey, D. R. (2001). Cognitive divergence and shared mental models in software development project teams. *Journal of Organizational Behavior, 22*, 135-144.

Levine, J. M., & Moreland, R. L. (1999). Knowledge transmission in work groups. In L. L. Thompson, J. M. Levine, & D. M. Messick (Eds.), *Shared cognition in organizations*. Mahwah, NJ: Earlbaum.

Liden, R. C., & Graen, G. (1980). Generalizability of the vertical dyad linkage model of leadership. *Academy of Management Journal, 23*, 451-465.

Liden, R. C., Wayne, S. J., & Sparrowe, R. T. (2000). An examination of the mediating role of psychological empowerment on the relations between the job, interpersonal relationships, and work outcomes. *Journal of Applied Psychology, 83*, 407-416.

Major, D. A., Kozlowski, S. W., Chao, G. T., & Gardner, P. D. (1995). A longitudinal investigation of newcomer expectations, early socialization outcomes, and the moderation effects of role development factors. *Journal of Applied Psychology, 80*, 418-431.

Manogram, P., & Conlon, E. J. (1993). *A leader-member exchange apaproach to explaining organizational citizenship behaviors*. Paper presented at the annual meeting of the Academy of Management, Atlanta, GA.

Masterson, S. S., Lewis, K., Goldman, B. M., & Taylor, M. S. (2000). Integrating justice and social exchange: The differing effects of fair procedures and treatment on work relationships. *Academy of Management Journal, 43*, 738-748.

McEvily, B., & Zaheer, A. (1999). Bridging ties: A source of firm heterogeneity in competitive capabilities. *Strategic Management Journal, 20*, 1133-1156.

McFadyen, M. A. & Cannella, A. A. (2004). Social capital and knowledge creation: Diminishing returns of the number and strength of exchange relationships. *Academy of Management Journal, 47*, 735-746.

Molm, L. D., Takahashi, N., & Peterson, G. (2000). Risk and trust in social exchange: An experimental test of a classical proposition. *American Journal of Sociology, 105*, 1396-1427.

Nahapiet, J., & Ghoshal, S. (1998). Social capital, intellectual capital, and the organizational advantage. *Academy of Management Review, 23*, 242-266.

Newell, S., Tansley, C., & Huang, J. (2004). Social capital and knowledge integration in an ERP project team: The importance of bridging and bonding. *British Journal of Management, 15*, 43-57.

Oh, H., Chung, M., & Labianca, G. (2004). Group social capital and group effectiveness: The role of informal socializing ties. *Academy of Management Journal, 47*, 8660-875.

Oh, H., Kilduff, M., & Brass, D. J. (1999). *Communal social capital, linking social capital, and economic outcomes*. Paper presented at the annual meeting of the Academy of Management, Chicago.

Podsakoff, P. M., MacKenzie, S. B., Paine, J. B., & Bachrach, D. G. (2000). Organizational citizenship behaviors: A critical review of the theoretical and empirical literature and suggestions for future research. *Journal of Management, 3*, 513-563.

Portes, A. (1998). Social capital: Its origins and applications in modern sociology. *Annual Review of Sociology, 24*, 1-24.

Portes, A., & Sensenbrenner, J. (1993). Embeddedness and immigration: Notes on the social determinants of economic action. *American Journal of Sociology, 98*, 1320-1350.

Putnam, R. (1993). *Making democracy work: Civic traditions in modern Italy.* Princeton, NJ: Princeton University Press.

Putnam, R. (1995). Bowling alone: America's declining social capital. *Journal of Democracy, 6*, 65-78.

Reagans, R., & Zuckerman, E. W. (2001). Networks, diversity, and productivity: The social capital of corporate R&D teams. *Organization Science, 12*, 502-517.

Reagans, R., Zuckerman, E. W., & McEvily, B. (2004). How to make the team: Social networks vs. demography as criteria for designing effective teams. *Administrative Science Quarterly, 49*, 101-133.

Salovey, P., & Mayer, J. D. (1990). Emotional intelligence. *Imagination, Cognition, and Personality, 9*, 185-211.

Scandura, T. A., & Schriesheim, C. A. (1994). Leader-member exchange and supervisor career mentoring as complementary constructs in leadership research. *Academy of Management Journal, 37*, 1588-1602.

Schriesheim, C. A., Neider, L. L., & Scandura, T. A. (1998). A within- and between-groups analysis of leader-member exchange as a correlate of delegation and as a moderator of delegation relationships with performance and satisfaction. *Academy of Management Journal, 41*, 298-318.

Seers, A. (1989). Team-member exchange quality: A new concept for role-making research. *Organizational Behavior and Human Decision Processes, 43*, 118-135.

Seibert, S. E., Kramer, M., & Liden, R. (2001). A social capital theory of career success. *Academy of Management Journal, 44*, 219-237.

Settoon, R. P., Bennett, N., & Liden, R. C. (1996). Social exchange in organizations: The differential effects of perceived organizational support and leader-member exchange. *Journal of Applied Psychology, 81*, 219-227.

Susskind, A. M., Miller, V. D., & Johnson, J. D. (1998). Downsizing and structural holes: Their impact on layoff survivors' perceptions of organizational chaos and openness to change. *Communications Research, 25*, 30-65.

Takahashi, N. (2000). The emergence of generalized exchange. *American Journal of Sociology, 105*, 1105-1134.

Thorndike, E. L. (1920). Intelligence and its uses. *Harper's Magazine, 140*, 227-235.

Tsai, W. (2000). Social capital, strategic relatedness and the formation of intraorganizational linkages. *Strategic Management Journal, 21*, 925-939.

Uhl-Bien, M., Graen, G. B., & Scandura, T. A. (2000). Implications of leader-member exchange (LMX) for strategic human resource management systems: Relationships as social capital for competitive advantage. In G. R. Ferris (Ed.), *Research in personnel and human resource management* (Vol. 18, pp. 137-185). Stamford, CT: JAI Press.

Uzzi, B. (1997). Social structure and competition in interfirm networks: The paradox of embeddedness. *Administrative Science Quarterly, 42*, 35-67.
Uzzi, B., & Gillespie, J. J. (2002). Knowledge spillover in corporate financing networks: Embeddedness and the firm's debt performance. *Strategic Management Journal, 23*, 595-618.
Wayne, S. J., & Green, S. A. (1993). The effects of leader-member exchange on employee citizenship and impression management behavior. *Human Relations, 46*, 1431-1440.
Wayne, S. J., Shore, L. M., & Liden, R. C. (1997). Perceived organizational support and leader-member exchange: A social exchange perspective. *Academy of Management Journal, 40*, 82-111.

CHAPTER 9

ORGANIZATIONAL CYNICISM

A Field Examination Using Global and Local Social Exchange Relationships and Workplace Outcomes

Pamela Brandes, Diya Das, and Michael Hadani

Recent conceptual work in organizational behavior has highlighted the importance of organizational cynicism in the workplace. However, few studies have empirically examined: (1) the importance of social exchange perceptions in influencing the cognitive and affective components of cynicism, and (2) the resulting impact of cognitive and affective cynicism on contemporary work behaviors. In this article, we investigate the importance of social exchange processes in understanding affective and cognitive cynicism, and some potential effects of affective and cognitive cynicism on work behaviors. We then test this theoretical framework based on data collected from a field study of 129 supervisor-subordinate dyads in a manufacturing organization. The data suggest that global social exchanges are better predictors of cognitive and affective cynicism than local social exchanges. The two components of cynicism also have different effects on work outcomes. Finally, we discuss how employees with high quality leader-member exchanges may express cynicism more or less as a function of overall trust in top management.

INTRODUCTION

The last two decades have ushered in a dramatic change in the notion of employee-organization relationships (Kissler, 1994; Tsui & Wu, 2005). Rampant mergers, acquisitions, corporate scandals, off-shoring of jobs, reengineering, and downsizing programs have flooded corporate life—resulting in mass layoffs, euphemistically labeled "rightsizings," and organizational restructurings which have left many employee-critics in their wake (Vogl, 1995). Increased turbulence in organizational life has created a multitude of organizational initiatives and a veritable "alphabet soup" of acronyms.

Frequent change that has not delivered in terms of outcomes has many employees noting inconsistencies between what management says and what it does. Hackneyed corporate values' statements that look good on a wall such as, "Our employees are our most important resource" often seem inconsistent with organization actions in practice (Stewart, 1996). For example, senior managers and corporate boards tell the workforce about the importance of cutting costs and freezing employee salaries while they earn multimillion-dollar bonuses. Teams are proclaimed by senior staff as the "new way to work," but organizational appraisal systems reward individual efforts in practice. Thus, many organizations send inconsistent or mixed messages to their workforce (Tsui & Wu, 2005). As a result, many employees have begun to reexamine corporate life and the worth of corporate loyalty. For many employees the cartoon strip character Dilbert has become a hero, symbolizing the frustrations and complexities of work life that have resulted from many of the above changes.

In light of the above, we focus on the "pervasive" phenomenon of cynicism within organizations as conceptualized by answering the following two questions. First, *how might social exchange processes be related to organizational cynicism?* As scholars have increasingly recognized the importance of the obligation of reciprocity between employees and organizations, social exchange processes have been recognized as potent predictors of employee attitudes and workplace behaviors (Coyle-Shapiro & Conway, 2005; Settoon, Bennett, & Liden, 1996). Specifically, social exchange theorists have identified multiple targets for employees' reciprocity assessments including one's supervisors, one's employing organization (Wayne, Shore, & Liden, 1997), as well as senior management. Due to changes in the nature of the employee-organization relationship, social exchange theory is uniquely positioned to provide insights to conditions that engender organizational cynicism. Second, *does organizational cynicism "matter?"* That is, how is organizational cynicism related to important work attitudes and behaviors? Organizational cynicism can have both direct and indirect influences on important work outcomes. Directly, as a negative attitude, organizational cynicism might subdue organizationally beneficial behaviors such as extra-role behaviors, in-role performance, and even employee involvement initiatives. Indirectly, organizational cynicism may affect important job attitudes such as organizational commitment and job satisfaction which, in turn, could affect job outcomes.

In response to these questions, the remainder of this paper is organized as follows. We first review theoretical and empirical work that focuses on organizational cynicism. Next, using social exchange theory we develop hypotheses relating global and local variants of social exchange processes to the affective and cognitive components of organizational cynicism. Here we explore both the direct effects of the social exchange variables on cynicism and their interactive effects. Then, we develop several hypotheses relating affective and cognitive cynicisms to both in and extra-role performance, as well as to employees' involvement in company improvement teams. Finally, based on a field study, we discuss our research procedure, results, findings, and offer suggestions on future cynicism research.

LITERATURE REVIEW

Organizational Cynicism

According to the Oxford English Dictionary (1989) a modern cynic is "one who shows a disposition to disbelieve in the sincerity or goodness of human motives and actions, and is wont to express this by sneers and sarcasms; a sneering faultfinder." A systematic exposition on organizational cynicism by Dean, Brandes, and Dharwadkar (1998) suggests it is a negative attitude toward one's employing organization comprising: a belief that the organization lacks integrity; negative affect toward one's employing organization; and disparaging and critical behaviors toward the organization that are consistent with these beliefs and affect (p. 345). Cynical *beliefs* refer to the beliefs held by the organizational cynics, i.e., the practices of their organizations are based on self-interest (e.g., Goldner, Ritti, & Ference, 1977). Organizationally cynical employees often hold that there are hidden motives for organizational actions, and thus, are unlikely to accept any official rationales advanced by management. Consequently, organizational cynics believe organizational actions lack fairness, honesty, and sincerity. *Affect* is an essential part of understanding attitudes and is often attached to the object of the belief (Eagly & Chaiken, 1993). Organizational cynicism includes intense emotions that follow from the judgments associated with cynical beliefs. For example, organizational cynics "may feel contempt for and anger toward their organization. They may also experience distress, disgust, and even shame when they think about their organization" (Dean et al., 1998, p. 346). Mishra and Spreitzer (1998, p. 569) suggest that cynical employees experience emotions like "anger, disgust, and moral outrage" (e.g., in the context of layoffs). Finally, cynical behavior occurs when organizationally cynical employees display negative, disparaging behavior toward their organizations, which includes strong criticisms of the organization, such as critical statements that reflect the organization's lack of honesty or sincerity in dealing with employees and customers. Employees' cynical behaviors also may include stinging, sarcastic humor, or other forms of badmouthing that targets the organization (e.g., Mishra & Spreitzer, 1998).

Since its formulation, organizational cynicism has, in whole or in its sub-dimensions, been previously studied in organizational behavior. For example, in terms of antecedents, Pugh, Skarlicki, and Passell (2003) show that psychological contract violations can predict (cognitive) organizational cynicism regarding a post-layoff employer. Chrobot-Mason (2003) also suggests that contract breaches affect employees' (cognitive) cynicism levels. In a similar vein, Johnson and O'Leary-Kelly (2003) find that cynicism mediates the relationship between contract breaches and emotional exhaustion. They show affective and cognitive cynicisms have discriminant validity from each other, as well as similar constructs such as negative affectivity, psychological contract breach, and trait cynicism. Following this stream of scholarship, we chose to focus on the affective and cognitive components of organizational cynicism.

HYPOTHESIS DEVELOPMENT

Antecedents of Organizational Cynicism: Social Exchange Relationships

Social exchange theory has served as an important theoretical basis for understanding the interactions that employees have with their supervisors as well as their organizations (Wayne et al., 1997). Social exchange theorists such as Blau (1964) suggest that social interactions create deferred obligations based on the notion of reciprocity (Gouldner, 1960). That is, over time, employees evaluate their balance of exchanges with various social referents in order to assess the benefits/costs relating to these repeated transactions. Employee assessments of these transactions influence attitudes and behaviors within organizations (Wayne et al., 1997). Social exchanges can also be conceptualized as occurring at global and local levels within organizations (Brandes, Dharwadkar, & Wheatley, 2004). Global exchanges are those that may not consist of direct interpersonal interactions between the employee and the targets of these exchanges, but would nonetheless have a global referent. This includes employees' perceptions of both perceived organizational support and top management. The perception of the quality of these variables has been shown to influence employees' attitudes and behaviors toward firms (Brandes et al., 2004; Eisenberger, Huntington, Hutchison, & Sowa, 1986). Local exchanges, on the other hand, refer to those exchanges that are based on a direct and primary contact between the employee and the targets of those exchanges. These would include leader member relations, and the interpersonal ties that employees have with members of other work groups within the organization. Thus the first part of our paper is an attempt to explore how these global and local exchange variables affect employees' cynical beliefs and cynical affect toward the organization.

Perceived Organizational Support (POS)

Using social exchange theory, Eisenberger et al. (1986) suggest that employees develop global beliefs about whether their employing organization values their contributions and cares about their well being, and they name this concept Perceived Organization Support (POS). Unlike leader-member exchange (in which an employee evaluates his or her partnership with a supervisor), in POS, the employee evaluates the quality of exchange with the organization at large. In other words, the "organization" is a partner to a social exchange relationship in which the employee evaluates the quality of exchange between the employee and his or her organization. Wayne et al. (1997) showed that while related, leader-member exchange and perceived organizational support were differentially related to outcomes, perceived organizational support was positively related to affective commitment, performance ratings, and organizational citizenship behavior, and was negatively related to intentions to quit. Moorman, Blakely, and Niehoff (1998) also found that POS was positively related to organizational and citizenship behaviors. POS evaluations are based on patterns of company decisions made not only by the employee's immediate superior, but also by other managers within the organization. It represents employees' evaluations of how the organization is committed to the employee (Rhoades & Eisenberger, 2002).

As managers and organizations demand more effort on the part of their employees, employees expect resources and support commensurate with these increased demands. We believe that employees who have global beliefs that managers have not provided adequate resources and support are more likely to be cynical. Not providing employees with adequate support suggests that employers have disregarded employees' well-being, goals, and values will result in higher organizational cynicism. Neglecting employee needs and providing mixed messages over what the company values will lead employees to question organization motives and engender feelings of resentment.

> **Hypothesis 1**: Perceived organizational support (POS) will be negatively related to affective and cognitive variants of organizational cynicism.

Trust in Senior Staff

Trust has been defined as "a willingness to be vulnerable to the actions of others," and is generally assessed by the likelihood of another party's readiness to take into account the interests of all parties concerned within a transaction (Hosmer, 1995; Mayer, Davis, & Schoorman, 1995). Senior staff members are obligated as trustees of the organization to protect the interests of all stakeholders, including employees. Employee beliefs about senior staff will no doubt have consequences for employee behaviors. Wayne et al. (1997) recall the two basic assumptions of Gouldner's notion of reciprocity, suggesting that (1) people should help those who have helped them, and (2) people should not injure those who have helped them. Clearly, most employees feel themselves to be vulnerable to the decisions and actions of senior managers. For example, employee survivors of organizational layoffs feel themselves particularly exposed to, and often disappointed by top management action (Brockner, Siegel, Daly, Tyler, & Martin, 1997). Employees expect that senior staff will act in the best interest of employees and will protect employee job security. Similarly, Mayer and Davis (1999) highlight the importance of the trust that employees have (or do not have) in their top management's actions.

Based on the above, those employees who feel that they have advanced the goals of senior staff are more likely to feel that senior staff is obligated to look out for employee interests. If, however, senior staff does not recognize employees' anticipation of future payback, employees are likely to have reduced trust in senior staff. Employees who believe they cannot trust their senior leadership are more likely to raise questions about where the organization is going, the apparent inconsistencies between organizational policies and practices, as well as be more negatively disposed toward the organization. For instance, top managers who claim, "Our employees are our greatest assets," yet take the first opportunity to offshore operations to lower cost international subsidiaries, may foster cynical reactions from employees. Top management may select a pet "technology project of the month," evangelizing how the package will "revolutionize the way we do business," yet the average employee may have barely learned last month's software or may work on an outdated computer. Employees may call into question the competence and reliability of senior staff, and express frustration and bewilderment with the inconsistency between the mandates and practices of senior staff. One can observe this cynicism amongst the reports of employee reactions following recent corporate scandals (Byrne, 2002; Pellet, 2002). The reactions of these employees lead us to believe that a lack of trust or a breach of trust with top management ignites cynicism in the employees. Thus, we posit that the lower the trust in top management, the higher will be the cynical beliefs and feelings that the employees would harbor toward the organization.

Hypothesis 2: Trust in senior staff will be negatively related to affective and cognitive variants of organizational cynicism.

Leader-Member Exchange (LMX)

LMX theory depicts an important social exchange process that emphasizes the importance of the differentiated dyadic relationships that supervisors create with their subordinates. In this approach, mature dyadic partnerships provide employees increased access to resources, information, and benefits within organizations. Significantly, these dyadic assessments are based on the cognitive evaluations that employees have about the quality of the working relationship that exists between the subordinate and their supervisor. Previously, LMX has been related to important employee attitudes such as satisfaction with supervisors, overall job satisfaction, and organizational commitment (see Gerstner & Day, 1997 for a review). In other words, individuals with higher-quality exchange relationships with their supervisors report greater attachment to their organizations and greater satisfaction with their work.

According to Graen and Uhl-Bien (1991), individuals who have high quality working relationships with their supervisors are more likely to receive essential resources, to be privy to insider information, and to be trusted with important tasks and responsibilities. Individuals who receive the resources, information, and respect associated with high quality relationships are less likely to be kept in the dark regarding important organizational priorities, allocations, and decisions. On the other hand, individuals with low quality relationships are less likely to hold their supervisor's knowledge, skills, and abilities in high regard and consequently, are more likely to experience negative affective and cognitive evaluations of their organizations. Furthermore, in trying to preserve attitudinal consistency and reduce cognitive dissonance between the underlying components of attitude and behavioral intentions, these individuals are more likely to act in a manner consistent with belief and affect (Festinger, 1957). In their theoretical study, Davis and Gardner (2004) proposed that the quality of LMX would be a key factor in the development of cynical attitudes amongst employees. In this study we extend their argument, testing the affective and behavioral aspects of organizational cynicism. We believe that low quality leader-member relationships would be instrumental in creating feelings and beliefs of cynicism amongst the employees.

> **Hypothesis 3:** Leader-member exchange (LMX) will be negatively related to affective and cognitive variants of organizational cynicism.

Ties Outside One's Work Group

One of the social exchanges that determine employee behavior at work is the ties that employees have outside their own work groups within organizations. Studies have shown that such ties lead to better organizational functioning (Cook, 1982; Krackhardt, 1992; Krackhardt & Hanson, 1993; Krackhardt & Brass, 1994). Brandes et al. (2004) showed these ties are associated with more citizenship behavior amongst employees. Ties outside one's work group provide employees with more information about the firm and its practices beyond information generated from one's own workgroup and supervisor.

We believe that such ties outside one's own workgroup can have a mitigating effect on the other aspects of social exchanges. The bonding generated therein would impact the level of cynicism within the employees. The greater the number of ties that the employees have, the greater the quality of information about organizational priorities and practices. Information from such ties keeps these employees "in the know" compared to employees who lack such ties. With greater information there would be greater trust (Sonnenberg, 1991) and, therefore fewer tendencies to doubt the motives of their organizations. Moreover, having more support outside one's own work group may dissipate any negative affect that arises out of one's work group experience, possibly reducing cynicism.

> **Hypothesis 4:** Ties outside of work groups will be negatively related to affective and cognitive variants of organizational cynicism.

Interaction of Local and Global Social Exchanges

While we have argued so far for the direct effects of the different local and global social exchange variables on cognitive and affective cynicism, there may be conditions under which local and global exchanges may interact, one perhaps compensating for the other. We had indicated that favorable evaluations of global and local exchanges would be associated with less cynicism. It might also be that poor quality global social exchanges could be compensated for by high quality local exchanges. In other words, assuming that organizational cynicism is generally deleterious for organizations (a point debated in Meyerson, 1990), it may be that combining the effects of global relationships with those at the local level might create conditions under which cynicism might be ameliorated. Similarly, those employees lacking quality global and local social exchanges may be the most cynical, and employees with high quality global and local ties may be among the least cynical.

For example, employees that have high quality relationships with supervisors may permit the employee to overcome shortcomings of poor global exchanges with the organization at large (POS) or with top management. Because local relationships are more proximate, they may compensate for poor, arm's length social transactions with the organization "at large." A high quality relationship with a supervisor may result in better information and resources even in the absence of poor support from management and senior management in general. Poor quality relationships both globally and locally should result in the most cynicism, but high quality leader-member relationships in combination with good global relationships should have the least cynicism overall.

> **Hypothesis 5:** LMX will moderate the relationship between global exchanges and cognitive and affective variants of cynicism.

Next we look into the other local exchange variable—ties with other groups—and explore how this likely interacts with the two global exchange variables. Brandes et al. (2004) showed how ties outside one's workgroup are a source of both information and support for an employee. Employees with low quality relationships with those outside their workgroup who also face low POS and/or low trust in senior staff are likely to have the worst cynicism levels. However, it may be that high quality relationships with others outside one's workgroup can compensate for poor quality POS and/or trust in senior management. Employees with strong information regarding organizational priorities may be able to compensate for low quality global relationships (as such information can provide more clarity or reduce inconsistencies or mixed messages), thereby resulting in reduced cynicism levels. Individuals with many ties outside one's workgroup would be able to generate greater information on the activities of the organization, in spite of poor quality global exchanges that would hopefully reduce feelings of dejection and cynicism.

> **Hypothesis 6:** Ties outside the workgroup will interact with global social exchanges such that ties will moderate the relationship between global social exchanges and cognitive and affective variants of cynicism.

Consequences of Organizational Cynicism

As a brief review, we have thus far considered the theoretical rationale for cynicism's relationship to social exchange processes. We now turn our attention to answering our second research question—empirically relating organizational cynicism to meaningful organizational outcomes. While we could consider a multitude of organizational outcomes, in the interest of brevity, we restrict our consideration to a limited, but essential, set of organizational behaviors and attitudes. Namely, we focus on some time-tested constructs such as organizational commitment and organizational citizenship behaviors as well as contemporary behaviors such as employee involvement in empowerment initiatives.

Organizational Commitment

Organizational commitment has long been an important employee attitude for investigation. Organizational commitment is a bond between the individual and the organization that focuses on the relative strength of an individual's identification with and involvement in a particular organization. Conceptually, it is characterized by (a) a strong belief in and acceptance of the organization's goals and values, (b) a willingness to exert considerable effort on behalf of the organization, and (c) a strong desire to maintain organizational membership (Steers, 1977). Researchers have focused on the calculative aspects of commitment (Allen & Meyer, 1990; Meyer, Allen, & Gellatly, 1990; Meyer, Paunonen, Gellatly, Goffin, & Jackson, 1989; Meyer & Allen, 1984) and have led to the confirmation of the multifaceted nature of commitment. Meta-analyses show that organizationally committed members have better job performance, perceive fewer job alternatives, have lower intentions to look for other jobs and to leave their current job, and have reduced tardiness and turnover (Mathieu & Zajac, 1990).

The question becomes, how is organizational cynicism related to organizational commitment? Conceptually and definitionally, organizational commitment assumes that the goals and values of the organization are consistent and non-questionable. Committed employees are more likely to put in effort on behalf of the organization and have pride in their organization. They would also believe that their organization inspires them to perform to their very best and provides them with the conditions that facilitate this performance. Finally, organizationally committed employees are concerned with the fate of their organization. In turbulent times, as employees have begun to question corporate life, there have not only been more negativity and frustration in the workplace, but also a new way of perceiving the organization. In this dynamic operating environment, employees are more likely to perceive inconsistencies within their organization's policies, goals, and practices, making them call into question the integrity of their organizations. Employees may experience frustration and irritation with the pace of change within their organizations. They may be more likely to complain about, criticize, and mock organizational initiatives. Organizationally cynical employees are less likely to accept the organization's values and goals or exert effort on behalf of the organization as these thoughts and action would create too much dissonance in their minds (Festinger, 1957). Cynical employees may also be more likely to look for other occupational alternatives, but perceive too few opportunities, and therefore stay within their given environment.

Hypothesis 7: Affective and cognitive cynicism will be negatively related to organizational commitment.

In-Role Performance

Williams and Anderson (1991) attempted to separate an employee's performance of in-role activities as distinct from extra-role or citizenship behaviors. They suggest that in-role activities are those that have direct performance implications—those activities that are rewarded by the organizational reward systems and structures. These activities are typically aimed at effective role performance and include the regular duties, responsibilities, and tasks concerning the individual's job in the organization. In the past several years, organizational researchers have frequently focused on extra-role behaviors perhaps at the expense of understanding an employee's in-role performance. While extra-role behaviors are no doubt important, in-role behaviors are critical in achieving organizational goals. In addition, what have previously been termed "extra-role behaviors" such as working long hours, attending professional meetings, and keeping informed of the latest developments in one's field, have all now become part and parcel of management expectations regarding adequate employee in-role performance.

Other organizational attitudes have been previously shown to relate to employee in-role performance. For example, job satisfaction, a commonly researched organizational attitude, has frequently been cited as a small, but significant predictor of in-role performance (Saari & Judge, 2004). Similarly, because organizational cynicism has been defined previously as an attitude, we anticipate that both the affective and cognitive aspects of organizational cynicism would also relate to employees' in-role performance. In this paper, following the theoretical understanding of the concept of cynicism as a generally negative workplace behavior, we would assume that it would affect both the in-role and the extra-role behaviors of the employees. Here, we argue that employees who believe that their organizations lack integrity and who possess negative feelings toward the organization are less likely to be effective in their in-role responsibilities and duties, as opposed to those employees who experience less frustration and believe in their organization's integrity.

> **Hypothesis 8:** Affective and cognitive cynicism will be negatively related to employee in-role behavior.

Extra-Role Behavior

Extra-role behavior, often referred to as Organizational Citizenship Behavior, is another concept that has enjoyed prominence within organizational studies (Konovsky & Douglas, 1994; Wat & Shaffer, 2005). Typically, extra-role behaviors have been described as organizationally beneficial acts that go beyond role requirements (Organ, 1988). Specifically, extra-role behaviors are defined as work related behaviors that are discretionary, not related to formal organizational reward systems and, in the aggregate, promote the effective functioning of the organization (Organ, 1988). Extra-role behaviors have been suggested as important elements of performance as they are part of the spontaneous and innovative behaviors that are also essential for effective organizations (Katz & Kahn, 1966; cited in Moorman, 1991).

Generally we expect individuals who are more organizationally cynical to be less likely to perform the types of behaviors listed above. Performing acts that advance the organization's objectives would cause cognitive dissonance in the minds of organizational cynics. An organizationally cynical individual is unlikely to perform beyond formal requirements for an organization that she or he believes is lacking in integrity. Such employees would generally sneer or speak disparagingly about the organization or attempt to thwart organizational efforts. One could scarcely imagine high OCB scorers to engage in such behaviors. This is consistent with work by Van Dyne, Graham, and Dienesch (1994) who suggest that cynicism (about human nature in general) was negatively related to the organizational citizenship behaviors of loyalty, social participation, and functional participation. Furthermore, Andersson and Bateman (1997), in their scenario study of employee cynicism, found that cynicism about a fictional company and cynicism about business in general resulted in a subject's reports that they would be (hypothetically) less likely to perform certain types of extra-role behaviors.

Extra-role behaviors assessed from the perspective of the employee are more likely to be tainted by employee concerns for social desirability. In order to combat this effect, it is essential to use an external perspective in validating employee responses. As supervisors are typically in the best position to observe employee behaviors, we expect that supervisors will also report reduced extra-role behavior on the part of their more organizationally cynical subordinates.

Hypothesis 9: Affective and cognitive cynicism will be negatively related to both employee and supervisory assessments of employee extra-role behaviors.

Employee Involvement

The last employee behavior that we would like to explore as affected by cynicism is employee involvement. The term "employee involvement" covers a fairly broad range of organizational initiatives. Lawler's (1988) typology of employee involvement provides us with a fairly comprehensive categorization of these activities. He states that most employee involvement activities would fall under the three categories of suggestion involvement, job involvement, and high involvement. Suggestion involvement seeks to get employee input on work processes through problem solving and idea generation, with the goal of improving organizational effectiveness. Job involvement requires additional employee input through job enrichment, teamwork, and enhanced decision making responsibility. Finally, high involvement programs empower employees to the highest extent wherein employees can help set organizational priorities and strategies, as well as provide mechanisms for evaluation and distribution of rewards. Thus, the basic premise of employee involvement is that by allowing employees to make decisions over how their work is done, employee commitment to the organization, performance, and satisfaction can all be increased (Cotton, 1993). Although the effects of involving employees in decision making have met with mixed interpretations, results generally suggest that organizations do realize modest increases in productivity, motivation, and job satisfaction when employee involvement programs are present (Cotton, Vollrath, Froggatt, Lengnick-Hall, & Jennings, 1988; Wagner, 1994).

Unfortunately, employee involvement is often accompanied by the simultaneous use of downsizing, restructuring, and re-engineering efforts (Mirvis, 1997). As competition increases, companies are forced to cut costs, trim workforces, and improve operational efficiency. Employee involvement efforts are sometimes read by employees as yet another attempt to extract more and more from a reduced, overextended workforce. This problem can be compounded by top management's more symbolic (rather than real) use of employee involvement. As individuals who are organizationally cynical question the integrity of their organizations, they believe that the true reasons for decisions may be incompletely disclosed or are subject to self interest. Organizational cynics may doubt the sincerity or motives behind management requests for participation in employee involvement. Emotionally, organizational cynics may feel isolated from their organizations, or feel indifferent about their participation in programs that advance the organization's interest. They may be embittered or frustrated with having believed in the possibility and promise of change, just to be disappointed later. Having these beliefs and affect makes cynical employees unlikely volunteers and infrequent participants in employee involvement programs. In fact, within the practical world, cynicism has been suspected as a barrier to empowerment and organizational change (Early, 1991). Furthermore, we expect that supervisors will notice reduced employee involvement in programs among organizationally cynical subordinates.

> **Hypothesis 10**: Affective and cognitive cynicism will be negatively related to both employee self assessments as well as supervisory reports of employee involvement.

METHOD

Setting and Sample

Hypotheses were tested in a field study conducted in a middle sized manufacturing organization. The initial survey was sent to all 465 members of the organization and was introduced with a letter from the CEO that asked employees for their input. Surveys were sent to the home addresses of respondents, and respondents were provided with postage paid envelopes so that they could return the surveys directly to the researchers at the university. Participation was voluntary, and confidentiality was assured in a cover letter from the researchers. Each survey was identified with a code number known only to the researchers and was used for matching purposes in the second phase of data collection. The employee data collection yielded 264 usable surveys for a participation rate of 57%.

The second data collection followed a similar procedure. Because several of the hypotheses required data on a given employee's activities, we identified all 76 supervisors in the organization. Again, surveys were mailed to supervisors at their home address and were returned in postage-paid to the researchers at the university. In order to reduce the reporting burden on supervisors, the number of surveys sent to each supervisor was limited to 4. To further reduce the reporting burden, a few scales were shortened in the supervisory survey. The effort of the two surveys yielded 129 usable matched supervisor/employee pairs for an overall response rate of 28%.

Measures

Affective and cognitive cynicisms. We used scales based on the theoretical definition proposed by Dean et al. (1998). Specifically, affect items reflect dimensions of negative emotions such as distress-anguish, anger-rage, and disgust-revulsion, and were adapted to reflect negative feelings employees might have regarding their organization (Izard, 1977). Similarly, belief items reflect cognitive evaluations that employees have about the integrity and sincerity of their organizations (Dean et al., 1998; Goldner et al., 1977). Both the affective and cognitive scales have been used in Johnson and O'Leary-Kelly (2003); the cognitive scale has been used in Chrobot-Mason (2003). Anchors for the seven-point cognitive cynicism scale reflect the frequency (1 = never, 7 = always) with which the employee believes the company, "does what it says it will do," and, "the extent to which its policies, goals, and practices are in common." Anchors for the seven-point affective cynicism scale deal with the frequency (1 = never to 7 = always) with which the employee feels irritation, aggravation, tension, and anxiety when thinking about their employing organization.

Outcome Variables

Organizational Commitment. This construct was measured using the Organizational Commitment Questionnaire by Mowday, Steers, and Porter (1979). Higher values reflect more attachment to the organization and more convergence with its goals.

In-role Performance. In-role performance was measured using the scale suggested by Williams and Anderson (1991). All six items were scored on a 7-point scale ranging from 1 = never to 7 = always. High scores reflected that the employee meets requirements and fulfills the responsibilities of the job. Full items for this and the following three constructs appear in Brandes et al. (2004).

Extra-role Performance. This construct was measured by the scale suggested by Williams and Anderson (1991). High scores on this reflected the supervisor's claims that his/her direct report takes on additional responsibilities, helps overburdened cohorts, volunteers for overtime and in general, exhibits behavior that can be termed as organizational citizenship. All the seven items were scored on a 7-point scale ranging from 1 = never to 7 = always.

Employee Involvement. This construct was measured by using a four-item scale suggested by Vance, Brooks, and Tesluk (1996). It assesses the supervisor's evaluation of the employee's engagement in company empowerment activities. The items were scored on a 7-point scale from 1 = strongly disagree to 7 = strongly agree.

Independent Variables

Leader Member Exchange. This construct was measured using the LMX-7 as recommended in Graen and Uhl-Bien's (1995) review article of the development of this construct. High scores on this scale reflect employee-supervisor relationships characterized by high levels of trust, respect, and mutual obligation. Supervisory assessments of leader-member exchange were also collected, but it is the direct report's assessment that is most relevant to most organizational research. Full items for the leader-member exchange scale and the following social exchange scales appear in Brandes et al. (2004).

Ties Outside Workgroup. This construct was developed adapting items from Granovetter (1973) and Mansour-Cole (1994). They assess the quality of interactions of employees with other employees within the organization but in different work groups. High scores on this scale reflect the willingness and motivation of the employees to form bonds with employees outside their departments. The items were scaled on a 7-point Likert scale with 1= strongly disagree to 7= strongly agree.

Perceived Organizational Support. This scale was taken from Settoon et al. (1996). Items in this scale reflect the extent to which an organization's management assists employees in carrying out their day to day activities and the extent to which management is concerned with employees' well-being, goals, and achievements. High values on this scale suggest that the respondent perceives a company's management as cognizant and supportive of the employee's goals and objectives.

Trust in Senior Staff. This scale was developed based on Robinson (1996) as well as theoretical work done by Tyler and Degoey (1996). Items in this scale reflect an employee's perceptions of the competency and integrity of an organization's executive leadership. High values suggest that employees have much faith in the company's executives. Employees were told that the senior staff of their employing organization included the company's six vice-presidents, the CEO, and the controller.

Controls

In order to assess the role of dispositional or trait-based cynicism, Wrightsman's Philosophies of Human Nature subscale (called "cynicism") was also included (Wrightsman, 1991). High values on this scale reflect beliefs that others are selfish and uncaring and cannot be trusted. In addition to personality cynicism, we also controlled for gender, department, time worked with supervisor, as well as tenure with the organization.

RESULTS

Analyses

Confirmatory factor analysis (Gerbing & Anderson, 1988) for all scales suggested unidimensional constructs with excellent reliabilities. Next, we considered descriptive statistics and zero-order correlations that are reported in Table 9.1. Finally, we used hierarchical regression analysis to test the hypotheses. In order to test Hypotheses 1-6, we entered the control variables in the first block, and used the social exchange theory variables in the second (global exchanges) and the third blocks (local exchanges), followed by centered interaction terms in the fourth block (tests of Hypotheses 5 and 6). To test Hypotheses 7 and 8, we entered the control variables in the first block, and included cynical affect and cognition variables in the second. In addition, we conducted change in R-squared tests to detect significant difference in models' explanatory power. Results are explained for the most parsimonious model that added statistically more variance.

Response Biases

We checked for several sources of possible non-response bias. Women participated in the survey at almost the same rate as their male counterparts (59.5% women, 56% men). A chi-square test confirmed that the divisional representation of our sample was similar to that of the organization at large. Furthermore, t-tests between the supervisory-rated performance of the sample of 129 subjects were compared with the performance of individuals for which we had supervisory data (but no accompanying employee-provided data); all these results showed no inherent differences between the two groups.

Controls

Although not the major focus of our study, it is interesting to note that personality cynicism often did affect the dependent variables, but was largely marginalized once other social exchange variables were included. Effects of years with supervisor as well as organizational tenure diminished once other social exchanges were included. The same can largely be said of gender, with the exception of affective cynicism where gender remained a strong predictor even when other social exchanges were included.

Test of Hypotheses

We ran hierarchical linear regression models to test our hypotheses. Results are listed for the preferred model (i.e., the one with that added a significant change in R-squared, or, Step 2 for the cognitive cynicism model, and Step 4 for the affective cynicism model). Hypothesis 1, which postulated that Perceived Organizational Support (POS) would be nega-

Table 9.1. Means, Standard Deviations, Scale Reliabilities, and Intercorrelations Among Variables

Variables	Mean	S.D.	1	2	3	4	5	6	7	8	9	10	11	12	13	14	15	16
1. Cognitive cynicism	3.22	1.22	(.86)															
2. Affective cynicism	4.18	1.07	.52***	(.80)														
3. In role performance (supervisor ratings)	5.59	0.97	-.10	-.03	(.93)													
4. Extra role performance (supervisor ratings)	4.73	1.08	-.02	.19*	.70***	(.91)												
5. Employee involvement (supervisor ratings)	3.74	1.60	-.08	.10	.38***	.57***	(.93)											
6. Organizational commitment (self report)	5.40	0.94	-.53***	-.37***	.21*	.10	.13	(.89)										
7. Organizational citizenship behaviors (self report)	5.51	0.99	-.12	.05	.07	.17*	.10	.48***	(.85)									
8. Employee involvement (self report)	4.45	1.28	-.25**	-.16†	.22*	.25**	.50***	.44***	.48***	(.87)								

Variable	Mean	SD	1	2	3	4	5	6	7	8	9	10	11	12	13	14	15	16
9. Years with supervisor	2.37	2.56	.04	.00	.08	.09	.04	.04	-.05	.04	(1.00)							
10. Years with company	3.88	2.06	.25**	.22*	-.02	.05	-.06	-.14	-.05	-.02	-.07	(1.00)						
11. Gender	0.86	0.35	-.18*	-.29**	.01	-.10	-.14	.10	-.16†	.10	.27*	.15†	(1.00)					
12. Personality cynicism	3.18	1.15	.23**	.08	-.06	-.07	-.20*	-.16†	-.22*	-.19*	.10	.14	.10	(.91)				
13. Perceived organizational support	4.48	1.18	-.56***	-.33***	.30**	.14†	.17†	.60***	.25**	.40***	.08	-.20*	.18*	-.29**	(.92)			
14. Trust in top management	4.64	1.29	-.65***	-.42***	.08	-.02	.18*	.59***	.28**	.38***	.05	-.28**	.10	-.34***	.66***	(.92)		
15. Leader member exchange	4.85	1.23	.51***	.33***	.38***	.38***	.23**	.28**	.14†	.21*	.16†	-.08	.06	-.20*	.51***	.33***	(.93)	
16. Social ties	5.24	.96	-.16†	.09	.22*	.27*	.23*	.21*	.31***	.35***	-.14	.01	-.05	-.08	.16†	.10	.17*	(.80)

Table 9.2. Hierarchical Regression Models for Cognitive and Affective Cynicism

Predictor	Cognitive Cynicism				Affective Cynicism			
	Step 1	Step 2	Step 3	Step 4	Step 1	Step 2	Step 3	Step 4
Controls								
Personality	.25**	.05	.05	.05	.06	-.07	-.06	-.05
Cynicism								
Gender	-.30**	-.12	.13	-.09	-.38***	-.27**	-.25*	-.21*
Yrs with supervisor	-.12	.01	.00	.01	-.03	.06	.08	.13
Yrs with company	.25**	.04	.06	.04	.31**	.18†	.16	.15
Global Exchanges								
Perceived organizational support (POS)		-.23*	-.23*	-.28*		-.10	-.16	-.24†
Trust in top management (TRUST)		-.44***	-.44***	-.42***		-.31**	-.31**	-.30**
Local Exchanges								
(LMX)			.04	.05			.04	.00
Social Ties (TIES)			-.07	-.07			.12	.14
Interactions								
LMX * POS				.07				.00
LMX * TRUST				-.11				-.22†
TIES * POS				.03				.07
TIES * TRUST				.10				.12
Adj. R^2	.19	.45	.45	.44	.13	.22	.22	.26
R^2	.24	.50	.50	.52	.19	.29	.30	.35
ΔR^2 over last step	.25***	.25***	.00	.01	.10***	.10***	.02	.05†

[a]Coefficients provided are standardized; † $p < .09$, * $p < .05$, ** $p < .001$, *** $p < .0001$.
Dummy codes for respondent's division are included but not reported for brevity.

Table 9.3. Hierarchical Regression Models for Employees' Self-Reported Organizational Commitment, Citizenship Behaviors and Employee Involvement

	Organizational Commitment		Extra Role Performance		Employee Involvement	
	Step 1	Step 2	Step 1	Step 2	Step 1	Step 2
Personality cynicism	-.15	-.03	-.21*	-.16*	-.16*	-.12
Gender	-.21†	.03	-.22*	-.23*	.22*	.19
Yrs with supervisor	.12	.06	-.09	-.11	.00	-.03
Yrs with company	-.18*	-.03	-.05	-.04	-.11	-.06
Cognitive cynicism		-.45***		-.21†		-.23†
Affective cynicism		-.13		.14		.05
Adj. R^2	.03	.25	.07	.09	.00	-.01
R^2	.10	.31	.14	.18	.08	.08
ΔR^2		.21***		.04		.00

Coefficients provided are standardized; † $p < .09$, * $p < .05$, ** $p < .001$, *** $p < .0001$.
Dummy codes for respondent's division are included but not reported for brevity.

Table 9.4. Hierarchical Regression Models for Supervisor's Assessment of Employees' in Role and Extra Role Performance, and Employee Involvement

	In Role Performance		Extra Role Performance		Employee Involvement	
	Step 1	Step 2	Step 1	Step 2	Step 1	Step 2
Personality cynicism	-.03	-.02	-.06	-.04	-.15†	-.14
Gender	.07	.06	-.09	-.03	.00	.03
Yrs with supervisor	.08	.08	.06	.05	.13	.13
Yrs with company	.01	.02	.07	.02	-.02	-.05
Cognitive cynicism		-.03		-.14		-.08
Affective cynicism		.00		.26*		.16
Adj. R^2	.07	.09	-.03	.00	.08	.08
R^2	.14	.18	.04	.08	.14	.16
ΔR^2		.04		.04†		.02

[a]Coefficients provided are standardized; † $p < .09$, * $p < .05$, ** $p < .001$, *** $p < .0001$.
Dummy codes for respondent's division are included but not reported for brevity.

Organizational Cynicism 213

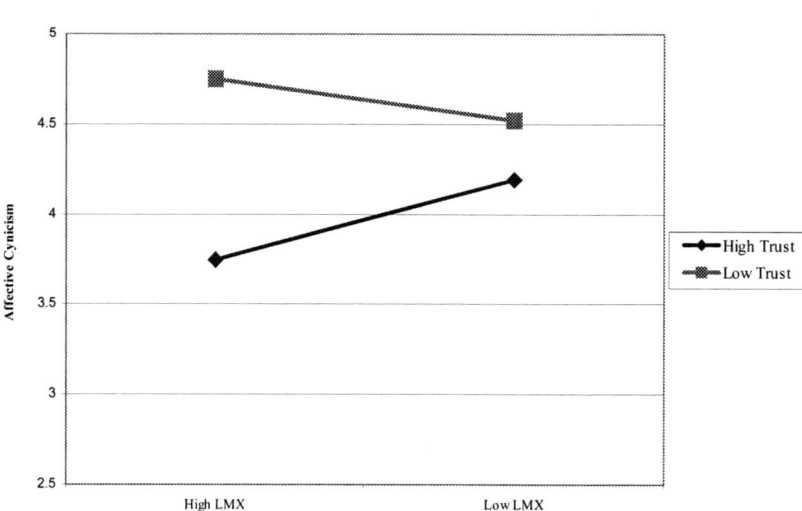

Figure 9.1. The interactive effect of LMX and trust in top management on affective cynicism.

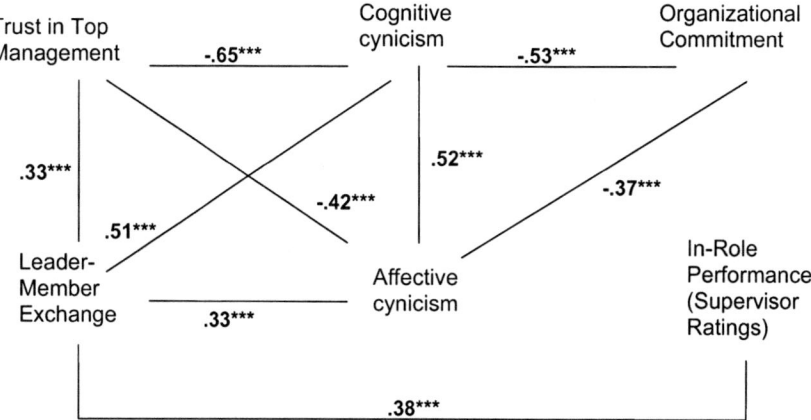

Figure 9.2. Overview of bivariate relationships between local social exchanges, cynicisms, and employee performance.

tively associated with cognitive and affective cynicism was supported. Specifically, POS was negatively associated with cognitive cynicism (ß = -.23, p < .05, step 2, Table 9.2) but only marginally related to affective cynicism (ß = -.24, p < .10, step 4, Table 9.2).

Hypothesis 2, which postulated that trust in senior staff would be negatively associated with cognitive and affective cynicism, was supported. Specifically trust in senior staff was negatively associated with cognitive cynicism (ß = -.44, p < .0001) and was negatively associated with affective cynicism (ß = -.30, p < .001).

Hypothesis 3, which postulated that Leader-Member Exchange (LMX) would be negatively associated with cognitive and affective cynicism, was not supported. Specifically LMX was not significantly associated with cognitive cynicism. Hypothesis 4, which predicted that both cognitive and affective cynicism would be positively related to ties outside the work group was also not supported.

Among the interactive effects, Hypothesis 5 was marginally supported. Namely, LMX quality interacted with the global exchange variable trust in senior management (ß = -.22, p < .10, Step 4, Table 9.2). A figure of this interaction delineates this relationship (See Figure 9.1). Although the interaction is marginally significant, the difference between extreme means are significant. Post hoc t-tests of means showed that the affective cynicism mean for high LMX and high trust were significantly lower than the affective cynicism mean for high LMX and low trust (Mean$_{\text{high lmx, high trust}}$ = 3.75, Mean$_{\text{high lmx, low trust}}$ = 4.80, t = 4.608, p <. 001), indicating how trust moderates the impact of LMX on affective cynicism. Hypothesis 6, which suggested that ties outside the work group would moderate the relationship between global ties and cynicism, was not supported.

We now turn our attention to the hypotheses related to our second research question regarding the outcomes of cynicism. Again, we focus on the results only for models in which adding the independent variables over the controls were associated with significant changes in R-squared (Tables 9.3 and 9.4). Hypothesis 7, which postulated that cognitive and affective cynicism would be negatively associated with organizational commitment, was supported for cognitive but not for affective cynicism. Specifically, cognitive cynicism was negatively associated with organizational commitment (ß = -.45, p < . 0001, step 2 Table 9.3) but affective cynicism was not significantly associated with organizational commitment.

Hypothesis 8 which postulated that cognitive and affective cynicism would be negatively associated with supervisors assessments of their direct reports' in-role performance was not supported for both measures of cynicism. Adding the effects of cognitive and affective cynicism provided no incremental increase in R-squared (Table 9.4).

Hypothesis 9 which postulated that cognitive and affective cynicism would be negatively associated with both employee and supervisory ratings of extra role performance was not supported, and an unexpected positive coefficient occurred. Specifically, affective cynicism was positively related with supervisors' assessments of extra role performance (ß = .26, $p < .05$, step 2, Table 9.4) but neither cognitive nor affective cynicisms added any incremental explanation of self-reported extra-role behavior beyond the controls.

Finally, Hypothesis 10, which suggested that the cynicisms would predict employee involvement in improvement efforts was not supported for either the self-report data or the supervisory data (Tables 9.3 and 9.4).

DISCUSSION

The results of the study are noteworthy for several reasons. First, the findings suggest that both trust in top management and perceived organizational support are powerful predictors of cognitive cynicism, and that trust in top management is also a significant predictor of affective cynicism. Our results also indicate that global social exchange variables are generally more powerful predictors of cynicism than local social exchanges. That being said, trust in top management does interact with LMX to produce an effect on affective cynicism. Finally, cognitive cynicism seems to affect one's organizational commitment. However, cognitive and affective cynicisms have little affect on employees' and supervisors' assessments of extra-role performance and support of employee involvement activities. We discuss these findings in detail.

Predictors of Organizational Cynicism

Among the four social exchange variables' correlations with the two cynicisms, trust in senior staff had the largest coefficient of correlation ($r = -.65$, $r = -.42$, all $p < .0001$ for cynical belief and affect respectively). Similarly, perceived organizational support was more moderately correlated with the dimensions of cynicism ($r = -.56$, $r = -.33$, $p < .0001$ for cynical belief and affect respectively). These correlations suggest that employee assessments of the organization are more influenced by impressions of senior staff trustworthiness and perceived organizational support than dyadic relations with one's supervisor. In other words, more generalized variants of social exchange explain more variation in organizational cynicism, versus more localized, dyadic relations with one's supervisor or other social ties. In the case of cognitive cynicism, global social exchanges explained significantly more variance than the controls in predicting cognitive and affective cynicisms.

Specifically, trust in an organization's senior staff was a stronger predictor of cognitive and affective cynicism than perceived organizational support. Previous research (Robinson, 1996) found that initial trust in one's employer influenced subsequent trust. For example, employees with high initial trust were less likely to experience a decline in trust, even after some implicit contract violations of the social exchange happened between the employee and the organization. We suggest that employees with high trust in senior staff are more likely to overlook issues that engender organizational cynicism, and thereby give senior staff members the benefit of the doubt. In addition, not all employees were willing to generalize across all senior staff members. Two employees suggested the following in an open-ended section of the survey.

> I don't feel that all senior staff can be stereotyped. Some are great, some are not.... It is difficult and unfair to evaluate senior staff as a whole. Misgivings about one or more members of senior staff will skew the ratings.

Thus the important issue seems to be that employees in this organization were normally cognizant of the senior staff in general, but may have had differing evaluations of specific members. Perhaps due to the company's moderate size, employees had some basic interactions with senior staff and sized them up accordingly. The findings suggest that the more trust employees have in senior staff, the less likely are they to be organizationally cynical.

Perceived organizational support was also instrumental in predicting employee beliefs. In fact, perceived organizational support refers to employee *beliefs* that the organization values his/her contributions and well-being. Most employees of the organization believed that the company provided moderate support for employees (mean = 4.48, std. = 1.18). These generalized beliefs about social exchange with one's organization are more likely to influence other evaluations based on beliefs and affect.

Finally, leader-member exchange or ties with other work groups were not related to organizational cynicism in a direct effect sense as judged by the significant interaction. In the case of leader-member exchange, employees were asked to evaluate the effectiveness of their working relationship with their supervisor. For example, items in the LMX scale asked employees "How would you characterize your working relationship with your supervisor?" or "How well does your supervisor recognize your potential?" In perceived organizational support, the questions focused on managers' concern and care of employees. As mentioned earlier, this is a more global assessment of the social exchange relationship. However, in the case of leader-member exchange, most employees have regular interactions with their supervisors that they may not have with managers or top management as a group. Thus, information gained from supervisor-subordinate relationships is distinctly different from the information gained from other groups. Evidently, a specific assessment of one's relationship with a supervisor does not generalize to one's assessment of the organization in a global sense.

However, when one's relationship with senior staff, taken in tandem with the quality of one's relationship with supervisors is considered, their ability to predict affective cynicism is greater than these variables considered alone. Namely, as previously suggested, high quality supervisory relationships, when combined with high quality social exchanges with senior staff, are best at reducing cynicism levels. Yet, low quality relationships with supervisors with simultaneously low quality relationships with senior staff created no less affective cynicism than mixed quality social exchanges. In other words, high quality relationships with senior staff are a good start for staving off cynicism, and that both high quality relationships with senior staff and with one's immediate supervisor are even better.

Work Outcomes and Organizational Cynicism

Organizational commitment was defined earlier based on the classic work of Porter, Steers, Mowday, and Boullian (1974) as the amount of goal congruence between the individual employee and their organization and the employee's resulting willingness to put in effort on behalf of the organization, and continue membership in it. Because organizationally cynical individuals were expected to question the organization's integrity and its values, as well as experience negative feelings, it was hypothesized that organizational cynicism would have a negative influence on organizational commitment.

Both the correlation coefficient and the standardized regression coefficient illustrate the negative relationship between organizational commitment and cognitive cynicism. This result implies that organizationally cynical employees tend to have lower levels of organizational commitment, may experience conflict with organizational goals, and may be more likely to leave their employing organization. This finding is important due to the indirect effects that cynicism could have on work outcomes (such as turnover, absenteeism, and productivity) that have been related to organizational commitment.

However, both affective and cognitive cynicism had no statistically significant effect on supervisors' reports of employees' in-role performance, nor on employees' willingness to engage in employee involvement and empowerment activities. Our results differ from that of Johnson and O'Leary-Kelly (2003), who found that an employee's in-role performance was negatively correlated (i.e., $r = -.21$, $p < .05$) with affective organizational cynicism. Johnson and O'Leary-Kelly (2003) found no linear relationship between cynicism (either affective or cognitive) and organizational citizenship behavior or in-role performance. In contrast, supervisors in our study noted MORE extra-role performance among those employees who were affectively cynical. A possible explanation is that employees who engage in excessive extra-role behaviors may feel overworked or underappreciated by their employers. Continually helping one's colleagues over and above one's expected in-role duties may contribute to feelings of irritation, aggravation, anxiety, and tension, which may eventually be turned toward one's employing organization.

LIMITATIONS AND FUTURE DIRECTIONS

While we believe that our findings should be viewed in the light of the specific organizational setting, we contend that the market experience of this organization is common to many other manufacturing organizations. Midwest Manufacturing was part of a highly dynamic, high-technology market, which faced major industry consolidation over the last two decades. Several employees remarked how multiple, recent initiatives (including employee involvement and information technology changes) had affected their workloads as well as their work priorities. An employee remarked:

> We are doing too many initiatives at the same time. I tracked many hours on a project that was not part of my core job. This issue is not being addressed corporately or divisionally.

Compared to many other studies, this study has the same limitations of being in one industry and one firm. In addition, we did not have access to complete performance, absenteeism, or turnover data.

It should also be noted that many of the results reported in Tables 9.3 and 9.4 (those measuring the effect of cynicism on work behaviors) were extremely close to significance, such that although the signs of the coefficients were appropriate, the associated p-values were less than .15 but were greater than .10. A more rigorous design and larger sample may have helped.

Another possibility for the largely null results regarding cynicism's contributions to in-role, extra-role, and employee involvement behaviors is that these relationships are actually nonlinear. For example, the relationship could best be described by an inverted "U" such that too little cynicism and its probing and questioning is related to poor performance, moderate levels are associated with optimal performance, but high levels are associated with unproductive critiques that reduce performance.

Future research in organizational cynicism might involve several different aspects. First, while supervisory data helped reduce the bias of self-report, future studies should try to enlist co-worker reports of employee behavior. However, this must be done in a tactful and nonthreatening manner. Supervisors are a good information source regarding employee work behaviors, but as more organizations move to team based structures, a more complete understanding of organizational cynicism might come from understanding how co-workers perceived their colleagues' behaviors. Additionally, we may want to relate organizational cynicism to other more specific, yet diverse, measures of employee performance.

In practical terms, we suggest that organizations' top managements should be particularly concerned about the implications of high quality leader-member exchanges. Time and again, research has demonstrated high quality leadership relationships are characterized by trust, respect, and mutual obligation between supervisors and followers. High quality relationships provide followers with better quality information about the state of affairs in organizations. These relationships may empower subordinates to make more helpful suggestions regarding organizational priorities. In addition, high quality leadership relationships have been shown to relate positively to employee performance, and can be a good source of information for making organizational improvement efforts (See Figure 9.2, a quick overview of the bivariate correlations).

However, being more knowledgeable of organizational priorities may either stave off cynicism by clarifying the motives of others, or actually enable cynicism by providing insights into a possible lack of integrity regarding managements' actions. Clearly, as our analysis indicates, high quality leader-member exchanges, in conjunction with high trust in top management, are associated with the lowest levels of cynicism. This reflects that when trust in top management is also high, the information gathered through high quality relationships can indeed stave off cynicism. High quality relationships in climates where senior leadership is trustworthy may provide a chance for both leaders and followers to let down their guard and "blow off steam" in a functional manner, thereby providing temporary, healthy distancing from organizational ambiguities that engender cynicism (e.g., Meyerson, 1990).

On the other hand, high quality relationships formed in a climate where employees place low trust in senior management is associated with greater levels of organizational cynicism. In fact, we find that employees are more cynical when they have good relationships with their supervisors and negative attitudes toward top management, indicating that information gained from this social exchange increases cynicism in low-trust organizational contexts. In practical terms, high quality exchanges may be a double-edged sword—when senior leadership is trustworthy with high LMX, we find lower cynicism; however, when senior leadership is untrustworthy, we find higher cynicism. In conclusion, our research indicates that both global and local leadership relationships may be important in shaping organizational cynicism.

REFERENCES

Allen, N. J., & Meyer, J. P. (1990). The measurement and antecedents of affective, continuance and normative commitment to the organization. *Journal of Occupational Psychology, 63*, 1-18.

Andersson, L., & Bateman, T. S. (1997). Cynicism in the work place: Some causes and effects. *Journal of Organizational Behavior, 18*, 449-470.

Blau, P. (1964). *Exchange and power in social life*. New York: Wiley.

Brandes, P., Dharwadkar, R., & Wheatley, K. (2004). Social exchanges within organizations and work outcomes: The importance of local and global relationships. *Group and Organization Management, 29*, 276-302.

Brockner, J., Siegel, P. A., Daly, J. P., Tyler, T., & Martin, C. (1997). When trust matters: The moderating effect of outcome favorability. *Administrative Science Quarterly, 42*, 558-583.

Byrne, J. A. (2002, August 26). After Enron: The ideal corporation following the abuses of the '90s, executives are learning that trust, integrity, and fairness do matter—and are crucial to the bottom line. *Business Week, 3796*, 68.

Chrobot-Mason, D. L. (2003). Keeping the promise: Psychological contract violations for minority employees. *Journal of Managerial Psychology, 18*, 22-46.

Cook, K. S. (1982). Network structures from an exchange perspective. In P. V. Marsden & N. Lin (Eds.), *Social structure and network analysis* (pp. 177-199). Beverly Hills, CA: Sage.

Cotton, J. L. (1993). *Employee involvement*. Beverly Hills, CA: Sage.

Cotton, J. L., Vollrath, K. L., Froggatt, M. L., Lengnick-Hall, M. L., & Jennings, K. R. (1988). Employee participation: Diverse forms and different outcomes. *Academy of Management Review, 1*, 8-22.

Coyle-Shapiro, J. A. M., & Conway, N. (2005). Exchanges relationships: Examining psychological contracts and perceived organizational support. *Journal of Applied Psychology, 90*, 774-781.

Davis, W. D., & Gardner, W. L. (2004). Perceptions of politics and organizational cynicism: An attributional and leader-member exchange perspective. *The Leadership Quarterly, 15,* 439-465.

Dean, J., Brandes, P., & Dharwadkar, R. (1998). Organizational cynicism. *Academy of Management Review, 23,* 341-352.

Eagly, A. H., & Chaiken, S. (1993). *The psychology of attitudes.* Fort Worth, TX: Harcourt Brace Jovanovich.

Early, V. (1991). Empowering organizations. *Executive Excellence, 8,* 13-14.

Eisenberger, R., Huntington, R., Hutchison, S., & Sowa, D. (1986). Perceived organizational support. *Journal of Applied Psychology, 71,* 500-507.

Festinger, L. (1957). *A theory of cognitive dissonance.* Stanford, CA: Stanford University Press.

Gerbing, D. W., & Anderson, J. C. (1988). An updated paradigm for scale development incorporating unidimensionality and its assessment. *Journal of Marketing Research, 25,* 186-192.

Gerstner, C. R., & Day, D. V. (1997). Meta-analytic review of leader-member exchange theory: Correlates and construct issues. *Journal of Applied Psychology, 82,* 827-844.

Goldner, F. H., Ritti, R. R., & Ference, T. P. (1977). The production of cynical knowledge in organizations. *American Sociological Review, 42,* 539-551.

Gouldner, A. W. (1960). The norm of reciprocity: A preliminary statement. *American Sociological Review, 25,* 161-179.

Graen, G. B., & Uhl-Bien, M. (1991). The transformation of professionals into self-managing and partially self-designing contributions: Toward a theory of leader-making. *Journal of Management Systems, 3,* 49-54.

Graen, G. B., & Uhl-Bien, M. (1995). Development of leader-member exchange (LMX) theory of leadership over 25 years: Applying a multi-level multi-domain perspective. *Leadership Quarterly, 6,* 219-247.

Granovetter, M. (1973). The strength of weak ties. *American Journal of Sociology, 78,* 1360-1380.

Hosmer, L. (1995). Trust: The connecting link between organizational theory and philosophical ethics. *Academy of Management Review, 20,* 379-403.

Izard, C. E. (1977). *Human emotions.* New York: Plenum Press.

Johnson, J., & O'Leary-Kelly, A. (2003). The effects of psychological contract breach and organizational cynicism: Not all social exchange violations are created equal. *Journal of Organizational Behavior, 24,* 627-647.

Katz, D., & Kahn, R. L. (1966). *The social psychology of organizations.* New York: Wiley.

Kissler, G. D. (1994). The new employment contract. *Human Resource Management, 33,* 335-353.

Konovsky, M.A., & Douglas, P.S. (1994). Citizenship behavior and social exchange. *Academy of Management Journal, 37,* 656-669.

Krackhardt, D. (1992). The strength of strong ties: The importance of philos in organizations. In R. Eccles & N. Nohria (Eds.), *Networks and organizations: Structure, form, and action* (pp. 216-239). Cambridge, MA: Harvard Business School Press.

Krackhardt, D., & Hanson, J. R. (1993). Informal networks: The company behind the chart. *Harvard Business Review, 71*, 104-111.

Krackhardt, D., & Brass, D. (1994). Intraorganizational networks: The micro side. In S. Wasserman & J. Galaskiewicz (Eds.), *Advances in network analysis* (pp. 207-229). Thousand Oaks, CA: Sage.

Lawler, E. E. (1988). Choosing an involvement strategy. *Academy of Management Executive, 2*, 195-205.

Mansour-Cole, D. (1994). *Reactions to one's lot: Exploring individual and group influences on perceptions of justice following an organizational transition.* Unpublished doctoral dissertation, University of Cincinnati.

Mathieu, J. E., & Zajac, D. M. (1990). A review and meta-analysis of the antecedents, correlates, and consequences of organizational commitment. *Psychological Bulletin, 108*, 171-194.

Mayer, R. C., & Davis, J. H. (1999). The effect of performance appraisal system on trust for management: A field quasi-experiment. *Journal of Applied Psychology, 84*, 123-136.

Mayer, R. C., Davis, J. H., & Schoorman, F. D. (1995). An integrative model of organizational trust. *Academy of Management Review, 20*, 709-734.

Meyer, J. P., & Allen, N. J. (1984). Testing the side bet theory of organizational commitment: Some methodological considerations. *Journal of Applied Psychology, 69*, 372-378.

Meyer, J. P., Allen, N. J., & Gellatly, I. R. (1990). Affective and continuance commitment to the organization: Evaluation of measures and analysis of concurrent and time-lagged relations. *Journal of Applied Psychology, 75*, 710-720.

Meyer, J. P., Paunonen, S. V., Gellatly, I. R., Goffin, R. D., & Jackson, D. N. (1989). Organizational commitment and job performance: It's the nature of the commitment that counts. *Journal of Applied Psychology, 74*, 152-156.

Meyerson, D. E. (1990). Uncovering socially undesirable emotions: experiences of ambiguity in organizations. *The American Behavioral Scientist, 33*(3), 296-307.

Mirvis, P. H. (1997). Human resource management: Leaders, laggards, and followers. *Academy of Management Executive, 11*, 43-56.

Mishra, A. K., & Spreitzer, G. M. (1998). Explaining how survivors respond to downsizing: The role of trust, empowerment, justice, and work redesign. *Academy of Management Review, 23*, 567-588.

Moorman, R. H. (1991). Relationship between organizational justice and organizational citizenship behaviors: Do fairness perceptions influence employee citizenship? *Journal of Applied Psychology, 76*, 845-855.

Moorman, R. H., Blakely, G. L., & Niehoff, P. B. (1998). Does perceived organizational support mediate the relationship between procedural justice and organizational citizenship behavior? *Academy of Management Journal, 41*, 351-357.

Mowday, R. T., Steers, R. M., & Porter, L. W. (1979). The measurement of organizational commitment. *Journal of Vocational Behavior, 14*, 224-247.

Organ, D. W. (1988). *Organizational citizenship behavior: The "good soldier" syndrome.* Lexington, MA: Lexington Books.

Pellet, J. (2002). Trust in an age of doubt. *Chief Executive, 180*, 60-67.

Porter, L. W., Steers, R. M., Mowday, R. T., & Boullian, P. V. (1974). Organizational commitment, job satisfaction, and turnover among psychiatric technicians. *Journal of Applied Psychology, 59,* 465-476.

Pugh, S. D., Skarlicki, D. P., & Passell, B. S. (2003). After the fall: Layoff victims' trust and cynicism in re-employment. *Journal of Occupational and Organizational Psychology, 76,* 201-212.

Rhoades L., & Eisenberger, R. (2002). Perceived organizational support: A review of the literature. *Journal of Applied Psychology, 87,* 698-714.

Robinson, S. L. (1996). Trust and breach of the psychological contract. *Administrative Science Quarterly, 41,* 574-599.

Saari, L. M., & Judge, T. M. (2004). Employee attitudes and job satisfaction. *Human Resource Management, 43,* 395-408.

Settoon, R. P., Bennett, N., & Liden, R. C. (1996). Social exchange in organizations: Perceived organizational support, leader-member exchange, and employee reciprocity. *Journal of Applied Psychology, 81,* 219-227.

Sonnenberg, F. K. (1991). Internal communication: Turning talk into action. *Journal of Business Strategy 12,* 52-55.

Steers, R. M. (1977). Antecedents and outcomes of organizational commitment. *Administrative Science Quarterly, 22,* 46-60.

Stewart, T. (1996, June 10). Why value statements don' work? *Fortune, 133*(11), 137-138.

Tsui, A. S. & Wu, J. B. (2005). The new employment relationship versus the mutual investment approach: Implications for human resource management. *Human Resource Management, 44,* 115-122.

Tyler, T. R., & Degoey, P. (1996). Trust in organizational authorities: The influence of motive attributions on willingness to accept decisions. In R. M. Kramer & T. R. Tyler (Eds.), *Trust in organizations: Frontiers of theory and research* (pp. 331-356). Thousand Oaks, CA: Sage.

Van Dyne, L., Graham, J. W., & Dienesch, R. M. (1994). Organizational citizenship behavior: Construct redefinition, measurement, and validation. *Academy of Management Journal, 37,* 765-802.

Vance, R. J., Brooks, S. M., & Tesluk, P. E. (1996). *Organizational cynicism, cynical cultures, and organizational change.* Working Paper, Pennsylvania State University.

Vogl, A. (1995). A future without jobs. *Across the Board, 32,* 42-46.

Wagner, III, J. A. (1994). Participation's effect on effort and performance: A reconsideration of research evidence. *Academy of Management Review, 19,* 312-320.

Wat, D., & Shaffer, M. A. (2005). Equity and relationship quality influences on organizational citizenship behaviors: The mediating role of trust in the supervisor and empowerment. *Personnel Review, 34,* 406-425.

Wayne, S. J., Shore, L. M., & Liden, R. C. (1997). Perceived organizational support and leader member exchange: A social exchange perspective. *Academy of Management Journal, 40,* 82-111.

Williams, L. J., & Anderson, S. E. (1991). Job satisfaction and organizational commitment as predictors of organizational citizenship and in-role behaviors. *Journal of Management, 17,* 601-617.

Wrightsman, L. S. (1991). Interpersonal trust and attitudes toward human nature. In J. P. Robinson, P. R. Shaver, & L. S. Wrightsman (Eds.), *Measures of personality and social psychological attitudes* (pp. 373-411). San Diego, CA: Academic Press.

CHAPTER 10

LEADER-MEMBER EXCHANGE AND SOLIDARITY BEHAVIOR

A Study of Reciprocity and Performance

B. Schyns, B. Kroon, and K. Sanders

The topic of this paper is the relationship between several different concepts that come from different theoretical backgrounds but refer to the same idea, namely, the reciprocal relationship between different actors within organizations. The concepts involved in this study are Leader-Member Exchange, Team-Member Exchange, as well as vertical and horizontal solidarity behavior. The results of our study indicate that the concepts are empirically differentiable, but are all related to team performance. This means that reciprocal relationships in organizations are definitely worth promoting.

INTRODUCTION

In this chapter, we will take a closer look at four concepts, namely, Leader-Member Exchange, Team-Member Exchange and horizontal and vertical solidarity behavior. Although all of these concepts refer either to the interaction between followers, and the interaction between leaders and followers, they originate from two totally different theoretical backgrounds. Leader-Member-Exchange (LMX) research is based on leadership theories and is a response to the critique that many approaches falsely assume that leaders show one and the same leadership style toward each follower. Team-Member Exchange (TMX) has been derived from LMX and focuses on the average relationship an individual follower has with his/her team. The final concepts, horizontal and vertical solidarity behavior, were developed in the context of a more typical European focus on the group, and stem from solidarity theories dealing with helping behavior in organizations.

Although the approaches that are being focused on in this paper have different theoretical backgrounds, they all refer to the norm of reciprocity in exchange processes within organizations (Blau, 1964). Granted, LMX and TMX focus more on the quality of a given relationship, be it between a leader and each of his / her followers or between team members themselves, whereas solidarity behavior refers to a specific behavior that constitutes the exchange and can also be regarded as an outcome of a good relationship quality.

Both LMX and solidarity behavior explicitly refer to the norm of reciprocity, which is the assumption that both parties are contributing to the exchange and that, in the long run, the exchange only stays stable if both parties perceive the respective other party to be contributing equally to the relationship. In the context of LMX, Sullivan, Mitchell, and Uhl-Bien (2003) claim that the norm of reciprocity "serves to initiate and stabilize social interaction among exchange parties" (p. 189). With respect to solidarity behavior, Koster (2005; Lambooij, 2005) claim that "(...) cooperative behavior of one actor will be responded to by a cooperative move of the other. It follows that employees will reciprocate solidarity received from both co-workers and their supervisors" (p. 56).

Both approaches also focus on behaviors or attitudes that go beyond the formal contracts between members of the exchange. Leaders establish high LMX relationships with members who are regarded as assistants and who receive and give more than is formally written down in their contracts (e.g., Graen & Cashman, 1975). Similarly, solidarity behavior, which refers to cooperation or helping behavior within organizations (Koster & Sanders, 2006), cannot and should not be formalized as formalizing this helping behavior can hinder employees from engaging in it voluntarily. In the solidarity behavior theory, as well as in its practical assessment, various actors and receivers are differentiated. For example, an employee can exert solidarity behavior toward a leader or his/her colleagues or can perceive solidarity behavior from his/her leader or colleagues (e.g.,

Koster, 2005; Lambooij, 2005; Sanders & Van Emmerik, 2004; Sanders, Van Emmerik, & Raub, 2005a; Sanders & Schyns, 2006).

Similar to LMX and solidarity behavior, a high quality Team-Member Exchange is something that cannot be put on paper and can hardly be explicitly demanded from team members. In addition, once again similar to LMX and solidarity behavior, it refers to reciprocity in organizations. Despite the fact that neither LMX nor TMX nor solidarity behavior can be part of a formal contract, high quality LMX and TMX relationships, as well as solidarity behavior, are desirable in organizations.

In this chapter, we will examine the relationship between LMX, TMX, and vertical and horizontal solidarity behavior. To begin with, we will describe the concepts, especially solidarity behavior, as this concept is less known to an American public. In terms of the relationship between the approaches, we will refer to theories of social exchange and reciprocity. Finally, we will report an empirical study on the relationship between LMX, TMX and solidarity behavior, as well as their relationship to team performance.

LMX AND TEAM-MEMBER EXCHANGE

The concept of LMX evolved from a critical evaluation of classic leadership research. Prior to the introduction of LMX, leadership research focused on assessing leaders' behaviors through their followers' ratings. Variance in these ratings was treated as error variance. Graen and colleagues, however, argued that the variance in follower ratings is meaningful (e.g., Dansereau, Graen, & Haga, 1975). According to them, the different ratings reflect the different behavior that leaders show toward individual followers. Graen argues that leadership is an interactive process, to which both leader and follower contribute. Graen's assertion meant that, for the first time in leadership research, the follower was seen as an active part of the leadership process. In his description of the process of developing LMX, Graen (2003) emphasizes that the leader may make a relationship offer to all (new) members, but that members individually decide whether or not they accept this offer. As a result, different relationships evolve within a work group. These relationships can be categorized with respect to their quality. Some followers have a higher quality relationship with their leader. Other followers have lower quality relationships with their leader (e.g., Graen & Scandura, 1987; Graen, 2003). The reciprocity differences between the subgroups lead to different interaction patterns and results (e.g., Graen, 2003): Some followers become valued assistants, receive more challenging tasks, and will, in return, put in more effort for the leader; Other followers, in contrast, are treated as "hired hands" and put in no extra effort for the leader (Graen & Uhl-Bien, 1995; Zalesny & Graen, 1987). The leader values the extra role performance of reciprocating followers and this is reflected in performance ratings (Gerstner & Day, 1997). It has to be noted, however, that this differentiation between members of a workgroup may describe a reality in most organizations, but need not be seen as a desirable state of affairs by less favored followers.

Although the exchange relationship between leader and member forms the basis for the development of LMX, the actual interaction processes between leader and member have not been the focus of recent LMX research. Instead, the relationship *quality* between leader and each individual member has received primary attention. This relationship quality is described using different dimensions. Graen and Uhl-Bien (1995) see the relationship quality as reflected in the dimensions respect, trust, and mutual obligation. According to these researchers, these dimensions are highly related and, as a consequence, LMX should be treated as a one-dimensional assessment.

Dienesch and Liden (1986), who refer back to the original exchange idea, extract three different dimensions for the relationship quality between leader and follower, namely, affect (friendly type of relationship between leader and follower), loyalty (willingness to defend each other in front of others), and contribution (follower's effort on behalf of the leader). Based on their empirical results, Liden and Maslyn (1998) add a fourth dimension, namely, professional respect, which refers to the evaluation of each other's competences.

Seers (1989) broadened the concept of LMX and introduced Team-Member Exchange (TMX). It refers to the relationship between members of a group. Sears defines Team-Member Exchange as "the individual member's perception of his or her exchange relationship with the peer group as a whole" (p. 119). Unlike LMX, TMX refers to an average relationship between a single person and a whole group and not to a dyadic relationship between two persons. TMX develops as a result of role expectations and the negotiation of roles within a group (Seers, Petty, & Cashman, 1995). The agreement between expectations and behavior reinforces the role that individuals develop within the team and, thus, defines the quality of the relationship within the team. Based on Seers' results, TMX can be defined by three factors, namely, quality of the working relationship with other team members, effectiveness of team meetings, and cohesiveness of a team as a whole. These factors can however be summed up in one dimension reflecting TMX.

SOLIDARITY BEHAVIOR

Within modern teams, employees enjoy a considerable amount of autonomy, perform more challenging tasks and experience more alignment between personal and organizational goals. The "price" for this autonomy seems to be that managers expect employees within a team to work together, to participate voluntarily, to cooperate willingly and submit to the mutual informal control needed to keep the organization running smoothly (Appelbaum & Batt, 1994; Handy, 1995; Wickens, 1995; see also Sanders et al., 2005a). In other words, the employer needs solidarity behavior from the employees. The assumption is made that solidarity behavior within (informal) relationships is characterized by a norm of reciprocity (Gouldner, 1960; Hechter, 1987; Sanders & Van Emmerik, 2004 Sanders & Schyns, 2006). Because the employee-employee relationship is qualitatively different from the employee-manager relationship (Smith, Carroll & Ashford, 1995), it is important to distinguish, both theoretically and empirically, between solidarity behavior from employees toward other employees (horizontal solidarity behavior), and solidarity behavior from employees to their managers (vertical solidarity behavior) (Koster, 2005; Sanders et al., 2005a; Sanders, Flache, Van der Vegt, & Van de Vliert, 2005b).

Compared to previous research on solidarity within organizations, this focus on solidarity is relatively new (see also Sanders et al., 2005b). Traditional research primarily involved the investigation of solidarity between employees in a conflict with management or in the enforcement of local work group norms.

As the term already indicates, solidarity behavior refers to the actual helping *behavior* shown or perceived by a person. Although the concept sounds more or less similar to Organizational Citizenship Behavior (Podsakoff, McKenzie, Paine & Bachrach, 2000), differences should be mentioned (Koster, 2005; Koster & Sanders, 2006). Koster and Sanders (2006) examined employee cooperation as a characteristic of the relationship instead of a characteristic of the employee. It is argued that, due to the reciprocation of solidarity behaviors, the solidarity behavior shown by the employee to the supervisor depends on the (perceived) behavior of the supervisor and, likewise, the solidarity behavior shown by the employee to other co-workers depends on the (perceived) behavior of the other coworkers. As can be seen in the assessment (see Appendix A), this reciprocity is reflected in the items in so far that they assess the same behavior twice: Once from the person toward the leader or coworkers and, once as the perception of the behavior from the leader or the co-workers toward the person.

Koster and Sanders (2006) investigated the structure of solidarity behavior using data from nine organizations ($n = 674$). Empirical evidence supports the assumption that solidarity is reciprocal in both horizontal and vertical relations.

An important characteristic of solidarity behavior is that it has significant costs and demands and represents a high personal sacrifice for the group, or for the other actor, at a point when it is not certain whether or not the behavior will be reciprocated. Consequently, solidarity behavior is threatened in the short term by the tempting possibility of opportunism (Raub, 1997; Sanders et al., 2005a,b). It is tempting for individuals to lean back and relax and "take a free-ride" on the work performed by others. However, solidarity behavior can be enhanced through long-term costs and benefits and the use of positive and negative sanctions, which, in the long run, offset short-term incentives for opportunistic behavior. For instance, opportunistic behavior can be discouraged by the prospect of future sanctions. The uncertainty as to whether or not the other person will at some point reciprocate ultimately closely links solidarity behavior—helping others, for instance—to issues of trust. And trust requires stable, enduring, close relationships (Raub & Weesie, 1990). Denison and Mishra (1995), and Tyler (2001), found that a certain degree of predictability of resources and rewards is essential for meaning and satisfaction in work. Such predictability is essential for the establishment of trust between workers and management (Fox, 1974; Granovetter, 1985). As relationships progress, individuals receive more information about the other, allowing them to formulate expectations about his or her reliability. When individuals are certain about their common future, solidarity behavior will thrive, due to the increasing benefits of solidarity as opposed to the growing costs of opportunism that emerge long-term (Koster, 2005; Sanders & van Emmerik, 2004).

Solidarity behavior can, therefore, be seen as a choice one makes in a particular work context. Examples of solidarity behavior exhibited by the employee toward the employer are willingness to work overtime, willingness to help colleagues with their job, and work efforts that go beyond obligations specified in the labor contract.

THE RELATIONSHIP BETWEEN LMX AND SOLIDARITY BEHAVIOR

Both LMX and vertical solidarity behavior refer to the exchange between leader and member. However, some differences between the concepts have to be highlighted. Solidarity behavior refers to a specific type of *behavior*, namely, helping behavior at the workplace. The concept differentiates between the actor and receiver of this behavior, that is, leader and follower or follower and colleagues. LMX, in contrast, presents an assessment of the relationship quality between leader and coworker, which can be assessed either from the leader's or the follower's perspective. Most often, the follower is asked to provide information on the relationship he or she shares with his/her leader. The different dimensions that are used in this context refer to attitudes (affect and respect) or the willingness to show a certain behavior (loyalty; Liden & Maslyn, 1998). Only the contribution dimension (Liden & Maslyn, 1998) comprises behavior. It focuses on the extra effort the follower executes on behalf of his/her leader. This dimension is probably most closely connected to the vertical solidarity behavior that a coworker exhibits toward a leader. Therefore, we expect that the relationship between LMX contribution and solidarity behavior coworker to leader is stronger than the one between LMX contribution and solidarity behavior leader to coworker. The LMX dimensions "affect" and "respect" also refer to something the follower contributes to the leader-member dyad and should therefore be related more strongly to solidarity behavior coworker to leader than to solidarity behavior leader to coworker. The case is different for loyalty. This dimension refers to a behavior that the leader executes on behalf of the follower. Therefore, it should be related more strongly to solidarity behavior leader to employee than to solidarity behavior employee to leader. The respective hypotheses read:

H1: There is a positive relationship between LMX and solidarity behavior employee to leader/solidarity behavior leader to employee.

H1a: The relationship between the LMX dimensions contribution, respect and affect and solidarity behavior employee to leader is stronger than the one between LMX and solidarity behavior leader to employee.

H1b: The relationship between the LMX dimension loyalty and solidarity behavior leader to employee is stronger than the one between LMX and solidarity behavior employee to leader.

THE RELATIONSHIP BETWEEN TMX AND SOLIDARITY BEHAVIOR

Solidarity behavior with respect to colleagues differentiates between actors and receivers (solidarity behavior employee to his or her colleagues/solidarity behavior of respective colleagues to employee). This differentiation cannot be found explicitly in TMX. However, the instrument which assesses TMX nevertheless does include items that refer to a self-rating and items that refer to a rating of the behavior of one's colleagues. Furthermore, instead of referring to behavior, TMX, similar to LMX, refers to a result of behaviors, namely, the quality of the working relationship and its cohesiveness. It also incorporates an outcome aspect, namely, the effectiveness of team meetings. When comparing TMX to horizontal solidarity behavior, the same logic applies as in the case with LMX and vertical solidarity behavior. This means that both refer to the same target (the work group) but comprise different aspects, namely, behavior versus relationship quality. Perceiving a good relationship quality to the team will stimulate solidarity behavior and, in turn, solidarity behavior will enhance relationship quality. Therefore, we assume that TMX and horizontal solidarity behavior reinforce each other. We expect:

> **H2:** There is a positive relationship between TMX and solidarity behavior employee to his or her colleagues/solidarity behavior colleagues to employee.

THE RELATIONSHIP BETWEEN LMX, TMX, SOLIDARITY BEHAVIOR AND TEAM PERFORMANCE

LMX research has frequently stressed that a high quality relationship is positively related to performance. Gerstner and Day (1997) conducted a meta-analysis and found that LMX in general is related to performance. Based on the multidimensional approach of LMX (Liden & Maslyn, 1998), Schyns and Paul (2005) showed that affect, respect, and loyalty are positively related to commitment and negatively related to turnover intention.

Similarly, employees' vertical solidarity (i.e., the solidarity of the employees with respect to their supervisors) is viewed as one of the most important success factors within modern organizations (Wickens, 1995). Indeed, research has shown that organizational solidarity is positively related to, for example, employees' performance (Sanders, Snijders, & Stokman, 1998; Lambooij, 2005), and negatively related to short-term absenteeism (Sanders, 2004; Sanders & Hoekstra, 1998; Sanders & Nauta, 2004).

Liden, Wayne, and Sparrow (2000) found that TMX is directly and positively related to performance. Theoretically, this is a similar process as in LMX, where the relationship quality impacts on cooperation and, eventually, enhances performance. With respect to team performance, Jordan,

Feild, and Armenakis (2002) found that TMX is positively related to team performance as rated by the supervisor.

Although all concepts involved in this study are considered to be success factors and supposed to be positively related to performance, we have to keep in mind that we decided to include a certain type of performance here, namely, team performance. It is therefore logical to assume that the dimensions referring directly to the team are more strongly related to team performance than the dimensions referring to leader behavior. Thus, our hypotheses read:

> **H3**: There is a positive relationship between LMX, TMX, solidarity behavior and team performance.
>
> **H3a**: The relationship between the dimensions referring to teams (TMX, solidarity behavior employee to his or her colleagues, and solidarity behavior colleagues to employee) and team performance is stronger than for the dimensions referring to the leader (LMX, solidarity behavior employee to leader, and solidarity behavior leader to employee).

METHOD

The data were gathered using a questionnaire and a convenience sample. Students received course credit for distributing the questionnaires amongst their acquaintances. The only condition for taking part in the study was that the participants were working and had a supervisor.

The sample consists of 360 employees from different companies and with different tasks. Of the participants, 185 were male, 174 were female. The average age was 35.6 years ($SD = 13.4$). Most of the participants ($N = 252$) had a tenured contract. The mean work hours per week were 30 hours ($SD = 12.1$).

Leader-Member Exchange was assessed using a Dutch translation of the multidimensional instrument introduced by Liden and Maslyn (1998). The instrument consists of twelve items, representing four dimensions, namely, affect, professional respect, loyalty, and contribution. Each dimension is assessed using three items. The answer categories range from 1 = *do not agree at all* to 5 = *agree completely*. The internal consistencies (Cronbach's alpha) for affect, professional respect, loyalty, and contribution were = .84, = .89, = .77, and = .61, respectively. This low alpha for contribution is not unusual in research (Maslyn & Uhl-Bien, 2001;

Schyns & Paul, 2005) Due to the low alpha, contribution was not used in further analyses.

Solidarity behavior consists of four dimensions: solidarity from employee to his/her colleagues, solidarity from employee to leader, solidarity from colleagues to employee, and solidarity from leader to employee (e.g., Koster, 2005; Lambooij, 2005; Sanders, Schyns, Koster, & Rotteveel, 2003). Each dimension consists of five items (see appendix 1). The answer categories range from 1 = *agree completely* to 7 = *do not agree at all*. The internal consistencies (Cronbach's alpha) were $a = .91$, $a = .89$, $a = .90$, and $a = .86$, respectively.

Team-Member Exchange is comprised of nine items. The one-dimensional scale used by Liden et al. (2000). The answer categories range from 1 = *do not agree at all* to 7 = *agree completely*. The internal consistency (Cronbach's alpha) was $a = .85$.

Team performance was measured by a nine item instrument of Costa (2001). Individuals provide a self-reflection about their team performance. The answers range from 1 = *do not agree at all*, to 5 = agree completely. The internal consistence (Cronbach's Alpha) was $a = .75$.

ANALYSES

For the testing of most of the hypotheses, Pearson correlations were run. However, some hypotheses refer to comparisons between two correlations. Here, we used a program provided by Hahn and Stöber (1999), which is based on a formula proposed by Meng, Rosenthal, and Rubin (1992) intended to help decide upon the extent to which two correlations are significantly different from each other. In addition, we conducted an explorative regression analysis to examine the variance accounted for by the different concepts.

PRELIMINARY RESULTS

Before testing our hypotheses, we conducted factor analyses in order to determine the extent to which the concepts are separable.

Factor Analyses LMX and Solidarity Behavior Employee to Leader/Leader to Employee

We conducted a Maximum likelihood factor analysis (oblimin rotation) with LMX and solidarity behavior Employee to Leader/Leader to

Employee. The eigenvalue criterion would have suggested a five-factor solution with the sixth factor just below 1. Therefore, and in line with theoretical arguments, we preset six factors in the factor analysis. The two different perspectives found in solidarity behavior load on different factors. The items referring to LMX load on four different factors. However, the contribution items load low which could have been expected given the low alpha of that dimension (see Table 10.1).

Factor Analyses TMX and Solidarity Behavior Employee to Colleagues/Colleagues to Employee

In a Maximum likelihood factor analysis (oblimin rotation) with TMX and solidarity behavior employee to colleagues/colleagues to employee, a three-factor solution initially emerged. The two different solidarity

Table 10.1. Factor Matrix LMX and Solidarity Behavior Employee to Leader/Leader to Employee (Initial 5 Factor-Solution)

	1	2	3	4	5	6
LMXA1	-.046	.037	.014	.755	.006	.006
LMXA2	.015	-.022	-.019	.880	-.036	-.096
LMXA3	-.106	.046	.107	.573	.022	.138
LMXL1	.002	.043	.012	.015	.005	.701
LMXL2	-.041	.019	.038	.091	-.030	.756
LMXL3	-.093	.000	.141	-.029	.033	.522
LMXC1	-.052	-.019	-.041	.052	.418	.101
LMXC2	.056	-.196	.042	.055	.149	.153
LMXC3	.065	-.071	.212	.288	.254	.085
LMXR1	-.014	-.000	.813	.001	.020	.016
LMXR2	.024	-.005	.879	.038	-.035	-.030
LMXR3	-.028	.019	.848	-.019	-.060	.058
SBCL1	.106	.634	-.027	.059	-.409	-.061
SBCL2	-.012	.764	.028	-.038	-.196	-.165
SBCL3	.063	.795	-.006	-.081	.162	.002
SBCL4	.255	.481	.001	-.025	-.345	.056
SBCL5	.031	.851	-.048	.024	.126	.124
SBLC1	.661	-.070	-.109	.003	-.343	.050
SBLC2	.580	.214	-.001	-.018	-.012	-.140
SBLC3	.593	.147	.014	-.106	.227	-.200
SBLC4	.751	-.016	-.032	-.121	-.069	-.024
SBLC5	.560	.131	-.146	-.056	.246	-.089

Table 10.2. Factor Matrix TMX and Solidarity Behavior Employee to Colleagues/Colleagues to Employee (Initial 3 Factor-Solution)

	1	2	3
TMX1	-.056	.316	-.258
TMX2	-.047	.602	.196
TMX3	-.011	.780	.095
TMX4	.062	.706	-.006
TMX5	-.003	.597	-.283
TMX6	.021	.416	-.320
TMX7	-.028	.615	-.146
TMX8	.009	.770	-.006
TMX9	.002	.782	.089
SBCWE1	.815	.088	-.068
SBCWE2	.916	-.049	-.227
SBCWE3	.796	.009	-.088
SBCWE4	.822	.017	-.024
SBCWE5	.832	.009	-.055
SBECW1	.553	-.036	.353
SBECW2	.658	-.136	.241
SBECW3	.532	-.057	.431
SBECW4	.514	-.060	.467
SBECW5	.609	-.076	.365

behavior perspectives load on one factor, with the items referring to solidarity behavior colleagues to employee also showing loadings on the third factor. The items referring to TMX load on one factor (see Table 10.2).

As the factor solution was ambiguous with respect solidarity behavior, we conducted a second factor analysis with only two factors. Here, TMX and solidarity behavior load clearly on separate factors (see Table 10.3).

RESULTS

The correlation table is reproduced in Table 10.4. As indicated in H1, the correlations between the LMX dimensions and solidarity behavior employee to leader/solidarity behavior leader to employee are positive (the negative sign is due to the reverse coding of the solidarity dimensions). As indicated in H1b, loyalty is indeed more strongly related to sol-

Table 10.3. Factor Matrix TMX and Solidarity Behavior Employee to Colleagues/Colleagues to Employee (2 Factor-Solution)

	1	2
TMX1	-.138	.398
TMX2	.036	.521
TMX3	.044	.736
TMX4	.085	.713
TMX5	-.082	.694
TMX6	-.076	.525
TMX7	-.057	.665
TMX8	.028	.768
TMX9	.055	.741
SBCWE1	.801	.163
SBCWE2	.827	.078
SBCWE3	.775	.091
SBCWE4	.823	.079
SBCWE5	.823	.084
SBECW1	.682	-.118
SBECW2	.741	-.177
SBECW3	.674	-.167
SBECW4	.671	-.181
SBECW5	.732	-.159

idarity leader to employee than to solidarity employee to leader. Contrary to our hypotheses, the same is true for affect and respect.

In line with H2, TMX is positively related to solidarity behavior employee to colleague and solidarity behavior colleague to employee. The latter is significantly higher than the former.

H3 referred to the relationship between LMX, TMX, solidarity behavior and team performance. As assumed, all relationships are positive. The correlations for TMX/solidarity behavior colleague to employee are somewhat higher than the other correlations, as was assumed in H3a. However, this is not true for solidarity behavior employee to colleague, contrasting H3a.

Table 10.5 shows that, after introducing LMX into a regression analysis, both solidarity behavior and TMX explain additional variance on team performance. In the final model, we find significant beta-coeffi-

Table 10.4. Intercorrelations

	1	2	3	4	5	6	7	8
1. Affect								
2. Respect	.53**							
3. Loyalty	.52**	.54**						
4. Solidarity Employee to Colleagues	-.08	-.06	-.08					
5. Solidarity Employee to Leader	-.29**	-.22**	-.29**	.71**				
6. Solidarity Colleagues to Employee	-.16**	-.09	-.15**	.75**	.65**			
7. Solidarity Leader to Employee	-.49**	-.46**	-.49**	.40**	.55**	.46**		
8. Team-Member Exchange	.22**	.20**	.16**	-.19**	-.25**	-.43**	-.21**	
9. Team performance	.21**	.25**	.20**	-.22**	-.20**	-.37**	-.24**	.37**

Note: ** $p < .01$ level (2-tailed).

Table 10.5. Regression Analysis With Team Performance as Dependent Variable

	Model 1				Model 2				Model 3			
	B	Beta	R^2	ΔR^2	B	Beta	R^2	ΔR^2	B	Beta	R^2	ΔR^2
(Constant)	2.80**		.06	.06**	3.26**		.21	.14**	2.61**		.24	.04**
Affect	0.04	.07			0.03	.04			-0.01	-.02*		
Respect	0.09	.17*			0.10	.18**			0.08	.15*		
Loyalty	0.04	.06			0.03	.05			0.03	.05		
Solidarity EM to C					0.03	.05			-0.00	.00		
Solidarity EM to L					0.04	.10			0.05	.11		
Solidarity C to EM					-0.22	-.47**			0.15	-.34**		
Solidarity L to EM					0.01	.03			-0.00	-.00		
Team-member exchange									0.13	.22**		

Note: * $p < .05$; ** $p < .01$; Solidarity CW to C = Solidarity Employee to Colleagues; Solidarity CW to L = Solidarity Employee to Leader; Solidarity C to CW = Solidarity Colleagues to Employee; Solidarity L to CW = Solidarity Leader to Employee.

cients for respect, contribution, solidarity behavior colleagues to employee and TMX on team performance.

SUMMARY AND DISCUSSION

The focus of this paper was on three different concepts and their relationship to each other. Up to now, research on LMX and TMX, on the one hand, and solidarity behavior, on the other hand, has been conducted independent of each other. Our paper is the first one examining their mutual relationship.

We found that LMX and solidarity behavior with respect to the leader are positively related, although not to an extent that would lead us to conclude that they are redundant. Contrary to our expectations, affect and respect were more strongly related to solidarity behavior leader to employee than to solidarity behavior employee to leader. We can interpret this in the following way: the more solidarity behavior a leader shows, the more he or she is liked and respected by his/her followers. Let us be aware, however, that we do not talk about objective solidarity behavior but the perception of the follower.

Similarly, TMX is more strongly related to solidarity behavior colleagues to employee than to solidarity behavior employee to colleagues, indicating again that a better relationship results from the behavior of others as perceived by the target person. Interestingly, in both cases of self-rated solidarity behavior, the relationships to LMX and TMX, respectively, are lower than for perceived solidarity behavior. It therefore seems that the relationship to others is more determined by their behavior as perceived by us, than by our own behavior.

In terms of team performance, the highest correlations were found between solidarity behavior colleagues to employee and TMX. This is logical given the type of performance we assessed here. For other types of performance, we can expect different relationships.

A certain limitation of our results is that the factor analysis did not differentiate between the two aspects of horizontal solidarity behavior, namely, the person's own behavior and his / her perception of the behavior of others. One reason for this could be that both horizontal solidarity behavior and TMX do not refer to dyadic relationships, but rather to a relationship to a group. Applying the critique that LMX research had on prior leadership research (Dansereau et al., 1975), we could assume that members share dyadic relationships rather than relationships with a whole group. Therefore, the assessment of horizontal solidarity behavior and TMX may reflect a group climate more than reciprocal behavior, indicating that a differentiation between one's own behavior and the behavior of others is less important.

CONCLUSIONS: RELATIONSHIPS BETWEEN THE CONSTRUCTS

Based on our results, we can conclude that solidarity behavior and LMX/TMX, although stemming from different traditions, are related to each other. The results of our last regression analysis show that horizontal solidarity behavior in particular adds to LMX and TMX. Vertical solidarity behavior is probably too similar to LMX to explain more variance in team performance. Interestingly, although LMX refers to the relationship quality between leader and member on different dimensions, some items do contain references to behavior. Solidarity behavior is specifically focused on behavior rather than on an attitude to another person. In principle, a person can show solidarity behavior toward someone with whom he or she does not share a good relationship quality. However, most of the time, both behavior and relationship quality will go hand in hand, as we can see reflected in the correlations we found between LMX and TMX, on the one hand, and solidarity behavior, on the other.

Our results also imply that both LMX/TMX and solidarity behavior contribute to team performance. This means that, although neither LMX/TMX nor solidarity behavior can be enforced in organizations, their presence helps to increase performance.

CONCLUSIONS: RECIPROCITY

The starting point of our chapter was the idea that both solidarity behavior and LMX/TMX refer to similar ideas, namely, reciprocity in organizations, but have a different theoretical background, namely, cooperation versus critique on group leadership approaches. In a way, solidarity behavior describes the behavior in terms of cooperation and LMX/TMX refer to the result of that behavior. Our empirical results underline that point and highlight the importance of solidarity. According to our results, it is very important what others do or better how we perceive what others do rather than how we perceive our own behavior. This underlines the significance of reciprocity: Only when others engage in behavior that we perceive as cooperative, we will be willing to invest in a relationship. On a much broader level, Torka (2003) showed this in the relationship between blue collar workers and their management: Blue collar workers highlighted that the management and white collar worker in general (thus, also clerks) did not show respect nor expressed friendliness toward them resulting in the blue collar workers themselves having feelings of "them and us" rather than feelings of "us, the company." Obviously, and this is reflected in the two concepts examined here, as far as their theoretical background is concerned, solidarity among employee and, especially, between employees and leaders has a certain tradition in Europe, at least in the Netherlands. This may also explain the still powerful position of national industrial relations including the unions that influence labor market law as well as collective agreements. In contrast, a concept such as LMX seems to ground more in the individualistic U.S. tradition of approaching employment relationship. For future research, it would be highly interesting to transfer this study to the U.S. context and examine the importance of solidarity behavior and the relationship between solidarity behavior and LMX/TMX in an American context.

APPENDIX: ASSESSMENT OF SOLIDARITY BEHAVIOR

Solidarity Employee To Supervisor

I help my supervisor to finish tasks

I am willing to help my supervisor when things went wrong that nobody is responsible for

I apologize when I have made a mistake regarding my supervisor

I try to equally divide the pleasant and unpleasant tasks between me and my supervisor

I live up to agreements with my supervisor

Solidarity Supervisor To Employee

Helps to finish team tasks

Is willing to help us when things went wrong that nobody is responsible for

Apologizes when something goes wrong

Divides to pleasant and unpleasant asks as fairly as possible

Lives up to agreements

Solidarity Employee to Colleagues

I help my team members to finish tasks

I am willing to help my team members when things that nobody is responsible for, went wrong

I apologize when I made a mistake regarding my team members

I try to divide the pleasant and unpleasant tasks as fairly as possible between me and my team members

I live up to my agreements concerning my team members

Solidarity Colleagues to Employee

Help to finish work in our team

Are willing to help when things that nobody is responsible for, went wrong

Apologize when they have made a mistake

Divide the pleasant and unpleasant tasks as fairly as possible

Live up to their agreements

REFERENCES

Appelbaum, E., & Batt, R. (1994). *The new American workplace*. Ithaca, NY: ILR Press.

Blau, P. (1955). *The dynamics of bureaucracy*. Chicago: University of Chicago Press.

Blau, P. (1964). *Exchange and power in social life*. New York: Wiley.

Costa, A. C. (2000). *A matter of trust: Effects on the performance and effectiveness of teams in organizations*. Dissertation, Tilburg: Kurt Lewin Institute.

Dansereau, F., Graen, G., & Haga, W. (1975). A vertical dyad linkage approach to leadership within formal organizations—A longitudinal investigation of the role making process. *Organizational Behavior and Human Performance, 13*, 46-78.

Denison, D. R., & Mishra, K. (1995). Toward a theory of organisational culture and {hyp} effectiveness. *Organisation Science, 6*, 204-223.

Dienesch, R. M. & Liden, R. C. (1986). Leader-member exchange model of leadership: A critique and further development. *Academy of Management Review, 11*, 618-634.

Fox, A. (1974). *Beyond contract: Work, power and trust relations*. London: Faber & Faber.

Gerstner, C. R., & Day, D. V. (1997). Meta-analytic review of leader-member exchange theory: Correlates and construct issues. *Journal of Applied Psychology, 82*, 827-844.

Gouldner, A. W. (1960). The norm of reciprocity: A preliminary statement. *American Sociological Review, 25*, 161-178.

Graen, G. B. (2003). Interpersonal workplace theory at the crossroads: LMX and transformational theory as special case of role making in work organizations. In G.B. Graen (Ed.), *Dealing with diversity, LMX leadership: The series* (Vol. I, pp. 145-182). Greenwich, CT: Information Age.

Graen, G. B., & Cashman, J. F. (1975). A role-making model of leadership in formal organizations: A developmental approach. In J. G. Hunt & L. L. Larson (Eds.), *Leadership frontiers* (pp. 143-165). Kent, OH: Kent State University.

Graen, G. B., & Scandura, T. A. (1987). Toward a psychology of dyadic organizing. In B.M. Staw & L.L. Cummings (Eds.), *Research in organizational behavior* (Vol. 9, pp. 175-208). Greenwich, CT: JAI Press.

Graen, G. B., & Uhl-Bien, M. (1995). Development of leader-member exchange (LMX) theory of leadership over 25 years: Applying a multi-level multi-domain perspective. *Leadership Quarterly, 6*, 219-247.

Granovetter, M. (1985). Economic action and social structure: The problem of embeddedness. *American Journal of Sociology, 91*, 481-510.

Hahn, A., & Stöber, J. (1999). Signifikanztest für zwei korrelierte Korrelationen (Significance test for two correlated correlations). http://userpage.fu-berlin.de/~ahahn/sigcorr.html.

Handy, C. (1995, May-June). Trust and the virtual organization. *Harvard Business Review*, 40-50.

Hechter, M. (1987). *Principles of group solidarity*. Berkeley: University of California Press.

Homans, G. C. (1974). *Social behaviour: Its elementary forms*. New York: Harcourt Brace Jovanovich.

Jordan, M. H., Feild, H. S., & Armenakis, A.A. (2002). The relationship of group process variables and team performance—A team-level analysis in a field setting. *Small Group Research, 30*, 121-150.

Koster, F. (2005). *For the time being*. Dissertation. Veendendaal: Universal Press.

Koster, F., & Sanders, K. (2006). Organizational citizens or reciprocal relationships? An empirical comparison of organizational citizenship behavior and organizational solidarity. *Personnel Review*.

Koster, F., Sanders, K., & Van Emmerik, H. (2003). Solidarity of temporary workers: the Effects of temporal and network embeddedness on solidarity behaviour of Ph.D. students. *The Netherlands Journal of Social Sciences, 38*, 65-80.

Lambooij, M. (2005). *Promoting Cooperation. Studies into the effects of long-term and short-term rewards on cooperation of employees*. Veendendaal: Universal Press.

Liden, R. C., & Maslyn, J. M. (1998). Multidimensionality of leader-member exchange: An empirical assessment through scale development. *Journal of Management, 24*, 43-72.

Liden, R. C., Wayne, S. J., & Sparrowe, R. T. (2000). An examination of the mediating role of psychological empowerment on the relation between the job, interpersonal relationships, and work outcomes. *Journal of Applied Psychology, 85*, 407-416.

Maslyn, J. M., & Uhl-Bien, M. (2001). Leader-member exchange and its dimensions: Effects of self-effort and other's effort on relationship quality. *Journal of Applied Psychology, 86*, 697-708.

Meng, X. -L., Rosenthal, R., & Rubin, D. B. (1992). Comparing correlated correlation coefficients. *Psychological Bulletin, 111*, 172-175.

Podsakoff, P. M., MacKenzie, S. B., Paine, J. B., & Bachrach, D. G. (2000). Organizational citizenship behaviors: A critical review of the theoretical and empirical literature and suggestions for future research. *Journal of Management, 26*, 513-563.

Raub, W., & Weesie, J. (1990). Reputation and efficiency in social interactions: An example of network effects. *American Journal of Sociology, 96*, 626-654.

Raub, W. (1997). *Samenwerking in duurzame relaties en sociale cohesie*. [Cooperation in long-term relationships and social cohesiveness] Amsterdam: Thesis Publishers.

Raub, W., & Weesie, J. (2000). The management of matches: A research program on solidarity in durable social relations. *The Netherlands Journal of Social Sciences, 36*, 71-88.

Roethlisberger, F. J., & Dickson, W. (1939). *Manager and the worker: An account of a research program conducted by the Western Electronic Company, Hawthorne Works, Chicago*. New York: Wiley.

Sanders, K. (2004). Playing truant within organizations: Informal relationships, work ethics, and absenteeism. *Journal of Managerial Psychology, 19*, 136-155.

Sanders, K., Flache, A., Van der Vegt, G., & Van de Vliert, E. (2005b). Solidarity behavior within modern organizations: A framing perspective on the effects of the employees' social embeddedness. In A. Flache, D. Fetchenhauer, A. P.

Buunk, & S. Lindenberg (Eds.), *Determinants and effect of solidarity: A framing perspective*. Dordrecht: Kluwer Academic Press.

Sanders, K., & Hoekstra, S. K. (1998). Informal networks and absenteeism within an organization. *Computational and Mathematical Organization Theory, 4*, 149-163.

Sanders, K., & Nauta, A. (2004). Social cohesiveness and absenteeism: The relationship between characteristics of employees and short-term absenteeism within an organization. *Small Group Research, 35*, 724-741.

Sanders, K., & Schyns, B. (2006). Trust, conflict and cooperative behaviour: Considering reciprocity within organizations. *Personnel Review*.

Sanders, K. Schyns, B., Koster, F., & Rotteveel, C. (2003). Het stimuleren van solidair gedrag: een kwestie van leiderschap? [Stimulating solidarity behaviour: A question of leadership?] *Gedrag en Organisatie, 16*, 237-254.

Sanders, K., Snijders, T., & Stokman, F. N. (1998). Editorial: effects and outcomes of informal relations within organizations. *Computational & Mathematical Organization Theory, 4*, 103-108.

Sanders, K., van Emmerik, I. J., & Raub, W. (2005a). Solidarität am Arbeitsplatz: Fiktion, Fakten und Kräfte [Solidarity at the workplace: Fiction, Facts and Forces]. In J. Berger (Ed.), *Zerreißt das Soziale Band. Beiträge zu einer aktuellen gesellschaftpolitischen Debatte* (pp. 121-142). Frankfurt/New York: Campus Verlag.

Sanders, K., & van Emmerik, H, (2004). Does modern organizations and governance threat solidarity? *Journal of Management and Governance, 8*, 351-372.

Schyns, B., & Paul, T. (2005). Dyadic leadership and organizational outcomes—Different results of different instruments? In G. B. Graen & J. A. Graen (Eds.), *Global organizing designs, LMX leadership: The series* (Vol. 3, pp. 175-205). Greenwich, CT: Information Age.

Seashore, S. E. (1954). *Group cohesiveness in the industrial work group*. Ann Arbor: University of Michigan Institute for Social Research.

Seers, A. (1989). Team-member exchange quality: A new construct for role-making research. *Organizational Behavior & Human Decision Process, 43*, 118-135.

Seers, A., Petty, M. M., & Cashman, J. F. (1995). Team-member exchange under team and traditional management. *Group and Organization Management, 20*, 18-38.

Smith, K. G., Carroll, S., & Ashford, S. (1995). Intra- en interorganisational cooperation: Toward a research agenda. *Journal of Applied Psychology, 38*, 633-655.

Sullivan, D. M., Mitchell, M. S., & Uhl-Bien, M. (2003). The new conduct of business: How LMX can help capitalize on cultural diversity. In G. B. Graen (Ed.), *Dealing with diversity, LMX leadership: The series* (Vol. 2, pp. 183-218). Greenwich, CT: Information Age.

Torka, N. (2003). *The influence of the labour contract on commitment*. Unpublished dissertation, University of Twente.

Wickens, P. D. (1995). *The ascendant organisation: Combining commitment and control for long-term, sustainable business success*. Basingstoke: Macmillan.

Zalesny, M. D., & Graen, G. B. (1987). Führungstheorien—Austauschtheorie. In A. Kieser, G. Reber, & R. Wunderer (Eds.), *Handwörterbuch der Führung* (pp. 962-978). Stuttgart: Poeschl.

CHAPTER 11

THE ROLE OF LMX AND COMMUNICATION IN THE GOAL SETTING PROCESS

David J. Henderson, Tanguy Dulac, and Robert C. Liden

In this chapter, we integrate LMX and goal setting theory to outline the ways in which LMX quality may influence the communication of goal assignments to subordinates and subsequently enhance goal commitment and performance. Specifically, we examine how LMX quality may affect subordinates' perceptions of their leaders' credibility as a source of information. Additionally, we suggest that the interpersonal familiarity gained in high quality LMXs facilitates the generation of messages, by the leader, that are useful and influential. Both leader credibility and the content of his or her goal-assigning communications have important implications for a subordinate's understanding of the goal and its purpose, cultivating task-specific self-efficacy, and rendering the achievement of a goal a personally meaningful endeavor for that subordinate. A model is presented that outlines the process through which LMX quality may be related to goal commitment. Through a discussion of these relationships, we contribute to a broader understanding of how LMX quality may augment the impact of communication exchanges that transpire in leader-member work relationships. Additionally, by examining the relationship between LMX quality and goal commitment, we provide insight into the ways in which LMX is positively related to subordinate performance.

INTRODUCTION

An important function of leadership is the direction of follower efforts toward achieving organizational objectives. Critical to this process is the development of interpersonal relationships "with followers that motivates them to bring their full attention, energy, and commitment to the collective endeavor" (Chemers, 2001, p. 382). The communication of performance goals by leaders to subordinates is one vehicle through which such influence attempts may be made (Locke & Latham, 1990). For these communications to prove an effective means of influence, they must generate a sense of commitment to engaging in behaviors that will lead to goal attainment. As an exchange between socially-connected actors, the content of and responses to goal assigning communications in leader-member dyads may be shaped by dynamics of the relationship, itself. Specifically, the production, interpretation, and attitudes resulting from goal assigning messages may be influenced by the exchange relationship quality that has developed in the dyad (Drake & Moberg, 1986).

LMX AND COMMUNICATIONS

Taking a leader-member exchange (LMX) approach to leadership (Graen & Uhl-Bien, 1995) allows for an examination of how leader-member communications might be influenced by characteristics of a dyad's exchange relationship. For example, leaders and members in poorer quality exchange relationships may lack personal familiarity with one another, thus constraining each partner's ability to adequately assess the other's task specific knowledge. This insufficient familiarity may result in leaders inferring that certain pieces of task-relevant information are not in need of direct communication, when, in fact, they are. Such a misjudgment might leave a subordinate feeling unprepared to engage in the activities required to attain a performance goal. On the other hand, messages emanating from leaders in better quality relationships may be assigned more credibility and contain more useful task-related information. Both of these factors might influence a subordinate's commitment to achieving assigned goals, and contribute his/her skills, knowledge, and abilities to the performance of the organization.

Born from the proposition that leaders do not use the same leadership style with all subordinates (Dansereau, Graen, & Haga, 1975), LMX quality has evolved into a means of describing the levels of interpersonal attraction, loyalty, perceived contribution, and professional respect present within leader-member dyads (Liden & Maslyn, 1998). As an indication of the quality of the exchange relationship that exists between leaders and followers, LMX has been shown, through meta-analytic results, to be related to such outcomes as job performance, role clarity, role conflict, satisfaction, commitment, and turnover intentions (Gerstner & Day, 1997). Additionally, empirical research has suggested that LMX may be related to the use of differential communication behaviors across leader-subordinate relationships (Fairhurst, 1993; Fairhurst & Chandler, 1989; Fairhurst & Rhea Hamlett, 2003; Waldron, 1991; Yrle, Hartman, & Galle, 2003). When considered together, these results bring to light the need to explore how outcomes associated with LMX might be related to specific characteristics of the communication exchanges that occur within leader-member dyads.

While the study of leader-subordinate communication has long been a focus of research (Jablin, 1979), there exist questions in the LMX literature as to *how* dyadic exchange relationship quality may be related to a leader's ability to influence subordinate attitudes and behaviors using effective communication tactics. In this chapter, we focus our attention on the ways in which LMX quality might shape both the content of and credibility granted to goal assigning messages flowing from leaders to subordinates. In doing so, we examine how these factors might be related to goal commitment. Through this endeavor, we aim to contribute to a more detailed understanding of how LMX quality impacts the interpersonal processes that occur within leader-member dyads, and the subsequent effects that these processes may have upon individual and organizational level outcomes.

GOAL SETTING COMMUNICATIONS AND GOAL COMMITMENT

While a number of individuals may participate in the generation of performance goals associated with unique, organizational roles, it is often leaders who are tasked with communicating these goals to their respective subordinates (Earley, 1986; Hollander, 1980). Locke and Latham (2002, p. 705) define a goal as an "object of aim or action." As such, goals are a means through which organizations can guide the behaviors of subordinates toward contributing to their central purpose. Goal setting theory (Locke & Latham, 1990) has emerged as a prominent framework for understanding the relationship between performance goals and individual behaviors. It posits that fostering goal commitment is an essential component of the goal setting process. As noted by Locke, Latham, and

Erez (1988, p. 23), "if there is no commitment to goals, then goal setting does not work."

For a communicated performance goal to lead to positive outcomes at the individual, unit, and organizational level, it must therefore effectuate goal commitment. Commitment refers to "one's attachment to or determination to reach a goal, regardless of where the goal came from" (Locke & Latham, 1990, p. 125). Both self-set and assigned goals require a degree of commitment if the goal is to lead to action. The results of a meta-analysis conducted by Klein, Wesson, Hollenbeck, and Alge (1999) suggest a positive relationship between goal commitment and performance and indicate that this relationship may be more pronounced when goals are more difficult.

According to Locke and Latham (1990), goal commitment may be influenced by an individual's aspiration to achieve a goal and perceptions that a goal is attainable. Klein and his colleagues (1999), in their meta-analysis, found that goal commitment was significantly and positively correlated with goal expectancy and attractiveness, offering indirect support for Locke and Latham's (1990) general propositions. In more detailed terms, Locke and Latham (1990) asserted that a number of factors, including authority figures, valence, and self-efficacy (Bandura, 1982), shape the attractiveness of a goal and the extent to which an individual holds expectations of achieving it. The communication exchanges, in which goal-assigning messages are relayed and received, offer opportunities for influencing goal commitment by clarifying the expectations associated with a goal and its general purpose, increasing the attractiveness of the rewards associated with goal attainment, and enhancing the task-specific self-efficacy of subordinates.

INTEGRATING LMX AND GOAL SETTING THEORIES

Organizational leaders play a critical role in shaping both the "attractiveness" of pursuing a goal, and an individual's perception that the goal is attainable. Locke and Latham (1990) provide a detailed discussion of the ways in which authority figures, such as leaders, might influence goal commitment. With respect to assigned goals, they state that commitment will be best fostered "when: (1) The authority figure is seen as legitimate; (2) The assigned goals imply associated rewards and punishments; (3) Goal assignment conveys (positive) self-efficacy information; (4) Goal assignment conveys (high) normative information; (5) Goal assignment fosters a sense of achievement; (6) The assigned goals imply opportunities for self-improvement; (7) The assigned goals challenge people to prove themselves; and (8) The authority figure is physically present, supportive, trustworthy, provides a convincing rationale for the goal, exerts reasonable pressure, and is knowledgeable and likeable," (pp. 135-136).

In view of Locke and Latham's (1990) propositions, it appears that integrating goal setting and LMX theory to account for goal commitment may be a fruitful endeavor. For instance, trust, mutual respect, liking, and support are all characteristics of prosperous LMX relationships (Graen, 2003; Graen & Uhl-Bien, 1995; Liden & Maslyn, 1998). Additionally, subordinates in high quality exchange relations may be more privy to information that is useful to their understanding of the goal they are being assigned, why the goal is important, and how the goal might be achieved. In fact, the results of an empirical study conducted by Klein and Kim (1998) suggest a positive relationship between LMX and commitment to assigned goals. As these researchers hypothesized, the degree of influence, support, encouragement, and rewards available in prosperous LMX relationships, as well an internalization of common goals within these relationships, served to enhance goal commitment.

Another method of accounting for the relationship between LMX and goal commitment is to consider the leader's function as a potential role-sender (Katz & Kahn, 1978) in goal-assigning exchanges and to explore the effects of LMX quality on the ways in which such messages are communicated and received. For instance, leader credibility impacts the extent to which a communicated message influences subordinate attitudes and behaviors (Hollander, 1964). When the goals that leaders assign are not viewed as emanating from a credible source, subordinates may dedicate less focus, and exhibit less desire to their pursuit. Credibility, in large, may be determined by the mutual trust and professional respect present within a dyadic relation, as well as the familiarity that a subordinate has gained with a leader's knowledge and expertise. Additionally, in order for leaders to provide useful information to a subordinate, a basis from which to gauge what information the subordinate needs, already holds, and what connections will be made between the two, must exist.

LMX quality serves as a means for determining both the credibility attached to the messages that leaders produce and the potential impact of the content that is found therein. Credibility will have a direct effect on goal commitment by influencing a subordinate's desire to attain a goal that has been assigned. Additionally, leaders who are able to provide useful information that clarifies the expectations and rewards associated with the goal, articulates its purpose, renders the goal personally meaningful, and nurtures task-specific self-efficacy will likely enhance goal commitment.

Figure 11.1 provides a graphical depiction of the proposed relationships between LMX, communication, goal commitment, and performance. In subsequent sections, the specific propositions implied by this model are

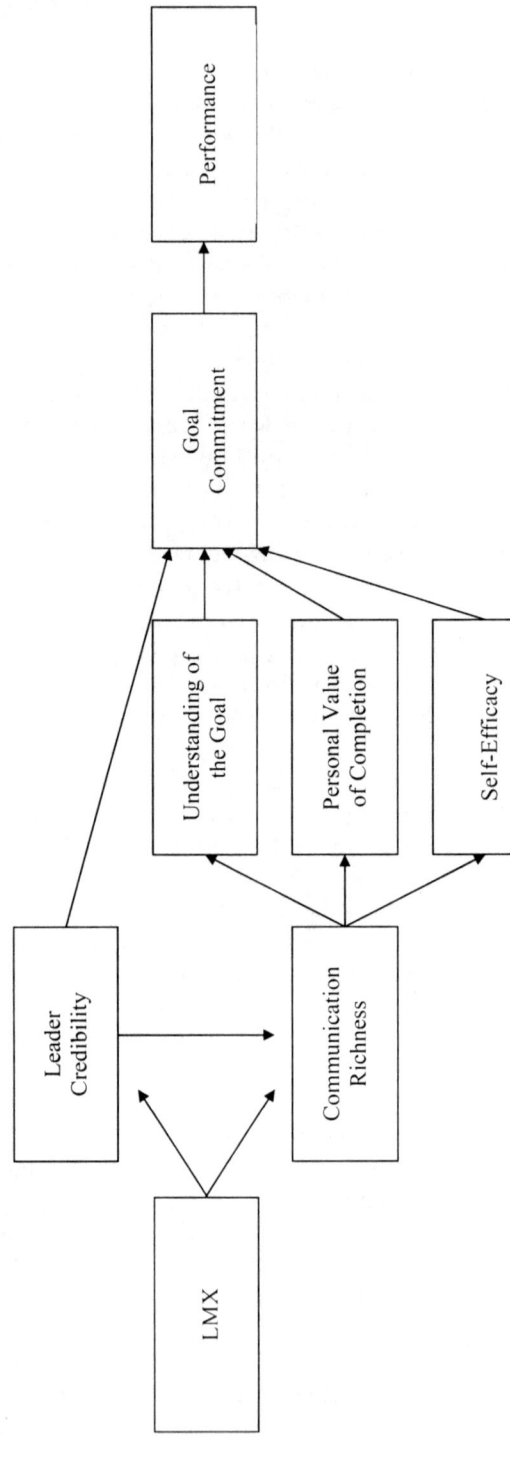

Figure 11.1. Processes linking LMX, subordinate goal commitment, and performance.

discussed, in detail. Before doing so, it is useful to examine the ways in which LMX quality might influence the communication exchanges that occur between leaders and subordinates. This discussion serves as a foundation for accounting for many of the relationships proposed by our model.

Effective Communication and Social Metacognition

The ability of a leader to communicate effectively has long been noted as a measure of leader competence (Riggio, Riggio, Salinas, & Cole, 2003). Followers, likewise, must also possess effective communication skills if messages exchanged within the dyad are to lead to beneficial outcomes. A distinguishing characteristic of successful communicators is their consideration of the thoughts and knowledge of their partners when formulating and interpreting messages. "Effective listeners interpret messages by considering what the speaker must have had in mind, and effective speakers produce messages by considering how their messages are likely to be interpreted" (Hewes & Planalp, 1987, p. 165). *Social metacognition* refers to the thoughts that one individual may have about the knowledge and cognitive processes of another individual (Hewes & Planalp, 1987).

Planalp and Hewes (1982) outlined six cognitive tasks that are vital to communication. Specifically, they stated that individuals "must be able to focus on the information they need, store it for later use, make inferences from it, retrieve it from memory when needed, and use it in selecting and implementing plans of action" (Planalp & Hewes, 1982, p. 57). Communicators must consider these processes, in addition to the knowledge of their partners, when exchanging messages. Through taking into account what messages might likely grab an individual's attention, what information another already holds, and the inferences that another is likely to make, both the comprehension and the influence of a message are enhanced. For example, a leader, when assigning a performance goal to a subordinate, must reflect on the knowledge the subordinate already has acquired as to the ways in which the goal might be attained. If these assessments are accurate, leaders are best able to fill in the gaps of what a subordinate may not know, and avoid repeating what a subordinate already does. When receiving messages, subordinates must make accurate assessments of their leaders' task and organizationally relevant knowledge if the leader is to be granted proper credibility.

Jost, Kruglanski, and Nelson (1998) noted that making accurate assessments of another's knowledge and cognition is vital for effective communication processes. Individuals may use thoughts about their own knowledge and cognitive processes as a basis for predicting those of others, and perceptions of similarity may intensify this effect (Jost et al., 1998). Communicators risk, though, making false-consensus biases (Ross, Greene, & House, 1977) when projecting their own thoughts, attitudes, and values onto others. Strong interpersonal exchange relationships between individuals may provide them with opportunities for gaining an awareness for the similarities and differences that exist between them, rendering them more sensitive to avoiding simple projections of their own characteristics onto their communication partners.

LMX and Social Metacognition

LMX quality may be directly related to the ability of both dyadic partners to make accurate inferences of each other's knowledge and cognitive processes. Waldron (1991) presented results to suggest that LMX quality may be related to a subordinate's use of *personal* upward maintenance tactics with their leaders. These tactics include conversations that are more "friendly" in nature and may include topics related to one's personal life and career ambitions. These results suggest a relationship between LMX quality and interpersonal familiarity in leader-subordinate dyads. High quality exchange relationships may be marked by a greater flow of messages, emanating from both leaders and members, relating to each partner's personal needs, values, concerns, and ambitions. Receipt of such personal information facilitates each partner's ability to gauge the knowledge and desires of the other. Through the course of interaction, leaders and subordinates may gain awareness for what captures the other's attention, how much information each generally remembers, and what types of inferences the other is likely to make.

LMX quality may also affect an individual's motivation to expend the cognitive energy required to contemplate the knowledge structures and cognitive processes of another. Because the salience of LMX relationships vary between both leaders and members, each party contributes a commensurate amount of effort toward meeting their mutual interests (Maslyn & Uhl-Bien, 2001). Such effort may present itself in energy dedicated to producing messages that contain information that is most beneficial to a dyadic partner. Liden, Wayne, and Stilwell (1993), in their empirical study of LMX development, found evidence to suggest that both leader and member expectations of each other were positively related to the LMX quality that emerged in the dyad. Expectations were measured as a function of the perceptions of future contributions, success, and similarity of the other. It follows that variability exists in the expectations held by both leaders and members regarding the perceived utility of each other's contributions to the relationship. Social exchange theory (Blau, 1964) supports this proposition, as social attraction, between individuals, is a function of an individual's needs and perceptions of another's ability to meet those needs. Therefore, following from Maslyn and Uhl-Bien (2001), individuals in lower quality exchange relationships may be less inclined to expend energy in seeking out cues that might enhance their communications, or integrate these cues into their production and interpretation processes.

Participation in Goal Assigning Communications

Following from empirical results demonstrating positive correlations between LMX and both empowerment (Liden, Wayne, & Sparrowe, 2000) and participative decision making (Scandura, Graen, & Novak, 1986), in higher quality exchange relations, subordinates may be more inclined to participate freely in a goal assigning communication exchanges. Fairhurst, Rogers, and Sarr (1987) found that LMX quality was related to the degree of dominance exhibited in communications from a leader to a subordinate. Communications in more prosperous leader-subordinate relationships may reflect decreased "power differences" within the dyad (Fairhurst, 1993). In fact, negotiation latitude was used as a means of distinguishing between "in-groups" and "out-groups" in early LMX research (e.g., Dansereau et al., 1975). For all of these reasons, exchange relationship quality may affect the level of comfort that a subordinate feels in voicing opinions and making direct requests for information from the leader.

LMX and Communication Richness

Prosperous exchange relationships between leaders and members will create relational contexts in which richer communications may arise between dyadic partners. For our purposes, we define communication richness as the degree to which messages between communication partners flow freely and are able to influence the attitudes and behaviors of the other. Additionally, communication richness refers to the level of useful content that is provided in messages exchanged between individuals and the degree to which these messages are clearly understood. We expect that the communication richness that is experienced in leader-member dyads will play an important role in accounting for subordinate commitment to goals that are assigned, therein.

Communications Influencing Goal Commitment

In reviewing the factors, as previously discussed, that Locke and Latham (1990) proposed to influence goal commitment, it is impossible to overlook the imperative role that communication plays in the goal setting process. In general, communication exchanges provide the vehicles through which leaders can influence a subordinate's desire to achieve a goal, as well as expectations of realizing the goal. Messages relayed from a leader to a member may include information linking the achievement of a goal to rewards and punishments, explanations of the rationale for a goal, and information as to the efforts required to achieve it. The extent to which a leader adequately provides this information to subordinates may have implications for the perceived importance of attaining a goal and subordinate self-efficacy. Additionally, through linking a goal to the achievement of personal desires and ambitions, a leader may render goal attainment more personally meaningful for subordinates. Finally, the mutual trust and respect present in leader-member dyads will have important consequences for the credibility assigned to the leader as a source of information.

The quality of the exchange relationship in which goal-setting messages are transferred between partners influences the manner in which these messages are produced, interpreted, and acted upon. We propose that LMX quality is directly related to a leader's ability to generate messages that are tailored to the individual needs and desires of subordinates. The absence of a strong interpersonal relationship between leaders and members may constrain the means through which leaders can use communication attempts to influence the behavior of subordinates. In the following sections, the relationships among LMX, credibility perceptions, communications of performance goals, and goal commitment are outlined.

Leader Credibility

Perceptions of credibility are driven by judgments of other individuals' trustworthiness and expertise (Petty & Wegener, 1998; Tsui, 1984). When leaders act as role-senders, communicating information regarding performance goals, their own credibility shapes subordinate focus and related attitudes toward the content of their messages (e.g., Earley, 1986). Prosperous LMX relations are marked by mutual trust and respect (Graen & Uhl-Bien, 1995; Liden & Maslyn, 1998), and thus it is likely that leaders in these types of relationships will be perceived as more credible by their subordinates. Additionally, through working closely with leaders, subordinates in high quality exchange relations may have more opportunities to witness, and gain familiarity with a leader's task and organizationally relevant expertise.

Perceptions of leader credibility have pervasive effects across leader-subordinate communication exchanges, affecting a leader's attempts at persuasion and influence (Hollander, 1964, 1980). If leaders are not viewed as credible sources of information and knowledge, then the individual, work unit and organizational-level usefulness of the goals they communicate may be called into question. Consistent with Locke and Latham (1990), we expect that leader trustworthiness, and thus subsequent credibility, has important implications for goal commitment. When a leader's credibility is questioned, one's desire to engage in behaviors aimed at achieving goals assigned by him or her diminishes.

> **Proposition 1**: LMX is positively related to subordinate perceptions of leader credibility. This credibility, in turn, results in heightened goal commitment and subsequent performance.

We contend that leader credibility also affects a leader's ability to enhance goal commitment through providing explanations regarding the goal, linking goal achievement to personally meaningful outcomes, and boosting self-efficacy. For any type of communication to have a positive impact on subordinate attitudes and behaviors, the leader must be viewed as a trustworthy and knowledgeable source of information. For example, if the honesty of messages that express confidence in a subordinate's abilities is questioned, the potential impact of these messages on subordinate self-efficacy may be limited. Likewise, persuasive messages that attempt to link goal achievement to furthering a subordinate's personal interests may have less influence on rendering goal attainment an attractive endeavor to the subordinate. Therefore, leader credibility might be viewed as contributing to the positive association between communication richness and LMX, as this richness, in part, refers to each party's ability to influence the attitudes and behaviors of the other through communication.

Understanding of the Goal

At a basic level, the communication of a goal assignment must result in a subordinate's clear understanding of the expectations and any rewards that are associated with a goal, its purpose, and the means through which the goal might be attained. Providing task-relevant information, such as how to accomplish a task and why the task is important, can influence goal acceptance and commitment (Earley, 1985, 1986; Locke & Latham, 2002). It is imperative that subordinates understand how their own work contributes to the more global operations of an organization (Katz & Kahn, 1978), as this understanding may affect the perceived importance of performance goals that are assigned to them. Additionally, subordinates must accurately understand the performance outputs expected of them, if goals are to effectively guide subordinate behavior toward contributing to the success of the organization. Furthermore, obtaining knowledge and strategies for achieving a goal influences subordinate's perceptions of goal attainability. In sum, fostering a clear understanding of the goals that subordinates are assigned is a vital aspect of the goal setting process. When leaders communicate goal assignments in a manner that facilitates this understanding, goal commitment is enhanced.

Taking into consideration another's knowledge, when exchanging messages, is an important component of the communication process (Krauss & Fussell, 1991). When communicating, individuals adapt their messages to the knowledge they believe their listeners to hold (Krauss & Fussell, 1991). It is through this process that speakers facilitate the comprehension and utility of their speech. Individuals may perceive knowledge to be shared among them on the basis of factors such as perceptions of similar network membership (Clark & Marshall, 1981). For instance, leaders may assume that all members of an organization or a profession share various pieces of knowledge. Thus, when forming messages, they may not include certain pieces of information because they infer this knowledge to be commonly held and not in need of direct expression. These assumptions can be problematic, though, if such information is *not* commonly held between leaders and their dyadic partners. Thus, leaders are in need of a means of forming accurate expectations regarding what knowledge their subordinates are likely to possess. By taking into consideration a unique subordinate's knowledge of the organization, goal specific performance expectations, and strategies for task completion, messages can be tailored to his/her individual information needs. Structuring messages in this manner will render them more meaningful and increase their potential to impact subordinate attitudes and behaviors.

Through perspective-taking (Krauss & Fussell, 1991), leaders may attempt to make assessments of the knowledge they anticipate their listeners to hold. Showing such consideration, when producing messages, may reduce a leader's tendency to project his or her *own* knowledge onto followers. As such, it allows a leader to gauge the types of explanations that must be given when communicating goal assignments. In order to view a situation through their subordinates' eyes, leaders must have familiarity with the thoughts, knowledge, and attitudes of their subordinates.

Otherwise, they risk making inaccurate evaluations of how subordinates may be perceiving, interpreting, and responding to a communication exchange. For instance, a leader in a low quality exchange relationship may be unaware of a subordinate's true understanding of how accomplishing a goal contributes to meeting organizational objectives. Thus, while this leader may believe that a subordinate understands the importance of the goal, and its relevance to the organization, this perception may be inaccurate.

High quality exchange relationships allow leaders the opportunity to familiarize themselves with the knowledge held by individual employees. The frequent interaction in these relationships grants a leader the possibility for gaining continual updates on any new information that a subordinate acquires. Additionally, open communication lines in high quality exchange relationships may increase the feedback that subordinates provide in discussions in which goals are assigned. Participation affords the subordinate the ability to ask for clarification when necessary information is lacking in the communication, or when misunderstandings arise. Speakers may reassess their listeners' knowledge on the basis of cues that are furnished during discussions (Krauss & Fussell, 1991). As such, feedback provides leaders with information about a subordinate's immediate perspective, and facilitates the production of messages that are tailored to a subordinate's information needs. As leaders acquire cues as to what knowledge a subordinate possesses, they can adapt their explanations, providing more or less information, as needed. The ability of a subordinate to provide feedback, and a leader's inference of a subordinate's knowledge on the basis of this feedback, facilitates the exchange of richer and more efficient communications.

As exchange relationships increase in quality, subordinates may also be more inclined to interact with the leader, after the initial discussion in which a goal is assigned, to ask for additional information (Fairhurst & Rhea Hamlett, 2003). It would be inappropriate to assume that leaders can influence subordinate goal commitment through their communications only during conversations when explicit goal assignments are made. Discussions that occur throughout the time period when subordinates are engaged in tasks aimed at goal attainment are also valuable opportunities for providing task-relevant information and clarification. Prior research (e.g., Kacmar, Witt, Zivnuska, & Gully, 2003; Schiemann, 1977) has suggested a positive correlation between LMX and communication frequency between leaders and subordinates. Thus, subordinates in high quality LMX relationships may have more opportunity to receive information that assists in their understanding of assigned goals. Leaders may be more inclined to follow-up with these subordinates, initiating opportunities for them to ask for clarifications or assistance. Subordinates in higher quality exchange relationships may also be more comfortable initiating opportunities for clarification, themselves. The credibility that they grant to their leaders may impact their desire to seek out assistance from him or her when in need of clarification. Additionally, because of their strong, interpersonal relationship with the leader, they may be less fearful that asking for clarification may signal incompetence, or lack of ability on their part.

In addition to more frequent communications, leaders and subordinates in higher quality exchange relationships may also enjoy longer and more detailed communication exchanges between them (Fairhurst & Rhea Hamlett, 2003). If lower quality relationships are lacking in mutual liking and social attraction, dyadic partners in these relationships may exhibit less desire to interact with one another for extended periods of time. Their interactions may be brief, and, as a result, less rich in information that may assist in a subordinate's understanding of a goal, its relevance, and the means through which it might be accomplished. Because of the importance this understanding plays in influencing a subordinate's desire to achieve a goal, as well as expectations of actual attainment, we propose:

> **Proposition 2:** LMX is positively related to communication richness between leaders and subordinates that serves to enhance subordinates' understanding of an assigned goal, its associated performance expectations, the means through which a goal can be achieved, and the importance of a goal to meeting organizational objectives. This understanding, in turn, results in heightened goal commitment and subsequent performance.

Personal Value of Attaining a Goal

The perceived value of the rewards associated with goal attainment may influence goal commitment (Locke & Latham, 1990). Leaders can enhance goal commitment, therefore, by rendering the achievement of a goal a personally meaningful endeavor to subordinates. A leader can accomplish this task by communicating a goal assignment in a way that facilitates linkages between rewards generated through goal attainment and their relevance to one's individual desires and aspirations. Communicating in this manner may improve a leader's ability to "grab" a subordinate's focus. Also, leader behavior that cultivates a subordinate's understanding that the achievement of goals is both rewarding and satisfying enhances interest and self-efficacy in tasks (House, 1996).

In order for leaders to render the achievement of a goal personally meaningful, some degree of leader familiarity with the individual needs and aspirations of their subordinates is required. Personal information acquired about subordinates facilitates the communication of goal assignments in a meaningful way. While in many cases, this may imply linking the achievement of a goal with personal career interests and intrinsic satisfaction, such appeals may not always prove effective. For example, subordinates who are motivated, in general, by immediate, monetary rewards, may be disinterested with assertions that meeting a goal will afford them "visibility within the organization" or an "opportunity to prove themselves." Due to the correspondence between LMX quality and communication frequency between leaders and subordinates (Kacmar et al., 2003), LMX should positively affect leaders' ability to make connections between rewards associated with achieving a goal and salient needs and desires of subordinates.

Given the positive association between LMX and communication frequency, increases in LMX quality may also result in a greater inclination for subordinates to pose questions and elicit information that will allow an accurate assessment of how the pursuit of a goal will meet their individual needs. Supporting this contention, Liden, Sparrowe, Erdogan, Gavino, and Maslyn (2002) found member feedback seeking from leaders to be positively related to LMX. Open-communication channels also contribute to furthering the amount of personal information that leaders may accrue regarding the ambitions of their subordinates. For instance, through conversations in which goals are assigned, leaders may learn of specific interests of their direct reports. This information may be taken into consideration and immediately acted upon by the leader through restructuring the specific nature of the goal and/or its associated rewards. Accounting for the relationship between valence and goal commitment (Locke, Latham, & Erez, 1988), we posit:

> **Proposition 3**: LMX is positively related to communication richness between leaders and subordinates that in turn serves to enhance the perceived, personal value of achieving a goal and subsequent goal commitment and performance.

Self-Efficacy

Self-efficacy refers to "judgments of how well one can execute courses of action required to deal with prospective situations" (Bandura, 1982, p. 122). These judgments may shape an individual's decisions regarding what pursuits to undertake, and affect an individual's determination to overcome challenges that are met while engaged in such pursuits (Bandura, 1982). Self-efficacy has been conceptualized as a task-specific (Gist & Mitchell, 1992) and domain specific trait, as well as a more generalized individual characteristic (Perrewé & Spector, 2002). For our purposes, we conceptualize self-efficacy as judgments corresponding with specific tasks that are required to attain an assigned goal. Both theory and the results of empirical research suggest a relationship between self-efficacy and goal commitment, such that an individual's perception that he or she has the ability to complete a goal may enhance commitment to it (Locke & Latham, 1990). Research also suggests a relationship between self-efficacy and in-role performance (Gist & Mitchell, 1992; Stajkovic & Luthans, 1998), highlighting the important individual and organizational level implications for creating an environment that is conducive to forming positive judgments regarding one's task-specific abilities.

Leaders, through their behavior toward subordinates, can influence perceptions of self-efficacy (Locke & Latham, 2002; Pillai & Williams, 2004). This process may occur in two important ways. First, leaders may provide cues, either directly or indirectly, as to the confidence they hold in a subordinate's abilities (Locke & Latham, 2002). Second, leaders can assist in clarifying the efforts required to accomplish a goal, allowing subordinates to make accurate judgments as to their ability to achieve them. An individual's assessment of efforts necessary to achieve a task can have important implications for self-efficacy (Gist & Mitchell, 1992). The ability to engage in both self-efficacy enhancing behaviors requires that the leader be viewed as credible and that he or she has sufficient familiarity with subordinates in order to communicate useful information.

Leaders may influence perceptions of self-efficacy by showing confidence in a subordinate's abilities (Eden, 1992). The act of assigning a difficult goal to an employee might indirectly imply confidence in a subordinate's ability to complete the task (Locke & Latham, 2002). Additionally, explicit communications may be generated that include direct assurances of a leader's confidence in a subordinate's performance abilities. Communications may also entail encouragement to apply the totality of these abilities to goal pursuit, such as "Give it your all, I know you can do it," types of messages. In lieu of such explicit communications, subordinates who enjoy positive relations with their leader may be better able to infer such confidence. Past communication exchanges or verbal rewards (such as "Good job, your work is always top notch") may be recalled and applied to this novel situation. Furthermore, subordinates in such relationships may be inclined to associate goal assignments with a leader's direct awareness for his or her competences. Such a subordinate may predict that a leader is aware of his or her capabilities and that the goal, itself, was generated with such an awareness in mind. In this sense, a subordinate may even view the goal as a type of social reward, in itself. Thoughts such as "He knows I'm competent, and that's why he's asked me to do this," may result from such an inference.

Likewise, information that is granted to subordinates that articulates the efforts necessary to complete a task may influence self-efficacy (Gist & Mitchell, 1992). An ambiguity may exist when a subordinate is assigned a goal, but is unaware of the required efforts that will be needed to attain it. In such a situation, individuals may waiver in their self-efficacy judgments, finding it difficult to commit to either perceptions of high or low task-ability. Past theorizing on the construct of self-efficacy suggests that supervisor explanations of the efforts necessary to achieve a goal may be particularly important with respect to novel tasks (Gist & Mitchell, 1992). The extent to which subordinates explicitly furnish information regarding the capabilities needed to attain a goal may enhance or diminish self-efficacy. Additionally, the degree to which a leader might accurately infer that a subordinate will link a present goal to one that was accomplished in the past, will affect his or her *need* to make the connection for the subordinate. Direct statements of information are not always necessary for them to be clearly understood by listeners (Hooper, 1981). For instance, if a leader expects that a subordinate will integrate the assignment of a goal with knowledge gained through past experience, he or she may not explicitly communicate such information. The accuracy with which these inferences are made will have consequences for self-efficacy.

Additionally, in order to generate messages that entail useful information as to the efforts that are required to accomplish a goal, a leader must have the motivation and ability to make accurate assessments of a subordinate's knowledge base. When a subordinate is unaware of all of the tasks associated with goal achievement, leaders can provide such information. Subordinates, in turn, may respond positively to this clarification, as it is necessary and useful (House, 1996). When this information is unnecessary, it may actually have negative consequences for self-efficacy. Communication of task-clarifying information that a subordinate already holds may indirectly signal a *lack* of confidence in a subordinate's abilities. Thus, a leader's accurate assessment of task-specific knowledge held by a subordinate will partially determine the influence that his or her communications may have on efficacy perceptions.

In summary, the communication event in which a leader assigns a goal to a subordinate offers an opportunity for the leader to influence a subordinate's task-specific self-efficacy. Because of the important relationship between an individual's perception that a goal is indeed attainable and goal commitment (Locke & Latham, 1990), we propose:

Proposition 4: LMX is positively related to communication richness between leaders and subordinates that serves to enhance subordinate self-efficacy and subsequent commitment to assigned goals and performance.

Goal Commitment and Performance

For difficult goals to incite high levels of performance, individuals must be committed to seeing them through (Hollenbeck, Williams, & Klein, 1989; Locke et al., 1988; Locke & Latham, 1990). If we presuppose that leaders set difficult goals for all of their subordinates, in an attempt to maximize employee outputs, then those subordinates who are most committed to achieving these goals should exhibit the highest levels of performance (Hollenbeck et al., 1989; Locke & Latham, 1990). As previously outlined, leaders can play an important role in enhancing goal commitment among their subordinates. As such, they are a critical source of continual influence that serves to *keep* subordinates dedicated to realizing ambitious performance objectives.

Although little empirical research has explored the effects of leader behaviors on the goal commitment to performance relationship, there is evidence to suggest that LMX quality does play a role in accounting for subordinate outcomes resulting from goal setting endeavors (e.g., Klein & Kim, 1998). According to Latham (2000, p. 113), "the organization needs to ensure that the time, money, people, and equipment necessary for goal attainment exist." Certainly, in many organizations, leaders hold the ability to ensure such provisions for their subordinates. Consistent with Klein and Kim (1998), we acknowledge that high quality exchange relationships with leaders offer members greater access to these resources, as well as elevated levels of social support that encourages them to exert their efforts toward goal attainment. Furthermore, we suggest that communication processes will play a significant function in ensuring that appropriate resources, explanations, and assistance are continually available to members. Over the duration of a member's pursuit of a performance goal, for example, frequent communication between leaders and members offers opportunities for asking for and providing clarification and feedback.

For these reasons, we propose that LMX quality supports not only the development, but also the *maintenance* of high levels of goal commitment. When faced with challenges, or a need for additional information, the availability of useful information and support from leaders keeps subordinates confident that goals can, indeed, be attained. Additionally, in moments when commitment may be in danger of decline, leaders can draw a subordinate's focus to the personal rewards associated with completion, in an attempt to keep the desire of task completion high. It would be interesting for future research to examine goal commitment longitudinally, to determine the extent to which LMX quality predicts the stability of high levels of goal commitment across the duration of a subordinate's pursuit of goal attainment. Overall, it is our contention that when a leader assigns performance goals that are equally difficult to a group of subordinates, the exchange relationship quality that is present between this leader and his or her unique subordinates will have important consequences for goal commitment and subsequent individual performance outcomes.

CONCLUSIONS

Now that a vast array of outcomes of LMX have been identified (Erdogan & Liden, 2002; Gerstner & Day, 1997; Graen, 2003; Liden, Sparrowe, & Wayne, 1997), research is needed that explores the processes underlying the documented associations between LMX and these outcomes. Perhaps of greatest importance to work organizations is the association between LMX and job performance. Given the established link between goal commitment and performance, our model of the processes through which LMX influences goal commitment also addresses the ways in which LMX may influence subordinate performance.

Despite the voluminous literature on goal setting, few studies have examined the role of leadership in subordinate goal commitment. Similarly, in the 30 years since it inception, path-goal theory of leadership remains inadequately tested (Schriesheim, Castro, Zhou, & DeChurch, 2006). Consistent with House and Mitchell (1974), we argue that leaders are instrumental in affecting subordinate goal acceptance and commitment. We further argue that it is the quality of the relationship between leader and subordinate and corresponding richness of communications that enable leaders to influence subordinate goal commitment. With the exception of a handful of researchers (e.g., Fairhurst, 1993; Fairhurst & Chandler, 1989; Fairhurst & Rhea Hamlett, 2003; Kacmar et al., 2003; Kramer, 2004; Lee, 2005; Lee & Jablin, 1995), communications have been ignored in the LMX literature. Unfortunately, as Fairhurst (2001, p. 419) laments, "marginalizing communication leaves researchers unable to explain the effects of social interaction fully," including its effects on goal commitment. Thus, we encourage researchers to examine the processes through which the quality of LMX relationships influences communications, which in turn affects goal commitment and subsequent performance.

In conducting this recommended research, it is imperative that researchers consider the way in which context influences the extent to which LMX and communications affect goal commitment. For example, organizational communications and communications with peers may provide sufficient information to the subordinate to comprehend the goal, its associated tasks, and outcomes. In such situations, communications from the leader that contain this information may be less influential in predicting goal commitment. In addition, culture may greatly influence the way in which leader-member relationships are perceived. Leaders may be afforded varying levels of status and power across cultures, rendering LMX quality more or less important with respect to the credibility that they are assigned and the impact that their messages may have on subordinate goal commitment and performance. Additionally, the differences in values and beliefs that exist across cultures may render the need for interpersonal familiarity between dyadic partners particularly important for the production of messages aimed at enhancing the attractiveness of goal achievement. Cultural differences in encoding and decoding communications messages should also be examined when exploring their mediating role in the association between LMX, goal commitment, and performance (Stohl, 2001).

Integrating both LMX and goal setting theory to account for subordinate commitment to assigned goals, and their subsequent performance, contributes to a better understanding of the fundamental role that leader-member relationships play in the goal setting process. When leaders communicate goal assignments to organizational members, these communications often arise and are exchanged within the dynamics of an existing social relationship. Exploring the effects of dyadic exchange relationship quality on the production, interpretation, and ultimate effectiveness of these messages is useful to furthering our understanding of how leaders might influence subordinate in-role behaviors. We invite goal setting scholars to join us in the worthy integration of these two theories that explicate individual performance in organizations.

REFERENCES

Bandura, A. (1982). Self-efficacy mechanism in human agency. *American Psychologist, 37*, 122-147.

Blau, P. M. (1964). *Exchange and power in social life*. New York: Wiley.

Chemers, M. M. (2001). Leader effectiveness: An integrative review. In M. A. Hogg & R. S. Tindale (Eds.), *Blackwell handbook of social psychology: Group processes* (pp. 376-399). Malden, MA: Blackwell.

Clark, H. H., & Marshall, C. E. (1981). Definite reference and mutual knowledge. In A. Joshi, B. Webber, & I. Sag (Eds.), *Elements of discourse understanding* (pp. 10-63). Cambridge: Cambridge University Press.

Dansereau, F., Graen, G., & Haga, W. J. (1975). A vertical dyad linkage approach to leadership within formal organizations: A longitudinal investigation of the role making process. *Organizational Behavior and Human Performance, 13*, 46-78.

Drake, B. H., & Moberg, D. J. (1986). Communicating influence attempts in dyads: Linguistic sedatives and palliatives. *Academy of Management Review, 11*, 567-584.

Earley, P. C. (1985). Influence of information, choice and task complexity upon goal acceptance, performance, and personal goals. *Journal of Applied Psychology, 70*, 481-491.

Earley, P. C. (1986). Supervisors and shop stewards as sources of contextual information in goal setting: A comparison of the United States with England. *Journal of Applied Psychology, 71*, 111-117.

Earley, P. C., & Lituchy, T. R. (1991). Delineating goal and efficacy effects: A test of three models. *Journal of Applied Psychology, 76*, 81-98.

Eden, D. (1992). Leadership and expectations: Pygmalion effects and other self-fulfilling prophecies in organizations. *Leadership Quarterly, 3*, 271-305.

Erdogan, B., & Liden, R. C. (2002). Social exchanges in the workplace: A review of recent developments and future research directions in leader-member exchange theory. In L. L. Neider & C. A. Schriesheim (Eds.), *Leadership* (pp. 65-114). Greenwich, CT: Information Age.

Fairhurst, G. T. (1993). The leader-member exchange patters of women leaders in industry: A discourse analysis. *Communication Monographs, 60*, 321-351.

Fairhurst, G. T. (2001). Dualisms in leadership research. In F.M. Jablin & L.L. Putnam (Eds.), *The new handbook of organizational communication* (pp. 379-439). Thousand Oaks, CA: Sage.

Fairhurst, G. T., & Chandler, T. A. (1989). Social structure in leader-member interaction. *Communication Monographs, 56*, 215-239.

Fairhurst, G. T., & Rhea Hamlett, S., (2003). The narrative basis of leader-member exchange. In G.B. Graen (Ed.), *Dealing with diversity: LMX leadership: The series* (Vol. 1, pp. 117-144). Greenwich, CT: Information Age.

Fairhurst, G. T., Rogers, L. E., & Sarr, R. A. (1987). Manager-subordinate control patterns and judgments about the relationship. In M. L. McLaughlin (Ed.), *Communication yearbook 10* (pp. 395-415). Beverly Hills, CA: Sage.

Gerstner, C. R., & Day, D. V. (1997). Meta-analytic review of leader-member exchange theory: Correlates and construct issues. *Journal of Applied Psychology, 82*, 827-844.

Gist, M. E., & Mitchell, T. R. (1992). Self-efficacy: A theoretical analysis of its determinants and malleability. *Academy of Management Review, 17*, 183-211.

Graen, G. B. (2003). Role making onto the starting work team using LMX leadership: Diversity as an asset. In G. B. Graen (Ed.), *Dealing with diversity: LMX leadership: The series* (Vol. 1, pp. 1-28). Greenwich, CT: Information Age.

Graen, G. B., & Uhl-Bien, M. (1995). Relationship-based approach to leadership: Development of leader-member exchange (LMX) theory of leadership over

25 years: Applying a multi-level multi-domain perspective. *Leadership Quarterly, 6,* 219-247.

Hewes, D., & Planalp, S. (1987). The individual's place in communication science. In. C. R. Berger & S. H. Chaffee (Eds.), *Handbook of communication science* (pp. 146-183). London: Sage.

Hollander, E. P. (1964). *Leaders, groups, and influence.* New York: Oxford University Press.

Hollander, E. P. (1980). Leadership and social exchange processes. In K. J. Gergen, M. S. Greenberg, & R. H. Willis (Eds.), *Social exchange: Advances in theory and research* (pp.103-118). New York: Plenum Press.

Hollenbeck, J. R., Williams, C. R., & Klein, H. J. (1989). An empirical examination of the antecedents of commitment to difficult goals. *Journal of Applied Psychology, 74,* 18-23.

House, R. (1996). Path-Goal theory of leadership: Lessons, legacy, and a reformulated theory, *Leadership Quarterly, 7,* 323-352.

House, R. J., & Mitchell, T. R. (1974). Path-goal theory of leadership. *Journal of Contemporary Business, 3,* 81-97.

Hopper, R. (1981). The taken-for-granted. *Human Communication Research, 7,* 195-211.

Jablin, F. M. (1979). Superior-subordinate communication: The state of the art. *Psychological Bulletin, 86,* 1201-1222.

Jost, J. T., Kruglanski, A. W., & Nelson, T. O. (1998). Social metacognition: An expansionist review. *Personality and Social Psychology Review, 2,* 137-154.

Kacmar, K. M., Witt, L. A., Zivnuska, S., & Gully, S. M. (2003). The interactive effect of leader-member exchange and communication frequency on performance ratings. *Journal of Applied Psychology, 88,* 764-772.

Katz, D., & Kahn, R. L. (1978). *The social psychology of organizations.* New York: John Wiley & Sons.

Klein, H. J., & Kim, J. S. (1998). A field study of the influence of situational constraints, leader-member exchange, and goal commitment on performance. *Academy of Management Journal, 41,* 88-95.

Klein, H. J., Wesson, M. J., Hollenbeck, J. R., & Alge, B. J. (1999). Goal commitment and the goal-setting process: Conceptual clarification and empirical synthesis. *Journal of Applied Psychology, 84,* 885-896.

Kramer, M. W. (2004). Toward a theory of dialectics in group communication: An ethnographic study of a community theater group. *Communication Monographs, 71,* 311-332.

Krauss, R. M., & Fussell, S. R. (1991). Perspective-taking in communication: Representations of others' knowledge in reference. *Social Cognition, 9,* 2-24.

Latham, G. P. (2000). Motivate employee performance through goal-setting. In E.A. Locke (Ed.), *The Blackwell handbook of principles of organizational behavior* (pp. 107-119). Oxford: Blackwell Publishers.

Lee, J. (2005). Communication as antecedents and consequences of LMX development globally: A new strong inference approach. In G. B. Graen & J. A. Graen (Eds.), *Global organizing designs, LMX leadership: The series* (Vol. 3, pp. 1-41). Greenwich, CT: Information Age.

Lee, J., & Jablin, F. M. (1995). Maintenance communication in superior-subordinate work relationships. *Human Communications Research, 22*, 220-257.

Liden, R. C., & Maslyn, J. M. (1998). Multidimensionality of leader-member exchange: An empirical assessment trough scale development. *Journal of Management, 24*, 43-72.

Liden, R. C., Sparrowe, R. T., Erdogan, B., Gavino, M., & Maslyn, J. M. (2002, August). *The role of proactive characteristics and behaviors on exchange relationships and outcomes.* Paper presented at the national meetings of the Academy of Management, Denver, CO.

Liden, R. C., Sparrowe, R. T., & Wayne, S. J. (1997). Leader-member exchange theory: The past and potential for the future. In G.R. Ferris (Ed.), *Research in personnel and human resources management* (Vol. 15, pp. 47-119). Greenwich, CT: JAI Press.

Liden, R. C. Wayne, S. J., & Sparrowe, R. T. (2000). An examination of the mediating role of psychological empowerment on the relations between the job, interpersonal relationships, and work outcomes. *Journal of Applied Psychology, 85*, 407-416.

Liden, R. C., Wayne, S. J., & Stilwell, D. (1993). A longitudinal study on the early development of leader-member exchanges. *Journal of Applied Psychology, 78*, 662-674.

Locke, E. A., & Latham, G. P. (1990). *A theory of goal setting and task performance.* Englewood Cliffs, NJ: Prentice-Hall.

Locke, E. A., & Latham, G. P. (2002). Building a practically useful theory of goal setting and task motivation: A 35-year odyssey. *American Psychologist, 57*, 705-717.

Locke, E. A., Latham, G. P., & Erez, M. (1988). The determinants of goal commitment. *Academy of Management Review, 13*, 23-39.

Maslyn, J. M., & Uhl-Bien, M. (2001). Leader-member exchange and its dimensions: Effects of self-effort and other's effort on relationship quality. *Journal of Applied Psychology, 86*, 697-708.

Perrewé, P.L., & Spector, P.E. (2002). Personality research in the organizational sciences. In G.R. Ferris & J.J. Martocchio (Eds.), *Research in personnel and human resources management* (Vol. 21, pp. 1-63). Oxford: JAI Press.

Petty, R. E., & Wegener, D. T. (1998). Attitude change: Multiple roles for persuasion variables. In D. T. Gilbert, S. T. Fiske, & G. Lindzey (Eds.), *The handbook of social psychology* (4th ed., pp. 323-390). Boston: McGraw-Hill.

Pillai, R., & Williams, E. A. (2004). Transformational leadership, self-efficacy, group cohesiveness, commitment, and performance. *Journal of Organizational Change Management, 17*, 144-159.

Planalp, S., & Hewes, D. (1982). A cognitive approach to communication theory: Cogito Ergo Dico? In M. Burgoon (Ed.), *Communication yearbook* (Vol. 5, pp. 49-77). New Brunswick, NJ: Transaction Books.

Riggio, R. E., Riggio, H. R., Salinas, C., & Cole, E. J. (2003). The role of social and emotional communication skills in leader emergence and effectiveness. *Group Dynamics: Theory, Research, and Practice, 7*, 83-103.

Ross, L., Greene, D., & House, P. (1977). The "false consensus effect": An egocentric bias in social perception and attribution processes. *Journal of Experimental Social Psychology, 13,* 279-301.

Scandura, T. A., Graen, G. B., & Novak, M. A. (1986). When managers decide not to decide autocratically: An investigation of leader-member exchange and decision influence. *Journal of Applied Psychology, 71,* 579-584.

Schiemann, W. A. (1977). *Structural and interpersonal effects on patterns of managerial communications: A longitudinal investigation.* S. Rains Wallace Award Doctoral Dissertation, University of Illinois.

Schriesheim, C. A., Castro, S. L., Zhou, X., & DeChurch, L. A. (2006) An investigation of path-goal and transformational leadership theory predictions at the individual level of analysis. *Leadership Quarterly, 17,* 21-38.

Stajkovic, A. D., & Luthans, F. (1998). Self-efficacy and work-related performance: A meta-analysis. *Psychological Bulletin, 124,* 240-261.

Stohl, C. (2001). Globalizing organizational communication. In F.M. Jablin & L.L. Putnam (Eds.), *The new handbook of organizational communication* (pp. 323-375). Thousand Oaks, CA: Sage.

Tsui, A. S. (1984). A role set analysis of managerial reputation. *Organizational Behavior & Human Performance, 34,* 64-96.

Waldron, V. R. (1991). Achieving communication goals in superior-subordinate relationships: The multi-functionality of upward maintenance tactics. *Communication Monographs, 58,* 289-306.

Yrle, A. C., Hartman, S. J., & Galle, W.P . (2003). Examining communication style and leader-member exchange: Considerations and concerns for managers. *International Journal of Management, 20,* 92-100.

CHAPTER 12

POST SIMON, MARCH, WEICK, AND GRAEN

New Leadership Sharing as a Key to Understanding Organizing

George B. Graen

Editing this LMX series continues to be a delightful and fulfilling journey for me. I have interacted on a deep-level with some of the brightest researchers in the field of face-to-face organizational innovation and been influenced by their work. My dream is to make a contribution to the integration of leadership sharing as a process to create social capital via networks for the benefit of team and larger networks including organizations. As a part of this integration process we have begun to show how the revised LMX-MMX leadership theory can be integrated with goal setting, organizational cynicism, emotional intelligence, social capital, and strategy. In this final chapter of the fourth volume of *LMX Leadership: The Series* I have attempted to show where we have been and where we are going.

PERSPECTIVE

In the United States when I came on the scene in the late 1950s, the leading business journals had long outgrown autobiographic stories of my years as CEO of General Bullmoose, were winding down a brief infatuation with decision sciences, and were already in a full-fledged affair with behavioral sciences. However, the behavioral sciences were being factored into the so-called "functional areas of business" (FAB) such as, finance, strategy, supervision and management, human resources, marketing, production, and engineering. Accordingly, the new Academy of Management also was divided into FAB. What FAB did was to partition organizational problems and solutions into separate departments of schools of business. This partitioning made little sense to Simon, March and Weick who conceived of organizations as decision systems designed and implemented by humans with little regard for FAB. Today, their continued efforts have begun to yield converts to their more research-based approach to the field of organizations. As I read Simon, March, and Weick, even the organizational behavior of strategizing was the result of a flow of behavior by human decision makers to detect and process events over time and space. They saw humans operating at many separate parts of many networks to energize the microsystems that are transformed into meso-systems that finally are converted into macro-systems. Humans employing technology, but following the general laws of the basic behavioral sciences, motivate these human networks.

Orton (2006) thinks that it is important to recognize that there might be three eras of leadership research—pre-culture studies (1970s), during-culture studies (1980s), and post-culture studies (1990s). There was a strong leadership research field in the 1960s and 1970s, then there was a withering critique of leadership theories (Selznick, 1957), and then there was a resurgence of new leadership theories, such as LMX. Although researchers in leadership trace their history as an unbroken progression, it is probably more honest to recognize their interdependence with culture researchers. If Selznick describes the decline of leadership and the rise of culture, Martin describes the decline of culture and the rise of leadership in her discussions of integrated, differentiated, and fragmented cultures (Martin, 1992; Meyerson & Martin, 1987). The observation that leaders need to become more complicated (Bartunek, Gordon, & Weathersby, 1983) to treat people differently in fragmented cultures clearly places LMX on the "new" or "post-culture" side of leadership research.

One important outcome of the "meltdown" of culture theories in the 1980s was the rise of research and practice on teamwork (Ancona & Caldwell, 1985; Gersick, 1988; Hackman, 1987; Katz, 1984). So I think the historical funnel here is (1) the meltdown of culture research, (2) leadership theories that explain fragmented cultures, (3) the leadership of teams within fragmented cultures, and (4) how a LMX perspective contributes to the study of the leadership of teams within fragmented cultures?

Volume 4 of *LMX Leadership: The Series* is focused on forwarding this view integrated with that of the legal view which assumes that organizations are entities that can contract for specific orderly human behavior. These legal entities can hire and compensate humans for outlined formal roles and ensure legal compliance with all written rules and procedures. This has been called the formal organization. Although lawyers love its perfectly defensible logic, it often does not predict human behavior. This has been understood by behavior science for a long time: Because many formal plans are incomplete, they become obsolete, even as general guides, and require unwritten human organizing to allow sense making.

It is my experience that organizations that find ways to legitimatize as formal those informal plans that delay obsolesce are the most competitive and well managed. In every organization, we as researchers must ask three general questions about our subject organizations: (1) What is the formal organization (written rules) and how is it enforced? (2) What is the informal organization (unwritten rules) and how does it operate? (3) How does the informal system keep critical parts of the formal system viable?

According to this view (Graen, 1976), humans react in two very different ways to formal roles in organizations. Some people enact "role-taking" (Katz & Kahn, 1978) in which humans accept all the formal rules and procedures religiously. Other people enact "role-making" (Graen, 1976) in which humans negotiate the rules and procedures as dynamic guidelines. Because the formal organization is a legal fiction designed to minimize exposure to lawsuits first and foremost and organizational efficiency and effectiveness secondly, the threat of punishment for role making is ever present. However, the market demands require that informal systems be developed and used. Thus, to make sense out of human systems, informal systems need to be understood along with the formal system demands factored into the equations. In this book we have focused on how the informal networks change the rules of the game for organizational members and change both the means and the ends for organizations.

Clearly, formal organization plans are incomplete as illustrated by the British labor unions tactic of "work to rule," by which union members only follow the written (formal) rules and take no informal action. Without needed informal actions, their organizations slowly grind to a halt. Human's are not intelligent enough to anticipate every contingency of complex organization's future situation, thus their formal plans for organizations need to be open to human sense making.

SMALL GAINS

This fourth volume carries on our outlining of the process and context of keys to unlocking the world of post Simon, March, and Weick called "Role Making." Once scholars and researchers discover this world, we hope that they can gradually document how frail humans continuously invent complex organizations from the inside. Next, we turn to commenting on our contributors.

We begin in chapter one with Kramer's endographic study over the life-cycle of real theatrical production. As an active participant observer, Kramer describes from the inside, using his carefully written notes, the gradual trust building process of successively increasing leadership sharing and the corresponding maturity on the LMX dimensions. He illustrates how LMX-MMX leaders ask for leadership sharing from cast and crew and carefully negotiate the sharing process over the life of the organization. These are concrete examples of how it is accomplished.

In the next chapter, Graen illuminates the components of LMX leadership theory that were illustrated by Kramer's cases including the need to expand LMX leadership theory to include the member to member exchanges (MMX). This inclusion requires new research on the team and larger networks that are partly driven by the new LMX-MMX theory generating social capital for the team or network and reciprocally being influenced by these same social networks. One way to look at an aspect of social capital is to see one's social capital network as a network of people who will be helpful when asked. Without social capital being developed with these people, they may be less than helpful. The infamous reply to a request for help on your work problems by those outside of your network is, "Sorry, it's not my job."

In chapter three Mayer and Piccolo follow with strong arguments for the integration of LMX-MMX leadership sharing with network theory and analysis. They argue and we agree that LMX should be examined with increasingly complex social network models and by expanding multi-level models. As we learn more about the pervasive influences of LMX and MMX on teams and larger networks, we need to also get back to the most revealing research design of LMX-MMX leadership, namely, the life cycle longitudinal design using network methods (Graen, 2003). These advanced programs of research and theory have already begun anew and the early results are promising (Graen, Hui, & Taylor, 2004; Sparrowe & Liden, 2005).

In chapter four, Gibbons and Grover provide a much needed review of the relevant parts of network analysis and its contributions to our understanding of the influences of networks on individuals and teams. The authors clearly illustrate how the network setting can make team leaders more or less capable and their teams more or less effective. Two critical questions one may ask of every participant in an organization are who do you go to for help on the job and who do you go to for advice on a personal problem? The first identifies a focal person's influence network (social capital) and the second question identifies the personal support network (personal capital). As shown by Sparrowe and Liden (2005) those members seen as more influential throughout the organization had strong LMX leadership with their leader and belonged to the same competence network as their leader.

In chapter five, Offstein, Madhavan, and Gnyawali guide us through the special domain of social triad. They outline the behavior that cannot be analyzed in a dyad. For example, units of three or more members allow coalition formation on various issues and the use of strategies and tactics. Moreover, the complete LMX-MMX triad is one of the critical units in network analysis and it has a lot to show researchers. Chapter six, Susskind, Behfar, and Borchgrevink present an approach to distant team leadership using communication network structures and teamwork. Many teams cut across great distances and different home organizations in the information age. We agree that more studies of this kind are needed.

Orton and Dhillon, in chapter seven, open wide the doors between leadership and strategy by making three requests of leadership: (1) Drag itself from its roots in outdated command and control to a post Simon, March, and Weick environment of loosely coupled networks and schizoid incoherence, (2) Begin mapping shared repertoire of meso-strategies used in organizations, and (3) Look for the connections between generic macro-strategies, meso-strategic options and micro-strategic actions over time.

Orton and Dhillon propose the integration of micro-meso-macro human problem finding, solving and implementing that I wrote about (Graen, 1989), but they have added something that could supply an integration of an organization's motivation with the motivation of its members over time and space. I find so much of generic macro strategizing is postdictive and grossly incomplete as they illustrate with Honda cases A, B, C and I could add D. In contrast, their predictive approach is a fresh breath. Simon, March and Weick viewed strategizing as a flow of actions by human decision makers to detected and process events over time and space. Because humans are imperfect organisms, operating with faulty information and crude processing technology in ever changing environments, their strategizing flows can be understood but not well predicted. They see the LMX-MMX theory to be well positioned to incorporate these concepts because of its roots in enactment research and role-making. We agree enthusiastically.

As summarized so neatly by Smith in chapter eight, the LMX-MMX leadership sharing phenomenon begins with the perceived utility of social capital derived from enriched working relations and the efficacy of attainment for two or more people leading to an agreement to exchange leadership. Success of initial collaborations lead to greater leadership sharing and social capital for all parties and an improved quality of LMX-MMX relations which leads to trust worthy behavior inside information sharing, and sharing of ties in working networks. These LMX-MMX improvements lead to social capital increases of relational, cognitive, and structural dimensions. Smith neatly integrates emotional intelligence into this developmental process of growing social capital.

In chapter nine Brandes, Das, and Hadani reserve a place for top management cynicism among the numerous influences of LMX leadership. Thus, the better the working relationship with one's leader, the more critical one can be about leadership at the top of the organization. However, this relationship is moderated by a follower's attitude of top management in which only the high LMX with negative attitudes toward top management are especially cynical. This fits into the overall model in which leaders allow those sharing leadership to speak their minds about top management.

Next, in chapter ten, Schyns, Kroon, and Sanders review the European concept of "solidarity behavior" in relation to LMX leadership. Solidarity is indicated by a follower's readiness to help the leader or team member. Solidarity may be related more closely to organizational citizen's behavior (OCB) than to LMX leadership. Also, LMX leadership works better in teams that prefer to share leadership and not only OCB.

Finally, in chapter eleven, Henderson, Dulac and Liden integrate LMX-MMX leadership with goal setting theory. They point out that the weakness of goal setting theory and research is that the process of difficult goal acceptance by followers is not well understood. It requires the proper motivation and support in real organizations. "Where do these come from?" asks LMX leadership. Unless leaders supply the proper motivation and support, difficult goals will not be accepted and subsequent strong performance will not follow. Henderson and his colleagues propose the long overdue marriage of goal setting with LMX-MMX leadership in which leadership sharing over time provides the necessary motivation, direction and support for goal acceptance and subsequent performance.

For example, in a classic study by Klein and Kim (1998) LMX leadership in a retail sales situation was strongly related to both very high and very low performance and this was in line with high or low goal acceptance. Because the piece-rate sales system rewarded annual increases in average annual sales, salespeople could maximize their income by alternately performing high one year and low the next. Clearly, the way the sales managers rewarded the high LMX followers was to allow them to perform very high and very low on alternative years. In this way, in any given year, high LMX followers would be very high or very low on sales improvement. Simple goal setting theory could only show that sales people do what they said they would do on performance. It could not explain the interaction of LMX and set goals on performance in a retail sales situation. High LMX followers who set high goals were the highest performers and those who set low goals were the lowest performers. My marketing colleagues tell me that this is a common result of this dominant sales incentive system. Leaders can reward those who share sales leadership by allowing them to perform at a very low level every other year and drive down the bogy (three-year moving average of annual sales). It is time that leader influenced goal settings be studied outside of the demand characteristics of the college sophomore laboratory in introductory psychology.

CONCLUSIONS

After considering all eleven separate original contributions to move the realization of our dream forward by small gains, my conclusions are as follows.

1. Most of organizational behavior or the behavior of humans in organizations is overdetermined by the rules and procedures of the formal organization enforced by legal contracts and agreements. That being stated, the most interesting and beneficial behavior is underdetermined and is called informal organization. Both are necessary for an organization's survival. Informal organization is governed by the nature of humans as self-aware, need satisfying, social creatures with limited rationality, imperfect information, creative imaginations, and deep-seated hopes and fears.
2. Informal organizations can be mapped in terms of networks of expertise, information, influence, and social capital at any point in time and overtime in terms of flows sensing relevant events, sense making, and implementation throughout the organization and its environments. As Orton and Dhillon described in chapter seven, the flows of strategy formulation goes from micro-actions to meso-options to macro-strategy for the purpose of continuously improving the organization's future. One key to this mapping process is the rigorous measurement of relationships between formal and informal influences on individual, team and network flows of behavior. Two different types of working relationships are LMX

and MMX with LMX being vertical and MMX being every direction but vertical. Research consistently documents that LMX relationships are social capital treasure chests of face-to-face leadership.

3. LMX leadership relations are granted by followers to leaders in exchange and in proportion for shared leadership. Thus, for a leader to grow his or her leadership influence to get the right things done the right way, he or she must find a way to share leadership with those ready and willing to invest it properly. Leaders who understand this multiplier effect are those who are most successful over their entire careers.

4. Those leaders who understand that MMX leadership sharing among members creates social capital throughout networks should encourage their associates and followers to do so for the good of their organization and their careers.

5. Leaders can destroy their social capital if they are not careful. Those who understand this and respect their followers will benefit from social capital.

6. Leaders who successfully grow influence in their networks also agree that those in their influence network can in turn influence them.

7. Certain people in organizations can form a "competence network" for a focal person. This is an influence network made up of people with abundant social capital that get "impossible" things done in bureaucracies (Graen, 1989).

8. We support the marriage of leadership theory and network analysis theory and hope that the new LMX-MMX theory of leadership sharing in teams and networks is a step in that direction. We have expected the goal to be reached soon after our early research showed that the LMX of one's leader with his or her boss limited the influence and social capital of a focal person (Graen, Cashman, Ginsburg, & Schiemann, 1977). The network up and down the chain of command made a difference for lower participants.

9. The impact of what a leader says to his or her follower depends on the particular leadership sharing LMX between the two (Wang & Law, 2005). A leader may use any of a number of transformation leadership styles, but the proof of the pudding is in the critical exchange of leadership. We shouldn't be fooled by the ease of training leaders to talk the "transformation" talk to followers and forget about the critical process of using authentic leadership sharing to grow leadership and other social capital. Clearly, it doesn't matter what the leader says about vision, if followers do not really

listen and buy in. We need to let a million flowers bloom to the understanding of more authentic leadership.

Finally, the new frontiers of leadership are keys to understanding the impact of informal organizational networks on the resultant behavior of organizations as micro-actions move to meso-options and to macro-strategizing. The door to putting human and organizational structures together is open and we hope that we have lit a few candles at the door.

A FINAL NOTE

The new "LMX-MMX theory of Sharing Network Leadership" has benefitted immeasurably from the many brilliant contributions of scholars to the successful integration of several loosely coupled research areas, such as, LMX leadership sharing, network theory, goal setting, emotional intelligence, mentoring, cynicism, March, Simon, and Weick, communications, strategy, multilevel theory, teamwork both local and distant, social capital and European solidarity. This integrated theory has taken a quantum leap in this volume IV of *LMX Leadership: The Series*. We are proud of the progress that we have made since the series began in 2003. As we look back and ask where we were in 2003, we thankfully can say, several light years back from where we are today. However, we are not finished and more research needs to be done. Herein lies many opportunities for researchers from pre-dissertation to endowed researchers to make real contributions to our understanding of the extremely powerful area of shared network leadership.

REFERENCES

Ancona, D. G., & Caldwell, D. F. (1985). *Boundary management in new product teams*. Paper presented at the Academy of Management, San Diego.

Bartunek, J. M., Gordon, J. R., & Weathersby, R. P. (1983). Developing 'complicated' understanding in administrators. *Academy of Management Review, 8*, 273-284.

Bougon, M., Weick, K. E., & Binkhorst, D. (1977). Cognition in organizations: An analysis of the Utrecht Jazz Orchestra. *Administrative Science Quarterly, 22*, 606-639.

Gersick, C. J. G. (1988). Time and transition in work teams: Toward a new model of group development. *Academy of Management Journal, 31*, 9-41.

Glynn, M. A. (2000). When cymbals become symbols: Conflict over organizational identity within a symphony orchestra. *Organization Science, 11*(3), 285-298.

Graen, G. B., (1976). Role making processes within complex organizations. In M.D. Dunnette (Ed.), *Handbook of industrial and organizational psychology* (pp. 1201-1245). Chicago: Rand McNally.

Graen, G. B. (1989). *Unwritten rules for your career: 15 secrets for fast-track success.* New York: Wiley.

Graen, G. B. (2003). Interpersonal workplace theory at the crossroads. In G. B. Graen (Ed.), *Dealing with diversity: LMX leadership: The series* (Vol. 1, pp. 145-182). Greenwich, CT: Information Age.

Graen, G. B., Cashman, J. F., Ginsburg, S., & Schiemann, W. (1977). Effects of linking-pin on the quality of working life of lower participants. *Administrative Science Quarterly, 22,* 491-504.

Graen, G. B., Hui, C., & Taylor, E. T. (2004). A new approach to team leadership: Upward, downward, and horizontal differentiation. In G.B. Graen (Ed.), *New frontiers of leadership: LMX leadership: The series* (Vol. 2, pp. 33-66). Greenwich, CT: Information Age.

Hackman, J. R. (1987). The design of work teams. In J.W. Lorsch (Ed.), *Handbook of organizational behavior* (pp. 315-342). Englewood Cliffs, NJ: Prentice-Hall.

Katz, R. (1984, January-February). As research teams grow older. *Research Management,* 23-28.

Klein, H. J., & Kim, J. S. (1998). A field study of the influence of situational constraints, leader-member exchange and goal commitment on performance. *Academy of Management Journal, 41,* 88-95.

Martin, J. (1992). *Cultures in organizations: Three perspectives.* New York: Oxford University Press.

Meyerson, D., & Martin, J. (1987). Cultural change: An integration of three different views. *Journal of Management Studies, 24,* 623-647.

Orton, J. D., & Dhillon, G. (2006). Macrostrategic, mesostrategic, and microstrategic leadership processes in loosely coupled networks. In G. B. Graen (Ed.), *Sharing network leadership: LMX leadership: The series* (Vol. 4, pp. 137-167). Greenwich, CT: Information Age.

Selznick, P. (1957). *Leadership in administration: A sociological interpretation.* New York: Harper & Row

Sparrowe, R. T., & Liden, R. C. (2005). Two routes to influence: Integrating leader-member exchange and network perspectives. *Administrative Science Quarterly, 50,* 4

Wang, H., & Law, K. S. (2005). Integrating LMX and member reactions (MDM): The joint effects on task performance and OCB. *Journal of Applied Psychology,* in press.

ABOUT THE AUTHORS

Kristin Behfar is an Assistant Professor Of Organization and Management at the Merage School of Business, University of California, Irvine. Prior to joining the Merage School of Business she was a post-doctoral fellow at the Kellogg School of Management, Northwestern University and completed her Ph.D. at the Johnson School of Management, Cornell University. Her research program focuses on work strategies and processes that predict sustainable performance outcomes in teams. Her work has appeared in *Organizational Behavior and Human Decision Processes* and *Organizational Research Methods*. She is the co-editor of *Conflict in Organizational Teams: New Directions in Theory and Practice*.

Carl P. Borchgrevink has a Ph.D. in Communication from Michigan State University, an MS in Hotel, Restaurant and Travel Administration from the University of Massachusetts, a Norwegian undergraduate degree from the Norwegian Hotel School, a culinary degree from Oslo Vocational School, and has a Norwegian Chef's Certificate (Kokkefagbrev). His research interests include Leader-Member Exchange, Service Management, Service Employee Persuasive Influence, Food and Beverage Operations and Management, and Menu Language. Prior to his academic career, Dr. Carl P. Borchgrevink, accumulated 14 years of hospitality business experience. The positions he held included Chef, Restaurant Manager, and Foodservice Manager.

Pamela Brandes is an Assistant Professor of Strategy and Human Resource Management at the Whitman School of Management at Syracuse University. Her main research and teaching interests include executive and non-executive employee compensation, corporate governance, and employee-organization linkages. She has published in *Academy of Management Review, Academy of Management Executive, Group and Organizational Behavior, Human Resource Management Review,* and *Journal of Business Research*. She completed her Ph.D. in Management from the University of Cincinnati.

Diya Das is a doctoral candidate in the department of Strategy and Human Resource Management at the Whitman School of Management at Syracuse University. Her main research interests include issues of social identities in global workplaces, executive compensation, employee surveillance, and the employee-organization interface. She has published in *Human Resource Management Review*. She has an Undergraduate Honors in Sociology from Presidency College, Calcutta, and a Masters from the Delhi School of Economics in Human Resources and Organizational Development.

Gurpreet Dhillon is Professor of Information Systems in the School of Business, Virginia Commonwealth University, Richmond. He holds a Ph.D. from the London School of Economics and Political Science, UK. His research interests include management of information security, ethical and legal implications of information technology. His research has been published in several journals including *Information Systems Research, Information & Management, Communications of the ACM, Computers & Security, European Journal of Information Systems, Information Systems Journal, and International Journal of Information Management* among others. Gurpreet has authored six books including *Principles of Information Systems Security: Text and Cases* (John Wiley, 2007). He is also the Editor-in-Chief of the *Journal of Information System Security*, is the North American Regional Editor of the *International Journal of Information Management* and sits on the editorial board of *MISQ Executive*. Gurpreet consults regularly with industry and government and has completed assignments for various organizations in India, Portugal, UK and the United States.

Tanguy Dulac is a Ph.D. student in the Louvain School of Management, Université catholique de Louvain (Belgium). He was awarded a fellowship from the Intercollegiate Center for Management Science, starting in September 2003, to conduct research on the development of the psychological contract during organizational socialization. His current research interests include the psychological contract, organizational socialization, and the strategic management of human capital.

Deborah Gibbons is an Assistant Professor at the Graduate School of Business and Public Policy in the Naval Postgraduate School. She received her Ph.D. in organizational behavior and theory from Carnegie Mellon University. Her research arena addresses antecedents, attributes, and outcomes of social networks at levels ranging from individual relationships through inter-organizational systems. Working at the individual and network levels, Deborah has partnered with several schools, the City of Atlanta government, and the U.S. Centers for Disease Control and Prevention to study effects of social relations and networks on innovation, attitudes, and knowledge dissemination. Recently, she has expanded this work to interventions that support stakeholders' participation in community-based networks and crisis management. Her current research involves assessment, benchmarking, and development of inter-organizational networks.

Devi R. Gnyawali is Associate Professor of Management at the R. B. Pamplin College of Business, Virginia Polytechnic Institute and State University (Virginia Tech). He received his Ph.D. in strategic management from the University of Pittsburgh. His research interests include competition and collaboration, inter-firm networks, learning and innovation. His research has been published in the *Academy of Management Review, Academy of Management Journal, Journal of Management, Human Resources Management Review, Journal of Engineering and Technology Management, Management Learning*, and other referred journals. His research has won awards from the *Academy of Management Review*, Strategic Management Society, and National Meetings of the Academy of Management.

George B. Graen is a founding member of the Society of Organizational Behavior (SOB), a Paul Harris Fellow and international volunteer of Rotary, and a member of Artists of Northwest Arkansas. He is a Grandad of four, Dad of two sons and 46 year husband of Joan and he continues his professional life as the internationally known father of several (popular and well established) methods for developing successful LMX leaders and followers and building effective LMX teams in organizations of all kinds. He grew up in North Minneapolis, married his high school sweetheart and served his country before going on to the University of Minnesota majoring in psychology and staying for all three degrees. He and his young family journeyed to the University of Illinois for 10 years, then to the University of Cincinnati for 20 years, before a stint at the University of Louisiana (Cajun U). During his career, he taught at Keio University in Tokyo and Nagoya University both in Japan, the University of Science and Technology in Hong Kong, and Dong Hua University in Shanghai,

China. He keeps busy editing *LMX Leadership: The Series* and doing LMX theory research and consulting globally.

Steven L. Grover (Ph.D., Columbia University) is a Chaired Professor of Management at the University of Otago in Dunedin New Zealand. He researches leader honesty and integrity and his publications have appeared in journals including *Administrative Science Quarterly, Academy of Management Journal, Organizational Behavior and Human Decision Processes,* and *the Journal of Applied Psychology.* Before moving to New Zealand he held positions at Indiana University and Georgia State University.

Michael Hadani is a doctoral candidate in the department of Strategy and Human Resource Management at the Whitman School of Management at Syracuse University. His main research interests include compensation and executive compensation, employee attitudes and the business-government interaction. He has published in the *Journal of Business Research*. He has an Undergraduate Honors in Psychology from the Hebrew University, Jerusalem, and a Masters in Organizational Psychology from the same institution.

David Henderson is currently pursuing a Ph.D. in Human Resource Management at the University of Illinois at Chicago. Prior to beginning his doctoral studies, David completed a Masters Degree in International Business, as well as a Masters Degree in French Language and Linguistics at the University of Florida. His research interests center around the study of leadership, social exchange, and culture.

Michael W. Kramer received his Ph.D. from the University of Texas at Austin in 1991. He is Professor and Chair of the Department of Communication at the University of Missouri-Columbia. He has over 20 years of experience teaching organizational and group communication courses at the undergraduate and graduate level. His research initially focused on using quantitative and interview methods to examine career transitions of organizational members, such as newcomers, transferees, those recently promoted, and those involved in mergers and acquisitions. He continues to explore how communication with supervisors and coworkers helps employees manage their uncertainty during the various transitions. He has more recently begun doing ethnographic research to examine communication processes, dialectical tensions, and issues of shared leadership in theater groups.

Brigitte Kroon (Msc, Radboud University Nijmegen, 1994) is a scholar of Human Resource Studies at Tilburg University, the Netherlands, were she teaches personnel testing and research skills. Her Ph.D. research examines the structuration of HRM practices in start-up organizations through social cognitive processes, especially in the interpersonal relations between founder and employees.

Robert C. Liden (Ph.D., University of Cincinnati) is Professor of Management at the University of Illinois at Chicago, where he is Director of the OB/HRM doctoral program. His research focuses on interpersonal processes as they relate to such topics as leadership, groups, career progression and employment interviews. He has over 50 publications in journals such as the *Academy of Management Journal, Academy of Management Review, Administrative Science Quarterly, Journal of Applied Psychology, Journal of Management, Journal of Organizational Behavior, Organizational Behavior and Human Decision Processes*, and *Personnel Psychology*. In 2000 he was inducted into the Academy of Management Journals' Hall of Fame as a charter bronze member. He won awards (with coauthors) for the best article published in the *Academy of Management Journal* during 2001, as well as the best article published in *Human Resource Management* during 2001. He has served on the editorial boards of the *Journal of Management* since 1994, *Leadership Quarterly* since 2004, and the *Academy of Management Journal* from 1994-1999. He was the 1999 Program Chair and 2000-01 Division Chair for the Academy of Management's Organizational Behavior Division.

Ravindranath (Ravi) Madhavan is Associate Professor of Business Administration at the Katz Graduate School of Business, University of Pittsburgh. He received his Ph.D. in strategic management from the University of Pittsburgh in 1996. His research focuses on the interaction structure of competitive advantage, i.e., how the structure of firm-to-firm interactions (including, but not limited to, alliance networks) influences competitive advantage. Ravi's papers have been published in the *Academy of Management Review, Academy of Management Journal, Strategic Management Journal, Journal of Management*, and the *Journal of International Business Studies*, as well as in other refereed journals. Ravi has received research funding from, among others, the Alfred P. Sloan Foundation, the National Science Foundation, and the International Business Center at the University of Pittsburgh.

David M. Mayer is an Assistant Professor of Management in the College of Business Administration at the University of Central Florida. He received his Ph.D., in industrial/organizational psychology from the University of Maryland. His research interests concern social and ethical issues in the workplace with a specific focus on organizational justice, workplace diversity, and business ethics and society. His research has been published in the *Academy of Management Journal*, *Journal of Applied Psychology*, and *Human Performance*.

Evan Offstein is an Assistant Professor of Business Management at Frostburg State University. A former Military Intelligence Officer, Offstein is a graduate of the United States Military Academy at West Point. He earned a Master's degree in administration from Central Michigan University and a doctorate in business from Virginia Tech. He has managed and led at profit and non-profit organizations to include Corning, Target Corporation, and the Virginia Military Institute. Offstein is also certified as a Senior Professional in Human Resources (SPHR). Professor Offstein has published in such outlets as *Human Resources Management Review*, the *Journal of Engineering and Technology Management*, *Journal of Managerial Psychology*, and *Business Communication Quarterly*. Notably, Offstein was a Strategic Management Society/McKinsey Finalist for Best Conference Paper in 2003 and was winner of the 2004 Best Doctoral Conference Paper in the Human Resources Division of the Academy Management (New Orleans).

James Douglas Orton, Ph.D. is an expert on the strategic management of loosely coupled networks, with a special research focus on the U.S. national security community. The literature review chapter for his dissertation at the University of Michigan, co-authored with his dissertation advisor Karl Weick and published in *Academy of Management Review* in 1990, is a foundation citation for the fields of network organizations and network strategies and has been cited over 700 times. From 1994-2000, Dr. Orton taught at HEC Paris Graduate Business School. While in Europe, Dr. Orton published articles on sense-making, decision-making, and strategy-making processes in loosely coupled networks in the *International Journal of Intelligence and Counterintelligence* (1995), *Scandinavian Journal of Management* (1996), *European Management Journal* (1997), *Journal of Management Studies* (2000), and *M@n@gement* (2001). Since returning to the United States, Dr. Orton has taught graduate strategic management courses at MIT's Sloan School of Management, UNLV, UC-Irvine, and UC-Riverside. From 1994-2006 Dr. Orton has maintained a research partnership with the George Washington University Executive Leadership Program and Center for the Study of Learning. He currently teaches in the new graduate program in the School of Business and Economics at Michigan Technological University.

Ronald F. Piccolo is an Assistant Professor in Management in the College of Business Administration at the University of Central Florida. He received a doctorate from the University of Florida, an MBA from the

Crummer Graduate School of Business at Rollins College, and a B.S. in mathematics from Stetson University. His research interests include leadership, cross-cultural studies, emotion, and risk. Ron has published in the *Journal of Applied Psychology*, the *Journal of Organizational Behavior*, and the *Academy of Management Journal*.

Karin Sanders is a Professor of Work and Organisational Psychology at the University of Twente, the Netherlands. Her main interests are the determinants and effects of solidarity behavior among employees, and between employees and supervisor within organisations; and the formal and informal governance structures to influence solidarity behavior. She published on this topic in a number of journals like *Journal of Governance and Management*, *Small Group Research*, and *Journal of Managerial Psychology*.

Birgit Schyns received her Ph.D. in psychology at the University of Leipzig, Germany in 2001. Her Ph.D. focused on preparedness for change, including LMX and occupational self-efficacy as antecedents. She is a reader in Organizational Behavior at the University of Parthmouth, U.K. Her research topics comprise leadership and career development. She has done research on antecedents and consequences of LMX in Germany and the Netherlands, as well as on biases in followers' perception of leadership (e.g., mood, personality, implicit leadership theories).

Melvin L. Smith is an Assistant Professor of Organizational Behavior at Case Western Reserve University's Weatherhead School of Management. He received his Ph.D. in organizational behavior and human resource management from the University of Pittsburgh. His research interests include social capital, social exchange relationships in organizations, and workplace well-being. Dr. Smith has provided training and/or consulting services to a number of organizations including Booz Allen Hamilton, H.J. Heinz, Roadway Express, University of Texas MD Anderson Cancer Center, University of Pittsburgh Medical Center, and a number of educational organizations. In addition, he has served as a visiting professor at ESADE Business School in Barcelona, Spain where he co-taught a senior executive education course on emotionally intelligent leadership.

Alex M. Susskind joined the faculty at Cornell's School of Hotel Administration in the Department of Food and Beverage Management in the Fall Semester of 1998. He earned his Ph.D. in Communication from Michigan State University with cognates in organizational communication and organizational behavior where he also earned his MBA with a concentration in personnel and human relations. Dr. Susskind earned his undergraduate degree at Purdue University from the Department of Restaurant, Hotel, and Institutional Management and is also a trained chef with a degree in Culinary Arts from The Culinary Institute of America in Hyde Park, New York. Professor Susskind has worked as a chef for both independent and multi-unit restaurant companies in the food and beverage, lodging, and resort segments of the hospitality industry and continues to act as food and beverage management consultant to hospitality operators across those segments. Dr. Susskind's research is based primarily in organizational communication and organizational behavior. He is currently researching: (a) the influence of customer-service provider interaction as it relates to organizational effectiveness and efficiency from the perspective of guests, employees, and managers; and (b) the influence of communication relationships upon individuals' work-related attitudes and perceptions surrounding organizational events and processes such as teamwork and downsizing. Professor Susskind's research has been published in leading hospitality-related journals such as the *Cornell Hotel and Restaurant Administration Quarterly*, the *International Journal of Hospitality Management*, the *Journal of Hospitality and Tourism Research*, and the *Journal of Travel Research*. His research has also been published in leading journals in the fields of communication and management such as *Communication Research* and the *Journal of Applied Psychology*.

Printed in the United States
89569LV00002B/48/A